An Interdisciplinary Primer in African Studies

An Interdisciplinary Primer in African Studies

Edited by Ishmael I. Munene

LEXINGTON BOOKS
Lanham • Boulder • New York • Toronto • Plymouth, UK

Published by Lexington Books
A wholly owned subsidiary of The Rowman & Littlefield Publishing Group, Inc.
4501 Forbes Boulevard, Suite 200, Lanham, Maryland 20706
http://www.lexingtonbooks.com

Estover Road, Plymouth PL6 7PY, United Kingdom

British Library Cataloguing in Publication Information Available

Library of Congress Cataloging-in-Publication Data

An interdisciplinary primer in African studies / edited by Ishmael I. Munene.
p. cm.
Includes bibliographical references and index.
ISBN 978-0-7391-6597-3 (cloth : alk. paper) — ISBN 978-0-7391-6598-0 (pbk. : alk. paper) — ISBN 978-0-7391-6887-5 (electronic)
1. Africa—Civilization—20th century. 2. Africa—Social life and customs. 3. Africa—Politics and government—1960- 4. Africa—Economic conditions—1960- I. Munene, Ishmael I.
DT30.5.I587 2011
960.3—dc22 2011021150

This book is dedicated to my Mom, Gladwell Wanjiku, and Dad, John Munene, in recompense. Love for everything education and inspiration to aspire for all knowledge that enlightens they did provide. —*Ishmael I. Munene*

Contents

List of Figures

Photospread

List of Tables

Acknowledgments

A number of individuals and institutions have immensely contributed to the fruition of this book. The work has been a labor of love, presenting an opportunity for all to offer their time and creative talents along with their intellectual resources to birth the matrix of the book. The list is too long to mention all, but I would like to mention a few who went beyond the call of duty in seeing the successful outcome of this publication.

First is my dear friend and colleague Mwalimu Abdul Karim Bangura of Howard University who was instrumental in conceptualizing the two-volume series on African Studies. He coordinated the editing of the two books and was a constant source of encouragement and inspiration at each roadblock that we encountered. Our editor at Lexington Books, Justin Race, deserves special commendation for his faith in the project, and support as well as needed recommendations throughout the production of the book. I also wish to thank Dr. Eric Otenyo of Northern Arizona University and Dr. Hannington Ochwada of Missouri State University for their willingness to serve as manuscript reviewers. I am also grateful to Eve Constance Paludan, editor at Bilby Research Center at Northern Arizona University, for her exemplary work in editing and typesetting the manuscript.

Several institutions were central to the success of this book. The African Studies and Research Forum (ASRF) of The Association of Third World Studies (ATWS) coordinated the commissioning of the chapters. The ATWS 26th Annual Conference held at Millersville, Pennsylvania, provided a stimulating intellectual atmosphere in which the chapters in this book were first presented and critiqued. I also thank the College of Education at Northern Arizona University for providing release time and travel funds that facilitated the completion of the book.

Finally, I am grateful to my wife, Eula C. Loney, and daughter, Grace Wangari Irungu, for their patience and understanding during the long hours I was away from them.

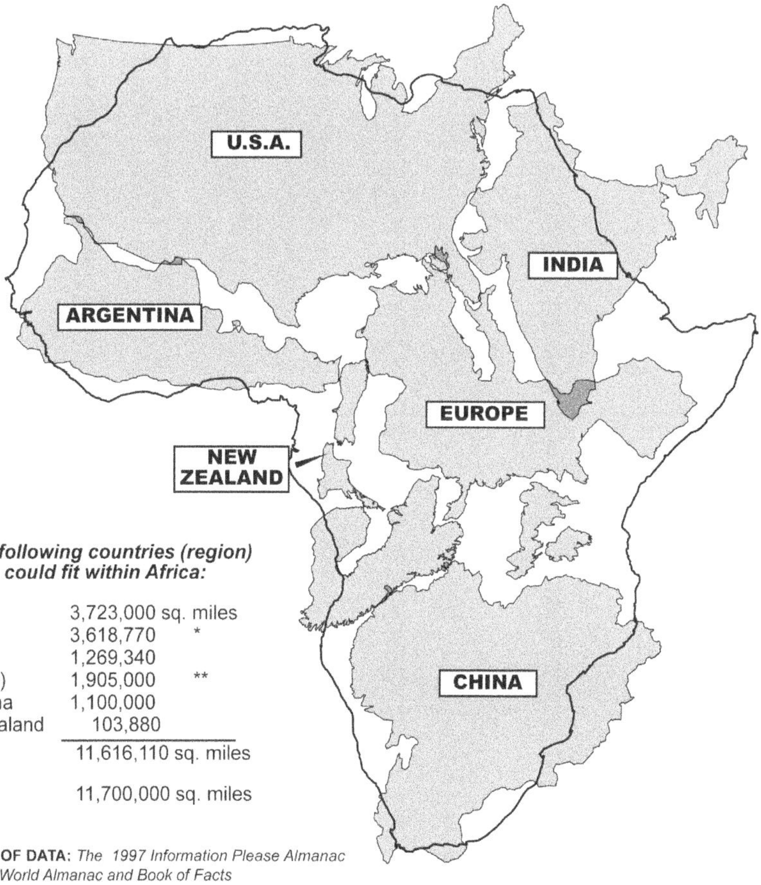

The following countries (region) could fit within Africa:

China	3,723,000 sq. miles	
U.S.A.	3,618,770	*
India	1,269,340	
(Europe)	1,905,000	**
Argentina	1,100,000	
New Zealand	103,880	
	11,616,110 sq. miles	
Africa	11,700,000 sq. miles	

SOURCE OF DATA: *The 1997 Information Please Almanac* and *1997 World Almanac and Book of Facts*
* Total, land and water, 50 states
***1997 Information Please Almanac*. Includes Iceland.
Excludes the former European Soviet Union and European Turkey.

Africa—Size

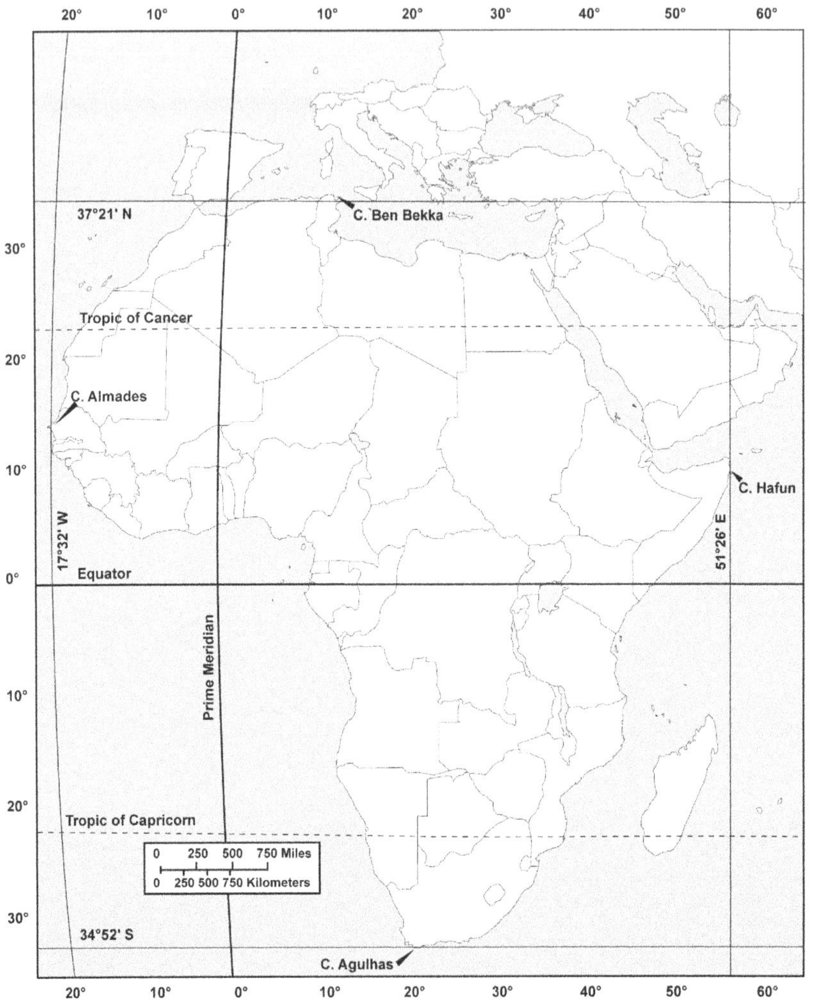

Africa—Showing Position

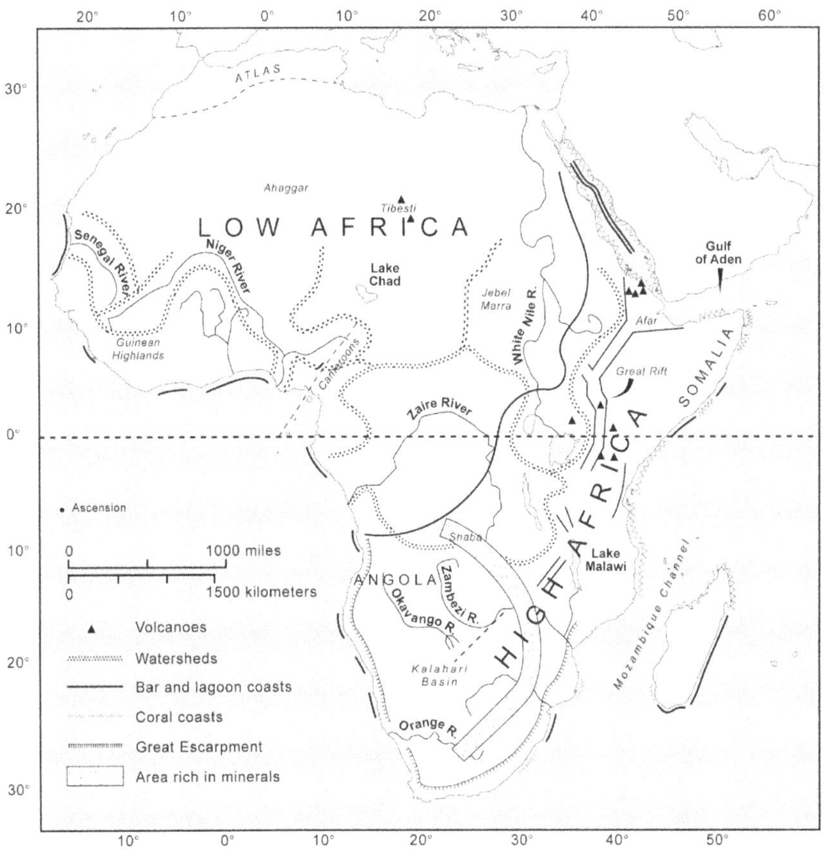

Africa—Showing Major Physical Features

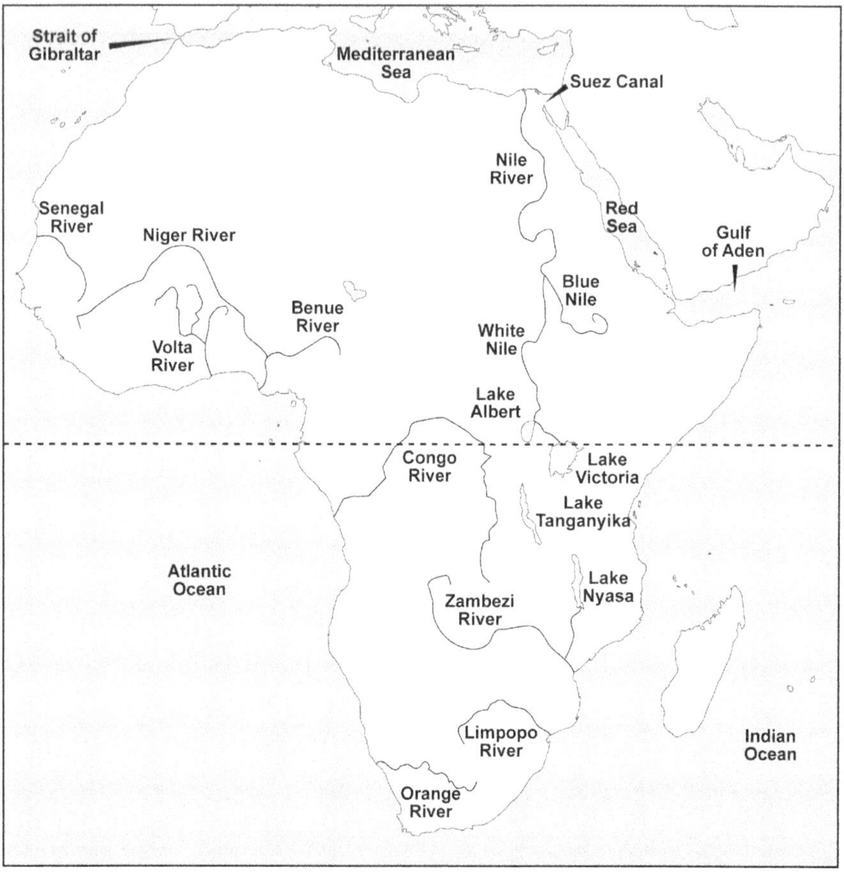

Major African Rivers and Lakes

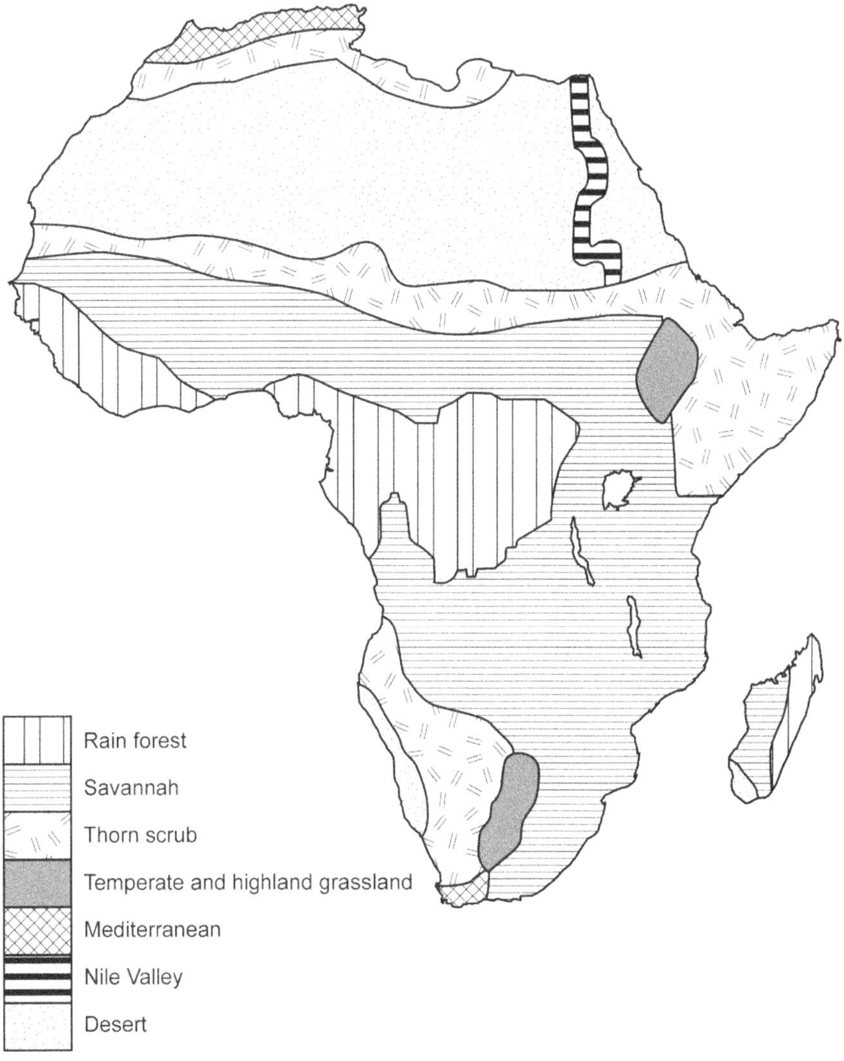

Africa—Showing Natural Vegetation

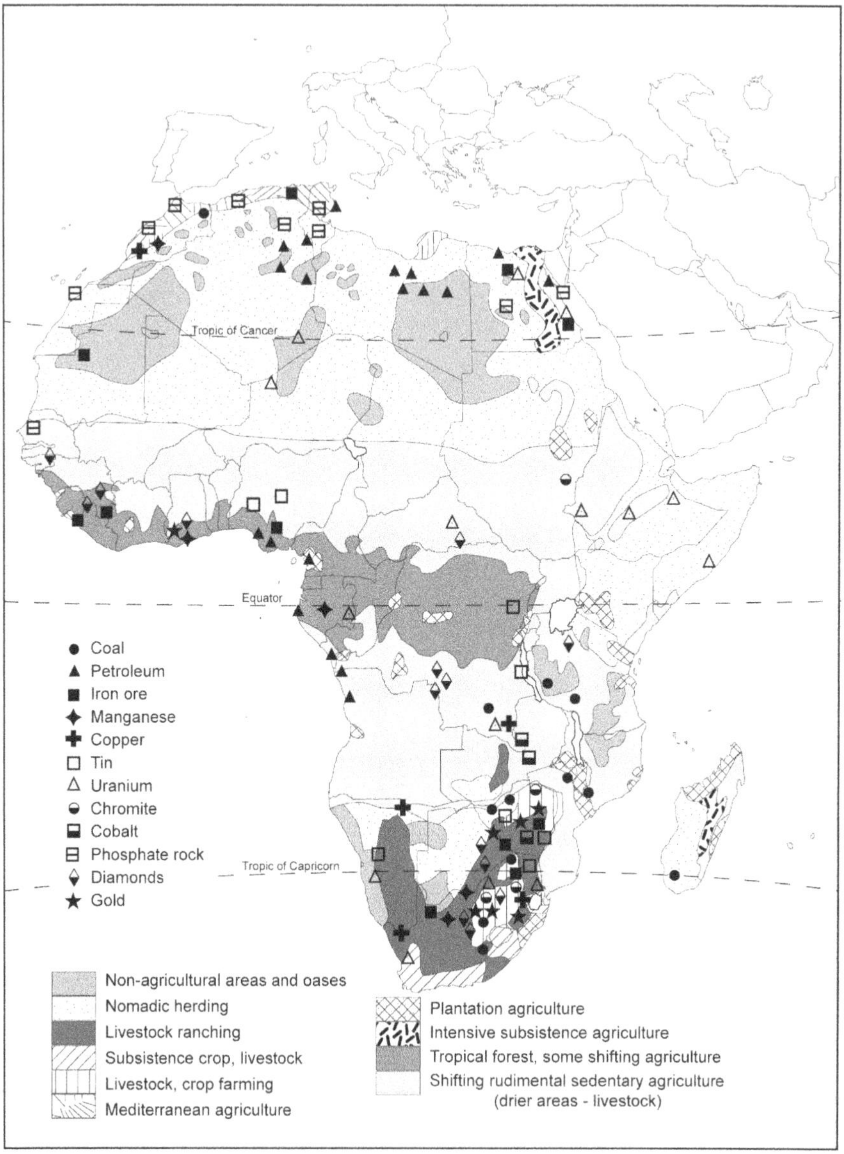

Africa—Showing Agricultural and Mineral Resources

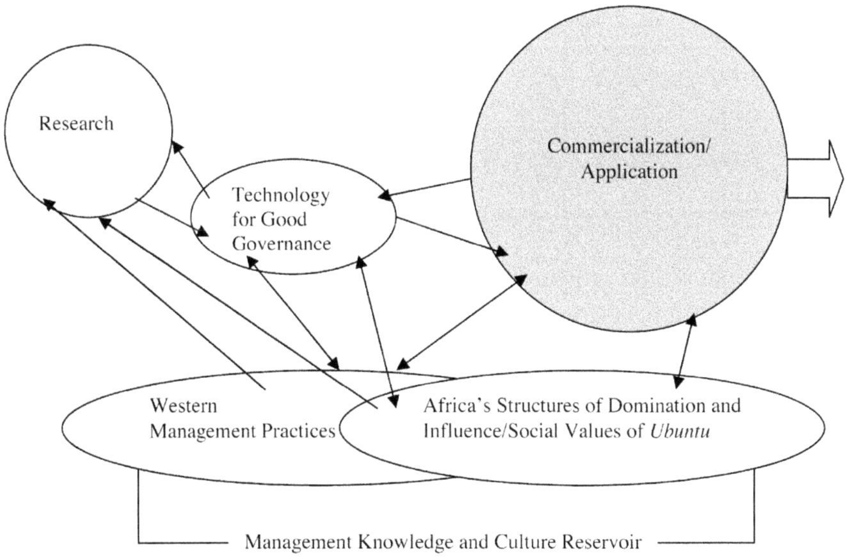

Figure 6.1. Application System of "Governance Management Model"

General Introduction

Ishmael I. Munene

Reconceptualizing African Studies

"You mean you have universities in Africa? I thought there were no colleges in Africa," my pastor, an African American, asked me soon after the morning worship in the late 1990s. During the worship service, I was accorded an opportunity, as a new congregant, to introduce myself to this largely African American congregation. In the introduction, I mentioned that I was teaching at the University of Nairobi prior to migrating to the United States. What followed after the surprising question from the pastor was a long silence, a moment of mutual embarrassment between the two of us. He could hardly believe that he knew so little about Africa, and neither could I comprehend how a person of African descent would be so ill-informed about Africa in a country where access to information is pervasive. Quickly, my mind raced back to three weeks prior to my coming to the US when I attended a luncheon at Kenyatta University, Kenya for my friend Joseph who was going to the US. Joseph was advised to take his doctoral studies seriously, and avoid African Americans who are lazy, violent, and mired in gangster activities. Just like my pastor, whose knowledge about Africa largely depended on international news media with its emphasis on pestilence, war, and hunger, so did Joseph's colleagues' information about America rely on folklore and Western movies with their largely negative depiction of the African American male. It is an insidious cycle. Just as African Americans are frustrated with African perceptions about them, so are Africans in America frustrated about the dismal knowledge many African Americans have about Africa. Addressing these knowledge chasms calls for concerted and collaborative efforts on both sides of the spectrum.

This book is part of the effort to address only one dimension of the problem, the dismal knowledge about Africa notable among American university students in particular and American public in general. The idea of the book emanated from the general observations by academics of African descent teaching in American universities about the superficial knowledge of Africa exhibited by university students. The knowledge was largely based on anecdotal snippets of mass media coverage of the continent without the benefit of in-depth grounding of the issues of historical context of the events. It was envisioned that an introductory text that is well illustrated, easy to read, and with sufficient depth in the coverage of pertinent issues germane to the continent would not only be widely accessible but would also go a long way toward addressing stereotypes about Africa.

Thus, the African research group, operating under the aegis of African Studies and Research Forum (ASRF) within the Association of Third World Studies (ATWS), took up the challenge which has translated into two volumes dedicated to an Afrocentric view of African issues. This is the second volume in the series; the first was *Contemporary Issues in African Studies* edited by George Kieh and Pita Agbese. Our focus in this volume is to explore the methodological approaches to the study of Africa by way of selected themes. Both projects were conceptualized by Abdul Karim Bangura who also coordinated the completion of publications. Though contributors in this volume also include colleagues based in Africa, most of the authors are academicians in the United States. Most of the chapters were presented at ATWS conferences in either Lima, Peru or Millersville, Pennsylvania (US) in 2007 and 2008, respectively. The two conferences provided a valuable space away from workplace settings for additional input, and critique as well as inspiration for writing on issues that are dear to the contributors.

Granted, African studies are not a new field of inquiry. Indeed, as an area of inquiry, African studies began the first time that Europeans came into contact with Africans. Nor is this volume a pioneer in seeking to refashion African studies in the Western world. Though a number of works have been produced since 1945, it is crucial at this time to mention a few recent ones that have made substantial contribution in reconstruction of the field in terms of concrete realities of the African experience. The two-volume seminal work edited by Paul Tiyambe Zeleza has been instrumental in exploring the changing contours of African studies from both thematic and disciplinary perspectives. In the first volume on disciplinary and interdisciplinary encounters, Zeleza situated the African studies in the ever-changing contexts of disciplinary and interdisciplinary knowledge production, dissemination, and consumption. He contended that like any field of study, African studies are subject to "concrete and conceptual, material and moral, political and discursive contexts which create the variations that are so evident across the world and across disciplines" (Zeleza, 2006, p. 3). In the second volume on global and transnational engagements, Zeleza (2007) dissected the internationalization of African studies, exploring ways in which Africa has engaged in international studies and international contexts. He argued, quite convincingly, that the continent has largely been studied by non-Africans and used a testing ground for shifting analytical paradigms, theoretical perspectives coupled with different national tendencies. Put simply, African influence in global production of knowledge on the continent has been marginal even as the region has become the experimental ground for shifting analytical fads.

In *Contested Terrains and Constructed Categories: Contemporary Africa in Focus*, editors Bond and Gibson presented a collection of essays focusing on the contested categories in politics, the economy, and civil society. The editors provided a brief introduction of the study of Africa as a scholarly discipline, capturing the contentious environment that informs the relationship between African and non-African scholars along with the politics of setting the research agenda. The editors identified three potent questions that are germane to any scholarship on Africa: First, which scholars are best suited and entitled to describe the daily lives of African peoples? Second, which theoretical frameworks best explain the political, social, and economic conditions of the continent? Finally, should the study of Africa include the entire continent or just Africa south of the Sahara? (Bond and Gibson, 2002, p. 2). The strength of this volume includes its contributors who include leading Africans with a distinguished record in African studies. The volume also presents specific case studies from Angola, Ghana, Madagascar, Nigeria, South Africa, and Zimbabwe. While dedicated to graduate and advanced study students, this book does more than serve as a college-level textbook; it compels students to think critically about all issues raised which also makes it handy for a general reader who is interested in reflecting on critical issues in Africa today.

Worthy of mention, too, but in the category of periodicals is the recent special issue of *Africa Development* dedicated to the critique of knowledge production on Africa in US universities as perceived by African doctoral students in America's universities. Edited by Godwin Murunga and Souleymane Diagne, the intent of the journal articles is to champion the contribution of what the editors term as the "fourth generation of African scholars" to scholarship as strategy to counter the continued disregard of the existence of African (including Black) epistemic communities that are actively engaged in knowledge production about Africa by Western scholars. The special issue provides a rich historical account of the development of African studies in American universities, and interrogates the delinking of African studies from African American studies. The editors note that the current state of affairs in American universities leave the impression that "...Africa has no community of scholars worth the name, or, if they have, their work is not worth reading" (Murunga and Diagne, 2008, p. 3).

These samplings of the various attempts by African and Afrocentric to deconstruct and reconstruct African studies is a by-product of its long and checkered history. The earliest writing about Africa and its people by Westerners, in the period just preceding colonialism, was spearheaded by explorers and missionaries. The fascination with people of a different race, cultural lifestyle, economic organization, and worship practices generated a caricature of a human genus that was in need of redemption and civilization in Europe. Books and newspaper accounts by David Livingston and Henry Stanley, among other missionaries and explorers, elicited strong images of a "noble savage." Africans were a people with neither history nor culture. Their tales of slave trade and its ramifications was the icing on the cake needed to make Christianity, civilization, and commerce (3 Cs) the beacon of European political, economic, and cultural invasion of Africa.

The colonization of Africa added another layer of Europeans fascinated by the study of Africa and its inhabitants. Anthropologists, with their emphasis on the study of the "other," a group that is radically distinct, invested time and resources investigating the customs, cultures, values, and languages of African colonial subjects. Long periods of residency in Africa by these colonial anthropologists followed by a short stint in Europe for report writing, ensured that these scholars expropriated significant intellectual artifacts from the continent. Further, anthropologists were instrumental in generating an "orientalized" image of the Africans, a situation that has defied attempts to rectify it (Mafeje, 1996; Mudimbe, 1988). African people became frozen in time, static and unchanging. African people were primitive, had no history. This contrasted with European societies that were civilized, modern, and with a history (Murunga, 2008).

These pre-colonial and colonial efforts in the study of Africa and its people have had lasting ideological, institutional, and policy ramifications. They concretized the ideology of racism with Africans being seen as an inferior race to their European counterparts. They also led to the institutionalization of the study of Africa as a distinct subspecialty, away from the study of "modern" disciplines such as history, economics, and geography. The establishment of institutions dedicated to this academic enterprise such as the School of Oriental and African Studies at the University of London was the crystallization of the efforts to relegate the study of Africa to a second-tier category of scholarship. It also led to a clear-cut bifurcation between African and Western societies; Africans were ahistorical and belonged to anthropology while Europeans had a history and were to be studied from a sociological perspective. Policy-wise, studies by colonial anthropologists proved critical in facilitating the colonial authorities' efforts to retain their hegemony over the African people, just as they provided the intellectual rationale for the pursuit of modernization as the colonial and post-colonial development policy for Africa.

So enduring have been these consequences that, notwithstanding the changes that have occurred in anthropology, Mafeje (1998) notes that it is impossible to deracialize anthropology as an academic discipline, given its historical notoriety. Hountondji (1997) has appropriately noted that colonial era experimentation with theoretical models resulted in the "theoretical extraversion" of the continent in which imported perspectives, paradigms and perversions still pervade not only the intellectual terrain about the region but continually influence policy prescriptions enunciated by foreign governments.

But if the colonial period provided a leeway for European scholars, especially British, to intensify their interest in Africa, then the aftermath of independence provided segue for American scholars to stamp their foothold on African studies. US interests were self-serving; Americans wanted to understand African ideological and organizational capacity that had so successfully led to the "winds of change" from European colonialism. This quest had a dual impetus, both closely related. First was the desire by the US to extend its sphere of influence over Africa as a counterweight to the Soviet Union's own imperial designs at the height of the cold war. Second was the desire to be at the forefront of any policy proscription for the continent articulated by multilateral institutions. Consequently, with the support of the US governments, American universities were encouraged and assisted to establish African Studies departments. The government also provided the initial seed funding for the establishment of the African Studies Association (ASA), the largest of such professional associations dedicated to the study of Africa in the world.

This development had important consequences for African Studies as a discipline. The emergent of a new class of African scholars, the "Africanist," became a distinct feature of US academic and policy terrains. These are white Americans with specific intellectual interest in African affairs. They have played a critical role in shaping US foreign policy towards Africa through their consultancy services to the State Department (Murunga, 2008; Zeleza, 2006). Africa has become an experimental ground for various theoretical proscriptions which have little bearing on the lives and experiences of the citizens. Theoretical postulates such as "patrimonialism, authoritarianism, prebendalism, tribalism, consociationalism, developmental democracy, ethnic antagonism, predatory elite, indigenous bourgeoisie, and comprador capitalism" (Ukaegbu, 1998, p. 329) are not indigenous to Africa and their application in the analysis of African situation leaves a lot to be desired. Of the many disastrous policy proscriptions for Africa with heavy input from American "Africanist," two stand out. The World Bank-led, Western-backed Structural Adjustment Programs (SAP) and the neoliberal approach to development were modeled along the American free market ideology. As Mafeje (2008) appropriately observed, it is the negative consequences of these policies of state retreat from development that inspired African economists to stake their intellectual against the World Bank.

An additional consequence was the shearing of bonds between the experiences of Africans and their African American counterparts. In his seminal writings on the experiences of black people, W. E. B. Du Bois noted the connection between the African American experiences and that of the Africans in the following terms:

> The history of the American Negro is the history of this strife—this longing to attain self-conscious manhood, to merge his double self into a better and truer self. In this merging he wishes neither of the older selves to be lost. He would not Africanize America, for America has too much to teach the world and Africa. He would not bleach his Negro soul in a flood of white Americanism, for he knows that Negro blood has a message for the world. He simply wishes to make it possible for a man to be both a Negro and an American, without being cursed and spit upon by his fellows, without having the doors of opportunity closed roughly in his face. (Cited in Wadsworth/Thomson Learning, 2000, p. 54)

The preponderance of white "Africanist" teachings about Africans turned off African Americans who found their niche in African American studies. The long historical bond among Africans and African Americans, nurtured during the independence struggle from European colonialism by the former, and the civil rights movement by the latter, both in the 50s and 60s, was no longer tenable. Interpreting African events and issues in the US largely became an occupation of white "Africanists."

In sum, the development of African studies in the West is inextricably interwoven in the history of Africa's intersection with the West. It is an interaction that has been less about benefiting Africans as it has been more about ideological and economic control of the Africans. It is in this contentious environment that Africans both, in both in the continent and in the diaspora, have increasingly began to redefine the discourse on Africa issues and events. This work builds on this tradition.

Discipline and Methodology in African Studies

In a landmark scathing attack on Area studies, of which African Studies is a key component, Robert Bates, while addressing the American Political Association, declared that "within the academy, the consensus has formed that area studies has failed to generate scientific knowledge" (Bates, 1996, p. 1). As one with a track record in research on Africa, Bates' attack was surprising as it was shocking. Yet, his statement was a desperate clarion call for donors to stop the hemorrhage of funds from area studies since political scientists had become more adept at incorporating social science methodologies in area studies in a more rigorous fashion. More importantly for us, Bates' remarks underscore the pressures that area studies face to conform to traditional academic disciplines. It also raises questions about the appropriate methodology and theoretical perspectives pertinent in area studies. These are complex and, at times, controversial issues in the academy today.

African studies has been undertaken from a variety of vantage points, disciplinary and interdisciplinary. This duality is an acknowledgment that issues are complex and no one discipline is sufficient to address them comprehensively. Increasingly, too, scholars in disciplines that were hitherto critical of interdisciplinary studies such as law, natural sciences, and social sciences have increasingly sought to examine issues from multiple disciplines. While advocates of interdisciplinary orientation contend that it provides space for new questions to be asked, new methodologies to be developed and new areas of inquiry to emerge, its critics argue that it is a threat to disciplinary boundaries, hierarchies and rigor (Zeleza, 2007). Whatever its criticism, interdisciplinary orientation has led to the emergence of new areas of inquiry including women's studies, environmental studies, peace and conflict studies, and technology studies in addition to area studies. These newer fields of inquiry have tended to infuse advocacy and activism as part of their offering, eschewing the conservatism that is inherent in the traditional academic disciplines.

Contributors to this volume have employed disciplinary orientations to analyze important issues germane to the continent. Obviously, there is plenty of cross-pollination not only in framing of the issues but also in methodological approaches. At times more than disciplinary perspective is employed in particular analysis. This approach reflects the increasing interdependence of disciplines in methodological approaches and theoretical orientations. Disciplines and interdisciplines are fluid and porous, reflecting the continued evolution of scholarship in the academy. This dynamism in scholarship is also a reflection of the increasing fluidity in society in general (Zeleza, 2007, p. 5). Interdisciplinary perspectives employed take a variety of imageries and approaches. In contrast to the purely single discipline orientation which stresses the importance of academic departments, and knowledge production that is geared towards academic publishing, interdisciplinary orientation stresses the importance of study centers or institutes along with a scholarly output that infuses a high degree of activism in policy and practice. Common examples include women's studies, environmental studies, peace studies, black studies and, increasingly, African studies.

Interdisciplinary approaches entail a variety of programmatic, paradigmatic, and pedagogical dimensions. The basic premise of any interdisciplinary study is a new area of inquiry constituted by two disciplines already in existence. Kochelmans (1998) has contrasted interdisciplinarity from other widely used approaches to research and scholarship including multidisciplinarity, pluridisciplinarity, crossdisciplinarity, and transdisciplinarity. Multidisciplinarity involves studying or engaging in more than one discipline that are not connected. Pluridisciplinarity is the act of competence in a particular discipline through the knowledge of other disciplines. In crossdisciplinarity, specialists from multiple disciplines collaborate to address a challenging issue but do not develop a common outlook on the same. Finally, transdisciplinarity is dedicated to the generation of theoretical or conceptual framework that cuts across scattered disciplines. Except for Bangura's chapter on *Ubuntu*, which is pluridisciplinary, the bulk of the work in this volume involves aspects of interdisciplinarity. Wasserstrom (2006) has identified five dimensions of interdisciplinarity, and three of which are discernible in this volume. Most contributors in this volume use exploratory interdisciplinarity in which ideas and methods from other disciplines are employed. However, Gire's chapter on African psychology would constitute what Wasserstrom defines as cross-over interdisciplinarity. In this interdisciplinary approach separate disciplines of African studies and psychology overlap to create a new area of African psychology. In Munene's chapter on higher education transformation as well as Zalanga's chapter on rural development in the neoliberal era, we see the use of paradigmatic interdisciplinarity whereby synthetic theories that operate across disciplines are widely used in the analysis. While both chapters make use of neoliberalism to explore the integration of African institutions and economies into the global systems, Zalanga extends the debate further by infusing a critical perspective that borrows heavily from Marxist theories.

"Where is the African in the study of Africa?" posed Anyidoho (2008) in highlighting the significance of insider scholarship in understanding the importance of politics of representation in African studies as well as the extant power differentials in African studies. Contributors in this volume are all of African descent, either resident in Africa or teaching and researching in North America. Unlike the case of scholars from other regions writing about their own areas of origin, knowledge produced by Africans about Africa has been treated with circumspection:

> Rather strikingly, in comparative terms it is remarkable that when Chinese study Chinese culture and society in their own terms and for their own purposes, western scholarship does not protest. This is because the sovereignty of Chinese scholarship on China is accepted. India and the Arab world have almost reached that point. Russians do not look west for understanding their society...Neither do the Japanese. (Prah, cited in Mafeje, 2008, p. 1)

Critics of African insider scholarship cite universalism, cosmopolitanism, and *créolité* as more useful constructs in identity politics. They are viewed as more encompassing, eschew the contradictions inherent in everyday life, and do not tie self to race, ethnicity, language, or race (Anyidoho, 2008). Insider scholarship is limiting in that it promotes a totalizing concept of identity, it leads to essentializing of groups (societal, national, cultural, or otherwise), and it runs the risk of reinforcing homogeneous stereotypes.

Notwithstanding these criticisms, the Afrocentric perspective employed by scholars in this volume is nothing more than a demand that Africans be at the center in the production of any knowledge about the continent. Only through this approach will realities that inform the African life be captured, and its authenticity assured. It is a political weapon that seeks to empower groups that have hitherto suffered intellectual subjugation reflected in Western-dominated scholarship and its attendant paradigms. Insider scholarship provides a safe haven for scholars from subordinated groups to present their perspectives to the Western world by tying themselves to specific national, cultural, and ethnic identity (Narayan, 1997) just as is the case with gender studies where the social gendered perspective is the legitimate analytical category. It is in this context that contributors to this volume have offered their scholarship.

Organization of the Book

The chapters in this book are compendium of essays that provide a broad overview of various thematic concerns pertinent to understanding of the complex character that is Africa. These themes are presented using an array of methodological and theoretical approaches including the requisite critiques. No claim is made to the exhaustiveness of these themes and methodological approaches in appreciating all there is about the socio-cultural, economic, and political realities of Africa among others but rather we seek to present an introductory snapshot of such themes and methodologies that could additional springboard for additional academic interrogation.

A geographical analysis of the continent is presented by Iheanyi Osondu in order to clarify some myths and misconceptions about the African landmass. He does this in the chapter entitled "The Geography of Africa." The 53-nation continent is only second to Asia in land size yet its physical landscape is far less complex than Asia and Europe. A number of mountains, valleys, and water bodies in the east, north, south, and west dot the landscape presenting a picturesque view of the landmass. This is accentuated by diverse climatic zones including equatorial, tropical Mediterranean, and desert conditions. Osondu goes on to show how the physical geography of Africa influences the various economic and human activities. This chapter should be an eye opener to the rich and varied climatic, physical, economic, and human attributes of a continent largely viewed from the prism of war, famine, and natural disasters. The chapter should also form a good background study to Kalipeni, et al. (2007) whose work focuses on human geography, which paints a complex picture of the interaction population, resources, and environment in Africa thereby challenging previous Africanist assumptions.

Geography also provides lenses for deconstructing ethnocentric views that perpetuate the myth of an inferior Africa, while at the same time illuminating significant cultural patterns and processes, regional variations in cultural elements, cultural diffusion, and how culture is reflected in the landscape. However, using geography to achieve these twin objectives requires utilization of the appropriate pedagogical tools. Ibipo Johnston-Anumonwo, in the chapter on "Countering Ethnocentricism in Teaching Human Geography of Africa," presents an array of pedagogical tools in human geography that could be used in Western countries to present a positive image about Africa. Johnston-Anumonwo's goal in the chapter is to cast Africa as "humanity's original cultural hearth, the origin and spread of various culture traits especially language and religion, the continuity and change in Africa's cultural evolution that exposes the interactions of indigenous influences with processes of modern cultural change that is manifested in Africa's cultural diversity."

The chapter is rich with examples of how history, literature, political developments, ethnic relations along with gender power structures can be used to teach Africa's human geography as a springboard in the deconstruction of negative stereotypes about the continent.

The nexus between indigenous rituals practices on the one hand and religion and spiritual matters on the other is examined by Ngozi Caleb Kamalu in "African Religions and Spirituality: The Case of Okija Shrine Worship in Eastern Nigeria." Customary practices are macabre including ritual killings, drinking of human blood, witchcraft, and extortions, among others. Participants and victims encompass a broad spectrum of the populace raising important questions as about shrine worship's continued sustenance and rejuvenation in Nigeria in this modern era. According to Kamalu, the resiliency arises from a plethora of factors the most prominent being religion, superstition, and poverty.

Rituals are designed to appease gods and deities who them offer protection against tragedies, and portend blessing for material and familial success for those who practice them. This strong belief in the power of deities is possible because of the strong belief in superstitions alongside widespread poverty. Resilience of ritual worship is one thing; the reason for its genesis in the first place is another. The author offers a reasoned critique of the failure of the British-inherited jurisprudence in Nigeria as the raison d'être for its origins. A legal system that is slow, corrupt, and complicated to most people has forced them to seek judicial recourse in the traditional region-cultural institutions of which the most prominent is the shrine worship system. In all, Kamalu's chapter is significant in revealing the cyclic nature of traditional institutions and practices in Africa. What was thought to have outlived its usefulness suddenly become important and even destructive, and in its wake, left modern state institutions confounded and in a state of confusion. This chapter epitomizes the dynamism of African religious practices, a far cry from when they were simply dismissed and condemned as inconsequential by self-righteous European missionaries and colonial anthropologists (Bongmba, 2007).

In "African Mathematics: From Bones to Computers," Mamokgethi Setati and Abdul Karim Bangura survey pre-colonial Africa's genius in use of mathematics in various cultural and economic endeavors. Conventional wisdom has it that pre-colonial Africa was deficient in scientific and mathematical knowledge whose legacy is reflected in the continent's poor economic performance. According to Setati and Bangura, Eurocentric scholars in particular have used mathematics as a weapon to insinuate European cultural superiority over Africans. Writings on the history of mathematics hardly mention the mathematical prowess of sub-Saharan communities; only a scant mention is made of Egyptian mathematical genius. Yet it is hardly impossible to ignore the great mathematical knowledge that ancient African societies exhibited in their day-to-day activities. A survey of these activities is the focus of Setati and Bangura's chapter.

What follows is a detailed exposition of the application by diverse African communities of the various branches of mathematical knowledge in labor, crafts, building construction, exploiting the solar system for calendaring, and graphic designs. An important aspect of this recollection in mathematical knowledge is the extensive use of fractals in graphic designs. Setati and Bangura show how fractals were extensively used in divination (fortunetelling), gaming, carvings, music, and fashion. Today, African fractals are evident in architecture, and art, politics, and religion. The authors end with a discussion of the African Fractals in Development project, a large-scale investigation of indigenous African science for education and development focusing on six areas: architecture for an indigenous science; an indigenous knowledge database; agro-ecology; technological expertise; science education; and financial stability.

James Gire explores the vexing question of whether African psychology is necessary, or even warranted, within the overall discipline of psychology. Indigenous psychology based on African reality has been a pet theme among many

Afrocentric scholars who, according to Gire in his chapter, "African Psychology: To Be or Not to Be," have criticized contemporary theories and models in psychology as being too Eurocentric to address the cultural contexts that are uniquely African. The author calls for a compromise between the two extreme positions contending that each complements the other, and any calls for psychology that is uniquely African presupposes the need for a new knowledge domain that is exclusive to a particular region and its people. It also presupposes that African psychology exists in opposition to psychology that is unique to other regions of the world. Using the works of Frantz Fanon, Bame Nsamenang, and Frank Eyetsemitan and James Gire, the author illustrates how African psychiatrists and psychologists have successfully used concepts, models, and theories from universal psychology to address the reality of African issues, problems, and challenges.

Gire concludes by stating unequivocally that the search for a distinctive African psychology is self-defeating ". . . since its seemingly universal dialogue which accompanies notions of diversity across psychological theories actually encourages particularism. What psychologists in Africa need to do is to engage the problems and issues of Africa with the powerful tools that psychology in general makes available to them."

Gire's explication, like the one by Ratele (2007) illustrates just how difficult it is for psychology to shed its Eurocentric heritage. The need to uncover universal laws of human behaviors has tended to color the cultural biases inherent in psychological theories espoused by psychologists of the yore. Ratele and Gire are critical of the narrowness of the issues examined in the discipline, which, in most instances, tend to sacrifice matters related to Africa at the altar of efficiency.

In "Model of Governance Management in Africa: An Integrated Approach of Blending Modern Management Methods with Africa's Cultural Mores for Greater Institutional Efficiency," Kenday Kamara makes a case for fusing Western management practices with Africa's cultural mores in order to address the continent's Achilles heel, administrative inadequacies. Africa is embroiled in poverty and economic development is hamstrung by a volatile governance environment that leads to managerial inefficiency in institutions of productivity. A way out of this morass, according to Kamara, is to recapture the very best in African cultural values along with the finest Western management thought in order to create viable "learning organizations" in Africa to successfully address organizational effectiveness and social change. Even though management thought and practices are culture-dependent, the author is confident that Western management thought has universal principles that are applicable to the African context.

According to Kamara, an overarching paradigm for infusing African cultural mores in management is the African world view of *Ubuntu*. The centrality of *Ubuntu* is its emphasis on collectivism, collaboration, caring, dignity, and respect. Both collective and collaborative spirits provide the foundation for generating mechanisms for mutual engagement and accountability in institutions.

The principle of caring is the engine for crafting a culture of empowerment and teamwork in the workplace as it places emphasis on bonding and the achievement of tasks collectively rather than individually. Compassion leads to helpfulness towards each other eventually leading to collegiality that is based on sharing and caring. Lastly, dignity and respect lead to a culture of positive expectations since there is no prospect of acting opportunistically to one's detriment. Kamara rounds up his argument for an African-based cultural orientation in management with a framework that leads to strong and visionary leadership, quality management, management by objectives, performance-based compensation system, and empowered performance for African institutions.

A Western-derived methodological approach that is deemed as being germane to the analysis of African societies and institutions is grounded theory. Along with case study, ethnography, and phenomenology, grounded theory is one of the four designs in qualitative research approach. Ishmael Munene, in "Transformation Turbulence: Grounded Theory and African Higher Education Transformation," argues that grounded theory is relevant to understanding African societies and institutions for it permits theory development, a necessary process for Afrocentric scholars keen to develop explanatory models authentic to the continent. This utility notwithstanding, its application in research studies in Africa has been circumscribed by the undue emphasis on quantitative approaches in the training of African researchers in Western institutions, coupled with the stress on theory affirmation and verification as opposed to theory generation in the social science epistemologies in the continent. Munene goes on to demonstrate the applicability of grounded theory in the study of an African university in Kenya undergoing structural transformation occasioned by rapid privatization and marketization. Using conceptual models derived from grounded theory methodology and empirical data from Kenyatta University, the researcher generates a theory of transformational turbulence to explain the causal conditions, the context, and the intervening conditions as well as the consequences of the market university in Africa in the neoliberal environment of higher education development.

Munene's study shows that the neoliberal reforms in higher education have impacted universities in ways that were unprecedented. While universities have identified new revenue sources following decrease in government subventions occasioned by external pressures from multilateral agencies, these revenue generation reforms have come at a great to the institutions. Not only have universities corporatized their governance structures, they have also commercialized academic activities. This, in turn, has led to increased incidents of disruption of learning, administrative disarticulation, institutional bifurcation along with exacerbating equity disparities among the student community. Munene's study is a good illustration of how empirical data can be used to study African institutions undergoing rapid transformations linked to global forces. It sits well with Ukaegbu (1998) for more empirical studies as a way of enhancing the status of African studies.

Samuel Zalanga also takes up the theme of neoliberalism and globalization as it relates to notion of development in Africa as public policy in his chapter titled, "Rural Development in the Era of Neoliberal Hegemony: Poststructuralist and Postcolonial Methodological Critique and Theoretical Analysis." He uses empirical data from the anthropological work of Katherine Snyder among the Iraqw Da'aw of northern Tanzania as a representative of the disempowered condition the subaltern class in Africa finds itself, and poststructuralist and postcolonial methodology and theoretical frameworks to critique the neoliberal model of development. Zalanga's point of departure is that neoliberal development models in Africa articulated by multilateral agencies like the World Bank and IMF and bilateral partners from the West, all of which are based on the market model of development and jettison the importance of local peoples knowledge, experience and context, have only served to leave the local populace poorer and insecure. He avers that "development" as presently conceived is not a neutral term but rather a loaded concept that encapsulates unequal power relations between advanced Western nations and institutions and developing countries in Africa among other regions.

To ameliorate this disjuncture between development and disempowerment in public policy in Africa, Zalanga advocates the use of institutional ethnography knowledge generation methodology as a means of incorporating perspectives from the marginalized class in the power discourses. Universal knowledge paradigms on development perpetuated by advanced countries are premised on inferiority of non-Western societies. He also argues that this research approach is in tandem with the call for incorporating "micro-level" experiences in any development policy that Foucault and Freire call for in order to empower the subjugated class to liberate themselves.

Development is also the central focus of Ivor Agyeman-Duah in his chapter, "Culture, Communication, and Socio-economic Development in Post-Colonial Ghana." Agyeman-Duah begins with an incisive overview of the role of culture in pre-colonial Ghana societies especially as it pertains to enhanced communication and social integration. In post-colonial Ghana, the author criticizes the political class failure to appreciate the role of culture in socioeconomic development along with policies that have only stressed the significance of cultural institutions and personalities. Since the turn of the century, Agyeman-Duah notes the increased attention to culture as an important variable in socio-economic development through the enactment of constitutional and legislative mechanisms to give legal foundation to cultural production activities coupled with the establishment of institutional infrastructures to facilitate the development and marketing of cultural products. While all these seems commendable, the author is not oblivious to its inherent contradictions where Ghana has to rely on advanced industrial countries and multilateral institutions such as the World Bank and IMF which saw no merit to the country's cultural heritage to finance these developments. Agyeman-Duah's chapter is in tandem with Nyamnjoh's (2007) call for communication research in Africa to focus on development restraints by global hegemonic forces while avoiding the tendency to blame the continent's socio-economic status on peoples' culture.

No study of Africa is complete without a critical examination of the political realities obtaining in the continent. In this context, two contributions are a most welcome addition to this primer. The first is Abdul Karim Bangura's chapter, "The African State, Dialectics of African Culture, and Representative Political Organization: An *Ubuntu*/Communal Paradigm." Just as in Kamara's work noted earlier which uses the *Ubuntu* paradigm, the core of this seminal work is to provide evidence that the *Ubuntu*/communal paradigm constitutes a more robust explanatory framework for understanding political underpinnings of the African nations and states. Employing an amalgam of multidisciplinary and interdisciplinary methodologies and perspectives including *Sankofa* and Pluridisciplinary research along with theories from political science, sociology, and peace studies, Bangura navigates the history of Africa from pre-independence to post-colonial eras to discount myths that ethnicity alone has been central to Africa's political quagmire. Instead, he makes a compelling case for appreciating the political quandary in light of oppressive colonial and post-colonial state formation mechanism that exploited the prevailing ethnic differences.

Using the pre- and post-colonial conflicts in South Africa, Liberia, Sierra Leone, and Rwanda as empirical case studies, the author shows how colonial powers manipulated ethnic groups to cement their hold on power so as to sustain economic exploitation of the continent. The post-colonial indigenous elite who took over the reins of power after the departure of the colonial powers employed similar divide–and-rule tactics to consolidate their hold on to power against an incipient opposition. This political arrangement led political conflagrations between those in power and the oppressed that resulted in massive inter-ethnic bloodletting. Bangura shows the inadequacies of Western jurisprudence in mediating the post conflict need for justice and forgiveness concurrently. It is here that the traditional African conflict resolution and justice system epitomized by *Ubuntu* has achieved a considerable measure of success. Bangura does not romanticize *Ubuntu*; he shows how societies are conflicted demonstrating clemency towards the perpetrators of heinous human rights abuses while at the same time having to live with a feeling that justice has not been done.

The second chapter that focuses on political developments is Nabie Conteh's "The Efficacies of Decision Making Styles in the African-centric Decision Making Process." In the chapter, Conteh uses computer simulations to test the efficacies of various decision making styles in the continent. Due to the preponderance of autocratic decision making in the political regime, the author tests whether this decision making style translates into significant improvement in outcomes in comparison to other decision making styles. Results from the computer simulations show that consultative decision making will yield the most productive and profitable results than all other decision making styles covered.

Taken together, the chapters in this volume present a kaleidoscopic view of Africa from a different thematic perspective. The chapters are bound by a passionate commitment to an Afrocentric viewpoint but without romanticizing the issues. This volume demonstrates the dynamism of the socio-economic, cultural, political, and psychological conditions in the continent, which is best understood from a variety of disciplinary and interdisciplinary parameters. The authors take pride in adding to the growing repertoire of Afrocentric studies of the motherland.

Bibliography

Anyidoho, N. A. "Identity and Knowledge Production in the Fourth Generation." *Africa Development*, XXXIII, 1 (Special Issue: The Politics of Knowledge Production in Africa: Nurturing the Fourth Generation), 25–39, 2008.

Bates, Robert H. "Letter from the President: Area Studies and the Discipline." *APSA-CP Newsletter*, 7, 1, Winter, 1–2, 1996.

Bond, George C., and Nigel C. Gibson. "Introduction: African Studies in Contention." In *Contested Terrains and Constructed Categories: Contemporary Africa in Focus*, edited by George C. Bond and Nigel C. Gibson. Boulder and Oxford: Westview Press, 1–36, 2002.

Bongmba, Elias K. "The Study of African Religions: A Sketch of the Past and Prospects for the Future." In *The Study of Africa Vol. 2: Global and Transnational* Engagements, edited by Paul T. Zeleza. Dakar, Senegal: CODESRIA Books, 338–374, 2007.

Hountondji, Paulin. "Introduction: Recentering Africa." In *Endogenous Knowledge: Research Trials*, edited by Paulin Hountondji. Dakar, Senegal: CODESRIA Books, 1–39, 1997.

Kalipeni, Ezekiel, Joseph R. Oppong, and Benjamin Ofori-Amoah. "Trajectories of Modern African Geography." In *The Study of Africa Vol. 2: Global and Transnational Engagements*, edited by Paul T. Zeleza, 233–273. Dakar, Senegal: CODESRIA Books, 2007.

Kochelmans, Joseph I. "Why Interdisciplinarity?" In *Interdisciplinarity: Essays from Literature*, edited by William H. Newell. New York: College Entrance Board, 2–22, 1998.

Mafeje, A. "Africanity: A Commentary by Way of Conclusion." *CODESRIA Bulletin*, 3 & 4, 111–113, 2008.

———. Anthropology in Post-Independent Africa: End of an Era and the Problem of Self-Redefinition. *African Sociological Review*, 2, 1, 1–43, 1998.

———. Anthropology and Independent Africans: Suicide or End of an Era? CODESRIA Monograph Series 4/96, 1996.

Mudimbe, Vumbi Y. *The Invention of Africa*. Bloomington: Indiana University Press, 1988.

Murunga, Godwin R. "Thoughts on Intellectual and Institutional Links Between African and Black Studies." *Africa Development*, XXXIII, 1 (Special Issue: The Politics of Knowledge Production in Africa: Nurturing the Fourth Generation), 40–66, 2008.

Murunga, Godwin R., and Souleymane B. Diagne. "Introduction." *Africa Development*, XXXIII, 1 (Special Issue: The Politics of Knowledge Production in Africa: Nurturing the Fourth Generation), 1–6, 2008.

Narayan, Uma. *Dislocating Cultures: Identities, Traditions, and Third-World Feminism*. New York: Routledge, 1997.

Nyamnjoh, Francis B. "Rethinking Communication Research and Development in Africa." In *The Study of Africa Vol. 1: Disciplinary and Interdisciplinary Encounters*, edited by Paul T. Zeleza, 393–416. Dakar, Senegal: CODESRIA Books, 2007.

Ratele, Kopano. "Psychology for a Contemporary Africa." In *The Study of Africa Vol. 2: Global and Transnational Engagements*, edited by Paul T. Zeleza, 274–296. Dakar, Senegal: CODESRIA Books, 2007.

Ukaegbu, Chikwendu C. "Commentary: Area Studies and the Disciplines." *Africa Today*, 45, 3/4 (January 1, 1998): 323–336.

Wadsworth/Thomson Learning (Firm). *Wadsworth Classic Readings in Sociology*. Belmont, CA: Wadsworth//Thomson Learning, 2000.

Wasserstrom, Jeffrey N. "Expanding on the I-Word." *The Chronicle of Higher Education*, January 20, 2006, B5.

Zeleza, Paul. "Introduction: The Disciplining of Africa." In *The Study of Africa Vol. 1: Disciplinary and Interdisciplinary Encounters*, edited by Paul T. Zeleza, 1–35. Dakar, Senegal: CODESRIA Books, 2006.

———. "Introduction: The Internationalization of African Knowledges." In *The Study of Africa Vol. 2: Global and Transnational Engagements*, edited by Paul T. Zeleza, 1–26. Dakar, Senegal: CODESRIA Books, 2007.

Chapter 1
An Outline Geography of Africa

Iheanyi N. Osondu

Introduction

The geography of Africa is not as complex as that of other continents such as Asia. However, Africa is so diverse that even educated outsiders are often confused by or lose sight of this diversity when discussing its geography. To many outsiders, Africa is the most poorly understood of all the world's regions. News media often portray Africa as a continent with many countries, wars, violence, diseases, and great poverty. Hollywood films still perpetuate the stereotyped images of Africa as a place teeming with wildlife and inhabited by dangerous and backward peoples (Hobbs, 2010; Stock, 2004). According to Adichie (2009) most outsiders have a single story of Africa.

Africa is not only a vast continent, to date archaeological findings show that it was also the cradle of human civilization (Ramsay, 2001). Geologically, Africa is the richest continent yet it is the least developed. Africa's diversity can be seen in the many ethnic groups or nationalities that make up the continent's population. Major ethnic groups in Africa include the Berber, Arabs, Taureg, Kanem, Mossi, Hausa, Fulani, Ashanti, Yoruba, Igbo, Ibibio, Fang, Mayumbe, Dinka, Massai, Fung, Ngoni, Ovambo, Herero, Tswana, Swazi, Xhosa, Zulu, Shone, and Bemba. In Africa, over a thousand languages are widely spoken. These languages belong to about four broader language groups or families. These groups include the Niger-Congo language family that is sometimes considered a subfamily of the Niger-Khordofanian. It includes many West African languages and approximately four hundred Bantu subfamily languages that fall into seven branches (Hobbs, 2010). These include the Benue-Congo, Kwa, Atlantic, Mande, Gur, Adamawa, and Khordofanian. Languages in the Benue-Congo group include Fulfulde, Chewa-Nyanja, Gikuyu, Kongo, Luba-Lulua, Makua, Ndebele, Rundi, Rwanda, Shone, Swahili, Xhosa, and Zulu. The languages in the Kwa group include Akan, Igbo, and Yoruba. The Afro-Asiatic language family includes Berber, Tuareg, Hausa, Amharic and Arabic. These are just the major languages. There are others that are too numerous to list. Furthermore, the continent is imbued with a variety of religious beliefs, arts, and music (Aryeetey-Attoh et al., 2010; de Blij et al., 2007; Grove, 1989). Major religious beliefs include Christianity, Islam, and traditional African worship. Hence, it is very difficult to generalize about Africa although various myths and misconceptions about Africa still exist, especially among those who know it least. Thus, this chapter attempts to present a brief geography of Africa, a great and diverse continent.

Size

The continent of Africa covers approximately 11.8 million square miles and accounts for 20.2 percent of total land area on earth, therefore, it is at the heart of the land hemisphere (de Blij et al., 2004). Comparatively, the continent of Africa is more than twice the size of the United States (Hobbs, 2010). Africa would add up to 12 million square miles if the entire adjacent islands—for example, Madagascar—were included. Hence, Africa is the second-largest continent in the world, next to Asia. Unlike the manner in which people unfamiliar with Africa refer to it, Africa is a continent, not a country. It is sometimes difficult to believe that the continent of Africa could accommodate within it the whole of Europe, China, New Zealand, Argentina, India, and the United States (Edge, 2006; Ramsay, 2001) but it could (See Map 1.1. Africa Showing Size in photospread).

Africa extends approximately 5,000 miles from the northernmost point at Cape Ben Bekka in Tunisia, on the Mediterranean coast to Cape Agulhas, at the southernmost tip in the Republic of South Africa (See Map 1.2. Position in photospread). The width of Africa, from the westernmost point at Cape Almedes to the easternmost tip at Cape Hafun is about 4,700 miles (Stock, 2004). Although Africa is the second-largest continent, it has one of the shortest coastlines for a land mass of its size.

Position

Africa lies across the Equator, which almost bisects it into two equal halves. It is separated from Europe by the Strait of Gibraltar in the Mediterranean Sea (near Tunisia) at about 37° 21' N. The Sinai peninsular at the northern end of the Red Sea (this had been cut due to the construction of the Suez Canal) separates Africa from Middle East Asia (George Philip and Son, 2003). To the west, Africa extends to 17° 32' West at Cape Almedes, by the Atlantic Ocean and to the east, it extends to Cape Hafun, on the Indian Ocean, 51° 26' E. Southwards, Africa extends to 34° 52'S (Adams et al., 1999). Africa is the only continent crossed by both the Equator and the Prime Meridian. Also considered as part of

Africa are the islands of Madagascar, one of the world's largest islands that is separated from the mainland by the Mozambique Channel, and other relatively small islands such as Mauritius, Reunion and the Seychelles, Comoros, São Tomé and Príncipe, Guinea Bissau, Equatorial Guinea, and the Canary Islands (still colonized by Spain).

Physical Features

The physical geography of Africa is less complex compared to that of other continents like Asia and Europe. Africa is made up of ancient crystalline rocks. The basement crystalline rocks are mostly composed of metamorphic and granitic rocks (Wright et al., 1985).

These older rock types cover a little over half of the continent. Other areas are covered by longer sedimentary rocks like in the Nile and Niger delta regions. It is important to note here that the older metamorphic and granitic rocks are dated at more than 500 million years and are therefore grouped among rocks of the pre-Cambrian era (Wright et al., 1985). Precambrian (before the Cambrian period) is the term that geologists use to refer to the period before the formation of the oldest rocks with recognizable fossils. It also refers to the period of all geologic processes prior to 600 million years ago. Generally, Africa is a plateau with an average elevation of 3,000 feet. As a result, Africa is usually referred to as the plateau continent (de Blij et al., 2004). Due to this high elevation, Africa, unlike other continents, has a very narrow coastal strip, with very few natural inlets such as the Sierra Leonean estuary. Fairly steep escarpments rise near the coast and extend into the interior. Due to this sharp drop in many coastal areas, African rivers that rise from the interior plunge over falls and rapids before reaching the coast; this limits their navigability. According to de Blij et al. (2004), Africa lacks prominent physical features that are seen in other landmasses such as a linear mountain range (See Map 1.3. Africa Showing Major Physical Features in photospread).

There are, however, areas above this general height of three thousand feet. Prominent among them are: the Atlas Mountains (13,665 ft.) in the northwest that runs from Morocco to Tunisia; the Tibesti plateau (10,712 ft.) in southern Algeria; and Ahaggar Plateau (9,541 ft.) in northern Chad. In West Africa there are the Guinea Highlands or the Fouta Djalon mountains; the Cameroon Mountains (13,353 ft.) on the Adamawa highlands) along the southern border between Nigeria and Cameroon; and the Jos Plateau in north Central Nigeria. In northeast Africa, the Ethiopian highland (15,157 ft.) is prominent. In East Africa, the East African highlands have mountains such as Mount Elgon (14,176 ft.), Mount Kenya (17,058 ft.), and Mount Kilimanjaro (19,341 ft.) (Stock, 2004). Mount Kilimanjaro is the highest mountain in Africa. Although it is situated along the Equator, the snow-capped summit is spectacular and attracts mountaineers from all over the globe. However, recent aerial photographs of the mountain show that the snow is gradually melting, perhaps due to global warming.

Other areas of high elevation in Africa include the Bié Plateau that is found mainly in southwestern Angola, and northern Namibia and the Drakensberg Mountain in southeastern South Africa with a peak at mont-aux-source reaching 10,768 feet (Aryeetey-Attoh et al., 2010; Pulsipher et al., 2008).

Apart from the highlands, there are also lowlands that present spectacular features. Example is the Somali-Djibouti lowland, and lowlands on either side of Mozambique Channel, as well as those along narrow coastal plains and river valleys. Along this low, narrow channel is found the lowest point in Africa, Lac Assal in the country of Djibouti, which is a crater lake 512 feet (-156 meters) below sea level. There is also the great East African Rift Valley with its deep and elongated lakes and beautiful scenery (Adams et al., 1999; Grove, 1989).

African Coastline

African coastline tends to be straight. Hence, there very few natural harbors. It is estimated that the African coastline is about 16,000 miles long, which is too short for a continent of its size. There are, however, a few remarkable natural inlets worth noting. Some natural inlets are found along the Gulf of Guinea. Prominent natural inlets include the estuary at the mouth of the Mesurado River in Liberia, where the Monrovia Harbor is presently situated. Another notable natural inlet is the estuary at the mouth of the Sierra Leone River, which has been estimated to be about four miles wide and is sheltered by the Sherbro Island. The third natural inlet is found in the lower part of the Gulf of Guinea, at the mouth of the Como (or Komo) and the Meberi River estuary in Gabon. Both rivers have their source in the Crystal Mountains to the northeast of the country. The place where both rivers empty into the Atlantic Ocean forms an estuary of about 40 miles long and 9 miles wide.

Another natural phenomenon that is closely associated with the African coastline is narrowness of the continental shelf. The continental shelf is the gently sloping, relatively shallow, submerged plain off the coast of a continent. It extends to a depth of about 600 ft. (about 100 fathoms) and with an average of about 50 miles (de Blij et al., 2004). Continental shelves are the treasure chests of the sea (Gabler et al., 2007). The shallowness allows for a deep penetration of sunlight and therefore, a good breeding ground for fishes and other sea creatures. Africa is one of the continents least endowed with a wide continental shelf except, perhaps, along the Namibia-Angola stretch of coastline; the Ghana and Guinea coasts in West Africa, and the Mauritania-Morocco coastline to the northwest (Aryeetey-Attoh et al., 2010). The continental shelf and all of the natural resources usually belong to the country whose coastline they form. Since African continental coastlines are narrow, they have been exploited by foreign fishermen like the Japanese, who, unchallenged, use illegal fishing nets along African coastlines and by so doing, put local fishermen out of work.

African Rivers

Although Africa's water resources are limited, there are many rivers in Africa that are worth examination. The very fact that Africa is a plateau affects the navigational use of these rivers. All of the major rivers in Africa have outlets to the sea or ocean except for Hadejia and Chari rivers that flow into Lake Chad and the Okavango River that flows into the Okavango Swamps and extends further south into the Makgadikadi pans. These are lakes of inland drainage.

The most notable river in Africa is the Nile River, estimated to be 41,000 miles long and arguably, the longest river in the world and the only river that flows from south to north (Adams et al., 1999). The Nile River rises from Lake Victoria in East Africa and flows northward as the White Nile to Omdurman and Khartoum (twin cities at its confluence) where it is joined by the Blue Nile that rises from Lake Tana on the Ethiopian highlands; it empties into the Mediterranean Sea as a delta in Egypt (Grove, 1989).

Other major rivers (See Map 1.3. Africa Showing Major Physical Features in photospread) include the Congo River which is 2,718 miles long. The Congo is the largest river (by volume) in Africa and drains much of central Africa. The Congo River originates from Zambia and flows northwest and then southwest before emptying into the Atlantic Ocean (Adams et al., 1999). The Niger River raises in the Fouta Djallon highlands and flows for 2,600 miles before it empties into the Gulf of Guinea in the Atlantic Ocean in a delta. Only the Nile and the Niger rivers are noted African rivers that have deltaic mouths; others have estuaries. The Zambezi River is 1,650 miles long and like the Congo River, originates from the highland in Zambia. The Zambezi River flows east and empties into the Indian Ocean in the Mozambique Channel. The Zambezi River is cut by many rapids and waterfalls. The most notable is Victoria Falls located at the border of Zimbabwe and Zambia (Adams et al., 1999; Strahler et al., 2006). The Orange River is the most notable river in southern Africa, with its tributary as the Vaal River; it extends for 1,300 miles (Stock, 2004). It rises from the foothills of the Drakensberg Mountains and flows west to the Atlantic Ocean. Others include the Senegal River (990 miles) and the Volta River, which is 930 miles long (in Ghana).

African Lakes

There are diverse lakes in Africa (See Map 1.4. Major African Rivers and Lakes in photospread). The largest lake in Africa and the third largest in the world is Lake Victoria. There are also Rift Valley lakes (created by tectonic action) such as deep-water lakes Malawi, Tanganyika, Albert, Turkana, and Nyamweru. In fact, Lake Tanganyika is the third-largest lake by volume and is also the second-deepest lake in the world; it contains approximately 1 percent of the world's fresh water. Its greatest depth measures 4,710 feet (Adams et al., 1999). There are also lakes created by volcanic action such as Lake Kivu and Lake Chala in Kenya. Lakes of inland drainage basins include Lake Okavango in Southern Africa and Lake Chad in West Africa (Adams et al., 1999).

Climate

Due to its position, Africa is almost wholly a tropical continent. As noted above, Africa is almost bisected into two equal halves by the Equator. The areas that lie outside the tropical zone are the extreme North and South (areas outside the Tropic of Cancer 23 ½ ⁰ North and Tropic of Capricorn 23 ½ ⁰ South). As a result of this there is a replication of climatic zones north and south of the Equator in Africa and temperatures are high everywhere in the continent. The exceptions are the higher elevations and during the winter seasons in the extreme north and south.

Another factor that affects the climate of Africa is the influence of air masses. The Southeast Trade Winds bring rainfall to most areas in West Africa from March to September. During this period, the ITCZ (Intertropical Convergence Zone) with its attendant low-pressure cell moves northward with the sun towards the Tropic of Cancer. In the south, high-pressure cell is most dominant. However, by January, the situation is reversed. In the north, the ITCZ moves south because at this time the low-pressure belt has moved over to the Tropic of Capricorn (Aryeetey-Attoh et al., 2010). Most of West Africa comes under the influence of the high-pressure belt. Also at this time, the extreme northern part receives rainfall from mid-latitude depressions. This wind, upon crossing the Sahara Desert, loses its moisture and picks up dust as it covers most of West Africa and brings the harmattan season. The harmattan wind is a dry, dusty wind that blows across West Africa from the Sahara; it carries dust that darkens the sky, lowers the temperatures, and reduces visibility (Aryeetey-Attoh et al., 2010; Stock, 2004).

In Africa, south of the Equator, onshore southwesterly winds bring heavy rainfall to the Congo Basin. In East Africa, tropical cyclones move onshore from the Indian Ocean. Areas in the eastern part of the island of Madagascar, parts of east Africa, and southern Africa receive large amounts of rainfall especially along the coastal margins. North and south of the Equator, Africa's rainy seasons last longer near the coast and diminish farther inland.

It should be noted that the Sahara Desert is affected by continentality, and to a lesser extent, the cold Canary Current to the northwest, off the coast of south Western Sahara and Mauritania. On the other hand, in the South, the Kalahari Desert is affected by the cold Benguela Current that washes the coast of Namibia (Grove, 1989).

Vegetation

The vegetation of Africa is less complex than that of most continents. The major vegetation belts in Africa are tropical rainforest, savanna grassland, tropical desert, temperate/Mediterranean vegetation, and mountain vegetation (See Map 1.5 Showing Major Natural Vegetation in photospread).

The Tropical Rainforest

The tropical rainforest is located on both sides of the Equator. Although there are slight changes in the fauna or biomes throughout the tropical world, they are made up of tall trees, usually found to have different levels or canopies. The tropical and subtropical rainforest regions experience year-round rainfall and high temperatures. The annual rainfall in this region is over 80 inches with double maxima. The tropical rainforest is mainly made up of evergreen forests with many varieties of plants and animals. In this region, trees grow quickly and many struggle to get sunlight. There are also many climbers and often, the lower part of the forest is not as crowded. A variety of birds and climbers often occupy the upper portion or canopy. There are also some deciduous plants especially in the subtropical zones (Grove, 1989). The tropical rainforest is an example of biodiversity.

Products of the tropical rainforest: The products of the tropical and subtropical rainforest include hardwood timber, rubber, cocoa, bananas and plantains, pawpaw, (papaya) palm tree, coconuts, cola nuts, rice (especially paddy rice), manioc or cassava, yams, maize, mangoes, cashews, sweet potatoes, pineapples, guavas, and peppers among others. This list is mainly agricultural resources that are produced for domestic consumption as well as for export. This zone supports plantation agriculture for crops such as bananas, cocoa, cashew, palm trees, rubber, and pineapples (Aryeetey-Attoh et al., 2010).

The Savanna Grassland

The savanna, sub-humid tropical grassland can be divided into three broad zones. The difference between the dry season and the rainy season is very pronounced in the savanna region. The dry seasons are longer and keep getting longer as the distances increases from the tropical forest zone (Stock, 2004).

The Guinea Savanna: This is the zone closest to the tropical rainforest. Here the annual rainfall is between 40–60 inches with summer maxima. The vegetation here is composed of very tall grasses like elephant grass. Additionally, this zone is interspersed with trees which are widely spaced and are shorter in height than those that are found in the tropical rainforest. However, trees in this zone are mostly clustered along river and stream banks.

The Sudan Savanna: The Sudan savanna is drier than the Guinea savanna. Rainfall here is less intense with summer maximum of 30–40 inches. There are fewer and shorter trees as well as grasses, compared to the Guinea savanna region (Stock, 2004).

The Sahel Savanna: Here the rainfall is much less than the other two savanna regions. The grasses are shorter (very low). The dry season is longer and rainy season shorter. The average annual rainfall is between 15 to 30 inches of rain per annum with a summer maxima. Trees are rare. Grasses are shorter with narrower blades which enables them to withstand the long dry seasons (Aryeetey-Attoh et al., 2010).

Products of the Savanna: The products of the savanna grassland region include shea-butter, peanuts (ground nuts) maize or corn, rice, sorghum, mangoes, different types of oranges, pineapples, millets, ginger, different types of dyes, gum arabic, pawpaw (papaya), and cashew and palm trees (especially in the wetter Guinea savanna region). Sisal is grown for export especially in East Africa.

The Tropical Desert

The tropical desert zone is found on both sides of the Equator. In the North, the Sahara Desert is very dominant. The Sahara Desert is the world's hottest desert. In the south, the Kalahari and Namib deserts are found in the southwest (Grove, 1989).

The Sahara Desert: Covering almost one third of the African continent and extending for approximately 3,500,000 square miles, the Sahara Desert is composed of a stretch of rocky plains with large, mobile sand dunes. The range in elevation varies from 100 feet below sea level to over 11,000 feet in the Ahaggar and Tibesti mountains (Stock, 2004). There are some regional deserts such as the Libyan, Nubian, and Western Desert in Egypt. The Sahara Desert is partly affected by continentality and overgrazing. For example, the southwest trade winds weaken and become less moist as they move further inland due in part to the vast expanse of land and the cold Canary Current off the cost of Mauritania and Western Sahara.

The Kalahari Desert: Covering approximately 100,000 square miles, it encompasses much of Botswana, western Namibia, and the southwestern regions of South Africa. However, along the coastal region, it is commonly known as the Namib Desert. The Kalahari is a desert plateau crossed by a swath of dry riverbeds. There are a few areas higher than the average plateau elevation. These include the Karas and Huns mountains. The Kalahari Desert is affected by the southwest trade winds which blow almost parallel to the coast and therefore, offshore. It is further denied moisture by the cold Benguela Current which washes the shores of south West Africa thus increasing the dryness (Adams et al., 1999).

Although the deserts are dry, there are fertile spots called oases. Oases are found in shallow depressions where local inhabitants dig wells in order to draw water from the subterranean water reservoir (Aryeetey-Attoh et al., 2010). In the Sahara Desert, a few underground rivers flow from the Atlas Mountain into the desert, thus helping to irrigate some of the oases. In addition, the Nile River, especially in Egypt, helps to provide water for irrigation and for other purposes.

In the Kalahari, the Okavango River provides the needed water for irrigation and wildlife. Large herds of wildlife are found in the Kalahari especially in the Gemsbok National Park. The Okavango River is a river of inland drainage. It does not have an outlet to the sea; rather, it empties itself into the sands of the Kalahari Desert in Botswana thus helping to irrigate approximately 15,000 km^2 (9,375 sq. miles) of desert (Adams et al., 1999). It is estimated that about 11 cubic kilometers (6.875 cubic miles) of water reach this inland delta annually. In fact, some of the water flows southward to create Lake Ngami. This lake, which is now a tourist attraction, is a haven for wildlife. It is worth noting that the waters of Okavango River and the river delta that it created experience seasonal flooding which begins about mid-summer in the north and about six months later in the south (Grove, 1989). However, due to excessive evaporation and high temperatures, water levels rise and fall. When the water level is low, islands appear in the delta, but when the volume is high, they disappear, especially during peak flood periods.

Moreover, since mean annual rainfall in the desert is less than 10 inches; oasis dwellers have long adopted different sophisticated methods of irrigation in order to cultivate some food crops. For example, they cultivate date palm, a tree that can withstand great heat, high rates of evaporation, and soil containing moderately high content of common salt (calcium chloride) solution. Other crops include tobacco, onions, small tomatoes, peas, beans, and melons. They also grow figs and vines which often manage to survive in the shades of the palms. Apart from crops, oasis dwellers also keep livestock. For example, they keep camels, chickens, and goats. The oasis can be compared to a truck stop where people who journey across the desert can replenish their food and water supplies as well as hay for their camels ("ships of the desert").

The Temperate/Mediterranean Vegetation

This vegetation type is found at the Northern and Southern tips of the continent. In this vegetation belt, annual rainfall is moderate, usually about 40–60 inches. In South Africa it is locally known as the Kraal. This is a climatic zone with cool summers and mild wet winters. Average annual temperature is approximately 55° F. Crops grown in this zone include wheat, rice, vines, grapes, and apples (Adams et al., 1999).

The Mountain Vegetation

The mountain vegetation zone can occur anywhere even in tropical rainforests. Altitude modifies the temperature and influences the vegetation type. At certain elevations, the forest at the foothills give way to grassland where cattle and other livestock are raised (Stock, 2004). The mountain vegetation region has been estimated to have over 4,000 plant species, 80 percent of which are mostly restricted to the higher altitude (Aryeetey-Attoh et al., 2010). On other slopes where the land gently rises, crops such as coffee and tea are grown in plantations (*shamba* in Kenya) for export as well as for local consumption. There are also coffee and tea plantations on the Guinea Highlands, the Bamenda Highlands, and the Ethiopian Highlands (Grove, 1989). On the Ethiopian Highland, a special brand of species of coffee indigenous to Ethiopia (*Coffea arabica*) is grown (Aryeetey-Attoh et al., 2010). *Coffea arabica* is considered to be a better coffee species than any other major commercially grown coffee species such as *Coffea canephora* (robusta). Recently, an American coffee chain, Starbucks, began negotiations with the Ethiopian government regarding the use of the trade name.

Also grown on the mountain vegetation zone is pyrethrum, especially on the

Kenyan highlands. Pyrethrum is a natural insecticide and is used in the manufacturing of different household insect sprays. In 1998, Kenya produced 90 percent (approximately 6,000 tons) of the world's pyrethrum. Tanzania is also producing a significant quantity of pyrethrum for the world market.

Natural Resources

Most of Africa is made up of ancient crystalline rocks dating from the Precambrian period. Such rocks include igneous rock such as granite and metamorphic rocks like schist, gneiss, and quartz. These old rocks, together with slightly younger sedimentary rocks such as sandstones and limestone, form the basement complex of the African continent and the source of large collection of its mineral resources.

Africa is an important source of several minerals and is the dominant source of supply for a few mineral commodities. In fact, it has been estimated that Africa produces half or more of the world's chromium, diamonds and platinum, and about 20 percent or more of the world's cobalt, gold, manganese, uranium, and titanium (See Map 1.6. Africa Showing Location of Natural and Agricultural Resources in photospread). Other minerals such as bauxite, phosphate, copper, and petroleum are also produced in large quantities, in South Africa, for example, especially in the Map 1.6. Africa Showing Location of Natural and Agricultural Resources.

Witwatersrand region and around the province of Orange Free State, gold is extracted from rich reefs. These reefs are made of layers of old metamorphosed sedimentary rocks. The same formation includes other minerals such as copper, platinum, chromium, iron ore, and coal. The Great Dyke ridge, which bisects Zimbabwe from the northeast, was formed when hot magma fizzed into older geological formation and slowly cooled, forming such minerals as chromium. The same process led to the formation of diamond-bearing kimberlite deposits in countries such as Democratic Republic of the Congo, Botswana, South Africa, Angola, Sierra Leone, and Liberia.

Other parts of Africa have large reserves of bauxite and aluminum, iron ore, manganese, graphite, lead, cobalt, mica, nickel, molybdenum, sulfur, tungsten, uranium, tin, vanadium, and zinc. There are sufficient reserves of petroleum and natural gas found in sedimentary rock basins south of the Atlas Mountains, in countries like Libya, Algeria, and Morocco. Another area of production is along the Atlantic Coast (both on shore and off shore) between Ivory Coast, Guinea Bissau, Niger Delta, Bakassi peninsula, Equatorial Guinea, Gabon, and Angola. The central Nile Valley, especially Southern Sudan, is an emerging center of petroleum production in the African interior.

Population

The total population of Africa was estimated at approximately 770 million (Hobbs, 2010). It should, however, be noted that Africa population is not evenly distributed due to a variety of ecological and historical / cultural factors (Stock, 2004). Moreover, national population densities vary from about 2 persons per square mile /kilometer in places like Namibia to approximately 337 persons per square mile/kilometer in a country like Rwanda. According to Stock (2004), the least densely populated countries; especially those with fewer than 10 persons per square mile/kilometer account for about 6.4 percent of the total ecumene in Africa but only occupy 30.8 percent of the total area. The ecumene is the livable portion of earth's surface that is permanently inhabited by human beings (de Blij, 2004). In addition, some countries such as Niger, Central African Republic, Burkina Faso, Mauritania, Mali, Chad, Gabon, Botswana, Angola, Namibia and Congo Republic have low densities that are very diverse. These countries are found throughout the continent and in all major biomes—tropical rainforests, Savanna, semi arid deserts and deserts.

On the other hand, countries with high population densities of over 80 persons per square mile/kilometer account for approximately one third of the population but occupy about 6.7 percent of the area (Stock, 2004). Even within the high density area there are areas with higher densities such as Nigeria. Nigeria alone account for about 60 percent of the high density group's total population and about 56 percent of its area (Stock, 2004). It is important to note that areas of high or low densities do not necessarily correspond with national units. Sometimes regions of exceptional densities cut across national boundaries. Additionally, there are substantial regional variations in population densities in almost all countries. For example, in Nigeria, several areas such as Igboland in the Southeast, Yoruba heartland in the South-west and the North central areas of Kano, Zaria and Sokoto have high population densities. Other areas with high population densities in Africa include the Nile valley in Egypt, the zone extending from Burundi and Rwanda to the northern shoreline of Lake Victoria and southern Uganda, Western Kenya, central Ethiopia as well as several pockets of South Africa (the apartheid created homelands), as well as the Islands of Cape Verde, Comoros, São Tomé and Príncipe (Stock, 2004). Generally there are pockets of high population densities along the coastal regions and in major urban centers especially in primate cities. Urban population in Africa was estimated at 33 percent. Overall population per square mile in Africa was estimated at 72 (Stock, 2004).

Regarding birth and death rates, a breakdown of available statistics shows that the number of births per thousand is 38 and deaths per thousand, is 14. This census data shows that the rate of natural increase in Africa was estimated at 2.5 percent per annum (Hobbs, 2010). It was further projected that between 2002 and 2050, the population of Africa will change by 13.2 percent. Hence, the projected population of Africa for the year 2025 was estimated at 1,281 million and

2050 at 1,845 million. It is important to emphasize that there was a time when African parents desired large families to utilize extra hands to work the farms and to care for the sick or elderly, but family sizes are changing; they decrease with education.

In addition, infant mortality rate was 86 with total fertility at 5.2 (Population Reference Bureau, 2004). Infant mortality rate is the annual number of deaths of infants under the age of 1 year per 1,000 live births. Table 1.1 presents the regional distribution of population in Africa. It shows that regional population is not evenly distributed. Furthermore, it shows that West and East Africa have the highest density or concentration of people on the African continent. In addition, the percentage of African population that is less than 15 years old was about 44 percent and those 65 years and above, 3 percent. This implies that a higher percentage of the African population is still young. In addition, life expectancy at birth for males is 52 years and for females, 54 years.

Table: 1.1. Regional Distribution of Population in Africa

Regions	Populations
North Africa	191 million
West Africa	263 million
East Africa	270 million
Central Africa	107 million
Southern Africa	53 million

Source: Compiled from World Population Data Sheet (Thomson/Brooks Cole, 2004).

The inference from Table 1.1's statistics shows that there is a high birth rate as well as a high death rate in Africa. Infant mortality is still high in Africa as well as low life expectancy. This could be attributed to many factors including lack of or poor development of health infrastructure, or even the availability of health services. While urbanization is fast growing in many African countries, the provision of social services does not keep pace with the rate of urban development (Moseley, 2009). African urban growth has been estimated at between 4–5 percent per annum (Fellmann et al., 2005). This is higher than that of any other region in the world. Diseases which could be prevented with the provision of basic social services such as electricity, portable or pipe-borne water, better sanitation, and hygienic methods, are still developing in Africa.

Hence, Africa is still largely rural with about 66 percent of the population classified as rural. According to Hobbs (2010) in some countries, rural population is as high as between 65 and 85 percent. However, it should be noted that Africa has one of the fastest rates of urbanization or urban growth rate at about 5 percent per annum (de Blij et al., 2007; Pulsipher et al., 2008).

African Urbanization

The history of urbanization in African can be traced back to city-states and empires that existed before the arrival of European colonialists. However, many African cities were built by European colonizers as centers of trade and government.

In recent decades, African cities have been growing very fast due to increasing rural-to-urban migration. According to Pulsipher et al. (2008), in the 1960s, only about 15 percent of Africans lived in cities but now it is estimated at about 34 percent. It should be noted that there is a great variation in the rate of urbanization between countries. African cities attracted a massive influx of rural migrants because rural areas offer very few jobs and little opportunity for upward social mobility. In addition, there is the presumption that life in the city offers a quick access to money and prestige. However, the truth is that most African urban dwellers work at very low wages, mostly in the informal sector (Rowntree et al., 2008).

Most African countries have one large primate city, which in most cases, is the capital city. However, there are other countries such as Nigeria and South Africa that have more than one primate city.

It is important to note here that many people outside Africa often view Africa as a region with dysfunctional countries and cities. As with all stereotypes, coupled with Hollywood's presentation of Africa as a place where lions roam the streets, it is difficult to dispel such images. Admittedly, there is some dysfunctionality existing in economic, cultural, political, and environmental spheres in the continent. For example, with the rate of urbanization accelerating from 15 percent in the 1960s to about 35 percent at the turn of the century, there are bound to be inequalities in the provision of urban social services (Brunn et al., 2003). The supply of urban housing and social amenities could not keep pace with the rate of rural to urban migration and urbanization, leading to poor housing quality and the growth of slums. In addition, a combination of large numbers of rural to urban migrants and widespread unemployment most often leads to overwhelming pressure for low-rent housing (Jordan-Bychkov et al., 2006). Most African governments have rarely been able to meet these needs through housing projects resulting in the growth of slums in some countries and squatter settlements in others. Moreover, since economic development cannot keep pace with either population growth or with urbanization, social and physical characteristics normally associated with urbanization and city growth failed to materialize. Hence, according to Brunn et al. (2003) most African cities present architectural kaleidoscopes of structures with great disparities in housing quality and urban social amenities. It is not uncommon to find shanty and slum dwellings without any major social amenities like piped or potable water, electricity, or central sewage systems, juxtapose with very expensive mansions with all comforts, comparable to those in Europe and the United States.

Conclusion

Despite its huge resources—human, natural as well as agricultural—Africa's identity to the outside world is defined by hunger, famine, refugees, and wars. Abundant resources have not been deployed to Africa's overall development. In fact, Africa is noted as the poorest continent with the annual per-capita income of less than $500 in many countries. Overall, little has been known about Africa and even now, not much is known; hence the writings of early eighteenth-century Irish satirist, Jonathan Swift (1667-1745), are still true:

> So geographers in Africa maps
> With savage pictures fill their gaps,
> And o'er uninhabitable downs
> Place elephants for want of towns. (Stock, 2004)

Bibliography

Adams, William M., Andrew S. Goudie, and Antony R. Orme. *The Physical Geography of Africa.* Oxford: Oxford University Press, 1999.

Adichie, N. Chimamanda. *The Danger of a Single Story*. Video. 2009. http://www.ted.com/talks/lang/eng/chimamanda_adichie_the_danger_of_a_single_story.html (accessed on July 23, 2010).

Aryeetey-Attoh, Samuel, Barbara E. McDade, Godson C. Obia, Joseph R. Oppong, William Y. Osei, Ian Yeboah, and Ibipo Johnston-Anumonwo. *Geography of Sub-Saharan Africa*, 3rd ed. New York: Prentice Hall, 2010.

Bergman, Edward F., and William H. Renwick. *Introduction to Geography: People, Places, and Environment*, 8th ed. Upper Saddle River, NJ: Pearson Prentice Hall, 2008.

Brunn, Stanley D., Jack F. Williams, and Donald J. Zeigler. *Cities of the World: World Regional Urban Development*, 3rd ed. Lanham, MD: Rowman & Littlefield Publishers, Inc., 2003.

Clawson, David L., Douglas L. Johnson, Viola Haarmann, and Merrill L. Johnson. (2007) *World Regional Geography*: A *Development Approach.* Upper Saddle River, NJ: Pearson/Prentice Hall, 2007.

de Blij, Harm J., and Roger M. Downs. *College Atlas of the World.* Washington, DC: National Geographic, 2007.

de Blij, Harm J., and Peter O. Muller. *The World Today: Concepts and Regions in Geography*, 3rd ed. New York: John Wiley & Sons Inc., 2007.

de Blij, Harm J., Peter O. Muller, and Richard S. Williams. *Physical Geography: The Global Environment,* 3rd ed. New York: Oxford University Press, 2004.

de Blij, Harm J., Alexander B. Murphy, and Erin H. Fouberg. *Human Geography: People, Place, and Culture,* 8th ed. New York: John Wiley and Sons, Inc., 2007.

Edge, Wayne. *Global Studies: Africa,* 11th ed. Guilford, CT: Dushkin/McGraw-Hill, 2006.

Fellmann, Jerome D., Arthur Getis, and Judith Getis. *Human Geography: Landscapes of Human Activities,* 6th ed. New York: McGraw Hill Higher Education, 2005.

Gabler, Robert E, James F. Petersen, and L. Michael Trapasso. *Essentials of Physical Geography*, 8th ed. Belmont, CA: Thomson Brooks/Cole, 2007.

George Philip & Son. *Oxford New Concise World Atlas.* New York: Oxford University Press, 2003.

Grove, Alfred T. *The Changing Geography of Africa*, 2nd ed. Oxford: Oxford University Press, 1989.

Hobbs, Joseph J. *Fundamentals of World Regional Geography*, 2nd ed. Belmont, CA: Thomson Brooks/Cole Cengage Learning, 2010.

Jordan-Bychkov, Terry G., Mona Domosh, Roderick P. Neumann, and Patricia L. Price. *The Human Mosaic: A Thematic Introduction to Cultural Geography*, 10th ed. New York: W. H. Freeman, 2006.

Moseley, William G. *Clashing Views on African Issues*, 3rd ed. Boston: McGraw Hill Higher Education, 2009.

Pulsipher, Lydia M., Alex Pulsipher, and Conrad Mac Goodwin. *World Regional Geography: Global Patterns, Local Lives,* 4th ed. New York: W. H. Freeman and Company, 2008.

Ramsay, F. Jeffress. *Global Studies: Africa*, 9th ed. Guilford, CT: McGraw-Hill/Dushkin, 2001.

Rowntree, Lester, Marie Price, and William Wyckoff. *Globalization and Diversity: Geography of a Changing World,* 2nd ed. Upper Saddle River, NJ: Pearson/Prentice Hall, 2008.

Stock, Robert F. *Africa South of the Sahara: A Geographical Interpretation*, 2nd ed. New York: Guilford Press, 2004.

Strahler, Alan, and Arthur Strahler. *Introducing Physical Geography,* 4th. ed. John Wiley & Sons, Inc., 2006.

Thomson/Brooks Cole. "World Population Data Sheet of the Population Reference Bureau." Belmont, CA: Brooks/Cole-Thomson Learning, 2002.

Wright J. B., D. A. Hastings, W. B. Jones, and H. R. Williams. *Geology and Mineral Resources of West Africa.* Boston: George Allen and Unwin, 1985.

Chapter 2
Countering Ethnocentrism in Teaching the Human Geography of Africa[1]

Ibipo Johnston-Anumonwo

Introduction

It is very gratifying to know that teachers of human and cultural geography courses have at their disposal a wide range of instructional materials on Africa to teach key concepts and facts to students in ways that do not portray a predominantly negative tone about the continent. While commending the improvements in prevailing methods and perspectives (e.g., Bastian and Parpart, 1999), one still notes that there are continuing ethnocentric perspectives about Africa that must be exposed, decried, and eradicated in order to engender a balanced knowledge of Africa's human geography. Ethnocentrism—the attitude or tendency to view one's culture, ethnic group, religion, or national background as superior to others by emphasizing cultural differences and promoting the converse assumption that all other groups are inherently inferior—has generated widespread misunderstanding and territorial conflict. Ethnocentrism hinders objectivity and the ability for people to learn from others but since education at its best stresses the equality of all people and similarities across humanity, it is one of the best ways to defuse ethnocentrism. This chapter discusses a variety of methods and content that can be effective in promoting a balanced perspective in teaching and learning about Africa. Six aspects are discussed as illustrations of positive content and approaches that countervail one-sided misrepresentations of Africa's human geography.

A standard human geography course outline typically consists of content on cultural patterns and processes, regional variations in cultural elements, cultural diffusion, and the ways by which culture is reflected in the landscape. Among the cultural geography topics that provide relevant teaching opportunities which are applicable to Africa are the exploration of evidence on Africa as humanity's original cultural hearth, the origin and spread of various culture traits, especially language and religion, and the continuity and change in Africa's cultural evolution that expose the interactions of indigenous influences with processes of modern cultural change that are manifested in Africa's cultural diversity.

Africa's Cultural Diversity: *Africa is Not a Country*

The provocative title of a book, *Africa is Not a Country* (Knight, 2000), is an attempt to correct the widespread error in US students' spatial perception (i.e., awareness of places). The volume and variety of African languages (not dialects) provide a perfect forum to teach about the African continent's cultural landscape as vast and variegated. Classic maps of Africa's languages (hundreds) and language distribution abound in textbooks and Internet sites. For cultural regions, readily available distribution maps of Africa's main religions offer broad distinctions between predominantly Muslim Northern Africa and predominantly Christian Southern Africa, with a central transition zone of a significant Muslim minority in much of Eastern and Central Africa and across the southern parts of West African countries. The study of Islam in Africa can be used to illustrate patterns and processes of cultural diffusion noting the geographical proximity to Islam's cultural hearth; diffusion types, paths, barriers, facilitators, and adopters; and Islamic influences a *lingua franca* like Swahili or upon built landscapes. Ali Mazrui's thesis of Africa's "triple heritage" and other African viewpoints on multiculturalism and cultural diversity (Odhiambo, 1997) should be included.

Culture, Conflict and Change in Africa—Colonialism and Imperialism: Include Historical Analyses

Geographic education materials for teaching Africa's human geography are most commendable in appropriately tackling the critique of colonialism. Human Geography textbooks can hardly be flawed for being ahistorical in analysis of colonialism in Africa. On the contrary, all current standard textbooks with references to colonialism in Africa provide a valid critique of the nature and effects of colonial contact (Myers, 2001). Classroom debates are an approach that further promotes critical thinking. Exposing students to contending scholarly analyses and opposing viewpoints about colonialism, gender, or political issues (Moseley, 2009) is enlightening. To supplement textbooks, novels about the colonial era are rich teaching tools. A classic novel is Chinua Achebe's *Things Fall Apart* (Achebe, 1994). Students can discuss the nature of cultural imperialism in Eastern Nigeria and decide whether or not they agree that the book's title is accurate.

In US classrooms, another way to use the book is to engage students in an activity that identifies similarities between Ibos and Americans. Through a comparison of several aspects in the way of life of the Ibos and contemporary Americans (traditions, values, daily activities, beliefs—both positive and negative), students identify and discuss far more similarities than differences and reach a conclusion about the story as representative of "human qualities common to all men of all times and places." It is a powerful exercise for defusing ethnocentrism. At the end of the story, a quick survey of "whose side are you on?" yields more students who are sympathetic of the Ibos.

Africa's Political Map: Discuss the Norm and Identify Alternative Examples

The topic of jurisdictional organization of space calls for a rethinking of the widely used assertion that colonial superimposition of boundaries caused Africa's instability (Myers 2001). This framework and its attendant dependence by textbooks and teachers on the classic map of Africa's ethnic groups may indeed be overused. Instead, in teaching spatial connections between patterns of ethnicity and political patterns, a more accurate stance is not only to link part of Africa's post-colonial political instability to the inherited colonial boundaries, but to also include and emphasize the exceptions. In this case, the exception is the norm—in the sense that the prevalent reality is one of nonboundary disputes among African nation states. Most African countries do not have boundary disputes in spite of retaining the arbitrary, imposed colonial boundaries.

When teaching relationships between culture and politics in contemporary Africa, important qualifiers should be highlighted. Ethiopia—one of a couple of well-known countries without prolonged European colonization, but whose reality since the 1970s is plagued with boundary conflicts with its mostly ethnically homogenous neighbors (Somalia and Eritrea)—offsets the overemphasis on a sole cultural causation thesis of European superimposed boundaries. Qualifying the prevalent reality and providing alternative examples allows critical thinking of connections between culture and Africa's political map. To simply claim that the resultant carving up of African space after the Berlin Conference is the source of Africa's political boundary conflicts is a wrong cultural deterministic viewpoint.

Ethnic Territorial Conflict: Social Construct and African Agency in Reconciliation

Africa's numerous ethnic and religious conflicts (in Nigeria, Kenya, South Africa, and Chad) provide teachers of human and cultural geography with ample case studies for elucidating geography concepts. Yet, one opportunity is teaching the historical basis of these conflicts. Rather than merely presenting the horrors of the past conflicts in Liberia and Sierra Leone, or the prolonged conflict in Darfur, the socially constructed character of the conflicts should be taught (Myers, 2001). Such an approach is both comprehensive and forward looking, in the sense that it more completely identifies the deep sources of the conflicts as well as focuses on the viewpoint that since the tensions were socially constructed, a viable approach for their resolution is to deconstruct the importance of ethnicity, religion, or language. This is a teaching approach that leaves students with a more hopeful vision of Africa rather than a hopeless one.

Another important theme to teach is the role of Africans and African governments in conflict resolution. Students should be taught about the many current initiatives in Africa that attempt to restore peace. These multilateral efforts illustrate cooperation and collaboration among African countries in solving Africa's problems (instead of the tendency to portray African nation states as constantly at war and in disagreement with each other). The example of ECOMOG in Liberia, with its mixed results, is a case in point.

Instead of focusing always and only on 1990s' ethnic cleansing in Rwanda and Burundi, the contemporary ethnic reconciliation efforts in these countries also offer an unusual teaching moment. Much is known and publicized about the dreadfulness of the conflict, but little attention is given to post-war efforts at peace building and reconciliation (a recent PBS documentary is especially useful in teaching about the role of African women in conflict resolution). A similar situation is the Biafra war: the terror of the thirty-month civil war is well known and taught, but little attention is given to the Nigerian government's resettlement and reconstruction efforts which were successful in healing some of the wounds and ethnic animosities. Post-conflict success stories enable the teaching of positive elements of Africa's human geography especially as it relates to democracy.

Democracy in Africa: Include Multiple Examples and Avoid Stereotypes

Perhaps the case study that can be most celebrated is the shift to a democratic regime in the Republic of South Africa. Geographers, like all other scholars correctly identify and teach the South African post-apartheid era as a positive change. After decades of the racist policy of apartheid, in 1994, South Africa conducted democratic elections in which all citizens were eligible to vote. The country's map no longer consists of the fragmented ethnic homelands (Bantustans), with its imprint of European-imposed boundary limits. Likewise, the country's Commission on Truth and Reconciliation can be presented for students to debate the pros and cons of this atypical approach to pardon ethnic-based misgivings. More illuminating case studies that portray African activists can be gleaned from a 2001 video appropriately titled *Hopes on the Horizon*.

The singular focus on South Africa's end of apartheid success story in teaching about Africa's human geography is problematic since many other equally significant democratic transformations on the continent are ignored. There are African countries where cultural factors do not constitute sources of tension. Rather, teachers should bring to students' attention the popular democratization movements in Benin Republic, Burkina Faso, Malawi, or Botswana since the inclusion of such less-known and less-taught examples in the human geography curriculum helps to expose students to more African countries and the more widespread reality, rather than the isolated depiction of what is going right in Africa (Chege, 1994).

Along with misrepresentations such as "Rwanda as Africa" (referred to as geographical simplification by Myers), teachers must avoid perpetuating out-of-date ideas and terminology that is associated with native, primitive, tribe, and race. Students should also become skeptical of an ethnocentric attitude that sees African women only as subjects of development. Rather, students should be exposed to teaching and learning perspectives that enable them to recognize African women in their true roles as active contributors to and sustainers of development as well as dynamic agents of change ranging from initiatives to restore the environment (a chance to celebrate the Nobel prize winner, Wangari Maathai—founder of the Green Belt Movement), to female-led geopolitical reforms across the continent.

Gender and Indigenous Culture: Emphasize Areal Variation and Societal Change

The topic of gender and development is an area where the teaching of Africa's human geography has shown satisfactory progress. But, from the geographer's perspective, it cannot be overemphasized that there are important variations across the continent due to differences in government policies, economic conditions, and attitudes about women, as well as in cultural values, all of which make it impossible to generalize about gender issues in Africa. Hence, teachers must use multiple methodologies and focus on multiple indicators if students are to grasp an accurate understanding of the multiple and changing roles of women throughout Africa.

Although women carry out much of Africa's agricultural tasks and despite increases in female-headed households, the stereotypical assumption of a male-headed household is still widespread, and development resources continue to be channeled disproportionately to African men. An exercise that asks students to attempt to fit female-typed tasks into standard census categories of gainful employment serves to impress upon the students the importance of complementing quantitative studies with studies based on qualitative inquiry. Census data abound of the extent of water pipes in a community but there are no censuses of the miles that women walk to the water wells or, of women's extensive activities in the informal economy. Thus, the contributions of African women remain either unaccounted for or discounted. Using widely documented and readily obtained conventional measures such as fertility and maternal mortality, students can generate their own maps that show the geography of women's conditions across Africa—they can use data on male-versus-female literacy rates or HIV infection rates to analyze the geography of gender, while the teachers stress regional variations. Longitudinal data should be used to emphasize that the total fertility rate has declined, and thereby counter the stubborn preconceived attitudes of static "cultural determinants" of high fertility in Africa. Show of exceptional cases: Mauritius, with a maternal mortality rate of 50 (per thousand), has sustained one of the best records for Africa.

To illustrate the influence of culture on human-environment relationships, Africa's agricultural crisis should be taught with an emphasis on gender. A full understanding of the multifaceted dimensions of Africa's food crisis must include an analysis of women's alienation from productive resources and continuing patriarchal views that it is a woman's traditional duty to perform the housework. Combined with role play in the classroom, *With These Hands: How Women Feed Africa* (a succinct video produced by the New Internationalist), gives rise to excellent opportunities for students to critically rethink the connections between gender and development. For example, the emphasis in development geography on production neglects social reproduction. Yet, failure to consider social reproduction means ignoring the lopsided gender division of labor within the home. Given the unequal gender division of household work, it is easier to understand why many rural African women have several children. By examining the household as a unit of analysis, intra-household gender relations are studied as part of the human, social, and cultural processes that shape African conditions.

Teachers can capitalize on the fact that students in introductory-level human geography courses vividly understand the significance of land, labor, and money (even time) as resources. So they can appreciate the argument that if African women have greater access to and control of productive resources, they will not need large numbers of children to ensure their social security. Students could comment on the novel, *Joys of Motherhood*, by Buchi Emecheta (1979), but this time, the charge is to explain why the title is ironic. Through these varied instructional materials and methods, students learn that African women's conditions and status as a "social periphery" is socially created; it is neither natural nor traditional. The image of African women as passive victims of development is one-sided, and they should not be thought of only as exhausted mothers of malnourished children who are in dire need of development aid. In fact, teachers must counter erroneous stereotypes on African ignorance, and feature African knowledge, indeed new knowledge, and indigenous innovations in agriculture (e.g., Davis, 1996). Hundreds of self-organized women's groups are active in environmental conservation programs, unsurprisingly because women are much more likely than men to be the ones whose responsibility is to obtain firewood for domestic fuel. Some implications are that: a) women have a greater interest in the long-term productivity of food and fuel resources; or b) women in refugee camps or war-torn areas face the danger of sexual abuse (Congo) and violence when fetching firewood (e.g., Darfur). Also, it is worth noting that at the governmental level most African countries have signed and ratified the UN convention on the elimination of all forces of discrimination against women—CEDAW.

Yet, case studies, not a sweeping coverage of the continent, better underscore continuing significance of indigenous culture in health care, or clarify that it is not African immoral sexuality and prostitution that causes HIV/AIDS, or expose the limits of many cross-cultural analyses (e.g., Nagel, 2001). In Africa, as elsewhere, by "excluding half the human in human geography" and ignoring the world of women, a non-gendered perspective for studying geographical patterns and processes provides an incomplete understanding of human geography. Further, if gender, like ethnicity, is taught as a social construct—a phenomenon that is created by society and that varies spatially and over time, then the main lesson that students learn is that these cultural elements and their impacts can be revised.

Conclusion

Regardless of whether the materials are textbooks, atlases, newspapers, magazines, internet websites, music, films, or guest speakers' critiques about Africa's representation in instructional materials and social science textbooks existed decades ago (e.g., Fuller, 1971) and more recently (e.g., Myers, 2001), when the goal is to defuse ethnocentrism in the teaching of the cultural geography of Africa, it is worth repeating more than thirty years later, that "in the last analysis, it is the purposeful selection, use and reuse of a wide variety of instructional materials that provide the key to worthwhile teaching and learning about Africa today" (Willmer, 1975, p. 224).

Note

1. Ibipo Johnston-Anumonwo, "Countering Ethnocentrism in Teaching the Human Geography of Africa," earlier version of paper presented at the annual meeting of International Geographical Union Commission on Geographical Education (IGU-CGE), 2006.

Bibliography

Achebe, Chinua. *Things Fall Apart*. New York: Knopf Doubleday, 1994.

Bastian, Misty L., and Jane L. Parpart (eds.). *Great Ideas for Teaching about Africa*. Boulder, CO: Lynne Rienner Publishers, 1999.

Chege, Michael. "What's Right with Africa?" *Current History*, no. 93, 583 (May 1994): 193–97.

Davis, Diana K. "Gender, Indigenous Knowledge and Pastoral Resource Use in Morocco." *Geographical Review*, 86, no. 2 (January 1, 1996): 284–88.

Emecheta, Buchi. *The Joys of Motherhood: A Novel*. New York, NY: George Braziller, 1979.

Fuller, Michael J. "Africa as Seen by World History Textbooks." *Social Education*, 35, no. 5 (May 1971): 466–73.

Knight, Margy Burns. *Africa is Not a Country*. Minneapolis, MN: Millbrook Press, 2000.

Moseley, William G. *Taking Sides: Clashing Views on African Issues*. New York, NY: McGraw-Hill (third edition), 2009.

Myers, Garth A. "Introductory Human Geography Textbook Representations of Africa." *Professional Geographer* 53, no. 4 (2001): 522–32.

Nagel, Mechthild. "On the Limits of Cross-cultural Feminist Analysis on Discourses about African Women." In *Issues in Africa and the African Diaspora in the 21st Century*, edited by Seth N. Asumah and Ibipo Johnston-Anumonwo, 53–79. Binghamton, NY: Global Publications Press, 2001.

Odhiambo, Atteno. "African Perspectives on Cultural Diversity and Multiculturalism." *Journal of Asian and African Studies*, 32, nos. 3 and 4 (1997): 185–201.

Willmer, John E. (ed.). *Africa: Teaching Perspectives and Approaches*. Tualatin, OR: Geographic and Area Studies Publications, 1975.

Chapter 3
African Religions and Spirituality: The Case of Okija Shrine Worship in Eastern Nigeria

Ngozi Caleb Kamalu

Introduction

In Nigeria, the majority are either Christians or Muslims. The former are primarily inhabitants in Eastern region of Nigeria. However, a small group of religious groups (animists) worship other traditional Nigerian religions. Most of the time, these people worship objects: rocks, rivers, hills/mountains, forests, and trees. In most cases, a sacred place called "shrine" is reserved for offerings and other forms of sacrifice. A shrine is often dedicated to a specific spirit or deity. A shrine is like an altar, temple, or a sacred place earmarked for the worship of a deity. At the center of shrine activity is the "ritual"—which is a prescribed order of performing rites, just like baptisms, marriages, church services, and proceedings at a traditional shrine. Most of the time, the objects used in sacrifices include but are not limited to cows, sheep, bulls, goats, dogs, fowl/chickens, and foodstuffs—fruits, maize, eggs, honey, and cassava. Drinks may even be offered to the deity—milk, water, leaves, and tobacco. Among the Igbo of Eastern Nigeria, shrines as places of traditional worship are scattered all over in different communities and with different names, histories, hierarchy, and allegiance.

The shrine is widely regarded as a religious institution and an essential ritual sacrifice among the Igbo of eastern Nigeria. It is also a visible symbol of cult and religious worship of the deity. Shrines exist in many forms. Some are more localized and smaller in size. These mainly serve the spiritual and ritual needs of the immediate family unit. On the other hand, communal shrines are usually large, higher in the pecking order and serve the ritual needs of a wider community. They are vital sacred institutions that contribute immensely to the community's sense of being. They are sited in large public squares where they could serve many community purposes, even though they are primarily for tribal worships. It has many stages specified for specific community services which include but are not limited to meetings, markets, festivals, wrestling, dancing, and other kinds of public observances. Many kindred take turns in keeping them clean. They are often surrounded by different kinds of prohibitions and taboos. They are symbols of reverence because of what they represent.

Primary Functions of the Shrine

According to the writing of N. S. S. Iwe, "Igbo Deities" (1988), the shrine serves many purposes:

(1) It commands a special moral and social place in Igbo society. Apart from its religious and cult role, it serves as the custodian of public morality and order in the community. For example, any violations of the moral code—commission of societal crimes like suicide, abortion, incest, stealing, and adultery are considered a letdown or abomination. The consequence is therefore an alienation of the deity, the protector of the community from omens. In such a case, a cleansing exercise is urgently needed to woo back the protective hands and favors of the divinities. Thus, only the performance of appropriate and befitting rites at the shrine will purify the transgressor and the land, appease the deities and ancestors, and thus restore the community to spiritual harmony and tranquility.

(2) In any inter-clan disputes involving rival claims to land, fathering of children out of wedlock, or adultery, the warring parties in the dispute may be required to appear publicly before the community shrine and its chief priest to swear before the authority of the shrine and the divinity in support of their claims. In some cases, depending on the preferences of the chief priests of the shrine, the principal rival claimants may appear alone, while in others the attendance is expanded to include all members of the claimants' immediate families who will be required to swear while standing with their feet placed in the "ritual" basket of *Amadioha* (god of thunder—a deity).

(3) Special occasions and ceremonies—marriage ceremonies, chieftaincies, yam festivals, New Year events and other forms of community celebration are usually begun and ended with the observance of relevant rites by the elders and priests at the shrines of the local deities.

(4) For the chief priests, community elders, and custodians, the shrine is often the center of periodic social gathering, interaction, and community planning. It is believed that the appeasement of the deity will help to secure the progress and harmony of the community which is under its watch. As Iwe noted,

"The shrine is to the Igbo traditional religion what the altar is to the Christian church."

The Root Causes of Shrine Worship in General

Why is it that shrine worship like that of Okija in eastern Nigeria persists or even flourishes? This is a challenging question to scholars of ethnic religions. But Nigerian scholar Nonso Okereaforezeke (2005) has advanced some of the explanations for sustenance and rejuvenation of shrine worship in eastern Nigeria. They include the following:

First, many Nigerians perceive the English system of law which was inherited at the time of independence to be ineffective and inefficient with regard to social control. Under the British law, disputes which are supposedly settled in court linger as the judgments are not usually accepted as final and supreme by parties to a case.

Second, the average Nigerian is alienated from the British-style system of law and justice as he perceives the system to be foreign. The same sentiment is also expressed by the well educated who appreciate the customary way even much more. The pride in the Nigerian traditional means of social justice appears to be appealing if not culturally reinforcing. This sheer pride, according to Okereaforezeke (2005), stimulates interest in shrine worship.

Moreover, the frustration over long delays in the rendering of justice in the English system of jurisprudence tends to stimulate interest in a system that is quick, relatively inexpensive, and finite. The Nigerian modern legal system is expensive, in terms of time spent and financial costs as well as reputation. Court cases linger for several years, not even to mention appeals and inherent counter-appeals. This type of frustration among the non-ruling class provides impetus to the search for an alternative legal system that renders speedy trial as, "justice delayed is justice denied."

Next, lack of knowledge and understanding of alternative systems and methods of justice help to drive shrine worship. Absence of formal education and travel beyond one's cultural boundaries—by many of the patrons of shrines and especially the Priests—helps to buttress their natural beliefs in shrine worship.

Also, the failure of the institutions of virtually all the Nigerian state and its constituent authorities have degraded substantially to the extent that the masses have lost confidence in them, including the court and criminal justice systems. This degree of decadence is attributed primarily to the rising corruption among politicians and law enforcement officials who pay only lip service to their constituents. Hence, there is great desire for alternative system of justice for the yearning, poor masses.

Furthermore, mixed signals by successive government officials provide impetus to the legitimization of the traditional systems of worship. The politicians and other elites not only patronize the gods for a number of reasons—including material wealth, political fortunes, and supernatural protection from perceived enemies—but they parade their loot while attributing such successes to their allegiance to the deities. Thus, these so-called exemplary and successful officials serve as models to the poor masses who crave for similar successes. This, in essence, helps to cement public support and attraction toward shrine-worship as their only means to acquire riches. It should be noted that the attitudes of these select officials contradict their oaths to uphold the rule of law.

Finally, fear and the underlying belief that the deity is a supreme being helps to sustain all sorts of traditional systems of worship, including shrine worship. Because of the degree of affinity people of all ethnic and religious persuasions render to deities as sources of success, life, and protection, the decisions rendered by the shrine priests in a case or dispute is regarded as final, binding, and supreme, as all parties to a dispute are not likely to appeal it.

The Ogwugwu Shrine of Okija

The Okija shrine is located in Okija town, near Onitsha, a bridge-head city in Eastern Nigeria. The shrine is popularly called, according to customary practice, "Ogwugwu" shrine. Ogwugwu in Igboland means "the valley." As a famous shrine in the area, Ogwugwu will be interchangeably called the "Okija" shrine. The Okija shrine has been of great interest and focus in recent months, in Nigeria as well as abroad. This is not the first time. The country is reeling from the notorious murder of a Nigerian boy in London—simply referred to as "Adam" by the British police. This incident exposed the dreadful and horrifying practices of ritual killing in Nigeria. As a backdrop, the floating, mutilated body of Adam was found by the British police in the River Thames, near London's famous Tower Bridge. Information based on forensic examination and the fact that Adam lived in South-West Nigeria and the nature of his mutilated body aroused the suspicion of the British police that it must be connected to ritual killing, which commonly makes news in Nigeria.

The British police went as far as visiting Nigeria in search of finding the killers. This eventually led to the arrest of a thirty-seven-year-old Sam Onogigovie and a number of others in connection with the killing. Ritual killing is not uncommon in Nigeria. Many people have become victims of ritual killers. These murderers are popularly called "head hunters."

In Igboland in particular, they are called *Ogbuisi* in Igbo native tongue. They hunt in search of human parts—breasts and sexual organs—at the behest of witch doctors, juju priests, and medicine men (*dibia*) that use them for sacrifices to the gods or for magic. Prior to this London incident, ritual killing in another part of Nigeria had made international news as well. In 1996, the police in Owerri, the capital of Imo state of Nigeria (also in eastern Nigeria) had arrested one Innocent Ekeanyanwu with the head of a boy whom police identified as Ikechukwu Okonkwo. This fellow was revealed to be in collaboration with a hotelier popularly known as "Otokoto." His famous hotel was also known as Otokoto hotel. Even the nearest bus stop in the city bore his name. In fact the name Otokoto became a capital city (Owerri) landmark to trucks, taxis, and motorcyclists as drop zones (motorcyclists used for taxi in Nigeria are called *okada*).

The expressed or tacit involvement of such rich and powerful people heightened the interest of the Nigerian police that it was the work of an organized syndicate. As the news of the incident spread like wildfire, violent protests erupted. In the fracas that ensued, Otokoto Hotel was burned down to the ground, including the looting of property belonging to the suspected killers by angry mobs when they heard of the news that he was implicated in ritual trade and killings and mutilated bodies either to be sold for ritual, profit, or procured and sold for organ transplant. Details of the Otokoto killings revealed the buried torso of Ikechukwu in the premises of Otokoto Hotel which was owned by Chief Duru. With this negative news about Nigeria commanding headlines throughout the mass media houses, including the internet, Nigeria as a country could no more resist the urge to fight this cankerworm eating into its social and moral fabric. Hence, the war of moral rejuvenation, renewal, and enlightenment was unleashed. A full investigation aimed at bringing the culprits to arrest and punishing them by bringing the full weight of the law was launched.

Nigeria in Desperate Search of Good International Image

This was a time when Nigeria most needed to put its acts together, and clean up its image. It was again, a time when the country was reeling from travel advisory warnings by major international airlines and other carriers. Even foreign nationals changed their travel plans for academic, research, Fulbright exchanges, and other business plans after apprising themselves of the Okija and Otokoto tragedies. Also, this was a time when Nigeria was asking for debt relief (forgiveness) from the international community—World Bank, International Monetary Fund (IMF), and the Paris Club. War on official corruption formed the cornerstone of the President Olusegun Obasanjo's campaign against public corruption at home—a war that was tainted by the respective arrests and trials of two Nigerian state governors in London on charges of money laundering. They are Mr. Joshua Dariye, Governor of Plateau State and Mr. Diepreye Alamieyeseigha, Governor of Bayelsa State. Also, it was not long after the debacle of the Miss World Pageant occurred; the event was disrupted by Muslim rioters and later moved to London, England, from Abuja, Nigeria. Also, Nigeria has been fighting tooth and nail to enhance its regional and global image through its unrelenting efforts to host All Africa games, World Cup, and if possible, the Olympic Games.

Furthermore, it has been in contention to fill the United Nations Security Seat on behalf of the African continent, in which South Africa, Egypt, and Nigeria made the short list among countries being seriously considered. In the same vein, Nigeria has not yet recovered from the black eye given to its international image, by the official reports of the Transparency International (2003), in its Corruption Perception Index data, which measured levels of corruption in 133 countries; found that Nigeria ranked 132 out of 133 nations surveyed. This puts Nigeria second to the most corrupt country, after Bangladesh. It also found itself in the same place in the 2001 study which also found it to be second to the most corrupt country on the surface of the earth, with Bangladesh at the top of the list. In 2004, its position remained constant as it made number 144 out of 145 as the most corrupt country. Bangladesh and Haiti tied for the last position of 144. However, in the 2005, Nigeria corruption perception index improved slightly. In this case to the position of the sixth most corrupt country. Then in the 2005 study by the World Bank, it was only trailed by Ethiopia as the second-poorest country in the world.

Leo Igwe, Head of the Nigerian Skeptics Society, posited some of the salient reasons why many people in Nigeria indulge in cult and ritual killings, and other barbaric acts and atrocities (2004). They are:

(a) Religion: Many believe in the existence of supernatural being, and that these beings could be influenced through ritual acts and rituals. These rituals are therefore designed to appease the gods and deities; and thus appease them in order that they may ward off their misfortunes and those of their family members—protect them from death and accidents, miscarriage, uphold their good luck, make them pass examinations, make them find good jobs, make them marry good wives/spouses, and bless them with children. They think that they will face punishment if they fail to do so. This explains why superstition, supernaturalism, etheism, and occultism are at the root of religious rituals in Nigeria.

(b) Superstition: Most of the beliefs in Nigeria are driven by lack of reason (passion), dogmas, myth, and magic. There are wide spread beliefs in ghosts, juju, charms, and witchcraft (voodoo). They believe that deities or even that magical objects have preferences for select sensitive portions of human body: head, breast, tongue, sexual organs, and eyes. When offerings are made to the deities with these sensitive human parts, the *juju*, charms, and deity are pleased with the individual subjects. Thus, they would double their watch and protection of their subjects and their family members—reward them with political fortunes in winning elections, guarantee them financial profits for their businesses (business expansion and profitability) and guard against business failures, protect them against AIDS, sickle-cell diseases, etc., and protect them against accidents. During wars, people would usually go to a fortune teller or medicine man (*juju*) for ritual sacrifices and cult prayer so that they would not die in war.

It is believed that the spirits (deities) possess the power to ward off bullets and bombs in their path. In some cases, it is also believed that those bullets could be diverted away from their subjects to the killing of "nonbelievers." Even young, single men solicit special handkerchiefs and powders whose colors and scents can attract beautiful girls toward them for dates and marriage. I remember my elementary school years in the 1960s in eastern Nigeria, where there were rumors and scares about handkerchiefs that people could use to make you follow them or that can make you go crazy (mad) if you enter into a fight with any magical figure with a handkerchief they used to call then "talisman." They believe that. In fact, rituals are perceived as an act of "spiritual fortification."

(c) Poverty: Many Nigerians engage in ritual killings and rituals for money. They believe in rituals performed with human blood or body parts which money cannot buy. In fact, things that signify the highest forms of sacrifice can only convince the gods of the level of reverence their subjects accord them. Hence, rituals performed with human blood or body parts would be preferable. In return, the gods will reward them with good luck. Make whatever they touch or involve in turn into gold—winning a lottery, doubling money through magical action, and making profit in business sales by attracting people with money and making them gullible to buy their products. Under the influence of the gods, the party buying the goods would be manipulated by the gods in such a way that they would be sold anything at any price. This phenomenon is always referred to as "blood money or ritual wealth" (wealth acquired through magic).

The Ogwugwu Shrine Snafu

The Ogwugwu Shrine of Okija commanded great international attention when in August 2004, Okija shrine came to the scrutiny of Nigeria and the world. The whole incident was generated when the Nigerian police, working on a tip, raided the shrine and discovered the scene of ritual killing, with several body parts, skulls, and more than fifty corpses, some partly mummified. The police found that all of the dead bodies were those of adults. Some were in coffins while others were headless, thus heightened a sense of curiosity and interest as a sign of ritual killing. The general belief was that most of the victims were businesspeople, civil servants, and politicians who were poisoned. The shrine worshipers were labeled cult worshippers of Arusi Okija. They were also believed to practice rituals in which people involved in disputes over business deals in particular were exhorted to settle them by drinking a form of poison with full assurance that only the guilty party would die.

History has it that Arusi Okija took its name from a local oracle god and the town "Okija." It is also believed that the ritual and practice of swallowing poison to test the guilt of a party in dispute is not new, but has been an enduring ancient practice. The practice was originally intended to deter crime. But most victims and their family members claim that the process has been hijacked by the shrine priests as money-making machine, where the priest and their sympathizers and collaborators kill and defraud people. They cite incidents where the chief priests would rub some poisonous substance on the vehicle of a claimant tagged to die—to induce an accident on his way home—or may place poison on the body on the claimant who dies without a struggle, and then the chief priests claim the deaths were was the work of the gods. In others, claimants were forced to drink concoctions after which they died.

This in fact brings back memories of the mass suicide tragedy of the Jim Jones cult—movement of Divine Socialism in Jonestown, Guyana. There was a description of a typical scenario in which a complainant who was cheated out of his business deal was summoned before the chief shrine priests to resolve the dispute. The believers who tend to respect and fear the summons say that over a long period there has been virtually full attendance by the respondents for fear that not showing up would draw the wrath of the deity, tantamount to a death sentence which they want to avoid in the first place. It is alleged that after the poisoning ritual, the community hands the body of the deceased (who is presumed the losing party) to the chief priest, including his personal property and money. This financial motive appears to corroborate the police twist of the story, that "only the richest of the party in the dispute is always guilty." Other suspicions of monetary interest came out of media reports that the Chief priest—so-called "Ndukwu"—owned property in a prime area of Lagos, Nigeria, worth millions of naira. It should be noted that a few years ago, Lagos topped the list of the most expensive cities in the world to live.

The incident in the Okija shrine raised a lot of interesting questions. First, are the victims of mental poisoning—"fear" which H. Spencer Lewis has written extensively about in his book, *Mental Poisoning,* according to social science researcher, Eric Roark (2004), in his critique titled, "Herbert Spencer's Evolutionary Individualism." In this exposé, Spencer explains the processes by which individuals could allow themselves to fall prey to the poison darts of subtle, sordid, and destructive situations. As Emmanuel U. Obi (2004) has also written very eloquently, this could be one of the reasons why the chief priest in the Okija shrine would label or attach name tags to the victims of the *arusi* (gods)—to instill fear in the minds of their victims, weaken them, and make them vulnerable to their tricks of extortion. The same could equally be said about the register which is kept, with the names and activities of all the claimants. Although negative stories of the event in the Okija shrine were strange to the world, the shrine hosted a number of prominent political clients from eastern Nigeria. The list included Dr. Chris Ngige, the sitting Governor of Anambra State and his estranged godfather, Chief Chris Uba. Both of these men had secretly visited the shrine when Ngige was a candidate for governor under the Peoples Democratic Party platform.

Revelations about all these ritual visits were made known in the wake of the aborted abduction of Ngige in what amounted to a coup. In the fracas, Ngige was forced to sign his handwritten letter of resignation. Other highly placed individuals acknowledged visiting the Ogwugwu shrine. They included Senator Chuma Nzeribe and Reverend Dr. Bonny Asuzu. Popular calls went out that the police should charge the operators of the shrine, including the priests. Even the Anambra police Commissioner, Felix Ogbaudu, alluded to the possibility that the only way to dissuade the public from patronizing the deity's priests would be to charge them with murder. But their lawyer Osita Ndukwu argued that there was nothing in Nigerian law that would suggest that the ministers of the shrine are responsible for the deaths of any attending parties, but that "only the gods are culpable." Pa Edimuo Ndukwu, the chief priest of the shrine, and his minister, James Obi, claimed that their ordeal with the police authorities had rather boosted the popularity of the deities.

The chief priest also claimed that this ancient (traditional) practice of worshipping deities is designed to kill only those who commit evil, lie to the gods, or the greedy oppressors who dispossess the poor of their land and for which they are reported to the deities to intervene. Furthermore, among the clientele of the shrine are businessmen who ask for profit ventures and favor in getting bank loans; politicians who ask for the favor of deities to win elections, land judicial and cabinet or ministerial appointments; travelers, pilots, and bus drivers who ask for divine protection against accidents; barren women seeking children; women in troubled marriage relationships; police officers for safety; exam takers who want to pass; employees who want to be promoted; school leavers who want to land prestigious and high-paying jobs; madmen who want to regain their sanity; and spouses who want a male offspring. Also according to the shrine priest, the identities of the parties are kept anonymous but they are firmly warned that the deity kills without the knowledge of the priest. However, it is the relatives of the guilty party who have the burden of reporting the death to the chief priest and requesting that the body, including his belongings and personal effects, be returned to the deity (*arusi*).

The chief priest further disclosed that the Ogwugwu Shrine of Okija was registered with the Corporate Affairs Commission of the State government as a cultural organization and granted full powers to arbitrate over local and cultural matters, and renewed annually in the sum of N50,000 (about $500 US). As such, the shrine is required by the government to keep accurate records of the dead, those whose family relations returned their corpses for deposition in the shrine, those who had vowed before the gods, those who received favor from them and those who are killed—complainants and respondents to the cases before the deity. As a matter of courtesy for lodging complaints, the complainants usually bring kola nuts, spirits, chalk, alligator pepper, fowl, drinks, or animals—goats, sheep, cows, cats, and dogs, etc., and some money to the chief priests; what is sacrificed to the idols by the priests depend primarily on what the chief priest recommends as desirable and appropriate.

Test of Nigeria's Legal System: Ogwugwu Shrine of Okija in Court

The legitimacy of and legality of shrine worship (including Okija shrine), belief in deities, the authority of shrine priests, and the authenticity of customary law and practices were tested in a landmark case in Nigeria. The case, which originated in a customary court, went all the way to the Nigerian Supreme Court. The case, Onyenye v. Ebere (2004), began at the Ukwa Customary Court. Ukwa is one of the Local Government Areas (LGA) of Abia State in Nigeria. The case was instituted by three plaintiffs who sued for themselves and on behalf of Umungede family of Owaza in Ukwa LGA. The "Ulogor" family of Owaza in Ukwa LGA was listed as the defendant. The dispute centered on ownership of a piece of customary land. The complainants claimed that the disputed land belonged to their ancestors, called Elechi, who pledged the land to the defendants' descendants. For unknown reasons, subsequent heads of the family of the plaintiffs failed to redeem the pledge until the first plaintiff's father, Ebere Oforji, acting as the head of the plaintiff's family, took it upon himself in that capacity to redeem the said pledged land. When the redemption money was offered to the defendants, they declined to accept it, claiming that the land in question was not on pledge to them. Shocked by this refusal, the plaintiffs, in deference to customary law and practice, deposited the redemption money with a *juju* in their locality.

The defendants, however, refused to swear to an oath before the *juju* to affirm their ownership of the disputed land as custom demands. Therefore, the *juju* priest before whom the dispute was taken ordered the respondents to provide within eight days any *juju* of their choice before whom they could swear. Thanks to their suggestion and acceptance of the Okija shrine, this choice of a foreign-based *juju* (Okija in Anambra State, about 100 miles away) by the defendant now appeared to be a vote of no confidence on the Ukwa (local) *juju*. With the consent of the plaintiff to take the oath, the Okija *juju* (Okija shrine) from Anambra State was transported to Ukwa in Abia State, where it was placed on the disputed land. The rule and effect of the oath is that the false claimant would die within a year. But, the plaintiffs who took the oath survived the one-year period. This automatically gave them exclusive possession of the disputed land in accordance with customs of Ukwa where the parties hail from and where the land in dispute was located. Not satisfied with the outcome, the defendants headed to the Ukwa Customary Court which awarded judgment to the plaintiffs. On appeal at the Customary Court of Appeal, Abia State, the decision of the trial Customary Court was set aside.

The plaintiff then appealed to the Court of Appeal which overturned the judgment of the Customary Court of Appeal and restored the decision of the Ukwa Customary Court. Refusing to yield possession of the land, the defendants appealed to the Nigerian Supreme Court. In dismissing the appeal, the apex court advanced a legal reasoning that where any party to a dispute alleges the existence of a customary law, such must be proved because the law of evidence "regards it as a fact, unless it can be noticed judicially." With respect to applicable custom in oath-taking before foreign *juju*, pursuant to customary arbitration, the Supreme Court further stated that "where a foreign juju is brought into a disputed land for the purpose of customary arbitration, it is the custom of the place where the land is located that should take precedent (prevail) in the determination of the outcome of the juju on the party to the oath." In essence, the ramification of the Supreme Court is that the following facts are sufficient and undisputable evidence of ownership by the appellants who initiated the appeal and as duly arrived at by the customary arbitration: (a) the land in dispute is in a different geographic jurisdiction, Ukwa in Abia State; (b) The *juju* was foreign (brought to the disputed land from a distant jurisdiction—Okija in Anambra State by the appellants); and (c) the defendants survived the one-year period allowed by Ukwa custom after taking the oath on the disputed land before the foreign *juju*.

In other words, the rationale behind the Supreme Court ruling was that the place of the origin of the *juju* sworn at Okija in Anambra State was totally irrelevant; and that what mattered most was that everything was done according to Ukwa custom. It was, in fact, the Ukwa custom and not that of Okija that was binding on the warring parties. Also, by virtue of this ruling, the Supreme Court recognized oath taking as a valid process of establishing truth of a matter or arbitration under customary law. Moreover, the Supreme Court in its reasoning in this ruling established the fact that decisions on parties are binding as long as the following conditions are met: (a) The two or more parties to a dispute voluntarily submit the issue of controversy between or among them to arbitration in accordance with customary law; (b) The parties agree expressly or tacitly that the decision of such arbitration would be accepted as final and binding on all parties; (c) It is no longer an option for either party to subsequently back out or withdraw from the decision once it is rendered or pronounced.

The Last Chapter of the Okija Saga: Court Verdict on Okija Priests

The raid of the Okija shrine was triggered by the petition filed by one chief Obed Igwe that the ancient shrine was being used for ritual killings. Following the raid by police on August 23, 2004, about forty persons believed to be high priests and patrons of the Okija shrine were arrested. Most people knew about the existence of the shrine, but not the extent of the horrific activities described in the petition. About forty persons believed to be high priests and patrons of the Okija shrine were arrested. Among them, two died shortly after they were released on bail by police, prior to court arraignment. The victims were identified by police as Edinmuo Ndukwu and Samuel Ebuodinma. The whole Okija drama raised a lot of salient questions for both the judicial system and government that are begging for answers. They include but are not limited to:

(a) The release of the identities of suspected patrons (influential and powerful politicians) and possibly victims of the shrines contained in 10 registers discovered by police in the shrine;

(b) The revelation of the full identities of the priests and what they were doing with human bodies;

(c) The establishment of the legality of the criminal code that forbids secret societies and groups that try by ordeal;

(d) The establishment of whether the Okija shrine operated along the lines of justice prejudicial to Nigeria's constitutional principles of justice;

(e) Whether or not the Okija shrine practices were inhuman and unnatural;

(f) The establishment of whether there is anything wrong with cannibalism and ritual sacrifice of human beings.

On August 23, 2005, exactly a year from the date of the police raid, the first chapter in the orgy of the shrine trial came to an end. On this date, the Ihiala Chief Magistrate Court discharged and acquitted thirty-eight high priests of the Okija shrine. The decision by Chief Magistrate Justina Anaukwu-Ohanehi relied strictly on a letter written to the court by the Anambra State Director of Public Prosecution, Mrs. Ada Unobuagha. The Director of Public Prosecution had stated *inter alia*: "Pursuant to section 252 of the Criminal Procedure laws cap 37 Revised Laws of Anambra State 1991, I am directed to inform you that the record of the proofs of evidence in respect of the above case does not in the opinion of the Honorable Attorney General disclose sufficient evidence to sustain the charge of murder against all the accused persons mentioned in charge No. MIH/IOC/2005." Henceforth, the Magistrate Court discharged and acquitted them for want of sufficient evidence to prosecute them.

Conclusion

The mystery of this judgment is that the gravity of the offense, notwithstanding, the prosecutor could not find any grounds to recommend common misdemeanor charges against the stakeholders of the shrine. Also unsettling is the fact that the date of ruling for the discharge and acquittal of all the shrine priests came exactly one year (the first anniversary) after the Okija shrine raid. Is this a coincidence or a set up? Additionally, the full identities of the names of patrons of the shrine which might include politicians and other people of power have not been officially disclosed until now. One certainty is that no individual, including the judges and prosecutors, wanted the challenge of this ancient practice of worship under their watch, not even the Supreme Court in the famous landmark case, Onyenye v. Ebere (2004), which reinforced the fact that customary law and tradition can be binding on parties in a dispute as long as they voluntarily submit the issues in question to arbitration according to customs and accept the arbitrators' decision as final and binding.

Perhaps the court judges did not want the wrath of the deities to descend on them and their families if they ruled against shrine worship or against their agents. This is perhaps a risk they cannot afford to take. As things now stand, there are genuine and compelling reasons why deity/shrine worship flourishes.

These factors include but not limited to outright fear, respect for culture, lack of confidence in Western-style justice, permanency of resolution, and cost. The practice of shrine worship is likely to grow as more people who lose faith in the modern system of justice turn to traditional methods of worship, social control, and justice for final answers.

The only way to contain this trend would be to sanitize the modern system. Even that alone would not stop the growing appeal of the traditional solution. All we can ask for now is that the customary/traditional practices be allowed to coexist with the modern system of jurisprudence.

Bibliography

Aluko, Mobolaji E. "Monday Quarter-backing: The Barbarous Acts of Okija," August 9, 2004. www.nigeriavillagesquare.com/content/3-200.html (accessed June 28, 2010).

Anderson, Allan. "The Gospel and African Religion." *International Review of Mission* 89 (2000): 373–83.

Anyanwu, H. Onyema "Why the Igbos Abandoned their Gods." *Africa Theological Journal* 14 (1985): 91–99.

Arinze, Francis A. *Sacrifice in Ibo Religion*. Ibadan, Nigeria: Ibadan University Press, 1970.

Awolalu, J. Onlosade. "The Concept of Death and Hereafter." *West African Religion* 18 (1979): 57–69.

Bujra, Janet. "Interview with Leo Igwe—A Nigerian Humanist by Janet Bujra, on Religion, Ideology & Conflict in Africa." *Review of African Political Economy* 33, no. 110 (September 2006): 740–43.

Dammann, Ernst. "A Tentative Philological Typology of Some African High Deities." *Journal of Religion in Africa* 2 (1969): 81–95.

Diala, Isidore. "Ritual and Mythological Recuperation in the Drama of Esiaba Irobi," *Research in African Literatures* 10, no. 4 (Winter 2005): 87–114.

Dzobo, Noah K. "African Ancestor Cult: A Theological Appraisal." *Reformed World* 38 (1985): 333–40.

Egbo, E. P. "Conflict Between Traditional Religion and Christianity in Igbo, South-Eastern Nigeria." *West African Religion* 10 (1971): 1–17.

———. "The Beginning of the End of Traditional Religion in Igboland." *Civilizations* 21 (1971): 1–12.

Ejizu, Christopher I. "Nigeria's Three Religions: Patterns and Prospects of their Interaction." *African Theological Journal* 17 (1988): 179–95.

Ekechukwu, Alexander. "The Problem of Suffering in Igbo Traditional Religion." *African Ecclesial Review* 24 (1982): 81–89.

Ezeanya, S. N. "The Osu (Cult-Slave) System in Igboland." *Journal of Religion in Africa* 1 (1967): 35–45.

Gaiya, Musa A. B. "The Inter-play between Religion and Culture in African Traditional Religion." *Jos Studies* 4 (1994): 1–18.

———. "Human Rights in African Indigenous Religion." *Bulletin of Ecumenical Theology* 4 (1991): 31–45.

Hickey, Raymond. "The Decline of African Traditional Religion." *The Outlook* 20 (1986): 36–41.

———. "Authentic African Religion." *AFER* 27 (1985): 216–24.

———. "Ministry in African Traditional Religion." *The Outlook* 18 (1982): 19–26.

Ifesieh, Emmanuel I. "The Concept of 'Chineke' as Reflected in Igbo Names and Proverbs, (A Case Study)." *Communio Viatorum* 26 (1983): 109–27.

Igwe, Leo. "Religion, Ideology and Conflict in Africa." *Review of African Political Economy* 33(110) (2006): 740–43.

———. "Ritual Killing and Pseudoscience in Nigeria." *Skeptical Inquirer* 14, no. 2, (June 2004).

Ilega, Daniel I. "Religion and Godless Nationalism in Colonial Nigeria: The Case of the God's Kingdom Society and the N.C.N.C." *Journal of Religion in Africa* 18, no. 2 (June 1988): 163–82.

Imasogie, Osadolor. "The Influence of African Traditional Religious Ideas of Worship in the Christian Worship Practices in Nigeria." *Ogbomosho Journal of Theology* 6 (1991): 17–23.

Isichei, Elizabeth. "On Masks and Audible Ghosts: Some Secret Male Cults in Central Nigeria." *Journal of Religion in Africa* 18 (1988): 42–70.

Iwe, Nwachukwiuke S. *Socio-Ethical Issues in Nigeria*. New York: Peter Lang Publishers, 1987.

———. "Igbo Deities." Ahịajọkụ Lecture Series, Onugaotu Colloquium, 1988.

Iwuagwu, A. O. "Chukwu: Towards a Definition of Igbo Traditional Religion." *West African Religion* 16 (1975): 26–34.

Kalu, Orji U. "Gods in Retreat: Models of Religious Change in Africa." *Nigerian Journal of Humanities* 1 (1974): 42–53.

Kibicho, Samuel G. "Revelation in African Religion." *Africa Theological Journal* 12 (1983): 166–77.

Kopytoff, Igor. "Ancestors as Elders." *Africa* 41 (1971): 128–42.

Metuh, Emefie I. "Ritual Dirt and Purification Rites among the Igbo." *Journal of Religion in Africa* 15 (1995): 3–24.

———. "The Theological Study of African Traditional Religion: Case Study of Igbo Theodicy." *Africa Theological Journal* 14 (1985): 55–65.

———. "The Religious Dimension of African Cosmogonies: A Case Study of Igbo of Nigeria." *West African Religion* 17 (1978): 9–102.

———. "The Religious Dimension of African Cosmogonies: A Case Study of Igbo of "Igbo World-view: A Premise for Christian/Traditional Religion Dialogue." *West African Religion* 13/14 (1972): 51–8.

Noon, John A. "A Preliminary Examination of Death Concept of the Ibo." *American Anthropologist* 44 (1944): 640.

Nyamiti, Charles. "African Ancestral Veneration and its Relevance to the African Churches." *African Christian Studies* 9 (1993): 14–37.

Obi, Emmanuel U. "Understanding the Okija Shrine Phenomenon and the Art of Mental Poisoning: Just Before the Rush to Judgment." August 14, 2004. www.gamji.com/article3000/News3838.htm (accessed June 29, 2010).

Okeke, G. E. "Ancestral Worship among the Igbo." *Communio Sanctorum* 27 (1984): 137–52.

Okereafoezeke, Nonso. "Relevance of African Traditional Jurisprudence on Control, Justice, and Law: A Critique of the Igbo Experience." *African Journal of Criminology and Justice Studies* 2, no. 1 (2006): 36–62.

———. "Foundations of Okija Justice." *Nigeria World*. March 1, 2005. www.nigeria world.com/articles/2005/mar/033.html (accessed June 29, 2010).

Onyenga, V. E. in *All Federal Weekly Law Report* (Nigeria) (2004): 981–1001.

Osovo, Onibere. "Christian Reactions to Indigenous Religion in Nigeria: The Ancestral Factor as a Case in Point." *Bulletin of African Theology* 5 (1981): 53–9.

Roark, Eric. "Herbert Spencer's Evolutionary Individualism." *Quarterly Journal of Ideology* 27, nos. 3 and 4 (2004): 1–31.

Ryan, Patrick J. "Arise O God! The Problem of 'Gods' in West Africa" *Journal of Religion in Africa* 11 (1980): 161–71.

Tamuno, Tekena N. "Traditional Methods of Crime Detection and Control in Nigeria." *Orita* 26 (1994): 25–41.

Topor, Wolor. "The Concept of God in the African Philosophy." *Journal of African Religion and Philosophy* 2 (1990): 1–6.

Tovagonze, Venance. "God-concept: 'Supreme Being' in African Tribal Religions." *Journal of Dharma* 17 (1992): 122–40.

Transparency International Corruption Perceptions. 2003. pp. 1–8. For full details of the TICPI 2003, visit http://www.Transparency.org/cpi/index.html#cpi

Uba, Christopher N. "Divinities and Ancestors in Igbo Traditional Religion." *Africa* 2 (1982): 90–105.

Ukpong, Justin S. "The Problem of God and Sacrifice in African Traditional Religion." *Journal of Religion in Africa* 14(1983): 187–203.

———. "Sacrificial Worship in Ibibio Traditional Religion." *Journal of Religion in Africa* 13 (1982): 161–88.

Uzoho, V. N. "The Sacred and the Profane in the Traditional Religion of Africa." *West African Religion* 15 (1974): 30–43.

Uzukwu, E. "The God of our Ancestor and African Unity." *African Ecclesial Review* 23 (1981): 344–52.

Yamsat, D. G. J. "The Concept of God and Spiritual Beings in Various Nigerian Traditional Religions." *TCNN Research Bulletin* 16 (1986): 27–29.

Zuesse, Evan M. "Divination and Deity in African Religions." *History of Religions* 15 (1975): 158–82.

Zvarevashe, Ignatius. "The Problem of Ancestors and Inculturation." *AFER* 29 (1987): 242–51.

Chapter 4
African Mathematics: From Bones to Computers

Mamokgethi Setati and Abdul Karim Bangura

Introduction

That mathematics—generally defined as the systematic study of quantities and relations through the use of numbers and symbols—pervades every branch of human knowledge is hardly a matter of dispute. It is a useful and fascinating field of inquiry, and it possesses the power to solve some of the deepest puzzles humans encounter.

Mathematics is used in everyday life in such simple ways as telling time or counting the change returned by a cashier. A customer in a supermarket employs mathematics when buying groceries. A wife and husband use mathematics to create their household budget or to keep track of their bank accounts. And children use mathematics in playing many of their games.

In business, mathematics is prevalent in all exchange transactions. Business entities need mathematics to establish and maintain their records. Bankers rely on mathematics to handle and invest money. Many businesses rely upon accountants to keep their records and statisticians to analyze large aggregates of data. And insurance companies rely upon actuaries to compute the rates charged for insurance.

In industry, almost all companies rely upon mathematics for their research and development. Many major industrial firms hire trained mathematicians. All engineering projects rely upon mathematics. For instance, designing a superhighway requires a great deal of mathematical analyses. Without extensive mathematical formulae and calculations, constructing a giant dam would be impossible. The fact that engineering students must take many mathematics courses highlights the importance of this field of study.

In science, mathematics pervades all aspects of the field. Without exact mathematical descriptions, formulae, and observations, most scientists will not be able to perform their tasks. Many scientific problems have become so complex that without a sound training in mathematics, one may not be able to solve them. The hard, behavioral, and social sciences all depend on mathematics to advance their disciplines.

Despite this extensive utilization of mathematics, it is not obvious to many that it is also a tool used to teach students that Europeans are culturally superior to Africans. Most books dealing with the history of mathematics devote only a few pages to ancient Egypt and to northern Africa during the Middle Ages. These books generally ignore the history of mathematics in Sub-Saharan Africa, giving the impression that this history either did not exist or, at least, is not knowable, traceable, or, even more absurd, that there was no mathematics at all in that part of Africa. To Eurocentric scholars, even the Africanity of Egyptian mathematics is often denied. But contrary to the popular Eurocentric view, one can neither racially nor geographically separate Egyptian civilization from its Black African roots.

That Africa was in the center of mathematics history for tens of thousands of years is undisputable. From the civilizations across the continent emerged contributions which would enrich both ancient and modern understanding of nature through mathematics. From the measurement used in the African forest kingdoms to the mathematics used in building the great stone complexes of Zimbabwe, the efficient irrigation technologies, central administration, the great accuracy of the dimensions of the pyramids, and the random number generation of the binary code that led to the invention of the computer, the achievements of Africans remain a fascination.

Since the 1970s, many books and articles on different topics that deal with African mathematics have been published. What we provide in this chapter are overviews of the various aspects of Africa's contributions to mathematics. This, we hope, will give the reader a comprehensive picture, albeit not detailed accounts and artistic representations, of African mathematics. The reader interested in greater details of a particular topic will be well served by the relevant references.

Beginnings: Mathematics of Bones

In Central Equatorial Africa's high mountains, bordering Uganda and the Republic of Congo, is Lake Edward. This small lake, measuring about 60 by 30 miles, is a source of the River Nile. While the area is sparsely populated today, about 6,000 to 9,000 years ago a fishing and agricultural settlement existed by its shores. The community only existed a few hundred years before being buried in a volcanic eruption. The place where the inhabitants' remains were found has a name now given to these people—Ishango. Among their remains discovered in 1960 is the oldest mathematical object, the Ishango Bone, which is now located on the ninth floor of the Royal Institute for Natural Sciences of Belgium in Brussels (Bogoshi et al., 1987; de Heinzelin, 1962).

An examination of the Ishango Bone shows that at one end is a piece of quartz writing. The bone also has a series of notches carved in groups. While it was first thought that the notches are some kind of tally marks as found to record counts all over the world, it was later determined that they are much more than a simple tally. The markings on rows (a) and (b) each add up to 60. Row (b) contains the prime numbers between 10 and 20 (11, 13, 17). Row (a) is quite consistent with a numeration system based on 10, as the notches are grouped as 21, 19, 11, 9 = 20 + 1, 20 - 1, 10 + 1, and 10 - 1. Finally, row (c) seems to illustrate the method of duplication used relatively more recently in Egyptian multiplication: eight groups of notches in the order of 7, 5, 5, 10, 8, 4, 6, 3. The last pair (6, 3) is spaced closer together, as are (8, 4), and (5, 5, 10) (Bogoshi et al., 1987; de Heinzelin, 1962).

According to Ron Eglash (1999), the doubling system in the Ishango Bone is fundamental to many of the counting systems of Africa in modern times as well. He adds that it is common, for example, to have the word for an even number 2N mean "N plus N" (e.g., the number 8 in the Shambaa language of Tanzania is *ne na ne*, literally "four and four"). He further mentions that a similar doubling takes place for the precisely articulated system of number hand gestures: for example, "four" represented by two groups of two fingers and "eight" by two groups of four. Andrea L. Petito (1982) finds that doubling was employed in multiplication and division techniques in West Africa, Richard J. Gillings (1972; 1982) shows the persistent use of powers of two in Ancient Egyptian mathematics as well, and Claudia Zaslavsky (1973; 1999, p. 50) provides archaeological evidence that Ancient Egypt's use of base-2 calculations derived from the use of base-2 in Sub-Saharan Africa.

Recent microscopic investigations illustrate more markings which seem to suggest that the Ishango Bone is also a lunar phase counter. Alexander Marshack (1972), for example, conducted a detailed microscopic examination of the bone and found markings of different indentations, shapes and sizes. His conclusion is that there is strong evidence of a close fit between different phases of the moon and the sequential notation contained on the bone, once the additional markings—visible only through the microscope—were taken into account. He further suggests that the different engravings represented markings of various shapes and sizes that may have been a calendar of events of ceremonies or rituals.

For George Gheverghese Joseph (1991; 2000), these conjectures about the Ishango Bone highlight three important aspects of proto-mathematics. The first is that the close link between mathematics and astronomy has a long history and is connected to the need felt even among early humans to record the passage of time, out of curiosity as well as practical necessity. The second is that there is no reason to believe that early humans' capacity to reason and conceptualize was any different from that of their modern counterparts. What has changed over time is the nature of the facts and relationships with which humans have to operate. Therefore, the creation of a complicated system of sequential notation based on a lunar calendar was well within the capacity of prehistoric humans, whose desire to keep track of the passage of time and changes in seasons was translated into observations of the changing aspects of the moon. The third is that in the absence of records, conjectures about mathematical pursuits of early humans have to be investigated in the light of their plausibility, the existence of convincing alternative explanations, and the quality of evidence available.

Also in the 1970s, during excavations near what is today called Border Cave in the Lebombo Mountains between South Africa and Swaziland, a small piece of the fibula of a baboon (dated approximately 35,000 BC) was found marked with 29 clearly defined notches. At more than 37,000 years old, the bone, which resembles the calendar sticks still in use by the Bushmen in Namibia, ranks with the oldest-known mathematical objects (www.math.buffalo.edu/mad/Ancient-Africa). It is suggested that since the Lebombo Bone was used as a lunar phase counter, then women may have been the first mathematicians, as keeping track of menstrual cycles requires a lunar calendar (*The Internet Encyclopedia of Science*, 2007).

Geometry South of the Sahara

It is not an overstatement to say that Paulus Gerdes has done the most amount of published work on geometry in Sub-Saharan Africa. The result of his many essays, which are written in English, French, German, and Portuguese, is his book, *Geometry from Africa: Mathematical and Educational Explorations* (1999). Consequently, the discussion in this section draws a great deal from Gerdes' work. Of course, other scholars' works about geometry south of the Sahara are used and referenced as well.

According to Gerdes, the development of geometrical thinking started early in African history, as early humans learned to "geometricize" in the context of their labor activities. For example, the hunter-gatherers of the Kalahari Desert in southern Africa learned to track animals, and learned to recognize and interpret spoors. They got to know that the shape of the spoor provided information on what animal passed by, how long ago, if it was hungry or not, etc. (Gerdes, 1999, p. 3). Such developments propelled Louis Liebenberg to posit that the critical attitude of contemporary Kalahari Desert trackers and the role of critical discussion in tracking suggest that the rationalist tradition of science may well have been practiced by hunter-gatherers long before the advent of the Greek philosophic schools (1990, p. 45).

The major question here, then, is the following: What evidence is available to support these claims? The discussion that follows in the rest of this section is a synopsis of as much of the available evidence as possible.

Rock paintings and engravings from all over Africa have been reported (Wilcox, 1984). Some of these artifacts date back several hundred years, and others several thousand years. They often have geometric structures. Other archaeological finds that indicate geometrical explorations by African hunters, farmers, and artisans are stone and metal tools and ceramics. Particularly exceptional are archaeological finds of perishable materials such as baskets, textiles, and wooden objects. The finds from the Tellem are extremely important, as they provide ideas of earlier geometrical explorations (Gerdes, 1999, p. 4).

Clear evidence of the exploration of forms, shapes, and symmetries exists in the archaeological finds from caves in the Cliff of Bandiagara in the center of Mali. The earliest buildings in the caves are cylindrical granaries made of mud coils that date from the third to the second century BC. During the eleventh century, the now-vanished people of the Tellem (as they are called by the Dogon who inhabited the region from the sixteenth century onward) entered the area from the south, probably from the rain forest. From the eleventh up to the fifteenth century, the Tellem buried their dead in the remaining old granaries and in new buildings they built in the caves. The dead were buried with wooden headrests, bows, quivers, hoes, musical instruments, baskets, gourds, leather sandals, boots, bags, amulets, woolen and cotton blankets, coifs, tunics, and fiber aprons (Gerdes, 1999, p. 6).

These perishable objects found in a reasonably good state of preservation in the caves belong to the oldest objects that have been preserved from Sub-Saharan Africa. Archaeologists and textile experts who have analyzed the Tellem textiles assert that no other region in the world has such a great variety of linear and geometrical patterns in cotton fabrics by means of a single color (the only one available: i.e., indigo). According to Rita Bolland (1991), the Tellem designs have been the object of search for infinite combinations which have persisted to this day.

To illustrate this search by Tellem weavers, Gerdes examines some patterns found on preserved fragments of tunics, sleeves, coifs and caps, woven in plain weave: i.e., the weave in which the horizontal and vertical threads cross each other one over, one under. According to Gerdes, the average width of the threads is 1 mm. The weavers alternated groups of natural white cotton threads with groups of blue, indigo-dyed, threads. From left to right, six vertical white threads are followed by four blue threads; from top to bottom, three horizontal white threads are followed by three blue threads. These yield a plane pattern. The basic rectangle has dimensions ten (= 6 + 4) by six (= 3 + 3), or (6 + 4) x (3 + 3) (Gerdes, 1999, pp. 6–7).

Gerdes adds that generally, the dimensions are $(m + n)$ X $(p + q)$, where m, n, p, and q are natural numbers. The Tellem weavers experimented with dimensions and found relationships between the dimensions and the (symmetry) properties of the patterns that resulted. In particular, the variation among the discovered plain-weave fragments suggests that the weavers knew the effect on the patterns of the selection of even and odd dimensions, in addition to how these dimensions ($m + n$) and ($p + q$) are produced. The Tellem patterns from the eleventh and twelfth centuries feature woven rectangles followed by fragments of respective plane patterns, which are two-color patterns in the sense that for each there is a rigid motion of the plane—translation, rotation, reflection—that reverses the blue and white colors (Gerdes, 1999, p. 7).

Furthermore, according to Gerdes, the Tellem weavers employed a variant of the plain weave, whereby in one direction double threads are used instead of single threads. In this way, the weavers were able to weave cloths with decorative and strip patterns. With woven cloth, the tailor could begin his/her work: drawing and cutting pieces; knotting, stitching and sewing them together; and decorating, for example, a tunic with a plaited band along the neck opening. Geometric knowledge is imperative in each of these activities. Decorative bands were plaited both with even and odd numbers of strings. Among the plaited bands discovered in the caves, there are on one hand bands made out of 4, 6, 8, and 14 strings, and, on the other hand, out of 5, 7, and 9 strings. The selection of an even or an odd number of strings and the weave, either plain or not, has implications for the visible decorative patterns. In addition, the Tellem weavers also produced blankets made of wool (Gerdes, 1999, pp. 9–11).

In his work on textiles from the Kingdom of Kuba in the eastern Kasai region of central Congo, Georges Meurant (1986) demonstrates that the region is one of the African cultural contexts that particularly have stimulated design with a strong geometric accent. The Kuba people are a conglomeration of various culturally related ethnic groups that include the Bushungo, the Ngongo, the Shoowa, and the Ngeende. The reign of King Shyaam a-Mbul (c. 1600–1620) contributed to the intensification of industrious and artistic activities involving copper and iron work, basket and mat weaving, construction of palaces, wood carving, embroidery, pottery and beadwork. Geometric designs decorate all of these objects.

Dorothy Washburn (1990), in her work on Bakuba raffia cloth, also in Congo, illustrates examples from Bushongo plane patterns. First, the men weave the plain light tan raffia cloth on a single-heddle loom. The women then employ geometric designs to embroider plush motifs on the plain cloth.

According to Gerdes, Bushongo two-color plane patterns display the structure of woven mats, the decorative pattern on the border of a loincloth, and patterns on women's bark cloth made up of light and dark rectangles, squares, triangles and rhombi sewn together. Among the Ngongo, the decoration of the walls of houses and palaces with mat-work is widespread. The plane patterns entail various symmetries. The sticks are woven together by the vertical lianas. Wooden cups are decorated with symmetrical patterns. An iron knife is decorated with copper in an axial symmetric pattern. Plaid band motifs occur frequently as decoration on wooden and metal objects, carved on gourds, as well as a female Bushoong tattoo. Plaited band motifs made out of only one continuous line are drawn by boys in the sand for amusement. Wood carving of other geometrical line algorithms, leading to strip patterns, exists. Gerdes also mentions Emil Torday and T. A. Joyce's 1910 recording of a "topological" puzzle that Torday saw in the Kuba capital. It consists of two pieces of calabash and a string arranged in a way that the player has to separate one of the calabash pieces from the string without cutting or untying the string (Gerdes, 1999, pp. 13–20).

Donald Crowe (1982) recounts that among the Akan peoples in the forests of present-day southern Ghana and eastern Côte d'Ivoire, the Ashanti Kingdom with its capital in Kumasi emerged dominant in the early eighteenth century. Before then, from the fourteenth century onwards, the city of Begho, just north of the forests, had been a major center of craft and commerce. Among the archaeological finds of Begho are the smoking pipes whose symmetries Crowe analyzed.

According to Gerdes, Ashanti women brought pottery to a high level of perfection by richly decorating them with geometric designs. A jar is decorated with an eight-fold symmetry design and a strip pattern. Other Ashanti cultural activities interwoven with geometrical ideas and experimentation are plaster (wall decoration), smith work (e.g., blades of the state swords) and the weaving and decoration of cloth. To weigh gold dust, the Ashanti have used weights often with animal or geometric forms. Gerdes also cites the first volume of N. Niangoran-Bouah's book, *The Akan World of Gold Weights* (1984), which beautifully displays many of the gold weights with various geometrical shapes and forms (Gerdes, 1999, pp. 20–23).

Gerdes further notes that among the decorated cloths produced by the Ashanti is the *adinkra*—a hand-stamped cloth made from white cotton fabric that is divided into rectangles which are filled up by a series of copies of the same stamp. Each stamp is made from a piece of calabash, with sticks glued to its back to serve as a handle. Gerdes also mentions that the best known West African fabric is the multi-colored *kente* cloth that is woven by the Ashanti in Ghana and the Ewe in Togo. *Kente* weavers use horizontal looms to produce long and narrow strips of cloth that are then sewn together to form square or rectangular pieces used to make robes. Gerdes cites Peter Adler and Nicholas Barnard's book, *African Majesty: The Textile Art of the Ashanti and Ewe* (1992), for its beautiful display of examples of *kente* cloth. The examples of the two-color patterns reveal that there exist translations, reflections, or rotations which reverse the colors of a particular pattern. Gerdes also cites many other works that provide information about weaving traditions in Sub-Saharan Africa and present colorful photographs of fabrics, many with geometric designs and patterns, examples of which he replicates in his own book (Gerdes, 1999, pp. 23–24).

Enid Schildkrout and Curtis Keim (1990) point out that in northeastern Congo, the Mangbetu ideal of feminine beauty included body-painting in geometric patterns. Women of the ruling class painted their bodies with *bianga*, a black juice made from the gardenia plant. Mangbetu women wore pieces of bark cloth upon the right shoulder; whenever a woman wanted to sit down, she would place her barkcloth upon the stool before doing so.

Gerdes presents two Mangbetu ceramic water bottles from the nineteenth century and examples of useful ivory carvings collected in 1918. He also displays Georg Schweinfurth's nineteenth-century engraving of the great hall of the court of King Mbuza, giving an idea of its geometrical structure. The hall was used for dancing and has rattles made from strips of palm fibers and filled with seeds used during dances. Gerdes further displays the plane pattern structure of a Mangbetu mural painting photographed before 1915 in Niangara (1999, pp. 29–31).

According to Gerdes, mural decoration is one of the cultural spheres most used for geometrical exploration in Africa. He notes that in West Africa and in southern Africa, it is mostly the women who decorate the walls of their houses with geometrical figures. Each year after the harvest, the women gather to restore and paint their mud dwellings which have been washed away clean by the rains. He also presents beautiful examples of geometrical mural decoration of a house front in Zinder (Niger), mural paintings from the Zande people in northeastern Congo, a Swahili plasterwork design from the northern Kenyan coastal region, a Nubian stencil wall painting, a beautifully plaited strip design that decorates part of the wall above the door of the house of a Bamileke chief in Cameroon, a wall decoration motif from Ghana, the roof structure of a Fulani house in Cameroon, a schematic plan of a large Massa farmhouse enclosure in Cameroon, and the circular settlement structure of Zulu cattle keepers in South Africa (Gerdes, 1999, pp. 31–33).

Also explored by Gerdes are examples of African mat and basket weaving with geometrical exploration. He displays a basket-bowl with ten-fold and a small pendant with five-fold axial symmetry produced by Swazi women using the coiled basket making technique, two coiled basketry motifs from Ovimbundu women in Angola, a Somali coiled basket, a detail of the wall of a plaited basket collected in 1910 in Niangara (noteworthy are the production and joining of woven "toothed squares" and with two-color symmetry), and strip patterns on baskets from the Tabwa people in southeastern Congo (Gerdes, 1999, pp. 34–36).

Using different materials, designs from mat and basket weaving are frequently applied and further developed in other contexts. Gerdes displays part of the cover of a bottle from Senegal (sections of leather is slit and woven with dried palm fibers), the decoration of a leather money purse from the Mali/Côte d'Ivoire border region and a leather bolster from Korhogo in the latter country, examples of leather appliqués with which Tuareg women in Niger decorate camel saddle bags, a painted strip pattern on a leather bracelet from Tamale in Ghana, a parchment of dyed skin that is richly decorated with geometric designs by female Hausa artisans in Nigeria, several leather shields from the Nandi and Kipsigis peoples in Kenya, a couple of leather shields from the Lukha of Sudan and the Zulu in South Africa, and several others from the Embu and Masai of Kenya and the Sonjo of Tanzania. To make a good sounding drum, it is imperative that the covering is fixed evenly to the drum's wall. Thus, the pins must be equally spaced. Stated mathematically, the holes in which the pins are nailed constitute a regular polygon. Gerdes illustrates this with a drum from Senegal (Gerdes, 1999, pp. 37–41).

The decoration of calabashes or gourds is another major domain for geometrical expression and exploration. The calabashes are cut open and emptied, and their shells dried in the sun until hard. The yellow surface is darkened or colored, and then designs are applied by incision and/or burning lines into it with a sharp hot metal like a knife or nail. Gerdes presents a design incised and burned onto a semi-spherical calabash from Kano in Nigeria, a burnt-in decoration on a palm wine calabash collected in 1898 in northwestern Cameroon, and some gourd decorations from Nigeria (Gerdes, 1999, p. 41).

Wood carving is another activity that summons geometrical exploration. African wooden boxes, seats, headrests, doorposts, pilasters, canoes and boats, spears, drums, pestles, spoons, cups, masks, and combs often have symmetric shapes, in addition to often being decorated with geometric designs. Gerdes displays many examples of these. Various other domains of African life that invite geometrical exploration, imagination and creativity include metalwork, tattooing and other forms of body decoration, hairstyles, string figures, and other games (Gerdes, 1999, pp. 42–47).

The so-called "Pythagorean Theorem" is certainly one of the most interesting and attractive theorems of early geometry. Although Pythagoras of Samos (sixth century BC) is credited with the theorem, the African Egyptologist from Senegal, Cheikh Anta Diop, has suggested that Pythagoras may have learned the theorem during his long stay in Egypt (Diop, 1980, pp. 436, 479). Gerdes and other scholars have shown how diverse African ornaments and artifacts may be used for the discovery of the Pythagorean Theorem and for finding proofs for it. They have also explored connections with related ideas and propositions such as Pappus' Theorem, similar right triangles, Latin and magic squares, and arithmetic modulo n.

Gerdes (1999, pp. 55–56) observes that in Mozambique, to fasten a cover of a basket, two plaited strips with little lassos at their ends are permanently fixed to the cover, and two cubic buttons are fastened to opposite sides of the basket. Each of the lassos is pulled down around the corresponding button in order to close the basket. Two strips of a palm leaf are used to weave a button. Once an initial knot is made, one continues, on the backside, to weave "one-over-one-under," building up successive layers of the button, until it has become more or less cubic.

One may arrive at the conclusion that $C = A + B$ that is, one arrives at the Pythagorean Theorem. One can also join the square designs to form a pattern in such a way that the oblique lines are continued. Comparing the areas, one may find the following: $S + T = U$.

In African decoration, there are designs or pattern details that display a fourfold symmetry: i.e., a rotational symmetry of 90° occurs frequently. Gerdes explores the idea that four points which correspond to one another under a fourfold symmetry always constitute the vertices of a square (1999, pp. 60–68).

Gerdes' first example is a traditional decorative design from Mozambique. He links four corresponding points on the circles by straight line segments and obtains a square. The corresponding points of intersection of these segments with the circles are also the vertices of a square. Instead of linking the four neighboring points of intersection points, Gerdes links the opposed intersection points and obtains a cross that divides the first square into four congruent parts. Both designs produced in this way lead easily to the Pythagorean proposition.

Demonstrably, let *a*, *b* and *c* denote the sides of the congruent right triangles. One may then compute the areas of the squares and triangles and analyze their relationships. As the side of the large square measures $a + b$, its area is $(a + b)^2$. The area of the large square is equal to the sum of the areas of the four right triangles ($4ab/2$) plus the area of the inscribed square (c^2). Therefore, $(a + b)^2 = 2ab + c^2$.

Taking into account the equality: $(a + b)^2 = 2ab + a^2 + b^2$, one may find $a^2 + b^2 = c^2$.

In essence, one arrives at the Pythagorean proposition.

Geometrically, Gerdes arrives at this result in other ways as well. For example, he rotates the upper-left right angle clockwise 90° about its lowest vertex. Similarly, he rotates the upper-right triangle counterclockwise 90° about its lowest vertex. He observes that the large square may be considered as composed of one square with side *a*, one square with side *b,* and four right triangles with sides *a, b,* and *c*. Initially, the same large square was composed of a square of side *c* circumscribed by four right triangles with sides *a, b,* and *c*. Therefore, the area of the square with side *c* is equal to the sum of the areas of the squares with sides *a* and *b*.

Gerdes then turns to the cross which divides the initial square into four quadrilaterals that are congruent because of the rotational symmetry. As the arms of the cross constitute the diagonals of a square, they are perpendicular. He let *p* be the side of the initial square and let *r* be the length of the arm of the cross. The four congruent quadrilaterals are joined in such a way that a new and larger square with side *r* appears. At its center, a square hole appears. He let *q* be its side. From the construction of the new square, it immediately follows that $r^2 = p^2 + q^2$.

As $q = a - b$, one sees that *p*, *q*, and *r* make up the side of a right angle. This reasoning can be used to arrive at a "dissection" proof for the Pythagorean proposition. According to E. S. Loomis, this proof was found for the first time (?) by Henry Perigal as late as 1873 (Loomis, 1968, 1972, p. 104).

Gerdes considers an arbitrary right triangle with sides *p, q,* and *r*. He let *p* be larger than *q*. He then draws squares on the legs. Through the center of the square of side *p*, he constructs a cross with one of its arms parallel to the hypotenuse of the right triangle. The four pieces into which the *p*-square is dissected are joined together with the *q*-square to obtain the *r*-square. Therefore, $r^2 = p^2 + q^2$.

The second example that Gerdes provides shows some Chokwe (in Angola) sand drawings with a fourfold symmetry. He easily transforms each drawing into one of the preceding Pythagorean designs.

The third example that Gerdes presents is a beautiful tiling from the Kuba people who inhabit the central part of the Congo basin, living in the Savannah south of the dense equatorial forest. The Kuba are famous for their metal products such as weapons and jewelry. Their villages themselves had specialized in the production of certain types of craft like wooden boxes and cups, copper pipes, raffia cloths, etc. Gerdes displays an interesting tessellation of the plane composed of "hooks" and squares, a design that appears traditionally on woven mats and on embroidered raffia textiles, and called *Mikope Ngoma* (i.e., the drums of King Mikope). Each square is embraced by four hooks, with a fourfold symmetry. When the corresponding vertices are linked, a square that has the same areas as the design is obtained.

Gerdes generalizes this design in such a way that the new square still has the same area as the design and that the corresponding right triangle is arbitrary with sides a, b and c. In this way, he finds that the area of the large square (c^2) is equal to the area of the small square plus two times the area of the rectangle formed by joining the hooks. As the small square has side $b - a$, and the rectangles have sides a and $(a/2) + [(b - a) + (a/2)]$, or b, one can conclude that: $c^2 = 2ab + (b - a)^2 = a^2 + b^2$, that is, one proves the Pythagorean Theorem.

The fourth example that Gerdes explores is the "elephants' defense" designs of the Kuba in Congo. Gerdes shows two tattooing motifs formerly used by the Ngongo, one of the ethnic groups that belonged to the Kuba Kingdom. When he draws lines between the ends of the tattooing motifs, he obtains a design similar to the Kuba engravings that the Bushongo (the dominant people in the old Kuba Kingdom) call *mwoong* (elephants' defense). They call the motif *ikwa-akl'imwoong* (deformed elephants' defense). When he places several copies of the design together, he discovers, "reinvents" and even proves, easily and geometrically, the Pythagorean Theorem.

When Gerdes employs the identity $(b - a)^2 = b^2 - 2ba + a^2$ and the formulae for the determination of the areas of squares and right angles, he arrives at the same conclusion. The area of the small central square is equal to $(b - a)^2$ and the combined areas of the four neighboring right triangles are $2ab$. Therefore:

$$c^2 = (b - a)^2 + 2ab = a^2 + b^2.$$

Gerdes offers an ornamental variant and generalization of the Pythagorean Theorem of the Kuba's elephants' defense pattern by employing a big rectangle composed of two pairs of similar triangles and a little rectangle at the center. By placing several copies of this variant together, he discovers/invents and proves the following generalization of the Pythagorean proposition:

$$cc' = aa' + bb'.$$

He arrives at the same conclusion by algebraic-geometrical reasoning as follows: the area of the central rectangle is equal to $(b' - a)(b - a')$ and the areas of the four neighboring right triangles are together $ab + a'b'$. Therefore:

$$cc' = (b' - a)(b - a') + a\,b + a'b' = a\,a' + b\,b'.$$

A combination of the Pythagorean proposition with its generalization yields the following: from $c^2 = a^2 + b^2$, $(c')^2 = (a')^2 + (b')^2$, and $cc' = aa' + bb'$, it follows algebraically easily that:

$$ab' = ba'$$

which implies that

$$a : b = a' : b'.$$

Stated in another way, the ratios of the sides, taken in the same order, of similar right triangles are equal.

Gerdes returns to the rectangular Kuba variant of the elephants' defense pattern to join some of the ornamental rectangles in order to derive a square. He shows two possibilities of obtaining a square of side $c + c'$. In both cases, a square "hole" appears in the center, whose sides measure $c' - c$. When he extends the sides that end at the vertices of the "hole" until they encounter other sides, four right triangles appear around the square "hole" and, together with the square "hole," they form a new square of side $(a' + b') - (a + b)$.

In both cases, around this new central square emerge four rectangles which comprise patterns that are similar to the Kuba tattooing discussed earlier. Since the large squares are congruent and the small squares are also congruent, Gerdes arrives at the conclusion that both designs themselves are also equal in area. Both are comprised of four rectangles. Therefore, the area (ab') of one of these rectangles of the first design is equal to the area $(a'b)$ of one of the rectangles of the second design: that is,

$$ab' = a'b.$$

Stated differently,

$$a : b = a'b.$$

As a result, Gerdes arrives geometrically at the conclusion that the ratios of the sides, taken in the same order, of similar right triangles are equal.

On the basis of the preceding results, it turns out to be easy to prove the Fundamental Theorem of Similar Triangles. Within the same context, Gerdes introduces the concepts of tangent, sine and cosine of an acute angle. Applying the generalization $cc' = aa' + bb'$ in the case of the triangles yields the trigonometric formula:

$$c = a\sin\alpha + b\sin\beta.$$

Gerdes moves from widespread decorative motif to a discovery of Pythagoras' and Pappus' theorems and an infinity of proofs. He begins by displaying variations of decorative motif with a long tradition all over Africa. He replicates M.-L. Bastin's examples of the designs of the Chokwe of Angola called *manda a mbaci* (tortoise-shield) (Bastin, 1961, pp. 114, 116), and Alfred Hauenstein's examples of the designs of the Ovimbunda also of Angola referred to as *olombungulu* (star), *ononguinguuinini* (ants), or *alende* (clouds) (Hauenstein, 1988, pp. 39, 50, 54).

Pointing to the number of unit squares on each row of the "star" or "toothed square," Gerdes shows that the area of the "star" is equal to the sum of areas of the 4 x 4 shaded square and 3 x 3 un-shaded square. A toothed square, especially one with many teeth, looks almost like a real square. The area of a toothed square (T) is equal to the sum of the areas of two smaller squares (A and B):

$$T = A + B.$$

From this, it can be concluded that the area of a toothed square (T) is equal to the area of a "real" square (C). Since $C = T$, it can be concluded that

$$A + B = C.$$

When Gerdes draws the oblique square (area C') together with the squares with areas A and B, in such a way that the squares become "neighbors," the Pythagorean proposition for the special case of the right triangle emerges. In essence, toothed squares may assume a heuristic value for the discovery of the Pythagorean proposition.

In his first proof, Gerdes lets A' and B' be two arbitrary squares. He dissects A' into nine little congruent squares and B' into 16 congruent squares, and joins the 25 pieces together. The toothed square obtained T' is equal in area (T) to the sum of the real squares A' and B':

$$T = A + B.$$

Once again, the toothed square is easily transformed into a real square C' of the same area, allowing one to arrive at

$A + B = C$ (i.e., the Pythagorean Theorem in all its generality).

For an infinity of proofs, Gerdes begins by dissecting A' and B' into n^2 and $(n + 1)^2$ congruent sub-squares for each (positive) integer of n. To each value of

n, there corresponds a proof of the Pythagorean proposition. Put differently, an infinite number of demonstrations of the theorem exist.

The truth of the Pythagorean proposition is almost immediately visible for relatively high values of n. One more demonstration of the theorem is delineated when one takes the limit $n \rightarrow \infty$. A very short, easily understandable proof is obtained for $n = 1$. Analogously, Pappus' generalization of the Pythagorean Theorem for parallelograms is proved in an infinite number of ways. E. S. Loomis provides 370 different proofs, each requiring its own figure, and he encourages others to find new proofs (1972, pp. 13, 269). Gerdes' reflection on a widespread African decorative motif leads him not only to an alternative, active way of introducing the Pythagorean proposition, but also to the generation of an infinite number of proofs of the theorem.

For the toothed squares, Gerdes counts the number of unit squares in each of the horizontal rows. Knowing that the total number of unit squares is a square number, in this case 4^2, he compares the two enumerations and finds:

$$1 + 2 + 3 + 4 + 3 + 2 + 1 = 4^2,$$

or, taking into account the visionary line:

$$(1 + 2 + 3 + 4) + (3 + 2 + 1) = 4^2.$$

It follows that:

$$(1 + 2 + 3) + (3 + 2 + 1) = 4^2 - 4,$$

and

$$1 + 2 + 3 = \frac{4^2 - 4}{2},$$

Experimentation with other toothed squares, varying the number of teeth on each side, leads Gerdes to the following extrapolation:

$$1 + 2 + 3 + \dots + (n - 1) = \frac{4^2 - n}{2},$$

where n denotes a natural number bigger than 1.

By counting all the unit squares of the toothed triangle, row by row, Gerdes finds 1 + 3 + 5 + 7. Comparing the two enumerations, he concludes that:

$$1 + 3 + 5 + 7 = 4^2.$$

Put differently, the sum of the first odd numbers is 4^2. Experimentation with other toothed triangles and comparison of the results leads to the discovery of the general result that the sum of the first n odd numbers is equal to n^2.

Moving from mat-weaving patterns to Pythagoras, Latin and magic squares, Gerdes considers a solution found by Chokwe mat makers from northeastern Angola. Each brown strand goes over one white strand and then under four white strands; two successive brown (from the left to the right) differ two in phase. He moves one unit to the right and two units down and calls it the (1, -2)-solution. In this way, the upper part of the detail of a Kuba mat from Congo displays the (1, 2)-solution. Also displayed are the (1, 3) and (1, 4)-solutions. Other solutions are possible if brown squares composed of more than one unit square are admitted.

Gerdes observes that all of these solutions generate tessellations of the plane. What they share in common is that four neighboring brown dots embrace a white square. When he draws straight lines through the centers of these neighboring white squares, a new square grid—an oblique one—is obtained. As each white square is divided by the lines of the new grid into four congruent quadrilaterals and, at the same time, each square of the oblique grid is composed of a brown square at its center, surrounded by four such congruent quadrilaterals, it follows that the area of the oblique square (C) is equal to the sum of the areas of one brown (A) and one white (B) square: $A + B = C$.

When the oblique grid is translated in such a way that its vertices coincide with vertices of the brown squares, one arrives at (2) $a^2 + b^2 = c^2$, i.e., at the Theorem of Pythagoras, where a, b, and c denote the lengths of the sides of the squares of area A, B, and C.

A variant is provided by Gerdes whereby the design formed by four neighboring brown dots and the embraced white square shows a rotational symmetry of 90°. The implication here is that any four corresponding points are the vertices of a square. A rearrangement of the white and brown squares leads once again to the Pythagorean Theorem.

Turning to the notion of periodicity and fundamental blocks, Gerdes uses the example of the Chokwe mat, in which the vertical brown strands pass always over one horizontal white strand and then under four white strands; the brown-and-white pattern repeats itself in the vertical direction after five (horizontal) strands. In the horizontal direction, each white strand passes under one brown strand and then over four brown strands. In the horizontal direction, the pattern also repeats itself after five strands. Thus, it can be stated that the pattern has period 5 in both directions (i.e., it can be considered as made up of equally colored 5 x 5 blocks). This fundamental 5 x 5 block contains just one little brown square in each row and each column.

To enumerate the unit squares, Gerdes goes from the left to the right, 1, 2, 3, 4, 5 the successive (brown) squares of a fundamental block. He then attributes, to each small square of a specific 5 X 5 block, a number 1, 2, 3, 4, or 5, in such a manner that it is different from the numbers that appear in the same horizontal, vertical or diagonal line. For the unit square marked by a circle, there is only one possibility: 5.

For a Latin square, Gerdes does the same for the unit squares of the same fundamental block and gets the 5 x 5 number square. In each row and each column, the numbers 1, 2, 3, 4 and 5 appear precisely once.

Gerdes then uses the Latin square to construct magic squares. A magic square is generally defined as a set of integers in serial order, beginning with 1, arranged in square formation so that the sum total of each row, column, and main diagonal is the same. Since the Latin square already has the property that the sum total of each row, column and main diagonal is the same, Gerdes adds 5 to five numbers (one in each row and each column), adds 10 to five other numbers (one in each row and each column), and then adds 15 and 20 in the same way, and obtains a magic square. The sum total of the rows, columns and main diagonal is 65.

These magic squares have additional properties. They are also "diabolic" or "pan-diagonal," meaning that the sum totals of the so-called "broken diagonals" are equal to the same constant 65. "Broken diagonals" refer to those that belong partly to a number square and partly to its equal neighboring number squares. When several equal magic squares of this type are joined, and then displace the 5 x 5 square, new magic squares are derived.

One of the magic squares has the additional property that each number on one of the four axes of the square, added to the number symmetrically opposite the square's center, gives the same: 12 + 18 + 14 + 16 = 7 + 23 = ... = 30. Reflecting one of the magic squares about its vertical axis, Gerdes gets one of the magic squares presented by Muhammad ibn Muhammad al Fulani al-Kishwani, an early eighteenth-century Fulani astronomer and mathematician from Katsina (now northern Nigeria) in his 1732 work, *A Treatise on the Magical Use of the Letters of the Alphabet,* written in Arabic (cited and discussed by Zaslavsky, 1973/1999, pp. 138–151).

For the Kuba design discussed earlier, Gerdes illustrates that it has the 5 x 5 block as the fundamental block. The alternative solutions have period 10 and period 17, respectively. As done before, by enumerating the successive small squares in the case of the 17 x 17 block yields Latin and magic squares.

Finally, for Arithmetic modulo *n*, Gerdes illustrates that in order to go one place to the right side of the Latin square for the Chokwe mat, he adds 3 modulo 5. In order to go one place up, he adds 1 modulo 5. When he goes one place diagonally down the right, he has to go one place to the right (+3) and then one place vertically downwards (-1); the result is +2. When he moves one place diagonally downwards to the left, he goes, for example, first one place vertically downwards (-1) and then one place left (-3); the end result is -4, but -4 = 1 modulo 5. Going from 2 to 5, he adds 3. When he passes through 4, he adds first 1 and then two times 3, and from 4 to 5, he adds first 3 and then subtracts two times 1. Comparing the two ways yields:

$$(1 + 2 \times 3) + (3 + 2 \times [-1]) = 3 \text{ (modulo 5)}$$

or

$$7 + 1 = 3 \text{ (modulo 5)}.$$

The other topics dealing with the Geometry of Sub-Saharan Africa are geometrical ideas in crafts and the *sona* sand drawing tradition of the Chokwe in southern-central Africa. For the former topic, scholars explore symmetrical wall decoration in Lesotho and South Africa; house strip patterns from Guinea, Mozambique, Senegal, and Uganda; and finite geometrical designs from the Lower Congo region. Exploration of a hexagonal basket weaving technique from Cameroon to Kenya, Congo to Madagascar and Mozambique, leads to connections between the underlying geometry and chemical models of recently discovered carbon molecules. Pentagrams are discovered in knots, and alternative ways are developed for rectangle constructions and for the determination of areas of circles and volumes of spatial figures, including a twisted decahedron. For the latter topic, scholars underscore the mathematical underpinnings of the *sona* tradition by developing the Geometry of Lunda-designs and Lunda-patters. A discussion of the intricate mathematics of these topics (hexahedra, octahedra, polyhedra, trigonometric function, Euler's Theorem, monolinearity, algorithms, nonlinearity, etc.) is beyond the scope of this chapter.

Numbers

Indeed, the most cited and revered work on African numeration systems is Claudia Zaslavsky's *Africa Counts: Numbers and Pattern in African Cultures* (1973, 1999). It is only fitting, therefore, that the discussion in this section draws heavily from Zaslavsky's work. Nonetheless, other scholars' works on African numeration systems are also used and referenced accordingly.

The economic development of a society, asserts Zaslavsky, ultimately determines the development of its numeration system. African systems of numeration, she adds, varied from a few number words to well-constructed systems with which counting extended into the millions. In many African cultures, a formal system of gesture counting accompanied the number words. Like other peoples around the world, Africans shared a belief in the special significance—for either good or evil—of certain numbers (Zaslavsky, 1973/1999, p. 30).

The people naturally required numerals of a higher order as their society's economy grew more sophisticated. In some cases, the people borrowed from neighboring societies; in other cases, neologisms were created. Due to reasons other than the expansion of the numeral system, number words or their meanings undergo alteration over time. As the needs of a society change, special number words associated with the counting of particular objects, such as cowrie currency, tend either to disappear from use or to assume more general application. Furthermore, when a written language is developed, the lengths of various expressions for a given concept in different language varieties are reduced to facilitate standardization in order to spread formal education among the people. For example, the cumbersome Sotho language (Southern Africa) construction for the number 99 changed from *mashome a robileng meno a le mong a (nang le) metso e robileng mono o le mong* (tens which bend one finger which have units which bend one finger) to *mashome a robong a metso o robong* (tens nine with a root that is nine) (Zaslavsky, 1973/1999, p. 38).

Even more fascinating is how these African numeration systems have survived in the Diaspora. Lorenzo D. Turner (1949/1969), for example, observes that the descendants of enslaved Africans brought to the coastal areas of South Carolina and Georgia during the eighteenth and nineteenth centuries still speak Gullah, a combination of the West African language of their ancestors (Sierra Leone and Liberia) and the English language. Among the Africanisms surviving among the Gullah speakers to the 1940s, according to Turner, were the numerals from one to ten in several West African languages and from one to 19 in the language of the Fulani people. The survival of these number words is a clear indication that the numerals constituted a vital part of the vocabulary of the enslaved Africans who brought their languages from Africa.

According to Zaslavsky, despite the wide distribution of peoples and the existence of about a thousand languages in Africa, the words for two, three and four are similar in an area covering about half of the continent. This area includes the Sudan—the region extending from the Sahara southward to the Gulf of Guinea, and from the Atlantic Ocean to the River Nile—and most of the southern part of the continent now inhabited by Bantu-speaking people. The 300 Bantu languages comprise a subgroup of the Niger-Congo family and bear a great resemblance to the languages of the western Sudanic peoples in terms of basic words. Both categories of languages had a common origin, and half of the Bantu-speaking peoples dispersed throughout the southern half of Africa from the areas of Nigeria and Cameroon (Zaslavsky, 1973/1999, p. 39).

Zaslavsky observes that the word for one exhibits great variety in African languages, while this is not the case for the words for two, three and four. The word for two is usually a form of *li* or *di*; the word for three contains the syllable *ta* or *sa*; and the word for four is generally a nasal consonant, like *ne*. The word for five has a variety of forms and is frequently the word for hand.

Zaslavsky quotes Marianne Schmidl (1915, p. 168) who observes the following about the Bantu numeration system:

> When we compare the number words from one to nine in the various Bantu languages, we find a similarity in the names for 2, 3, 4, and 5, while the corresponding gestures differ considerably. The basic stems are:

2 *-vili* or *–vali*
3 *–tatu*
4 *–na*
5 *–tano*
...There are various expressions for "one," but generally they are related to -*mwe* (quoted in Zaslavsky, 1973/1999, p. 39).

Contrastingly, observes Zaslavsky, there are wide variations in the words for 6, 7, 8, and 9. Thus, she suggests that it is necessary to deal separately with the various branches of the Bantu language when analyzing these numbers (1973/1999, p. 39).

In some cases, the numbers 6, 7, 8, and 9 are expressed as a simple addition to five. For example, in the Kwanyama language (southwestern Africa), one finds the following:

6 *tano-na-mwe*
7 *tano-na-vali*
8 *tano-na-tatu*
9 *tano-na-ne*

In other cases, the composition of one with five to express six may not be so obvious. As Maurice Delafosse (1929) observes, in the Malinke language spoken on the upper Niger River, six is expressed by *woro* or *wolo*, where *wo* is an abbreviation of the word for five and *ro* or *lo* is a shortened form of one (also cited in Zaslavsky, 1973/1999, p. 41).

In many African languages, the words for six through nine are derived directly from the gestures of these numbers and are based on several different systems of gesture counting. Interestingly, the Manlike word for nine, *kononto*, means literally "to the one of the belly," a reference to the nine months of pregnancy (Zaslavsky, 1973/1999, p. 42).

Beginning with the five-ten system, the Sudanic and Bantu branches of the Niger-Congo language family diverge on the choice of the secondary base. The former generally use 20, and the latter favor ten. Most Bantu languages employ *kumi* or *longo* for ten, albeit it is not the original meaning. Number words for a hundred, a thousand and higher place values were rarely employed, except in association with specific objects to be counted. For example, in the Ziba language: 100 *tsikumu* was used to refer to a string of 100 cowrie shells; 1,000 *lukimi* was used to refer to a bundle of ten strings of cowrie currency; 10,000 *kakumi* was used to refer to a heap of ten bundles.

These same words were applied to other objects, or new words were invented, as the need arose (Zaslavsky, 1973/1999, p. 42).

In terms of the five-20 or quinquavigesimal system, for the African languages which build on 20 as a secondary base, ten may be an independent word or it may mean two hands or two fives. This is followed by an expression denoting ten and one, and so on to 15, which may be two hands and one hand or ten and one hand, or even an independent word, as in the Djola language of Guinea-Bissau, where the word means "to bow." Some languages continue to add one, two, etc. to the word for 15 until 20 is reached. The word for 20 in some languages means literally "man complete." In the Banda language of Central Africa, the word for 15 means "three fists" and the word for 20 means "take one person." The same method is repeated by adding to the word for 20 to form the numerals from 21 to 39. The number 40 is expressed as "two men complete," and 100 is "five men complete"—in essence, all of the digits on the hands and feet have been counted five times (Zaslavsky, 1973/1999, p. 42–43). And as Delafosse points out, a Malinke expression for 40 is *dibi*, meaning "a mattress," the union of the 40 digits, as the husband and wife lie on the same mattress and have a total of 40 digits between them (1929, p. 389). This is the basic form of the quinquavigesimal system found in many languages of the Sudan region: Djola, Balante, and Nalu in the west; Yoruba, Nupe, and Efik in Nigeria; Vai and Kru in Liberia and Sierra Leone; and the Nuba language of the eastern Sudan.

As a numeration system develops, special words are either introduced or existing words acquire new meanings. For example, the Malinke word *keme*, meaning "a large number," came to denote 100 and was employed in counting cowrie currency instead of the more cumbersome expression "five men complete" (Zaslavsky, 1973/1999, p. 43).

The Igbo (Nigeria) numeration system is based on 20. The number 30 is expressed as the sum of 20 and ten, 50 is 40 and ten, and similarly for the larger numbers. In most language varieties, the formation of the numbers in any place value is by addition of the digits from one to nine to the appropriate word for the multiple of ten (Zaslavsky, 1973/1999, p. 43). Roy Abraham (1967) reports an alternative method in the Igbo numerical system (i.e., 16, 17, 18, and 19) can be formed by deducting 4, 3, 2 and 1, respectively, from 20, and similarly for those of the higher place values. The Igbo numeration system also has a special word for the square of 20: 400 is *nu*; the square for 400, or 160,000, is expressed as *nnu khuru nnu*, translated as "400 meets 400." An "uncountably" large number is referred to as *pughu* (Zaslavsky, 1973/1999, p. 43).

The Yoruba of southwest Nigeria have a unique system based on 20. It illustrates an unusual subtractive principle still in effect to this day. As Scott W. Williams points out, the vigesimal (base 20) scale of the Yoruba in Nigeria was present around 1000 AD during the foundation of the Oyo Kingdom. This numerical system hinges heavily upon subtraction. It has different names for the numbers from one (*okan*) to ten (*eewa*). The numbers 11 (*ookanla*) to 14 (*eerinla*) could be translated as "one more than ten" to "four more than ten." But when 15 (*aarundinlogun*) is reached the convention changes, so that 15 to 19 (*ookandinlogun*) are expressed as "20 less five" to "20 less one," respectively, where 20 is *oogun*. Similarly, the numbers 21 to 24 are expressed as subtractions from 30 (*ogbon*). At 35 (*aarundinlogoji*), however, there is a change in the way the first multiple of 20 is referred to: 40 is expressed as "two 20s" (*ogoji*) while 60 (*ogota*), "three 20s," and 80 (*ogerin*), "four 20s," and so on to 200 (*igba*) for "ten 20s." It is the naming of some of the intermediate numbers that the subtraction principle becomes prominent. The following are examples:

45 = (20*3) - 10 - 5
50 = (20*3) - 10
108 = (20*6) - 10 - 2
300 = 20*(20 - 5)
318 = 400 - (20*4) - 2
525 = (200*3) - (20*4) - 2

All the numbers from 200 to 2,000, except those that can be directly related to 400 (*irinwo*), are treated as multiples of 200. From the name *egbewa* (2,000), names are constructed similar to the preceding examples. Indeed, the Yoruba numeral system is quite complicated, as the expression of small terms involves considerable feats of mathematical manipulation (math.buffalo.edu/mad/Ancient-Africa/).

In terms of linguistic change, the Arabic influence is evident in the Hausa numerical system of northern Nigeria. While nineteenth-century linguists classified the Hausa numerical system as quinary-vigesimal, but having a base of 12 for the formation of words for 13 through 18, later sources show a clear relationship to the decimal Arabic system for the numeral starting with 20 as well as the Arabic word for six (*shida*). Another aspect of the Hausa numeration system is the use of a subtraction principle for compound numbers ending in eight and nine: for example, 18 = 20 - 2; 19 = 20 - 1 (Zaslavsky, 1973/1999, p. 45). W. L. Migeod (1911) reports three designations for 20 in use at the same time in the Hausa numeration system: (1) *hauiya*, a special word for 20 cowrie shells used as currency; (2) the plural of *goma*, the word for ten; and (3) *ashirin*, the Arabic word for 20. The following are the Hausa number words in current use, according to Zaslavsky: 1 *daya*, 2 *biyu*, 3 *uku*, 4 *hudu*, 5 *biyar*, 6 *shida* (from Arabic), 7 *bakwi*, 8 *takwas*, 9 *tara*, 10 *goma*, 19 *goma sha tara*, 20 *ashirin* (from Arabic), 30 *talatin* (from Arabic), and 100 *dari* (1973/1999, p. 45).

There also exist other numerical systems with unusual number bases in Africa. For the Bram and Mankanye people of Guinea-Bissau, five is denoted by the word for "hand," ten is "two hands," nine is "hand and hand less one," and 19 is expressed as "two hands and hand and hand less one," which is definitely a quinary system. But 12 is "six times two." The Bram and Mankanye carry the idea further with 24 = 6 x 4. Their neighbors, the Balante, employ six to delineate the numerals from seven to 12: 7 = 6 + 1, 8 = 6 + 2, etc. For the Ga people of Ghana, both seven and eight are based upon six: 7 = 6 + 1 and 8 = 6 + 2 (Zaslavsky, 1973/1999, p. 46).

The Huku of Central Africa display the greatest variety, as they base their numerical system on four and six (Zaslavsky, 1973/1999, p. 46):

7 = 6 + 1
8 = 6 + 2

9 = (2 X 4) + 1
10 is an independent word
13 = 12 + 1
16 = (2 X 4) X 2
17 = (2 X 4) X 2 + 1
20 = 2 X 10

Other aspects of African numerical systems that have been thoroughly investigated include gesture counting, taboos and mysticisms, the concept of time, numbers and money, weights and measures, games, magic squares, patterns and shapes, and histories of various numerical systems. Due to space limitations, however, these aspects are not discussed in this chapter.

Beginnings of Written Mathematics: Egypt

According to Williams, as early as 4800 BC, the Egyptians had developed a calendar. In 4200 BC, their mathematics and astronomy scholars produced a 365-day calendar (12 months of 30 days plus five feast days). By the time of the Egyptian mace in 3100 BC, various agricultural communities along the banks of the River Nile were united by a Nubian, King Menes, who founded a dynasty of thirty-two Pharaohs and lasted three thousand years. For more than half that time, areas of modern Israel and Syria as well as the Nile Valley were part of Egypt. To rule effectively, the Egyptians had to develop an extensive and efficient administration for collecting taxes, taking census, and maintaining a large army. Since all of these activities required mathematics, the Egyptians at first employed counting glyphs. But even by 2000 BC, the hieratic glyphs were being used by Egyptians (www.math.buffalo.edu/mad/Ancient-Africa/).

Williams adds that from Herodotus, the Greek (500 BC), one learns that the Pharaoh Ramses II (1300 BC) divided the land into lots and gave each man a square piece of equal size, from the produce of which he exacted an annual tax. If a man reported that his holding was damaged by the encroachment of the river, the Pharaoh would send inspectors and surveyors to measure the extent of the damage to assess the extent of the loss. The data would then be used to set a fair proportion of his property tax. This may be the way in which geometry was invented and subsequently reached Greece.

Furthermore, Williams notes that another Greek, Democritus (410 BC), while boasting, made a high estimation of Egyptian mathematics. According to him, no one surpassed him in the construction of lines with the help of a ruler and compass, not even the so-called "rope stretchers" (surveyors) among the Egyptians.

Among the many strands of African mathematics, the Egyptian one has been studied and written about the most. Among the topics dealing with Egyptian mathematics that have been investigated are the sources, number recording, arithmetic, algebra, and geometry. George Gheverghese Joseph has discussed these aspects in his book, *The Crest of the Peacock: Non-European Roots of Mathematics* (1991/2000). What follows in the rest of this section is a synopsis of his presentation.

Time has not been kind to Egyptian mathematical sources recorded on papyri. Nonetheless, the papyrus is quite a bit more durable than the palm leaves, bark and bamboo used in writing materials by the ancient Chinese and Indians. There are two major sources and a number of minor ones on Egyptian Mathematics. A majority of the minor sources preserve the mathematics of later epochs of Egyptian history: the Hellenistic (332–39 BC) and Roman (30 BC–385 AD). The most important major source is the Ahmes (or Ahmose) Papyrus, named after the scribe who composed it, in about 1650 BC, from a work three centuries older. It is also referred to as the Rhind Mathematical Papyrus, after the British collector who acquired it in 1858 and subsequently donated it to the British Museum. The second major source is the Moscow Papyrus written around 1850 BC; it was taken to Russia in the middle of the twentieth century, ending up in Moscow's Museum of Fine Arts. Between the two papyri, there are 112 mathematical problems with their solutions (Joseph 1991/2000, pp. 59–60).

Among the minor sources, there is the Egyptian mace head from the early third millennium BC which contains the war booty of the Pharaoh Namer: 120,000 prisoners; 400,000 oxen; and 1,422,000 goats. Recording these numbers required a highly developed system of numerals that allowed counting to continue indefinitely by the introduction of a new system whenever necessary. Other minor sources include the Egyptian Leather Roll, a table consisting of 26 decompositions into unit fractions, from the same period as the Ahmes Papyrus; the Berlin Papyrus which contains two problems of simultaneous equations, one of second degree; the Reisner Papyri, consisting of four worm-eaten rolls which record volume calculations relating to temples, from around 1800 BC; and the Kahun Papyrus, containing six scattered mathematical fragments, not all of which have been deciphered, from around 1800 BC (Joseph 1991/2000, p. 60).

According to Ahmes, his material came from an earlier document belonging to the Middle Kingdom (2000–1800 BC), and he suggests that the knowledge may ultimately have been derived from Imhotep (c. 2650 BC), the legendary architect and physician to Pharaoh Zoser of the Third Dynasty. The opening sentence of the Ahmes Papyrus is a testament that it is "a thorough study of all things, insight into all that exists, knowledge of all the obscure secrets" (Joseph 1991/2000, pp. 60–61). It contains 87 mathematical problems and their solutions, making it the most comprehensive source of early Egyptian Mathematics. There are 25 problems, among them two notable results of Egyptian Mathematics: (1) the formula for the truncated square pyramid (or frustum) and (2) a remarkable solution to the problem of finding the curved surface area of a hemisphere (Joseph 1991/2000, p. 61).

The dominant impression in many textbooks on the history of Mathematics that only one scheme of numeration, the hieroglyphic (pictorial), was employed in ancient Egypt is incorrect. Instead, at least three different notational systems existed: (1) hieroglyphic, (2) hieratic (symbolic), and (c) demotic (popular). The first two numeration systems appeared quite early in Egyptian history. The hieratic notation was used in both the Ahmes and Moscow Papyri, while the demotic variant was a popular adaptation of the hieratic notation and became important during the Greek and Roman periods of Egyptian history (Joseph 1991/2000, p. 61).

In the hieroglyphic system, characters represented objects, some easily recognizable. Special symbols were employed to represent each power of 10 from 1 to 10^7. A unit was therefore commonly written as a single vertical stroke; when written in detail, however, it was shown as a short piece of rope. A long piece of rope in the shape of a horseshoe was used to represent the number ten, and a coil of rope was employed for 100. Quite in keeping with the important role of the "rope stretchers" (i.e., surveyors) in ancient Egypt, the overriding motif in all of these cases seems to have been a rope whose length and shape determined the magnitude of the number represented. A thousand was represented by a pictograph that resembles a lotus flower, although the plant sign formed the initial of *khaa*, which means cord. The number 10,000 was represented by a crooked finger; 100,000 was represented by a stylized tadpole; 1,000,000 was represented by a man with arms upraised; and 10,000,000 was represented by a rising sun. Any number can be written by using these symbols additively (Joseph 1991/2000, pp. 61–62).

The hieroglyphs were arranged in descending order of magnitude from right to left. To add two numbers, an individual made a collection of each set of symbols that appeared in both numbers and replaced them with the next higher symbol as necessary. To subtract, the process for addition was reversed and the higher hieroglyph is replaced by the lower one accordingly (Joseph 1991/2000, p. 62).

The hieratic representation was similar to the hieroglyphic process, since it (i.e., the hieratic process) was additive and based on powers of ten. But the former was far more economical, as a number of identical hieroglyphs were replaced with fewer symbols, or just one symbol. For example, 999 would require 27 symbols in hieroglyphs compared to six in hieratic. While this process was more taxing on memory, its economy, speed, conciseness and greater suitability for writing with pen and ink must have precipitated its early adoption in ancient Egypt. From the point of view of the history of mathematics, the hieratic system may have inspired the development of the alphabetic Greek number system around the middle of the first millennium BC (Joseph 1991/2000, pp. 62–63).

A great feat of the Egyptian method of duplication or division is that it requires prior knowledge of only addition and the two times table. Every integer can be expressed as the sum of integral powers. Thus,

$$15 = 2^0 + 2^1 + 2^2 + 2^3$$

$$23 = 2^0 + 2^1 + 2^2 + 2^4$$

The confidence with which the ancient Egyptians approached all forms of multiplication by this process suggests that they were aware of this general rule (Joseph 1991/2000, pp. 63–64).

This ancient method of multiplication was the foundation for Egyptian calculation. The Greeks employed it with some modification and it continued to be used by Europeans well into the Middle Ages. A modern variation of the method is still popular among rural communities in Russia, Ethiopia and the Near East (Joseph, 1991/2000, p. 65).

The ancient Egyptian process of division was closely related to the method of multiplication. For example, a division *x/y* is introduced by the words "reckon with *y* so as to obtain *x*." So for the Egyptian scribe, instead of thinking, "dividing 696 by 29," he would say to himself, "Starting with 29, how many times should I add it to itself to get 696?" If a scribe were to encounter a problem of not being able to get any combination of the numbers in the right-hand column to add up to the value of the dividend, he would introduce fractions. In essence, the writing method of the ancient Egyptians did not allow any unambiguous way of expressing fractions; consequently, they tackled the problem in quite an ingenious way (Joseph, 1991/2000, pp. 65–66).

Operating with unit fractions is a singular feature of Egyptian mathematics that cannot be found in any other mathematical tradition. A large proportion of ancient Egyptian calculations utilized such operations. The great emphasis on fractions hinged on two reasons. The first reason is that since the society did not use money, transactions having to be carried out in kind, there was a need for accurate calculations with fractions, particularly in practical problems such as division of food, parceling out land, and mixing different ingredients for beer and bread. The second reason emerged from the particular character of Egyptian Arithmetic: i.e., the process of halving in division often led to fractions (Joseph, 1991/2000, pp. 66–67).

The utility of unit fractions in arithmetical operations and the peculiar system of multiplication yielded a third aspect of Egyptian computation: i.e., every multiplication and division involving unit fractions invariably led to the problem of how to double unit fractions. Doubling a unit fraction with an even denominator is a simple matter of halving the denominator. Therefore, doubling 1/2, 1/4, 1/6 and 1/8 yields 1, 1/2, 1/3 and 1/4. Doubling 1/3 raised no difficulty, since 2/3 had its own hieroglyphic or hieratic symbol. Difficulty arose when doubling unit fractions with other odd denominations. Since it was difficult in Egyptian computation to write two times $1/n$ as $1/n + 1/n$, the need arose to develop a table that provided the appropriate unit fractions that summed to $2/n$, where $n = 5, 7, 9, \ldots$ The major purpose of constructing the $2/n$ table was to use it for multiplication and division (Joseph, 1991/2000, p. 68).

In order to deal with "problems of completion," the ancient Egyptians developed a method known as "red auxiliaries" (so named because the scribes wrote these numbers in red ink). The approach is analogous, but not equivalent, to the present-day method of least common denominator. First, the Egyptians took the denominator of the smallest unit fraction as a reference number and then multiplied each of the fractions by this number to obtain "red auxiliaries." They proceeded to calculate by how much the sum of these auxiliaries fell short of the reference number. This shortfall quantity was then expressed as a fraction of the reference number to get the complement. If the shortfall quantity turned out to be an awkward fraction, a further search was done for a reference number that would result in more manageable auxiliaries (Joseph, 1991/2000, pp. 71–72).

Rules devised by mathematicians for solving problems about numbers of one kind or another can be classified into three types. In the early stages, the ancient Egyptian rhetorical type, which gave birth to the two that followed, developed rules that were expressed verbally and consisted of detailed instructions about what was to be done to obtain the solution to a problem. In time, the prose of this rhetorical form of algebra paved the way for the use of abbreviations for recurring quantities and operations, ushering the appearance of "syncopated algebra." Traces of this algebra can be found in the works of the Alexandrian mathematician, Diophantus (c. 250 AD). During the past 500 years, there has developed "symbolic algebra" by which, with the aid of letters and signs of operation and relation (+, - , x, ÷, =), problems are stated in such a form that the rules of solution may be applied consistently and systematically (Joseph, 1991/2000, p. 76).

A series is the sum of a sequence of terms, and the most common types are the arithmetic and geometric series. In an arithmetic progression (AP), each term after the first (usually denoted by a) is obtained by adding a fixed number, called the common difference (usually denoted by d), to the preceding term. For example, 1, 2, 3, 5, 7, 9. . . is an AP with $a = 1$ and $d = 2$. For a geometric progression (GP), each term after the first (a) is formed from the preceding term by multiplying by a fixed number called the common ratio (usually denoted by r). For example, 1, 2, 4, 8, 16 . . .is a GP with $a = 1$ and $r = 2$. The ancient Egyptian method was based on operations with the basic GP 1, 2, 4, 8. . . and an understanding that any multiplier may be expressed as the sum of elements of the sequence (Joseph, 1991/2000, p. 79).

When it comes to the great achievements of Egyptian Geometry, there is general agreement on two: (1) the approximation to the area of the circle and (2) the derivation of the rule for calculating the volume of a truncated pyramid. Some disagreement arises over the third: the correct formula for the surfaced area of a hemisphere.

In the Egyptian method of calculating the area of a circle, the implicit estimate of π can be worked out quite easily by equating A with A^E:

$$\pi d^2/4 = (8d/9)^2$$

from which the following is obtained:

$$\pi = 4(8/9)^2 = 256/81 = (16/9)^2 \simeq 3.1605$$

This is nearly the value that is obtained by taking $d = 9$ in the expression $A^E = (8d/9)^2$ (Joseph 1991/2000, pp. 82–83).

The Egyptian knowledge of the correct formula for the volume of a truncated square pyramid is the zenith of Egyptian Geometry. The Egyptian approach is correctly based on the following formula:

$$V = (a^2 + ab + b^2)h/3$$

Three major explanations have been advanced for how the Egyptians arrived at the correct formula for the volume of a truncated pyramid. The first explanation is that the truncated pyramid was cut up into smaller and simpler solids whose volumes were then estimated before putting them back together. The reduction of the sum of the volumes of all the component solids to the final formula would require a very high degree of algebraic knowledge and sophistication (Joseph 1991/2000, p. 87).

The second explanation is that the Egyptians had discovered empirically that the volume of a truncated pyramid can be derived as the product of the height of the frustum, h, and the Heronian mean (the Heronian mean of two positive numbers x and y is given by $(x + y + \sqrt{xy})/3$) of the areas of the bases a^2 and b^2. This explanation is supported by the Alexandrian mathematician Heron (or Hero) of the first century AD, whose work, *Metrica*, contains a useful synthesis of Egyptian, Greek, and Babylonian traditions. Book II of the work details the volume calculations of prisms, pyramids, cones, parallelepipeds, and other solids. The method for calculating the volume of a truncated pyramid using the mean derived directly from the Egyptian mathematical tradition (Joseph 1991/2000, p. 87).

The final explanation is that the volume of a truncated pyramid was calculated as the difference between an original complete pyramid and a smaller one removed from its top. This explanation has been said to be the most plausible of the three, given the concrete approach to Geometry favored by the Egyptians. Regardless of how the Egyptians came to the discovery of this formula, it remains to this day a lasting testimony of their mathematical ingenuity (Joseph, 1991/2000, p. 87).

The Maghrebian Tradition

Thanks to Ahmed Djebbar (1995), there now exists a comprehensive survey of the mathematical tradition of the Maghreb (North Africa) from the ninth to the eighteenth century. This section is a summary of Djebbar's work.

From the ninth to the eleventh centuries, which is the period of the installation and consolidation of Muslim power in the first cities of Spain and the Maghreb, Medicine and Calculation were the first scientific endeavors to benefit from teaching, followed by the publication of works, to respond to the needs of certain higher-rank people of society and to lawyers for the resolution of certain problems such as those involved in land measurement or in the partitioning of inheritance. The eminent role played by Kairouan (Holy City in northern Tunisia) in the theological debates during the Aghlabid epoch (800–910) attracted numerous intellectuals from the East to Ifriqiya (city in today's western Libya), among them men of science educated in arithmetical and geometrical techniques used to solve problems of land measurement and inheritance. As in other regions of the Islamic world, the patronage in favor of scientific activities existed in the Maghreb between the ninth and eleventh century and functioned in the image of that of the great metropolis of the East: buying books, financing production of manuscripts, remuneration for scholars, and construction of schools and institutions (Djebbar, 1995).

Very little is known about the mathematical activities of the Maghreb during the tenth century. It appears that the patronage system started by the Aghlabids in the ninth century was continued and benefited Mathematics and Astronomy, especially during the first two decades of the government of the Fatimid caliph al-Mucizz (953–975). Specialists often underlined the importance of the political and economic history of twelfth century Maghreb. Therefore, it is reasonable to suggest that their importance extended to other spheres of social life as well. The cultural and scientific history of this era, however, remains vastly unexplored (Djebbar, 1995).

One of the most outstanding mathematicians of the Maghrebian tradition was Abu al-Qasim al-Qurash. He was a specialist in Algebra and in the Science of Inheritance, in addition to his expertise in certain religious sciences. In Algebra, al-Qurash is known for his commentary on the book of the great Egyptian mathematician Abu Kamil (d. 930). Its importance is confirmed by the historian Ibn Khaldun (d. 1406) who considered it as one of the best treatises written on the book. This work of al-Qurash was not a simple commentary on a famous treatise of the Algebra of its time. Indeed, some new elements were introduced in the commentary. Beginning at the level of presentation, al-Qurash provides the objects and the operations of Algebra before explaining the solution of the canonical equations followed by the demonstration of the existence of the solutions of these equations. Al-Qurash distinguished himself from his predecessors in the classification of six canonical equations and in the demonstrations. This work continued to be studied and taught up till the fourteenth century (Djebbar, 1995).

In the domain of inheritance, al-Qurash is known for having elaborated a new method based on the decomposition of the numbers in prime factors in order to reduce the fractions that intervene in the distribution of a given inheritance to the same denominator. His approach was quickly appreciated by mathematicians who wrote the handbooks explaining the method and showing its utility through the presentation of concrete problems of inheritance (Djebbar, 1995).

Another outstanding mathematician of the Maghrebian tradition was al-Hassa. This mathematician was also well-known as a reader of the Qur'an, as an inheritance specialist, and as a high-ranking citizen since he was given the title of *Shaykh al-Jamaa* (Chief of the Community). He lived for some time at Sebta (in the Extreme Maghreb) with other mathematicians of this city (Djebbar, 1995).

Two of al-Hassa's books have survived. The first book titled *Book of Proof and Recall* is a handbook of calculation treating numeration, arithmetical operations on whole numbers and on fractions, extraction of the exact or approximate square root of a whole of fractionary number and summation of progressions of whole numbers (natural, even, or odd), and of their squares and cubes. The book occupies an important place in the history of mathematics for the following three reasons: (1) the manual remains the most ancient work of calculation representing simultaneously the tradition of the Maghreb and that of Muslim Spain; (2) it is wherein one finds a symbolic writing of fractions, which utilizes the horizontal bar and the dust ciphers—i.e., the ancestors of the digits that we use today; it is the only Maghrebian work of calculation known to have circulated in the scientific foyers of south Europe, as Moses Ibn Tibbon realized, in 1271, a Hebrew translation of it (Djebbar, 1995).

The second work is titled *The Complete Book on the Art of Number*. Only the first part of this book that contains 117 folios was recovered and identified in 1986. Its content takes up themes in the first book dealing with whole numbers, by developing them, and presents new chapters on the decomposition of a number in prime factors, the common divisors and multiples, and the extraction of the exact cubic root of a whole number. The second part of the work, which has not been recovered, is said to be dedicated to operations of fractions; the summation of the different categories of whole numbers; and the exposition of the algorithms that facilitate the calculation of perfect, deficient, abundant, and amicable numbers (Djebbar, 1995).

A third member of the Maghrebian mathematical tradition of the twelfth century is Ibn al-Yasamin, who is relatively better known than the preceding two. Al-Yasamin's mother was a Black African and his father was a Berber. For a long time, this mathematician was only known for his minor work of 62 lines, *Poem on Algebra*. It was the success of this poem that prompted him to write a similar one that deals with the roots of numbers and another one that summarizes the method of false position (Djebbar, 1995).

Al-Yasamin's work titled *Fecundation of the Spirits with the Symbols of the Dust Ciphers* is much more important than the three poems, at both the quantitative and qualitative levels. It is a book of more than 200 folios that deal equally with the classical chapters of the Sciences of Calculation and certain chapters of Geometry relative to the calculation of areas. Indeed, it is among the works of the Muslim West that link these two subjects. Its importance hinges equally upon the nature of his materials and mathematical instruments which make it an original book and certainly also significant to this period of transition when three mathematical practices ran in parallel before flowing together into the same stream: that of the East, of Muslim Spain, and of the Maghreb (Djebbar, 1995).

As an example, the following elements contribute to the originality of the work and to its anchorage in the great Arabic mathematical tradition of the ninth-eleventh centuries: in Arithmetic, and contrarily to the Maghrebian tradition that would continue from the fourteenth century onward, Ibn al-Yasamin treats first multiplication and division before addition and subtraction. In the domain of fractions, he shows, relative to the reading of certain expressions, besides the fraction bar, that the rest of the symbolism was not yet definitively fixed at this epoch. This book is also the oldest that contains both the objects and the operations of Algebra which permit the writing and solution of equations or abstract manipulation of polynomials (Djebbar, 1995).

A fourth major contributor to Maghrebian mathematics was Ahmad Ibn Muncim, who was born in Dénia (on the east coast of Spain, near Valencia) but spent a great deal of his life in Marrakech (Morocco). Ibn Muncim was considered one of the best specialists in Geometry and Number Theory during his time. This mathematician started studying medicine at the age of thirty and practiced it in Marrakech while teaching and conducting research. He published many works on diverse subjects that include Euclidian Geometry, calculation, construction of magic squares, Number Theory and Combinatorics. He explored two very important areas of geometry: (1) the intersections of solids whose bases are curves different from conic sections and (2) curves obtained by the projection of these intersections of solids on a given plane (Djebbar, 1995).

Ibn Muncim also informed readers in the Maghreb from the twelfth century onwards about the book of al-Mu'taman (d. 1085) titled *The Book of Perfection*, which is essentially dedicated to Geometry but with the first chapter dealing with Number Theory. This important work was transmitted from the Almohad capital. Later, Maimonides (d. 1204) taught the content of the book of al-Mu'taman in Cairo and also in Fez where he stayed for some time. During the thirteenth and fourteenth centuries, certain chapters of the work continued to be studied in the Extreme Maghreb, particularly by Ibn al-Banna who refers to it explicitly in his *Epistle on the Calculation of Areas* and, a little later, by Ibn Haydar (Djebbar, 1995).

With regard to the content of *The Book of Perfection*, it shows that it does not only concern a simple return to techniques and earlier mathematical results from the Andalusian tradition or transmitted by it. Instead, one finds new trends and results whose origins are to be found in the activities of the Almohad capital or in the preoccupations of its intellectual environment. More precisely, one discovers in it, along with the classical chapters on arithmetical operations, other mathematical operations like the one on the study of figurate numbers, the one on the determination of amicable numbers and, in particular, the one on enumeration of all words of a language utilizing a given alphabet. It is in this work that Ibn Muncim's most important contribution lies, as he dedicates a chapter of nineteen pages that contain the important combinatorial propositions and trends which will be rediscovered in Europe only in the sixteenth and seventeenth centuries in particular by Cardano (d. 1576), Mersenne (d. 1648), Frénicle (d. 1675) and Pascal (d. 1662). One may reasonably propose that it was the reinvigoration of Arabic linguistic and grammatical activities in Marrakech that brought the problems of enumeration to the order of the day. It is also reasonable to suggest that Ibn Muncim's way of solving these combinatorial problems by utilizing the concrete model of threads of silk of different colors finds its origins in the industrial or commercial environment of Marrakech (Djebbar, 1995).

Ibn Muncim had students, and one of them, ash-Sharuf, wrote a book titled *The Canon of Calculation* in which he incorporated the combinatorial results of his teacher. Ash-Sharuf, in turn, taught Combinatorics to his pupils, among them was the famous Ibn al-Banna (we will deal a bit more with his own mathematical contributions later). In fact, in Ibn al-Banna's little work titled *Advertisement to the Intelligentsia*, he evokes explicitly one of the methods of Ibn Muncin—that of the arithmetic triangle—to enumerate all words which are possible to pronounce when one utilizes the twenty-eight letters of the Arabic alphabet. But he does not stop here; he introduces three original contributions in this area. The first, which is the most important, concerns the announcement and the demonstration, for the first time, of the formula of factorials giving the combinations of n letters of a given alphabet taking p at a time, without utilizing the arithmetic triangle, a result that will be established once again by Pascal three centuries later. Second, Ibn al-Banna establishes, as far as possible, the relations that exist among the figurative numbers of Nicomachus, the combinations of n objects taking p at a time, and the sums of certain progressions of whole numbers. Third, Ibn al-Banna utilizes the techniques or the trends for combinatorial type to solve certain problems outside mathematics and which lead to enumerations with constraints: for example, the determination of the number of possible readings of a given phrase, taking into account the rules of the Arabic grammar, or of the number of prayers that a Muslim has to say to compensate for the forgetting of a certain number among them (Djebbar, 1995).

In the history of the scientific activities in the Maghreb, the fourteenth century marked a privileged moment, both for the quantitative importance of the mathematical production and for the content of this production and influence that it would have, during many centuries, on the teaching of mathematics in the whole of North Africa and sometimes even in certain regions of Sub-Saharan Africa. The majority of the mathematical production of this century is a return—in the form of commentaries, summaries or developments—to a part of what had already been discovered or assimilated during the preceding centuries. New contributions were indeed exceptional. Thus, a fifth major contributor to the Maghrebian mathematical tradition and one of the last innovators of the great Arab mathematical tradition and one of the initiators of a new tradition of teaching mathematics, based on the commentary, is Ibn al-Banna (Djebbar, 1995).

Born in Marrakech in 1256, Ibn al-Banna grew up there and acquired an excellent training in various disciplines. He also lived and taught for some time in Fez which became, after the fall of the Almohads, the capital of the dynasty of the Merinids. Fez tried to rival, on an intellectual level, Marrakech, the only city which had the privilege of having been, for almost two centuries (1062–1248), the capital of the entire Maghreb, including vast Sub-Saharan African zones. A strong scientific tradition was established in Fez (Djebbar, 1995).

Ibn al-Banna was the last of the Maghrebian mathematicians that were involved in research, to the extent that he tackled problems which were new for the epoch, and that he contributed original solutions and advanced new ideas. Already mentioned is his contribution to Combinatorics which lies in the prolongation of research activities and preoccupations of Ibn Muncim. Equally interesting elements are found in his *The Lifting of the Veil* in which he establishes the results that let us understand that during his epoch, the problems of enumeration were not only related to the field of language. He also introduces a new trend in Algebra concerning the justification of the existence of solutions to the canonical equations of al-Khwarizm and he continues with a reflection on bases different from ten that would have been started by Ibn Muncim (Djebbar, 1995).

The importance and prestige of Ibn al-Banna did not only come from his mathematical works. In fact, he distinguished himself from his Maghrebian predecessors by the richness and diversity of his production. Of the more than 100 titles of writings that are attributed to him, only 32 concern mathematics and astronomy. The others deal with disciplines that are very distant from one another, such as Linguistics, Rhetoric, Astrology, Grammar and Logic (Djebbar, 1995).

Among Ibn al-Banna's scientific writings, those related to the Science of Calculation seem to have assured his scientific notoriety. These writings include *The Abridgment*, *The Four Works on Calculation*, and *The Lifting of the Veil*. It is *The Abridgment* that illustrates the trend and conceptions of Ibn al-Banna, at the level of the ordering of the chapters, the conciseness, the rigor, the formulation, and the absence of all symbolism. The factors that led Ibn al-Banna to inaugurate this type of very condensed manual, in comparison to the great collections of the twelfth and thirteenth centuries, are perhaps not strictly pedagogical. This might have been the consequence of the whole training of Ibn al-Banna and in particular of his mystical guiding that favored a certain esotericism in addition to the difficulty and the abstract character of mathematical notions and techniques (Djebbar, 1995).

The encyclopedic nature of Ibn al-Banna's production may have contributed to his social status, as he was honored by the Merinid power. This led him to leave Marrakech for Fez at the invitation of the sultan of that era. It was this dual status, scientific and social, that helped Ibn al-Banna to solve the problems that preoccupied his contemporaries, and which led him to publish an original book, *Advertisement to the Intelligentsia*, whose contents might be related (because of some of its aspects) to Ethnomathematics. The first part of the book contains the precise mathematical answers to questions that touch varied domains of everyday life such as the composition of medicaments, the calculation of the drop of irrigation canals, the arithmetical explanation of a *sura* (verse) of the Qur'an concerning inheritance, the determination of the hour of the third daily prayer, the explanation of frauds linked to instruments of measurement, the enumeration of delayed prayers which have to be said in a precise order, the exact calculation of legal tax in the case of a delayed payment, etc. The second part of the book, which belongs to the ancient tradition of cultural mathematics, combines a collection of little arithmetical problems presented in the form of poetic riddles. Before Ibn al-Banna, mathematicians had also solved problems related to everyday life; but often, the concrete aspect of a problem was no more than a dressing-up of arithmetical or abstract algebraic exercises. This is not the case for the 17 mathematical problems explored by Ibn al-Banna (Djebbar, 1995).

At the level of the great orientations of mathematical activity during the Middle Ages, Ibn al-Banna appeared as the starting point of a whole tradition that extends to the different regions of North Africa and as far as Egypt, and which remained in Muslim Spain. This tradition is that of commentaries, which have been the object of a comparative study of their contents that reveal both quantitative and qualitative differences. At the quantitative level, one finds short commentaries that explain definitions and algorithms by means of examples without leaving the cadre of the work. At the other extreme, one finds treatises for which the content of the work seems to be just a pretext or a guideline to permit their authors to expose in their own way, while sometimes criticizing Ibn al-Banna severely, the themes dealt with by him and others he had deliberately abandoned. At the qualitative level, these commentaries are distinguishable from one another by the utilization or not of arithmetical and algebraic symbolism and by the recourse or not to the explanation or to the critique of certain definitions, to the demonstration of the propositions evoked by Ibn al-Banna and to the justification of the validity of the algorithms that he exposed (Djebbar, 1995).

The detailed analysis of the most important chapters of these commentaries makes it possible for Djebbar to make further remarks concerning the nature of mathematics taught in the Maghreb during the era. First, the level of the mathematics that is exposed is not lower than that of the previous period, but missing are certain themes that had been taught during the tenth century, such as the extraction of the approximate cubic root of a number, or the computation of new pairs of amicable numbers. This phenomenon was already perceptible in the work of Ibn al-Banna and it was only to extend from the fourteenth century onwards. Second, missing are new contributions in these commentaries, either on the theoretical plane or at the level of the applications of earlier ideas and techniques. The most meaningful novelty is situated at the level of written expression with the progressive use of a relatively elaborate symbolism. Finally, the commentaries of the fourteenth and fifteenth centuries concern the wording and composition of their content and the style that is employed. At this level, two trends are perceptible: (1) the trend characterized by stereotypical formulations which correspond to the usual style of mathematics and (2) the trend which is more rhetorical and is of a higher cultural level in the measure where the authors prolong and complete their mathematical explanations with grammatical, literary or philosophical commentaries. In the domain of Algebra, the works of Ibn al-Banna and other Maghrebian mathematicians continued to be taught in cities such as Fez, Tlemcen, Sebta and Tunis (Djebbar, 1995).

Maghrebian mathematical production of the period that extends from the beginning of the sixteenth century to the end of the nineteenth century has not been well studied. The known number of mathematicians who lived in the Maghreb after the fifteenth century surpasses 150. The disciplines they dealt with are Metrical Geometry, Calculation, magical squares, and the distribution of inheritance, as far as mathematics is concerned, and the calculation of time, the determination of the direction of Mecca and the description of astronomical instruments, as far as astronomy is concerned (Djabbar, 1995).

Restricting the discussion to mathematics, the content of the production during this period differs from the earlier mathematical writings in form and standard. The level of the writings is lower than that of the works of the fifteenth century, which are themselves less rich, with respect to ideas and techniques, than the works of the thirteenth and fourteenth centuries. This situation corresponds well to the other sectors' intellectual activities in the whole of North Africa. Among the internal factors that were the origins of this long process of decline of mathematical activities are the slowing down and later termination of research and the allure of a qualitative change in the content of the works of teaching that were progressively limited to the exhibition of techniques and results without any demonstration. These internal factors were induced by external ones that were economic in nature, such as the dying out of the African gold routes, the loss of control over sea routes and political spheres, such as the repeated offensives against the coast of North Africa by the new powers of southern Europe: i.e., Spain, Portugal, and certain Italian city-states (Djebbar, 1995).

Therefore, it is not surprising that this long process of degradation had indirect effects on mathematics through the progressive contraction of its domain and of its field of application. Consequently, the only activities that remained for the mathematicians, besides teaching and elaboration of manuals, were those of mathematical practices directly related to activities or preoccupations of a religious nature, such as the distribution of inheritance and donations to rightful claimants, the determination of time for the fixing of moments for prayer, and the construction and use of astronomical instruments such as the quart of sine and the astrolabe (Djebbar, 1995).

The absence of research in mathematics, the contraction of its field of application and the reduction of the content of the programs led to the appearance and development, both in the Maghreb and in Egypt, of the practice of publishing, on a single mathematical subject, a series of works that only differ in style (poetry or prose), volume (book or summary), or form (detailed commentary or glosses). This tendency had already emerged during the second half of the fifteenth century in the Extreme Maghreb. It continued at least until the eighteenth century. Notwithstanding the absence of originality of these numerous works, however, they constitute precious material for the history of scientific teaching in North Africa (Djabbar, 1995).

The preceding review of ten centuries of mathematical activities in the Maghreb makes it possible for Djebbar to provide a few concluding commentaries. First, the mathematical practice in the Maghreb inscribes itself essentially in the Arab tradition. Second, it was essentially the cities of the Extreme Maghreb (in particular Sebta, Fez, and Marrakech) which took the relay from Muslim Spain in mathematical activity from the twelfth century onwards until the end of the fourteenth century. After this period, there was a greater intervention of two other scientific poles: (1) Tlemcen in the Central Maghreb and (2) Tunis in Ifriqiya. Third, the role of the Maghreb in the diffusion of Arab Mathematics first influenced southern Europe in a direct manner as a result of translations, such as the unique example of the Hebrew translations of the books and in the indirect manner by which the assimilation of local teaching was realized in Arabic followed by the elaboration of manuals or treatises in Latin and Hebrew. The most famous example that illustrates this phenomenon and is still little studied is that of the Italian scholar named Fibonacci (Leonardo of Pisa). As he says himself, he was trained in Bougie (one of the Maghrebian scientific poles of the twelfth century) when he was young and later reproduced in his *Liber Abbaci* certain aspects of the Maghrebian mathematical tradition and in particular with respect to the symbolism and computation of fractions. The transmission of the mathematical writings of the Maghreb essentially went into two other directions. The first direction is that of the East, more precisely Egypt, where the writings were the object of commentaries. The second direction is that of Sub-Saharan Africa. It seems that it was the Extreme Maghreb that was the principal relay for this particular transmission that essentially concerned the Science of Computation and Astronomy. This is confirmed by the manuscripts that are today in the library of Timbuktu (Mali). Among these manuscripts, only one, treating computation, is attributed to a scholar from the region. It concerns a mathematician from Arawan (Mali) who lived after the sixteenth century, as he refers in his writing to an arithmetical poem titled "The White Pearl" written by a mathematician of the Central Maghreb. The other manuscripts are either mathematical poems or astronomical writings (Djebbar, 1995).

Fractals

The major focus of this section is on the evidence of the existence of fractals in African designs in terms of symmetric chaos. But before one delves into such a discussion, it makes sense to begin with a brief discussion of the fractal process itself and the connection between chaos and African fractals.

The fractal process is a graphical approach whereby the regions are subdivided until the sub-regions are less than one screen pixel in size. In essence, the strength of a fractal process is that no matter how small a region gets, one can still generate more detail simply by evaluating the procedure on the new, smaller region.

Thus, a fractal process is a special case of procedural process in that a fractal object generally has to be *self-similar*: that is, as one generates finer and finer object detail, that detail begins to look like the object itself. A procedural process is that instead of defining and storing a large data set of points to describe a shape, a procedure for computing the value (color, intensity, and shape) at any given point, given previously computed values for surrounding points, is defined. A good example pointed out by Christopher Watkins and Larry Sharp (1992, p. 86) is a leaf. The branching patterns of a leaf look very similar to the shape of the leaf itself. A careful examination of the branches with a magnifying glass reveals that the branches have finer branches, which in turn have finer branches, and so on.

The following discussion draws greatly from the findings of Eglash (1997, 1999), who has done the most work in this area, and Bangura's work titled *Chaos Theory and African Fractals* (2000). As Eglash (1999) points out, the most mathematically significant aspect of doubling in African religion occurs in the divination ("fortunetelling") techniques of vodum and its religious relatives. The Ifa system, for example, is characteristic of what mathematicians would call "stochastic," that is, it operates by pure chance. It is based on tossing pairs of flat shells or seeds split into two. Each lands open-side or closed-side. They are connected by a doubled chain to make four pairs. Each group of four pairs gives one of the sixteen divination symbols that tell the future of the diviner's client.

Nonetheless, a closely related divination system called Cadena has a non-stochastic element, or what mathematicians would refer to as "deterministic chaos." Cadena is based on a symbolic code in which each symbol, represented by a set of four vertical dashed lines drawn in the sand, stand for some archetypical concept (desire, travel, health, etc.) with which narratives about the future are assembled.

The Bamana divination, like the Cantor set (pathological curves), is based on recursion. Bamana divination begins with four horizontal dashed lines, drawn rapidly, so that there is some random variation in the number of dashes in each. The dashes are then connected in pairs, such that each of the four lines is left with either one dash or none. The narrative symbol is then constructed as a column of four vertical marks, with double vertical lines representing an even number dashes and single lines representing an odd number. There are two possible marks in four positions, thus 16 possible symbols. The random symbol production is repeated four times.

Both tarumbeta and owari mathematical game boards' marching-group dynamics are governed by triangular numbers. What is special about these types of cellular automata boards is the underlying concept of recursion—the way in which a kind of mathematical feedback loop can generate new structures in space and new dynamics in time.

Legba, god of chaos or "god of crossroads," is represented by a fork because the answer could be either yes or no—one never knows which path he will take. For divination, in which a "path" (question) is often pushed for further questions, the image becomes one of endless bifurcation. The bifurcating uncertainties of Legba are like a positive feedback loop, amplifying deviation and noise (i.e., random variation).

In the iconic carvings of the Baule, a contrast between a negative feedback loop, to create stability, and the positive feedback of uncontrolled disorder exists. For example, a carving of two caimans (relatives of the alligator) biting each other's tail depicts the chief and the people in balance—if one bites, the other will bite back. Another example is a carving showing that power creates the appetite for more power—little fish are eaten by bigger fish, which then become even bigger fish.

A form of music indigenous to Nigeria has something like a white noise (i.e., random noise with the highest algorithmic complexity) distribution of sounds. For example, the random music of the Birom is a flute ensemble designed to allow each musician to express individual feelings through whatever idiosyncratic noise (or even silence) s/he chooses. This results in an indeterminate process in which the sounds produced by the players are not obstructed by the conscious attempt to organize the rhythms and harmonies.

In Yoruba folktale, one learns about the trickster Eshu as the "lord of random." There is a coupling between the orderly work of Olirun and the unpredictable spirit of Eshu, similar to the negative feedback/positive feedback mentioned earlier.

From this relatively small number of examples, it is quite obvious that African Fractal Geometry is not a singular body of knowledge, but rather a pattern of resemblance that can be seen when a variety of African mathematical ideas and practices is described. And, indeed, it is not the only pattern possible. In short, it makes sense to see African fractals as just another moment in a historical sequence.

Elaborate cornrow braids on an African woman's head can be viewed as more than an affinity with culture or a fashion statement. The intricate patterns are also useful for learning about African fractals—geometric patterns that are repeated on smaller and smaller scales to produce intricate designs that are beyond the scope of classical or Euclidean Geometry, which refers to the "ordinary" system of geometry based on the parallel postulate—i.e., a basic assumption that states whether through a point P, not on a given line l, there exists none, one, or more than one line parallel to the given line l.

Fractal geometry has emerged as one of the most exciting frontiers in the fusion between mathematics and information technology. Fractals can be observed in many of the swirling patterns produced by computer graphics, and they have become a vital tool for modeling in the natural sciences. While fractal geometry can allow one to get into the far reaches of high tech science, its patterns are surprisingly common in traditional African designs. Also, some of the basic concepts in fractal geometry are fundamental to African knowledge systems: quantitative techniques, symbolic systems, engineering, architecture, games, traditional hairstyling, textiles, sculpture, painting, carving, metalwork, and religion.

Eglash demonstrated the principle with a tool on his Web site that allows one to create computer-generated graphics simulating the fractal branching patterns found in braided hairstyles (csdt.rpi.edu/african/afractal/afractal.htm). Eglash's book, *African Fractals: Modern Computing and Indigenous Design*, explores how fractals are evident in all levels of African society, including architecture and art, politics, and religion.

As Eglash explains, although most people learn Euclidean Geometry in school, few study fractal geometry (because it is difficult), which plays a significant role in the computer modeling processes in the hard sciences. Meanwhile, Eglash adds, fractal geometry has long been a theme in Africa, with a wide variety of local cultural associations, including kinship, labor practices, politics, and religion.

Eglash's research began in the 1980s while investigating settlement architecture in Central and West Africa. Aerial photographs of various settlement compounds revealed that many were composed of circular structures enclosed in other circles, or rectangles within rectangles, and that the compounds were likely to have street patterns in which broad avenues branched into very small footpaths.

As Eglash notes, at first he thought it was just from unconscious social dynamics. But during his field work, he adds, he found that fractal designs also appear in a wide variety of intentional designs—carving, hairstyling, metalwork, painting, textiles—and the recursive process of fractal algorithms are even employed in African quantitative systems. Eglash adds that in the design rationales and cultural semantics of many African geometric figures, as well as in indigenous quantitative systems (additive progression, doubling sequences, binary recursion) and symbolic systems (ionic symbols for feedback loops, equiangular spirals, infinity), there are abstract ideas and formal structures that closely parallel some of the fundamental aspects of fractal geometry. These results, he concludes, are congruent with recent developments in complex systems theory, which suggest that pre-modern, non-state societies were neither utterly anarchic, nor frozen in static order, but rather utilized an adaptive flexibility that capitalized on the nonlinear aspects of ecological dynamics.

While in Africa, Eglash encountered some of the most complex fractal systems that exist in religious activities, such as the sequence of symbols used in sand divination, a method of fortune telling found in Senegal. Some of his other findings include the use of sophisticated mathematical ideas in everyday objects. In the arid region of the Sahel, artisans produce windscreens by utilizing a scaling design that gives them the maximum effect—keeping out the wind-driven dust—for the minimum amount of effort and material.

A number of advancements are taking place in the study of African fractals. The prominent ones are discussed in the following paragraphs. What the following discussion shows is how modern computational tools are being used for mathematical experimentation and theorizing about African fractals.

The African Fractals in Development project is about a boot-strapping approach to investigating indigenous African science for education and development. The principal investigator of the project is Ron Eglash. The co-principal investigators are Christian Sina Diatta and Egondu Onyejekwe. The former is the director of the Institut de Technologie Nucléaire Appliquée at Universite

Cheikh Anta Diop of Dakar, Senegal. He is originally from the lower Casamance, and he coordinates links between the rural sites and university activities. The latter is a computer scientist at Ohio State University, and he manages links between Diatta's operations at the university and the support activities in the United States through the African Women Global Network. In addition, Nfally Badiane, a graduate student in anthropology at the Universite Cheikh Anta Diop of Dakar, is in charge of the Ziguinchor operations.

The project began with Eglash's visual observation that aerial photos of traditional African settlements tend to have a fractal structure (scaling in street branching, recursive rectangular enclosures, circles of circular dwellings, etc.). This was quantitatively confirmed in Eglash and Broadwell (1989), where they applied a two-dimensional Fourier transform (an analysis of frequencies that may be embedded in a body of data) to digitized photo images to estimate the fractal dimension from the slope of the spectral density function. Subsequent study by Eglash (including a year of field work under the Fulbright program in Central and West Africa) revealed that these architectural fractals result from intentional designs, not simply unconscious social dynamics, and that recursive scaling structures can be found in other areas of African material culture.

The major objective of the investigators is to test the possibility that indigenous knowledge can be employed in a boot-strapping approach to development. The investigators conceptualize "boot-strapping" as a development approach in which one begins with indigenous knowledge under local control, and self-installs modern technological abilities.

The project focuses on the creation of an indigenous science center in the city of Ziguinchor, in the lower Casamance region of Senegal. The choice of this site hinged on the excellent examples of fractal Ethnomathematics (mathematical practices of identifiable groups) in the area (Eglash, Diatta, and Badiane 1994). The goals of the center are as follows: (1) utilize indigenous knowledge for the benefit of the people and natural environment of the region; (2) create such benefits by combining indigenous knowledge with modern scientific frameworks and technological capabilities; (3) minimize the need for external support and maximize the potential for expansion; (4) create a model for other indigenous science centers in other regions, with the expectation that a network of these institutions could promote inter-ethnic cooperation and political stability.

In terms of methodology, while the indigenous center itself is used to define local problems, the investigators began their work with some obvious challenges. To begin with, increasing salinization of the area has led to a decreasing quality of life. Next, external economic pressures (e.g., the move to cash-crop production for export and tourism) and the migration to cities have disrupted many of the beneficial attributes of traditional life in the area (e.g., gender equality), increased disease (e.g., AIDS), and damaged the environment. The highly decentralized social structure of the Djola and the long historical conflicts with the north render policy recommendations particularly ineffective. Thus, the investigators believe that by encouraging the development of indigenous knowledge in modern technological frameworks, the Djola will be able to carry out their own empirical studies, educational projects and technological production to meet the challenges. Thus, the project's methodology focuses on the following six aspects:

1. *Architecture for an indigenous science*. The physical location of the center embodies the philosophy of the project, employing local materials and labor, and utilizing indigenous design practices. For instance, the French non-governmental organization (NGO) ENDA has devised a modern water collecting system based on the traditional Djola impluvia. At the same time, it makes use of recycled materials and generates solar electricity and heating. It is believed that these factors will ensure that the center will not shut down due to lack of utilities once the initial funding period is completed, while creating an infrastructure for its research facilities, school room, visitors' center, and educational office.

2. *An indigenous knowledge database*. A difficulty with indigenous knowledge research noted by the investigators is the separation between projects and institutions. They point out that, for example, traditional agricultural practices have been studied in the Casamance region by projects under Senegalese, American, French, Italian and Arabic governments, in addition to those of NGOs. Ethnobotany, ethnomedicine, and ethnomathematics of the local culture is not under-researched, but rather research findings are so widely diffused that this information is not readily available. The investigators believe that the advent of computer technology will remedy this problem. By linking a multimedia database at the science center in Ziguinchor with a similar facility at the University of Dakar, investigators hope to synthesize past research together with contemporary studies, access university resources, and facilitate Internet communication with the global research community.

3. *Agro-ecology*. Since botanical knowledge is quite extensive in traditional Djola culture, the investigators believe that this suggests an obvious application to recent developments in combining ecological biodiversity with agricultural practices and nutritional concerns. They cite the example of gastropod consumption being increasingly common due to the salinity increase. They also suggest that it could be possible to identify which species could best be harvested, or even cultivated, and thus encourage use of indigenous species while improving local food supplies and decreasing the motivation of forest destruction. They add that, most importantly, such innovations could be derived experimentally by the local population, which could increase the chances of them being widely disseminated and utilized. And they note that long-term records of the experiments and their results would be maintained in the database.

4. *Technological expertise*. The extreme degree of the recycling of artificial materials is one of the notable characteristics of contemporary African life.

However, while this is true of construction and craft materials, it is not so of electronics. By providing an electronics shop, the investigators foresee the science center as being able to recycle cast-off electronic items, build up a parts supply, and even produce its own instrumentation. One example they note is that of salinity which can be monitored from widespread sites throughout the Casamance, if simple instrumentation is widely available. Oscilloscopes could then be created from cast-off television parts, meaning that similar electronic shops could be set up elsewhere. Junk dealers even sell computer parts nowadays.

A side benefit from this expertise is that technological syncretism could be made available to the arts. For now, the growth of discos means only Euro-American audio technology and light shows, but traditional African artists could also take advantage of electronic media as well, acting as a force for cultural survival in the face of the Western cultural encroachment.

5. *Science education.* For the investigators, the utilization of traditional knowledge in math, science and engineering education is perhaps the most important function of the center. They cite the example of the Djola who are excellent musicians and have developed a "whistle language" as well as a drum communication system that allows them to communicate over long distances. According to the investigators, these attributes make the Djola vocabulary rich in analogs for oscillation, frequency, phase, and other elements of signal processing. Indeed, this is an excellent basis for physics education. The investigators plan to develop an introduction to basic physics, using amplified sound from Ekonting visually displayed on an oscilloscope, to demonstrate how the modern physics concepts are translated by the Djola indigenous knowledge system. They made a request to the Tektronix Foundation to donate an oscilloscope for the task. Portland's Black Educational Center also expressed an interest in participating in an exchange program to further develop the physics lab for encouraging more African American students to become interested in math and science. The investigators also point out that since it is widely acknowledged that some version of the Ekonting is the precursor of the American banjo, the connection to America heritage, both African and European, is quite profound.

For the investigators, here again, the major aspect for developing such a synthesis is to facilitate local empowerment. Students will be poised to use indigenous knowledge to learn ecology, medical sciences, and physical sciences in ways that encourage both the continuation of Djola tradition and prepare them for an increasingly technological world.

6. *Financial stability.* The investigators stress the need for independence from external funding to ensure the future of the project. They prefer self-generated income. They note that, for example, the Casamance has a large number of annual visitors, but presently there is no effort to create what is called "green tourism," despite an intense interest in both the natural and the cultural facets of the area. The investigators believe that such efforts would easily dovetail with the educational activities of the center.

When Eglash returned from Africa, one of his colleagues advised him to focus on scaling patterns in African hairstyles. An enthusiastic group of students at Evergreen State University volunteered their programming skills to help create a multimedia lesson on African fractals. The former Hairstyle Storyboard Web site utilized a style referred to as "the braids of threads," from Yaoundé, Cameroon, to explicate branching fractals.

The "fractal hairstyles" module guided users, step by step, through the creation of a three-dimensional fractal, beginning with the initial design and then mathematically determining the ratio of each iteration. The major goal of the principal investigators of this project (Ron Eglash, Gloria Glimer, T. Q. Berg, and Jaron Sampson) was to combine the images, software and video on African fractals.

One can learn about African fractals from a video project titled "Math and Science through the Eyes of Culture." Produced by the Nebraska Telecommunication Network, the video is distributed by GPN (acronym not spelled out). Narrated by the host, Julie Valentine, the video focuses on the works of three brilliant, contemporary scholars. The first is Tom Hull, a lecturer in mathematics who specializes in calculus and analytical geometry, who demonstrates how origami (arts and science of folding paper; the word is Japanese in origin, but the activity itself dates back thousands of years) can be used to explain some of the intricate aspects of geometry. The second is Eloy Rodriguez, a professor of environmental science at Cornell University, who shows how herbs from Africa and Latin America can be utilized in modern medical practices. And the third is Eglash who demonstrates the existence of fractals in African designs and offers a video at his Web site (csdt.rpi.edu/african/afractal/afractal.htm).

Developed for the Macintosh computer and designed to accompany Eglash's book (1999), the FractaSketch African Edition software is an interactive color tool for designing and drawing intricate African fractals. Users create fractals from basic shapes that they enter graphically. In addition, the program comes with many ready-to-use fractal images, from natural-looking objects to order and chaos. The program provides infinite drawing levels, proportional line thickness capabilities, and the ability to compute fractal dimensions and save images in either "Compact Format," PostScript® or in PICT file format. Some of the program's expansions include the following: color transition tools; window linking—a tool to allow fractal shapes created in one window to link with fractal shapes created in others; support of multiple frame generation—great for animation movies; extensive editing and object control; and high resolution printing output.

The producer of the software program, which comes in either disk version or as an email attachment, is Bernt Wahl at Dynamic Software (www.wahl.org/fe/).

The study of African fractals has also found a home at the International Study Group on Ethnomathematics (ISGEm). This organization was founded in 1985 by math educators Gloria Gilmer, Umbiratan D'Ambrosio, and Rick Scott. Since then, the organization has sponsored programs and business meetings at the annual conferences of the National Council of Teachers of Mathematics (NCTM-USA) and at the International Congress of Mathematics Education (ICME). In 1990, ISGEm became an affiliate of NCTM-USA. ISGEm publishes two newsletters each year.

D'Ambrosio coined the term Ethnomathematics to describe the mathematical practices of identifiable groups—for example, African Fractals. Ethnomathematics is sometimes used specifically for small-scale indigenous societies; but in its broadest sense, the "ethno" prefix can refer to any group, be it a national society, a labor community, a religious tradition, a professional class, etc. The focus is therefore on the culture in which mathematics arises. While mathematics is often associated with the study of "universals," it is nevertheless important to recognize that often something that is thought of as being universal is merely universal to those who share a culture and a historical perspective.

Thus, the mathematical practices that are being emphasized by ISGEm include not only formal symbolic systems, but also spatial designs, practical construction techniques, calculation methods, measurement in time and space, specific methods of reasoning and inferring, and other cognitive and material activities. ISGEm thrives on the now-abundant empirical evidence to support the notion that people in all societies devise their own ways of doing mathematics, no matter their technological level or what they may have learned in school. The organization therefore strives to increase people's understanding of the cultural diversity of mathematical practices, and to make this knowledge applicable to education and to development (isgem.rpi.edu/pl/ethnomathematics-web).

Work on African fractals has also found space in *Virtual Dimension*, an anti-manifesto of the so-called digital revolution, which critically examines the connections between emerging technologies, architecture, production, critical theory, the body, and society's current obsession with cyberspace. The objective of this forum is to facilitate an open arena/site from which to project an interdisciplinary event of all that is digital, mediated, and prosthetic. In essence, no manuscript exists. Rather, it is an assemblage of loosely disseminated fragments, critiques, and tactics which are infinitely porous, and thus represent a series of de-stratified architectural/cultural positions, thresholds, and fields.

Essays, interviews, QuickTimeVR, video, hypertext, and digital images are incorporated throughout the project in order to create ruptures or fissures that are equivalent to the streams of consciousness in the Joycian sense (this is akin to literalist James Joyce's line in *Finnegan's Wake*, "Three quarks of Muster Mark!" when he postulated their existence). The purpose of employing the multimedia platform of printed text and CD-ROM is to make explicit and literalize the modalities, ideas, and processes inherent in the digital and virtual media themselves. It is through this fusion of fuzzy aggregates that multiplicities and the "will to virtuality," the absence of presence, can best be understood.

Conclusion

The Negro was likewise eliminated from the teaching of science. The beginnings of science in various parts of the Orient were mentioned, but the Africans' early advancement in this field was omitted. Students were not told that ancient Africans of the interior knew sufficient science to concoct poisons for arrowheads, to mix durable colors for paintings, and to extract metals from nature and refine them for development in the industrial arts. Very little was said about the chemistry in the method of Egyptian embalming which was the product of the mixed breeds of Northern Africa, now known in the modern world as "colored people" (Woodson, 1933, pp. 18–19).

As the great African scholar Carter G. Woodson correctly intimated in the preceding excerpt, the African past has been shrouded in myths and misconceptions in the West. One of the most pervasive and pernicious of these myths and misconceptions is the notion of Africans as inactive agents in history. It is therefore hoped that this chapter will, in a small way, contribute towards rendering obsolete these myths and misconceptions.

So, why should anyone learn about African Mathematics? The answer is simple: No matter one's race or ethnicity, her/his great, great, great ancestors came from Africa—the continent where scientific thought first emanated. Thus, it is a good idea to know (a) how mathematical ideas are expressed in African cultures and (b) how mathematics permeate all levels of African society, including art and architecture, religion, politics, quantitative techniques, games, and symbolic systems. Indeed, it is not mere coincidence that Benoit B. Mandelbrot, who is dubbed the father of fractals, was influenced by the work of Georg Cantor, who studied in Egypt; Cantor, in turn, was influenced by the work of Fibonacci, who was educated in Tunisia. In addition, Mandelbrot reported that he was inspired by H. E. Hurst's work on flood variations over several centuries and concluded that it could be characterized in terms of a scaling component. H. E. Hurst, it turns out, lived for sixty-two years in Egypt and was able to demonstrate long-term scaling in Nile flood records because of the accurate "nilometer" readings recorded for fifteen centuries.

Also, as Scott W. Williams pointed out, the notion of purely Eurocentric origins of mathematics is no longer tenable. The oldest (35,000 BC) mathematical object was discovered in Swaziland; the oldest example of arithmetic (6000 BC) was found in Zaire; the 4,000-year-old so-called Moscow papyrus contains geometry from the Middle Kingdom of Egypt, the consequence of the formula for the *volume of a truncated square pyramid* (generalizations about the area of a circle). From Herodotus (450 BC) to Proclus (400 BC) to Aristotle (350 BC), we learn that Egypt was the cradle of mathematics, astronomy and surveying. The earliest, great Western mathematicians, including Pythagoras (500 BC), Thales (530 BC), and Exodus (the teacher of Aristotle), all learned much of their mathematics from Egypt.

Thus, this chapter also confirms what Ivan Van Sertima proffered several decades ago:

> A mathematical system is not always recoverable, is not always blessed with historical continuity like that found among the Yoruba and a number of large African communities. It may be hidden in architectural design, like the Granary of the Master of Pure Earth (among the Dogon) or in abstract patterns, like that obtained from the combination of two geometric operations, translation and reflection on an axis (as in decorations on bowls and cloths of the Kuba of the Congo) or in measuring systems (like the exquisite brass weights for measuring gold dust currency among the Ashante) or in the complex network games the Shongo children play or in mathematical recreations, which are the delight of many Africans (1983, p. 15).

Indeed, African Mathematics is present in all of these aspects pointed out by Sertima. Yet still, we are only at the preliminary stage of a vast field that awaits further investigation.

Bibliography

Abraham, Roy. *The Principles of Ibo*. Ibadan, Nigeria: University of Ibadan Press, 1967.

Adler, Peter, and Nicholas Barnard. *African Majesty: The Textile Art of the Ashanti and Ewe*. London, UK: Thames and Hudson, 1992.

Bangura, Abdul Karim. *Chaos Theory and African Fractals*. Washington, DC: The African Institution, 2000.

Bastin, Marie-Louise. *Art Décoratif Tshokwe*. Lisbon, Portugal: Publiçaões Culturais da Companhia de Diamantes de Angolas, 1961.

Bogoshi, Jonas, Kevin Naidoo, and John Webb. "The oldest mathematical artifact." *Math Gazette* 71 (1987): 458.

Bolland, Rita. *Tellem Textiles: Archaeological Finds from Buried Caves in Mali's Bandiagara Cliff*. Bamako, Mali: Musée National/Amsterdam, Holland: Tropenmuseum, 1991.

Crowe, Donald. "The Geometry of African Art III: The Smoking Pipes of Begho." In *The Geometric Vein, the Coxeter Festchrift* edited by C. Davis et al. New York, NY: Springer Verlag, 1982.

de Heinzelin de Braucourt, Jean. "de Ishango." *Scientific American* 206, no. 6 (June 1962): 105–16.

Delafosse, Maurica. *La Langue Mandingue et ses Dialectes*, vol. 1. Paris, France: Librarie Orientaliste, Paul Guenther, 1929.

Diop, Cheikh Anta. *Civilisation ou Barbarie: Anthrologies sans Complainsance*. Paris, France: Présence Africaine, 1980.

Djebbar, Ahmed. "On Mathematical Activities in North Africa since the 9th century." (1995) *AMUCHA Newsletter 15*. www.math.buffalo.edu/mad/AMU/amuchmapdf/amuchma15.pdf (accessed July 6, 2010).

Eglash, Ron. *African Fractals: Modern Computing and Indigenous Design*. New Brunswick, NJ: Rutgers University Press, 1999.

———."Fractals in African Settlement Architecture." *Complexity* 4 (November–

December 1998): 2.

———. "Geometric Algorithms in Mangbetu Design." *Mathematics Teacher* 91, no. 5 (May 1998): 376–81.

Eglash, Ron, and P. Broadwell. "Fractals in Architecture." In *Exploring Fractals on the Macintosh*, edited by Bernt Wahl. New York: Addison-Wesley, 1995.

Eglash, Ron, Christian Diatta, and Nfally Badiane. "Fractal structure in jola material culture." *Ekistics* 61, 368/369 (September–December 1994): 367–71.

Eglash, Ron, and Peter Broadwell. "Fractal geometry in traditional African architecture." *Dynamics Newsletter* (June 1989): 1–10.

Gerdes, Paulus. *Geometry from Africa: Mathematical and Educational Explorations*. Washington, DC: The Mathematical Association of America, 1999.

Gillings, Richard J. 1982. *Mathematics in the Time of the Pharaohs*. New York, NY: Dover Press.

———. *Mathematics in the Time of the Pharaohs*. Cambridge, MA: Massachusetts Institute of Technology Press, 1972.

Joseph, George Gheverghese. *The Crest of the Peacock: Non-European Roots of Mathematics*. New York, NY: Penguin Books, 1991, 2000.

Hauenstein, Alfred. *Examen de Motifs Décoratifs chez les Ovimbundu et Tchokwe d'Angola*. Coimbra, Portugal: Universidade de Coimbra, 1988.

Liebenberg, Louis. *The Art of Tracking: The Origin of Science*. Claremont, South Africa: David Philip Publications, 1990.

Loomis, Elisha S. *The Pythagorean Proposition*. Reston, VA: National Council of Teachers of Mathematics, 1968/1972.

Meurant, Georges. *Shoowa Design: African Textiles from the Kingdom of Kuba*. London, UK: Thames and Hudson, 1986.

Migeod, W. L. *Languages of West Africa*, 2 vols. London, UK: Kegan Paul, Trench, Trubner, 1911.

Niangoran-Bouah, N. *L'univers Akan des Poids a Peser l'Or* (The Akan World of Gold Weights). Abidjan, Côte d'Ivoire: Les Nouvelles Editions Africaines, 1984.

Petito, Andrea L. 1982. "Practical arithmetic and transfer: A study among West African tribesmen." *Journal of Cross-Cultural Psychology* 13:15–28.

Schildkrout, Enid, and Curtis Keim, eds. *African Reflections: Art from Northeastern Zaire*. New York, NY: American Museum of Natural History, 1990.

Schmidl, Marianne. "Zahl und zahlen in Afrika." *Mitteilugen der Anthropologischen Gesellschaftin Wein* 45 (1915): 165–209.

Schweinfurth, Georg. *The Heart of Africa: Three Years' Travels and Adventures in the Unexplored Regions of Central Africa from 1868 to 1871*, 2 vols. New York, NY: Harpers and Brothers, 1874.

Sertima, I. V., ed. *Blacks in Science: Ancient and Modern*. New Brunswick, NJ: Transaction Books, 1983.

The Internet Encyclopedia of Science. "Lebombo Bone." www.daviddarling.info/encyclopedia/L/Lebombo_bone.html (accessed July 25, 2007).

Turner, Lorenzo D. *Africanisms in the Gullah Dialect*. New York, NY: Arno Press, 1949, 1969.

Washburn, Dorothy. *Style, Classification and Ethnicity: Design Categories on Bakuba Raffia Cloth*. Philadelphia, PA: American Philosophical Society, 1990.

Watkins, Christopher D., and Larry Sharp (M. Finlay, ed.). *Programming in 3 Dimensions*. San Mateo, CA: M&T Books, 1992.

Wilcox, A. R. *The Rock Art of Africa*. New York, NY: Holmes and Meier, 1984.

Woodson, Carter G. *Mis-education of the Negro*. Washington, DC: The Associated Publishers, Inc., 1933.
Zaslavsky, C. *Africa Counts: Number and Pattern in African Culture*. New York: Prindle, Weber and Schmidt, 1973, 1999.

Web Sites

http://csdt.rpi.edu/african/afractal/afractal.htm
http://imagiware.com/mancala/
http://isgem.rpi.edu/pl/ethnomathematics-web
http://math.buffalo.edu/mad/Ancient-Africa/
http://math.truman.edu/~thammond/history/SubSaharanAfrica.html
http://tqd.advanced.org/3288/chaos.html
http://wahl.org/fe/

Chapter 5
African Psychology: To Be or Not to Be?

James T. Gire

Introduction

There is an interesting debate among psychologists in Africa as to whether there ought to be an indigenous psychology that is based on African reality or simply to modify and include African phenomena in the general psychology that would encompass, and thus be applicable to, African issues. This chapter attempts to highlight some of the pertinent issues and, presenting some research findings and positions, hopes to integrate the two positions in a manner that would enhance the "relevance" and utility of psychology in the African context. Very little by way of theoretical formulations about behavior has involved Africa or has been constructed using data or processes based on analyses of African issues. Within psychology, it has been taken for granted that specific behaviors have identifiable underlying mechanisms that explain them, and these are presumed to be fairly universal, therefore, utilizing information from ecologically and culturally diverse systems has been presumed (based on how psychology has gone about theory formulation) to be unnecessary. Thus, theories and concepts formulated largely in the West are expected to be appropriately applicable to the African situation. As a discipline, "mainstream" psychology, reflecting the Euro-American domination of the discipline, has been viewed as being fairly narrow in its focus on data and the conceptions of the person and his or her interpersonal networks. Increasingly, psychologists have questioned the extent to which laws and theories within the discipline can be generalized across cultures. Problems have arisen from researchers operating in different environments who have found results different from those obtained in the "mainstream" (Bond, 1988). The inability to replicate some of these results has led to critical voices that point to the limitations of a social science that fails to include indigenous psychologies, cultural context, and methodological pluralism (Tedeschi, 1988).

This discontent, not only with the narrow focus of the discipline but also the inability to generalize the results of research findings and theories to non-Western settings, has led to the development of cross-cultural psychology as an area of study within psychology, one of whose major objectives is "to help establish universal psychological principles that govern human behavior" (Lonner, 1987, p. 380); and to the establishment of *Division 52: International Psychology* within the American Psychological Association (APA). Even if it was not responsible for the quest to diversify theory formulation within psychology, this articulation from Kuhn (1962) in his seminal and influential book, *The Structure of Scientific Revolutions*, certainly sustained that effort:

> Finally, at a still higher level, there is another set of commitments without which no man is a scientist. The scientist must, for example, be concerned to understand the world and extend the precision and scope with which it has been ordered. That commitment must, in turn, lead him to scrutinize, either for himself or through colleagues, some aspect of nature in great empirical detail. And, if that scrutiny displays pockets of apparent disorder, then these must challenge him to a new refinement of his observational techniques or to a further articulation of his theories. Undoubtedly there are still other rules like these, ones which have held for scientists at all times. (p. 42)

The realization that eco-cultural variables play a role in the conceptualization of psychological theories led to efforts to try to argue for the development of psychological paradigms that are relevant to, and address the unique realities of African worldview. The argument is that since the current "mainstream" psychology is a Euro-American enterprise that focuses on its own cultural environment as the main subject matter, similar processes should apply to Africa, and by extension, other populations. However, there are those even within Africa who are not persuaded by this logic. According to this position, the scientific study of human behavior is an abstract, theoretical endeavor that is oriented to understanding psychological processes in general. Therefore, if current theorizing does not encompass variables from other eco-cultural systems, these simply need to be added to the equation in order for such a theory to be "relevant" since the major goal is to arrive at universal laws governing behavior everywhere.

In this chapter, I try to identify the nuances in the debate and suggest that the issues in this discourse are more complex than a simple dichotomy between universal versus African psychology. As Moll (2002) surmises, the positions range from the defense of psychology as a universally applicable and neutral set of scientific propositions capable of contributing to African problems, but needing to be extended (e.g., Biesheuvel, 1991) through attempts to build stratified models to emphasize the relationship between the individual and social change in Africa to eliminate the reductionist features of Western psychology (e.g., Gilbert, 1989) to arguments that relevance should be the application of psychology to uniquely African problems in place of the more disintegrative agenda of indigenous psychology (Nell, 1990) or a psychology so universal that it is decontextualized from its distinctive political-ideological context (Dawes, 1986). I argue that there is room on this table for the two extreme positions to occupy and complement each other because to state that a psychology that is purely African needs to be developed is to suggest a new domain of knowledge both unique to a particular region and its occupants; it also suggests that such an African psychology exists in opposition to a psychology that is unique to another geographical region and its people(s). However, there is already a substantial literature in Africa that has emerged out of efforts to combat problems distinct to the African context using the methods of universal psychology, suggesting that such principles are not (always) incompatible with African realities. This second point is consistent with the views of the influential Béninois philosopher, Paulin Hountondji, who opposes the notion of any form of knowledge and practice as essential only to Africa. Indeed, the debate within psychology is not that different from, and has, in fact, been influenced by a similar debate in philosophy. Therefore, I will present briefly, the main elements in the philosophical arena as a prelude to the primary arguments in psychology so as to place the psychology debate in a wider African context.

African versus Universal Philosophy

As with psychologists in Africa, there is a lively debate among African philosophers as to whether it is feasible to have an authentic African philosophy. The major elements in the debate have been summarized by Dismas Masolo (1994) in which he presents the case of a body of knowledge in search for an identity. Some of the prominent participants in the debate include: Paulin Hountondji (1983), H. Odera Oruka, (1981, 1990), Akin Makinde (1988) and Peter Bodunrin (1981). At one end of the spectrum is what Oruka classifies as the ethnographic school of philosophy that regards local community and cultural features as imperative for a system of philosophy. According to this view,

> African societies are fundamentally distinct and different from the western societies …The role of scientific models in the West is similar to, or taken by, the interaction of forces or, practically, by gods and spirits in African culture … Philosophy for the African is a practical identification with the intuition and unquestionable values and idioms of the cultural mass … African philosophy is hence, the reverse of the thought that comes as the outcome of theoretically and deductively reached inference. African philosophy is an experience common and obvious to all members of the stock. (Oruka, 1987, p. 58)

Mbiti (1990) is a proponent of the above viewpoint and considers the main role of African philosophy as an explication of the indigenous knowledge system or outlook of a particular African community or Africa as a whole since there is only one African traditional religion. Therefore, African philosophy is expected to work primarily with evidence from the myths, folk-wisdom, and proverbs of the collective mass of the people. The irony of this position, according to Hountondji (1983) is that the form of philosophy proposed here owes much of its theories and methodologies to European anthropologists, ethnographers, and missionaries who formulated the concept of collective philosophies of life. Thus, the key element in this proposal is an opposition to the notion of universal systems of philosophy, which paradoxically, is deemed un-African and is usually termed Eurocentric.

Curiously, the very issue in the debate about the viability of African philosophy is whether it is desirable to equate a universal system of philosophy with a local, culturally and geographically specific philosophical literature. Oruka captures this paradox rather succinctly:

> The West might have shown much explicit advance in the fields of science and philosophy, thanks to their longevity in the practice of writing, but neither science nor philosophy is the perverse of Europeans and a mere imposed innovation on the Africans. … African philosophy is still not seen as represented by the texts and thoughts of her scholars (modern, traditional, literate or illiterate) but by the myths and images of the mass culture. Africa cannot, by the laws of history, regain her dignity and make a contribution to human civilization if she ignores her own past and traditions. But, she will equally be handicapped if she abandons science and logic, in the so-called Western sense, as things that are unAfrican. (1987, p. 66)

To summarize, Oruka argues that African history and traditions have already made major contributions to universal scientific knowledge. And, just as insular "African" theories and epistemologies are inconsistent with developing human knowledge, distorted "Western" knowledge claims are equally narrowly conceived and thus are incapable of presenting themselves as representatives of the whole.

Amin (1989), in his thesis on Eurocentrism, argues against the narrow view of provincialism that he finds in both Europe-centered and African-centered attitudes toward the world. Amin suggests that Eurocentrism, as an ideology, projects Western models of humanity and society as the only solution to the challenges of our time. In the same vein, however, an ideology like Afrocentrism essentially supports this dominant form of imperialism because it "reacts to the challenge by a desperate evasion, in a two-fold cultural involution, Eurocentric and provincialist in the West, and "inverted Eurocentric" in the third world. More than ever, the need for a universalism capable of meeting the challenge makes a critical examination of both of these modes of thought necessary" (p. 78). Amin argues further that this position also creates an equally provincialist mode in the third world and that this quest for provincialism fuels a misguided pursuit of diversity:

> The Eurocentric universalism of capitalism is not critiqued in order to allow the construction of a new universalism; all aspirations for universalism are rejected in favor of a "right to difference" (in this case, differences of culture and forms of social organization) invoked as a means of avoiding the real problem. This is

> what I call "provincialism," very much in fashion today. The view that any person has the right – and even the power – to judge others is replaced by attention to relativity of those judgments. Without a doubt, such judgments can be erroneous, superficial, hasty, or relative. No case is ever definitely closed; debate always continues. But that is precisely the point. It is necessary to pursue debate and not avoid it on the grounds that the views that anyone forms about others are, and always will be false: that the French will never understand the Chinese, that men will never understand women, etc; or, in other words, that there is no human species, but only "people." (Amin, 1989, pp. 146–147)

Amin marshals a defense of universal inquiry in social theory and other intellectual endeavors by suggesting that the explanation of human societies and human action should be by means of common explanatory principles and a unified conceptual system, and the elaboration of a research program that addresses humanity as a whole. This implies the rejection of the handed-down conception of Eurocentrism as well as any notions that we might have about forms of knowledge that are essential to Africa or any particular geographical or socio-cultural context. Amin proposes, essentially, that both Eurocentrism and Afrocentrism entail each other, and in the process expose each other's theoretical inadequacy, thus enabling us to begin the effort of developing Africa in a universal system of thought.

One of Hountondji's main concerns, as articulated in *African Philosophy: Myth and Reality,* is to encourage, and to understand the necessary philosophical conditions for the development of the human and social sciences in the African context. He argues that the tendency among many African intellectuals to reduce psychology, philosophy, social theory and the like in and of Africa to folklore is today the biggest single impediment to the development of such knowledge for it limits research and theoretical discourse to a set of questions and issues that are generated primarily by European and American conceptions of Africa rather than by the priorities and needs of African society itself. This is a paradox since a human science that portrays itself as uniquely "African" actually encourages some "sort of a collective cultural exhibitionism which compels the "Third World" intellectual to "defend and illustrate" the peculiarities of his tradition "for the benefit of a Western public" (1983, p. 67). Thus, the supposedly universal dialogue that accompanies notions of diversity across psychological theories actually encourages particularism. This is the critical point in Hountondji's position on the debate about African philosophy. This summation of Hountondji's viewpoint is central to the debate on African psychology:

> My own view is that this universality must be preserved – not because philosophy must necessarily develop the same themes or even the same questions from one country or continent to another, but because these differences of *content* are meaningful precisely and only as differences of *content*, which, as such, refer back to the essential unity of a discipline, of a single style of inquiry. (1983, p. 56)

African/Cultural Psychology or Universal Psychology?

Our review of the debate on the desirability for an African philosophy provides an appropriate context for evaluating the corresponding arguments in psychology. We will begin with the position calling for a psychology that is distinctively African. Expressing frustration with the inability of current "mainstream" theories to explain African phenomena, Akotia and Olowu (2002) suggest that it is only when Africans begin to develop their own theories and epistemologies that they can properly understand what is meaningful to African people. They argued that indigenous psychology will be instrumental to the understanding of local phenomena. This position argues that there ought to be an African psychology that is rooted in the continent's unique epistemologies, knowledge systems, and identities. By contrast, Durojaiye (1993) argued that there is no such thing as an African psychology, or for that matter, a psychology that is particular to any region or country. Rather, he suggests that there should be a psychology that is engaged with issues or problems about Africa. The following quote aptly captures his position in the debate:

> Twice in my career as a psychologist and in my life as an African the question has been put to me, 'What about African psychology? Do you not have your own concepts and psychological processes?' The first time was in 1973 at Ibadan. The second time was in 1986 in Trinidad. On both occasions I was not ashamed to say that I do not know of any African psychological processes that are distinct from those found anywhere in the world. I still do not know of any. I know of how psychology has been manifested and operationalized in Africa, and I know of psychology in Africa. (p. 211)

Other psychologists in Africa that have tried to establish the basic parameters of the debate have viewed it as a distinction between "relevance" and ethnopsychology (Nell, 1990), or whether the notion of an African psychology is a myth or reality (Moll, 2002). The contribution by Nell (1990) dwelt mainly on the issue of whether "mainstream" psychology that is based on predominantly Euro-American concepts and theories was relevant to Africa, particularly South Africa, or if, indeed, an ethnically derived psychology was required. One of the first justifications for the call by some for the establishment of indigenous psychology has been the notion that mainstream psychology was irrelevant to African affairs. Speaking particularly within the context of South Africa, but a position that can be easily extrapolated to the rest of Africa, and for that matter, any geographical or cultural system regarded as different from the Euro-American tradition, Holdstock (1981) pointedly suggested that psychology would certainly rate highly among the most irrelevant endeavors in South African society of the day. Echoing the same sentiments but clarifying exactly what is meant by relevance, Dawes (1986) stated that relevance entailed an ability to expose the interests which are served by the uncritical psychological theory and practice, and to call for a reconceptualization of the subject matter of psychology which takes account of the social/ideological discourses which structure the individual person, the psychologist as theorist, researcher and practitioner, and the knowledge which they produce" (p. 34).

Although there are many interpretations to the relevance theme, the one that has been more strident and thus inflamed the debate is the view that equates relevance with indigenous. This interpretation of relevance underlies the comments by Holdstock (1981) when he justified his characterization of psychology as being irrelevant to Africa by indicating that psychologists in Africa tend to adhere to an exclusively Western approach to psychology and have failed to expose students in Africa to "Africa's psychological rhythm" (p. 126). Candland (1980) stated it more succinctly when he lamented that "we have assisted in the devaluation of the literature and scholarship of other cultures, leaving the impression that there is nothing to be learned from them, at least nothing called psychology. Do we believe there is no Arab or Indian psychology merely because there are no such courses in the college catalogue?" (p. 196).

The implication from the above viewpoints which are echoed by others (e.g., Moghaddam, 1987; Sinha, 1984) is that there is some sort of both a unique reality and a unique reservoir of wisdom in these third world countries. It implies further, that Westerners or non-Western psychologists whose education and practice in steeped in that tradition, who attempt to conduct research or deliver psychological services in the African arena risk damaging, rather than helping, their clients. Nell (1990) strongly opposes this quest for an ethnopsychology and its sister term, ethnopsychiatry, and presents three main criticisms of this approach.

First, Nell argues that invocations needed to achieve this kind of relevance would end up being harmful to psychology. It would, for example, inculcate the feeling of helplessness among psychologists who may come to believe that their psychology was out of tune with Africa, and that being irrelevant, would feel at best peripheral to the true needs of the people they wish to serve, or worse, that they would actively harm these same people they seek to help. Furthermore, ethnopsychology would encourage and support the notion that until the psychologist is fluent in the vernacular, and is an authority on indigenous customs or beliefs, he or she would be unable to effectively apply his or her knowledge and skills. Therefore, psychologists who do not deem themselves sufficiently proficient in cross-cultural psychology may misattribute real failures in negotiating skills and failed therapeutic encounters to cultural differences rather than their legitimate failure.

The second criticism advanced by Nell is the suggestion that the quest to develop "an indigenous third world psychology" (Moghaddam, 1987) is content free. Essentially, these proponents of ethnopsychology reject the Western model but do not provide an adequate set of operational definitions of what exactly constitutes relevance, and also fail to provide a coherent research agenda for the development of an indigenous psychology.

The third criticism is that the new indigenous, Third-World psychology lacks both the content and agenda precisely because the task it creates for itself is impossible, since the relevance agenda rests on a fundamental misunderstanding of psychology and human nature.

Based on the foregoing, this debate on African psychology can be categorized into three main positions: the first position argues for a distinctive, unique folk imagination that is essential to Africa, and that this produces forms of knowledge with their own theories and epistemologies. This implies that the African mind:

> [R]eveals itself through what may rightly be called a congenital trait of sociality or sociability. It further reveals itself as a virtuous natural endowment of patience and tolerance. And lastly, it manifests itself as a natural disposition of mutual sympathy and acceptance. These three areas then appear to serve as important landmarks in the general description of the phenomenology of the African mind. (Nyasani, 1997, p. 57)

The second position can be said to represent the Eurocentric viewpoint that essentially suggests that the answer to the question of universalism exists, and the West has already discovered it. According to Amin (1989), it is akin to saying "imitate the West, the best of all possible worlds" (p. xii). This type of position does not encourage analysis of the origins and shortcomings of particular ways of thinking that amount in the provincialisms of the West, such as thinking about psychological problems in terms of operational definitions or flat monocausal, neurological or genetic determinants. Eurocentric knowledge practices equate to a particular distortion of a universe of psychological procedures and principles.

The third position suggests that we ought to pursue a truly universal system of psychological knowledge, a knowledge that transcends all narrow provincialisms, be they Eurocentric, Afrocentric, or orientalist. This last position, to which I associate, implies that knowledge generated in Africa is intricately part of universal knowledge systems. It encompasses the notion that the prevailing fragmentation of psychology by identifying the different variations with particular peoples or geographic locales is undesirable in the quest toward evolving a coherent science of the human organism, an essentially global species (Nsamenang, 1990). In other words, universal psychology does not equate to Euro-American psychology, characterized by the instrumentalist notions of causality implicit in experimental methodology; neither does it equate to the putative, primeval African psychology. Both of these conceptions are distortions of the depth of knowledge required to build an encompassing psychological account of human reality.

To extrapolate Hountondji's thoughts in philosophy to psychology, African psychology is a myth if it is conceived as a product of theories and epistemologies that are unique to a singular people, nation or continent. There cannot be a coherent psychological theory that is unique to Africa, but only a universal psychology that is engaged with the problems and issues of Africa. Viewed from this perspective, African psychology is a reality, since there is ample literature in psychology that demonstrates this reality. I will make reference to works by Fanon, Nsamenang, and Eyetsemitan and Gire, to buttress this point.

Fanon's Psychoanalytic Application to Africa

Frantz Fanon (1925–1961) is most known for is contribution to the anti-colonial and revolutionary thought, especially in the African context, and to the psychology of racial and colonial oppression. Beginning with his first publication, *Black Skin, White Masks*, written in the early fifties and concluding with The *Wretched of the Earth*, published just before his death, Fanon makes an incisive analysis of how the historically bounded experience of colonialism, specifically, the relationship between the colonizer and the colonized can be normalized as psychology. Even though both books are essentially political manifestos, they also would rank among the classics of psychology in Africa because they are powerful examples of how universal systems of psychological thought, when applied to the issues of Africa, are enriched and elaborated in ways that would not have been possible if they had been confined to the West. Unquestionably, psychoanalysis has an indelibly African flavor after Fanon (Moll, 2002).

Fanon was born in Martinique and received his education in France—he trained as a psychiatrist in Lyon, France—but his theoretical work was formed during his engagement with Africa. While serving as the head of a psychiatry department at an Algerian hospital, Fanon encountered patients subjected to racist abuse, chained to beds in racially segregated wards, and other forms of torture to the point where by the time the war broke out, he came to the conclusion that colonial society—which was the cause of his patients' problems, rather the systems—ought to be his focus. He then decided to resign his appointment and join the liberation movement.

Fanon's psychology of colonial domination is exemplified in his letter of resignation in which he averred that "if psychiatry is the medical technique that aims to enable man no longer to be a stranger to his own environment, I owe it to myself to affirm that the Arab, permanently an alien in his own country, lives in a state of absolute depersonalization ...The events in Algeria are the logical outcome of an abortive attempt to decerebralize a people" (Fanon, 1967a, p. 53).

Thus, Fanon argued that colonial conditions create a massive "psychoexistential complex" (1967b, p. 14) from the moment of colonial conquest, which alienates the black man from himself. In other words, the combination of racism and colonialism generate a pernicious collective state of mind that blinds the black man to his own identity and subjects him unconsciously to a universalized white norm: he acquires a white mask. This contribution served as a precursor to much of contemporary sociocultural psychology that is concerned with the psychological internalization of social structure: "If there is an inferiority complex, it is the outcome of a double process: primarily, economic; subsequently, the internalization—or, better, the epidermalization—of this inferiority" (1967b, p. 13). In subsequent analyses, Fanon examines how this psychic complex explains the failure of nationalism to achieve liberation in post-colonial contexts.

In *The Wretched of the Earth*, Fanon devotes one section that discusses "colonial war and mental disorders" (1963). In all this, Fanon draws extensively from the works of Sigmund and Anna Freud, Adler, Jung, and a number of other clinicians, and mobilizes a range of concepts drawn from the analysis of the unconscious mind to develop his theory. He often develops tensions between its major theorists to help open up his own explanatory constructs of the unconscious. Thus, while Fanon produces a compelling anti-colonial psychology, and thus anti-Eurocentric psychology, he does so by developing the universal theoretical potentials of psychoanalysis. At the same time, he does not hesitate to criticize psychoanalytic notions when they do fail to adequately model the realities of the colonial or African experience.

Nsamenang's Contributions in Developmental Psychology

Bame Nsamenang is widely regarded as the first African psychologist, and one among few from outside the West, to provide a systematic account of the psychological development of children that is not sourced in Euro-American psychological cultural realities. Most of his significant work is contained in *Human Development in Cultural Context* (Nsamenang, 1992) in which he seeks "to stir up interest and systematic exploration of distinctly indigenous patterns of development so that the developmental research in the third world contexts may fertilize and expand the visions, methods, and knowledge of psychology beyond current (Western) molds" (1992, p. 4).

Working primarily from the Human Development Center in Bamenda, Cameroon, he developed what he terms a "West African ontogeny" that is distinct from the ontogenetic accounts of human development that dominate "mainstream" psychology. Making a careful analysis of the everyday life activities of west and east African peoples, he derived the following hierarchy of "socio-ontogenetic life stages": Spiritual selfhood—period of the newborn—social priming—social apprenticing—social entrée—social induction/internment—adulthood—old age/death—ancestral selfhood (Nsamenang, 1992, p. 148). He argues that these stages of development are generated by processes of *functional maturation* in a particular sociocultural context, "the product of a socialization with emphasis on the notions of locus of authority, seniority and filial service" (1992, p. 148).

Some of these notions are quite inconsistent with many normative conventions taken for granted in "mainstream" psychology. One of these is his suggestion that child labor should not be considered an evil to be eliminated in African society. He goes to great length to emphasize that child labor should not be taken as justification for exploitative child labor practices, but that when applied appropriately, child work is a necessary part of the developmental ontogeny of societies in Africa, suggesting that "child work is an indigenous mechanism for social integration and the core process by which children learn roles and skills" (Nsamenang, 1992, p. 156). Interestingly, research by Eyetsemitan and Gire (2003), to be discussed in the section, would provide some validation to the relativity of what is deemed child labor.

The second example relates to Nsamenang's suggestion that it is inappropriate to expect African fathers to be sensitive, caring, nurturing and involved with their children. They should also not be necessarily held responsible for the maintenance and welfare of their children (Nsamenang, 2000a). Rather, fathers play what may be characterized as a networking role, ensuring that children are inserted in a kinship system that entails socialization into extended family contexts, childcare by siblings and relatives and maternal responsibility for "independent ways to support themselves and their children." Thus, the African cultural norm demands that fathers be involved differently since they are an "important link between children and the social network of kin and neighbors, a group whose importance is reflected in the care of the child growing up in a sociological field of kin. In this field, fathers and mothers play different roles in educating and socializing children" (2000a, p. 6).

Nsamenang argues that including cultural variables from different societies will not only enhance our understanding of local psychological phenomena, but will also expand our vision of psychological functioning across diverse cultures. It would, for example, help question models derived primarily from the studies of Western populations. His commitment is to the development of a universal psychology that is applicable as much to any sociocultural context as to Africa itself so that it would "broaden theoretical and empirical models to incorporate the modes of behavior and developmental paths of representative segments of research niches—and in the long run to consider how the data we obtain reflect or fit the universal condition of *Homo sapiens*" (1992, p. 16). Finally, he argues that the systematic development of psychological research in Africa will help to transcend the current narrow mainstream. According to him, "the way to proceed is to acknowledge the achievements of mainstream psychology, accept it as indigenous Western psychology, but hybrid it and nurture it into a science that truly captures human diversity" (2000b, p. 2). This implies a continual theoretical movement of global, universal explanatory principles out of and into Africa. The following quote embodies Nsamenang's perspective in this debate:

> The call for the indigenization of psychology does not contradict the remark that variants of psychology should not be identified by geographic, racial, or ethnic source. To regard psychology as a science that can study behavioral development in all human societies is not to deny the remarkable variability in the ecocultures that shape and elaborate world views and basic personality attrib

> utes in diverse directions and channels. The emphasis should be on employing sound scientific methodology to explore, understand and describe developmental and behavioral phenomena in context. (1992, p. 13)

Eyetsemitan and Gire on Adult Development and Aging

Whereas Nsamenang focused on the early part of human development, Eyetsemitan and Gire (2003) concentrated on the adult development and aging side of the developmental spectrum. Both individuals were colleagues at the University of Jos, Nigeria, in the early years of their academic careers and had been grappling with the inadequacy of applying the dominant Western theories to the African reality, especially as they pertained to adult development, and in particular, to the developmental trajectories espoused in theories such as Erikson's (1950, 1959) stage theory of personality. This theory, while used widely, was considered to be lacking in cross-cultural empirical support, particularly at the higher-level stages (Church and Lonner, 1998).

A full exposition by Eyetsemitan and Gire is contained in their 2003 book, *Aging and Adult Development in the Developing World: Applying Western Theories and Concepts*. In addition to reviewing work from both the developed and the developing world in terms of those aspects that could be directly applied versus those that needed re-thinking, the authors also conducted a study utilizing participants from seven countries in the developing world, including two countries from Africa (Botswana and Nigeria). Eyetsemitan and Gire suggest that development occurs in context, and to have a full and relevant explanation that would be applicable to specific environments, one has to take into account the ecocultural context in which such development occurs. People across all cultures age; however, the determination as to when or what constitutes aging, as well as the experiences of aging are influenced by culture. These authors obtained the age demarcations for the three stages of adult development—early adulthood, middle adulthood, and late adulthood—from the developing world and compared them with Erikson's stages. Whereas Erickson's stages ranged from 17-45, 40-65, and 65 years and above for early, middle, and late adulthood stages, the average ages for the developing world were 19-31, 32-45, and 49-65 years, respectively. What was more interesting was that in each country, the age range for each stage was lower for females compared to males, with the early adulthood stage for females in some instances presumed to have a starting point of 15 years!

The discussion of these results echoed an important point stated earlier from the work of Nsamenang—the issue of child labor. Given the disparities in the developmental trajectories between the "developed" and "developing" countries, some misunderstandings might arise with regard to discussions concerning child labor. This is significant because each of the developmental stages is associated with role requirements. One of those roles expected of in the early adulthood stage in the developing world is to start jobs and to have children. Thus, what constitutes unacceptable child labor in one setting could be deemed a role-appropriate function in another setting. Yet, both societies may rightly frown upon child labor. The same situation applies to role functions in the late adulthood stage. Whereas growing old is associated with such attributes as being wise, resolving disputes and presiding over functions at ceremonies in the developing world (leading some to exaggerate their age), less appealing experiences such as role losses and diminished opportunities characterize the elderly in the developed world, which can result in feelings of despair or bitterness.

These differences in developmental trajectories and roles associated with the corresponding stages of adult development do not represent differences in the psychology of the respective ecologies in which these studies have been undertaken. Rather, these are similar psychological processes that may differ by virtue of ecology, language, learning, experiences, and social interactions, and adaptations.

Conclusion

Is psychology going to lay claim to the essential unity of a single discipline or fragmented science? The answer appears to depend on the resolution of the debate. If psychology as a scientific enterprise fails, it would be due to an absence of thematic and methodological coherence. In this case, country by country and culture by culture demand for a unique local psychology in parallel to local literatures could be warranted. However, if psychology does have scientific coherence in the way that philosophy, medicine or chemistry do, then an even stronger case for the rejection of indigenous psychologies can be made. An essential unity of method and thematic content will prevail in psychology across countries and cultures, demonstrating only changes in emphasis and application.

It would seem then, that the pursuit of a distinctive African psychology is self-defeating since its seemingly universal dialogue which accompanies notions of diversity across psychological theories actually encourages particularism. What psychologists in Africa need to do is engage the problems and issues of Africa with the powerful tools that psychology in general makes available to them. Applying the thoughts of Hountondji (1983) on philosophy to psychology, African psychology is a myth if it is conceived as a product of theories and epistemologies that are unique to a single people, nation or continent. There cannot be a coherent psychological theory that is particular to Africa, but only a universal psychology engaged in the problems and issues of Africa. If conceptualized in this manner, African psychology is a reality; there already is a good deal of literature in psychology that bears this out. The challenge is to keep pace with the application of the one psychology we know to the unique problems facing populations and planners in Africa and, indeed, the developing world.

Bibliography

Akotia, Charity S., and Akinsola Olowu. "Towards an African-centered Psychology: Voices from Continental African Psychologists." *Psych Discourse* 31, no. 10 (2000): 7–12.

Amin, Samir. *Eurocentrism.* London: Zed Books, 1989.

Biesheuvel, Simon. "Neutrality, Relevance and Accountability in Psychological Research and Practice in South Africa." *South African Journal of Psychology* 21, no. 4 (1991): 131–40.

Bodunrin, Peter O. "The Question of African Philosophy." *Philosophy* 56 (1981): 161–79.

Bond, Michael H. "Introduction." In *The Cross-cultural Challenge to Social Psychology (Vol. 11) Cross-Cultural Research & Methodology Series*, edited by Michael H. Bond, 9–13. Newbury Park: Sage, 1988.

Candland, Douglas K. "Speaking Words and Doing Deeds." *American Psychologist 35* (1980): 191–98.

Church, A. Timothy, and Walter J. Lonner. "The Cross-Cultural Perspective in the Study of Personality: Rationale and Current Research." *Journal of Cross-Cultural Psychology 29* (1998): 32–62.

Dawes, Andrew R. L. "The Notion of a Relevant Psychology with Particular Reference to Africanist Pragmatic Initiatives." *Psychology in Society* 5 (1986): 28–48.

Durojaiye, Michael O. A. "Indigenous Psychology in Africa." In *Indigenous Psychologies: Research and Experience in Cultural Context*, edited by Uichol Kim and John W. Berry, 211–20. Newbury Park: Sage, 1993.

Erikson, Erik H. *Identity and the Life Cycle.* New York: Norton, 1959.

———. *Childhood and Society.* New York: Norton, 1950.

Eyetsemitan, Frank E., and James T. Gire. *Aging and Adult Development in the Developing World: Applying Western Theories and Concepts.* Westport, CT: Praeger, 2003.

Fanon, Frantz. *Toward the African Revolution* (Political essays). New York: Grove Press (Translated by Haakon Chevalier), 1967a.

———. *Black Skin, White Masks.* New York: Grove Press (Translated by Charles Lam Markmann), 1967b.

———. *The Wretched of the Earth.* New York: Grove Press (Translated by Constance Farrington), 1963.

Gilbert, A. J. "Things Fall Apart? Psychological Theory in the Context of Rapid Social Change." *South African Journal of Psychology* 19, no. 2 (1989): 91–100.

Holdstock, T. Len. "Psychology in South Africa Belongs to the Colonial Era: Arrogance or Ignorance?" *South African Journal of Psychology* 11 (1981): 123–29.

Hountondji, Paulin J. *African Philosophy: Myth and Reality.* London: Hutchinson University Library for Africa, 1983.

Kuhn, Thomas S. *The Structure of Scientific Revolutions.* Chicago: University of Chicago Press, 1962.

Lonner, Walter J. Introduction to "The Generalizability of Social Psychological Laws and Theories across Cultures." *Journal of Cross-Cultural Psychology* 18 (1987): 379–82.

Makinde, M. Akin. *African Philosophy, Culture and Traditional Medicine.* Athens: Ohio University Press, 1988.

Masolo, Dismas A. *African Philosophy in Search of Identity.* Edinburgh: Edinburgh University Press, 1994.

Mbiti, John. *African Religions and Philosophy*. London: Heinemann, 1990.
Moghaddam, Fathali M. "Psychology in the Three Worlds: As Reflected by the Crisis in Social Psychology and the Move towards Indigenous Third-World Psychology." *American Psychologist* 42, no. 10 (1987): 912–20.
Moll, Ian C. "African Psychology: Myth and Reality." *South African Journal of Psychology* 32, no. 1 (2002): 9–16.
Nell, Victor. "One World, One Psychology: 'Relevance' and Ethnopsychology." *South African Journal of Psychology* 20, no. 3 (1990): 129–40.
Nsamenang, A. Bame. *Fathers, Families and Child Well-being in Cameroon: A Review of the Literature*. Philadelphia: National Center on Fathers and Families, 2000a.
———. "Issues in Indigenous Approaches to Developmental Research in Sub-Saharan Africa." *Newsletter of the International Society for the Study of Behavioral Development* 37, no. 1 (2000b): 1–4.
———. "Factors Influencing the Development of Psychology in Sub-Saharan Africa." *International Journal of Psychology* 30, no. 6 (1995): 729–39.
———. *Human Development in Cultural Context: A Third World Perspective*. Newbury Park: Sage, 1992.
———. "What's in a Name?" *Journal of African Psychology* 1, no. 3 (1990): 1–5.
Nyasani, Joseph M. *The African Psyche*. Nairobi: University of Nairobi Press, 1997.
Oruka, H. Odera (Ed.). *Sage Philosophy: Indigenous Thinkers and Modern Debate on African Philosophy*. New York: E. J. Brill, 1990.
———. "African Philosophy: A Brief Personal History and Critical Debates." In *Contemporary Philosophy: A New Survey*, edited by Guttorm Fløistad. Dordrecht: M. Nijhoff, 1987.
———. "Four Trends in African Philosophy." In *Philosophy in the Present Situation in Africa*, edited by Alwin Diemer. Wiesbaden: Franz Steiner Verlag, 1981.
Sinha, Jai B. P. "Toward Partnership for Relevant Research in the Third World." *International Journal of Psychology* 19, nos. 1–2 (April 1984): 169–77.
Tedeschi, James T. "How Does One Describe a Platypus? An Outsider's Questions for Cross-Cultural Social Psychology." In *The Cross-Cultural Challenge to Social Psychology (Vol. 11) Cross-Cultural Research and Methodology Series*, edited by Michael H. Bond, 14–28. Newbury Park: Sage, 1988.

Chapter 6
Model of "Governance Management" in Africa: An Integrated Approach of Blending Modern Management Methods with Africa's Cultural Mores for Greater Institutional Efficiency

Kenday S. Kamara

Introduction

Research in organizational sociology suggests that a flexible, organic, and decentralized organization can lose its "structure of legitimacy" when it fails to construct, justify and stabilize the obedience of the people (Courpasson, 2000). The process is political. And "authority" is the instrument of "structure of legitimacy" used. But organizations in Africa have not fully understood the political means of responsibly utilizing this instrument of authority to build a social order producing efficiency both for those in power and for subordinates. There is reasonable agreement among scholars that Africa is overwhelmed by "administrative inadequacies" (Keenleyside, cited by Bongyu, 2006, para. 7). Africa is in a vicious poverty cycle that obligates policy makers to seek self-reliant systems with checks and balances and massive commitment geared toward managing public organizations effectively, and of solving intractable public problems that have a strong management component. This study thus attempts to put together an application prospectus of a Western-oriented, culture-friendly, performance driven model of "governance management" for Africa. The study seeks to build on the groundbreaking work on organizational theory by Goldratt

(2004), Machiavelli (1950), Selznick (1957), Senge (1990), Simon (1976), and others by linking the insights of their management studies and related theoretical work on the dynamic, social nature of organizations to African management thought.

The study suggests the incorporation of Western management practice into Africa's "structures of domination" (Weber, 1968, p. 68). These approaches are adapted from a Western universal best practice perspective of management and mapped on African cultural values to create "learning organizations" (Senge, 1990, p. 3) in Africa that might help in dealing with issues embedded in Africa's local context and lead to organizational effectiveness and social change. The relationship between Western management ideals and Africa's cultural structuring and functioning receives attention in this study. After brief historical considerations of organizational management from a Western perspective and the nature of African cultural frameworks, the study interprets and analyzes social, managerial, ethical strategies gleaned from Western organizational management approaches to outline an integrated African management approach. These interpretations and analysis lead to a presentation of specific purposes that re-engineered mechanisms of African management thought can serve.

The study outlines the rationale for a competence-based view of organizational management and proposes a globalization-of-practice approach to address a number of important institutional challenges: bribery and corruption, leveraging and stretching competence across functions and departmental units, and accelerating innovation. The purpose is to develop new knowledge by combining ideas from the reservoir of organizational management knowledge in the West with African cultural principles. This grouping of knowledge and cultural practices does define the conception of applied management and decision knowledge in new ways that invents a bridge to twenty-first century governance in Africa, and generating new insights for theory and practice. Though management is culture-dependent (Burns, 1978; Dia, 1991; Drucker, 1969; Hofstede, 1993), to the extent that theories of management developed in a given culture reflect the main patterns of that culture, it appears reasonable to think that despite these cultural dimensions, some aspects of theories of management developed in the West may apply to the African context (Bahemuka and Brockingdon, 2004; C. D. Beugré and Offodile, 2001; Geertz, 1963; Mangaliso, 2001).

Several studies (Drucker, 1969; Kiggundu, 1988; Mangaliso, 2001; Saleh, 1985; World Bank, 1989) have underscored the role of management in poverty reduction, economic growth and development. The surge in violent conflict in the world in the last quarter century has also raised questions about relationships between economic factors and conflict risks. This is found to be especially true because many of the areas in which new conflicts were breaking out were in economic decline, notably in sub-Saharan African and the post-socialist world. The central finding of an ambitious World Bank (2006) research agenda led by respected Oxford University professor Paul Collier does provide some of the answers to this view. Economic factors are found to be central in all dimensions of violent conflicts. Poor economic policies are said to predispose these countries to conflict experiences (World Bank, 2006). And in all cases, management—contended as the main vehicle of economic growth (Drucker, 1969)—is inadequate and does not integrate the cultural inheritance of these societies, making economic development impossible in these conflict-ridden countries. "Although this assumption may overstate the impact of management on economic development, the case of Japan and the newly industrialized nations of the Pacific Rim that relied heavily on their own cultures to assimilate Western managerial practices, bears important lessons for African countries" (Beugré and Offodile, 2001, p. 536). A process of Westernization by benchmarking universal management best practices, therefore, can be done without losing the sense of community and kinship that is the foundation of many African communities. This means, Africans can aspire for Western materialism without internalizing individualism. Japan, for instance, is not just merely a:

> copy of the West but succeeded to create a highly successful system by simply using what is useful wherever it comes from combined with her own social system. Today, Japan has a better social structure, much lower crime, and a higher standard of living than virtually any "Western" nation. (N'dongko, 1999, p. 102)

The study is divided into five sections. The first section considers the evolution of Western management thought (i.e., historical considerations of organizational management from a Western perspective). The second section discusses African cultural archetypes. The third section looks at the concept of *ubuntu* and current managerial practices in sub-Saharan Africa. The fourth section presents an application prospectus of a Western-oriented, culture-friendly, performance driven model of "governance management" for Africa. This section shows how principles from organizational behavior are valuable for developing an alternative paradigm of management that takes seriously the social and cultural dimensions of Africa, especially ideas of collectivism and respect and dignity that may be at stake. Finally, the study discusses some policy implications of an alternative, social-economy view with suggestions for further research.

Evolution of Western Management Thought

To bring Western management ideas into focus, most of the scholars who have looked into the history and ideology of work, Lipset (1990), Runciman (2001), Taylor (1919), Tsutsui (2001), Tylor (2005), and Werthiem (2004) have drawn attention to the magnificent creations of work as an indication of the proper planning that leads to wonderful results. They believe work in any society is crucial in determining the society's level of economic growth.

And along the way, paradigms to define concept of labor have also evolved over the years. This evolution of paradigms is what Babbage (1969) has described as the "continual progression of labor, [in the form of] knowledge and experience which is also seen as humanity's greatest power" (p. 119). Karl Marx makes sense of this progression and social progress to have evolved to be exploited by capital, and out of which the state and class society has been institutionalized (cited by Quelch, 1995).

With the institutionalization of class society comes with it the different paradigms that have been used to define work patterns to enhance production. Taylorism (1919), for instance, is a science of management that has been a significant part of organizations from the early part of the twentieth century and has been polished by major American corporations for the last ninety years.

Frederick Taylor (1919) wrote *The Principles of Scientific Management* in 1911, these principles became known as Taylorism. Some of the principles of Taylorism include:

- A daily task—each person in every organization should have a clearly defined, large task which should take one day to complete;
- Standard conditions—the worker should have standard tools and conditions to complete the task;
- High pay for success—significant should be paid for successful completion of the task;
- High loss for failure—failure for completing the task should be personally costly;
- Tasks in large sophisticated organizations should be made difficult so as to require skilled, accomplished workers. (Taylor, 1919, p. 53)

Taylorism changed how organizations functioned (Babbage, 1969). By adopting Frederick Taylor's science of management, organizations became hierarchical and fixed (Pruijt, 1997). Manufacturing and office work became split and offices became compartmentalized. However, the sine qua non of Taylorism is that organizations were product or outcome focused, not customer or employee focused (Tsutsui, 2001).

Peter F. Drucker (1993) also made tremendous impact on management thinking and practice worldwide. His management thought, is today most organizations' trusted guide. With his trademark clarity, vision and humanity, Drucker sets out his ideas on a broad swath of key topics and concepts basic to organizations. For example, Drucker (1969, 1988, 1993) touched on issues like dignity and status of the worker, corporate purpose, corporate contribution to and harmonization with community, management compensation and succession, worker training and development, benefits of decentralization, suggestion plans, re-engineering, workers as resources not costs, etc. Unlike Taylor (1919), Drucker (2001) appreciates the importance of "people who work with their minds rather than their hands" (p. 34). Drucker believes a company is its people. Many of the ideas he introduced have long since become popularized and accepted.

By and large, Western nations have witnessed remarkable changes in work environments (Daniels and Daniels, 2004). The legendary management consultants mentioned in this study, Taylor (1919) and Drucker (1969, 1988, 1993), have made their mark in the science of management to show how organizations should be run. Today, technology, corporate restructuring, downsizing, and re-engineering have all had their roles in this evolutionary process and they continue to influence the design and shape of work environments (Mitter and Rowbotham, 1995). Further, network and "systems thinking" (Senge, 1990, p. 23) rather than linearity have recently dominated the debate on innovation when it came to the question whether innovation can be induced by organizational preliminaries. Senge's (1990) *Fifth Discipline* brings word of "learning organizations" (p. 3) organizations—where people continually expand their capacity to create the results they truly desire, where new and expansive patterns of thinking are nurtured, where collective aspiration is set free, and where people are continually learning how to learn together. Fundamental change may also be coming from a cultural shift in how people think about themselves at work (Senge, 1990). The ideal Western or Japanese worker today is entrepreneurial, creative and shows a desire to constantly innovate (Drucker, 1993). A hundred years ago these themes nevertheless manifested in how and where people came together to work (Taylor, 1919). Companies at the turn of the twentieth century had fewer location options and fewer resources, they however learned to modify and make do with what existed (Pruijt, 1997). For many, that meant a family labor pool and a home office. This scenario was better represented by architect Charles Loring in 1930 when he said that "The offices of our grandfathers were without steel frames and files, without elevators and radiators without telephones and without skirts" (cited by Babbage, 1969, p. 52).

African Social and Cultural Archetypes

Africa's pre-colonial past and its people's philosophy of life, expectations, and values of the community are not irrelevant to, but indeed important for understanding the questions of legitimacy of governance in Africa (Saleh, 1985). Africa was known to be the earth's oldest inhabited territory, with fossil evidence of human occupation perhaps as early as 7 million years ago, and an early and an uninterrupted transition from Stone Age to the Iron Age (Davidson, 1969). And Africa was never a unified region, but rather populated by peoples of diverse and differing cultures (Kiggundu, 1991). The great diversity that characterizes her pre-colonial era is the result of the existence of a plethora of small family groups of hunter-gatherers sharing historical and linguistic connections such as the San and Bantu-speaking people of central and southern Africa (Davidson, 1969). Many pan-African scholars consider this historical and linguistic diversity fundamental in their discussions about Africa. These scholars have also argued that current problems of Africa, are in fact, the result of the enslavement and sometimes mass destruction of communities by whites. The scramble by Europeans for African territories in the 1870s they also explain, arbitrarily demarcated Africa without due regard to the diversity that characterizes her pre-colonial era's communo-cultural identities.

People of African descent conceive and suggest a heightened awareness and strong attachment to African cultural values (including ethical values) (Nzelibe, 1986; Prinsloo, 1995; Saleh, 1985). The importance of cultural identity, evidenced by the manifesting pride for continuity of African cultural tradition in contemporary society has been emphasized repeatedly by Griffiths (2004), Asante (1991), N'dongko (1999), Nzelibe (1986), Karenga (1983), and Kiggundu (1991). In large measure, culture determines quality of life for people of African descent. It consists primarily of the symbolic, ideational, and intangible aspects of human societies (Banks, 1989). For Damen (1987) culture is "mankind's primary adaptive mechanism" (p. 367) based on learned and shared human patterns or models for living; which Kroeber and Kluckhohn (1952) describe as "historically created designs for living which exist at any given time as potential guides for the behavior of men" (p. 47). Lederach (1995) somewhat sees "culture [as] the shared knowledge and schemes created by a set of people for perceiving, interpreting, expressing, and responding to the social realities around them" (p. 9).

At the organizational level, it is these symbolic, ideational, learned and shared models and schemes of living prevailing in the larger society that filter through work habits creating new configurations of actors. These shared patterns define the fundamental dissimilarities in value priorities of Western versus African societies that encapsulate them. However, despite the diversity in the African cultural milieu, the persistence of a strong ethical tradition projecting certain common features of African cultures inherited from the African traditional milieu is felt. Kiggundu (1991), Ndaba (1994), Prinsloo (1995) and others have written extensively about the reality of common features across the ethnic diversity and have stressed the sense of communalism and its pervasiveness in African society. A fundamental unity, for instance, is found in cultural ethics and cultural habits (Ndaba, 1994). A unity of human relationship underlies traditional African ethics, and in this regard, African ethics places considerable value on conformity of the individual to the extended family, in order to preserve the unity of human relationship (Prinsloo, 1995).

Also rooted in traditions are the cultural values of the peoples of Africa, i.e. the collective identities that grow out of the values, social realities and life-world of the individuals experiencing them (Kiggungu, 1991). They are linked by shared values that are fundamental features of African identity and culture. So far, preparing a comprehensive "laundry list" of the components of the diverse African cultural patterns would be a task beyond the scope of this KAM. Therefore, the study discusses these cultural patterns in brief under the following sub-headings: respect and morality, the extended family, collectivism and ethnic-based alliances, traditional economic system, deference to authority, and politics.

Respect and Morality

Demonstration of respect and filial piety to elders are the hallmarks of African culture, tradition and moral underpinnings (Ndaba, 1994). Within the African cultural stream, the elder is a wise, dignified, and powerful figure who keeps the culture alive and guides the young (Poole and Van de Ven, 1989). The elder is a treasure of the family and the society, seen as the most authentic expression of Africa's long-standing traditions. Africans truly believe that filial piety is the first of all moral kindness and gratitude (Asante, 1991). The general point is that wisdom has traditionally been associated with old age. Veneration of elders and ancestors is an aspect of African philosophy which pervades the lives of African people and still shapes interpersonal relationships in most African countries (Beugré and Offodile, 1995).

The Extended Family

As in every culture and society, families and communities are important aspects (Elliott and Merrill, 1934). In Africa, it is the extended family system that epitomizes the traditional values of the region (Mangaliso, 2001). The extended family defines the individual as being attached to an ethnic group that involves not merely a sense of psychological belonging but also a sense of sacredness. What is emphasized here of being typical of the extended family is a "primordial attachment" (Geertz, 1963, p. 109) that stems from being born into a particular religious community, speaking a particular language, or even a dialect of a language, and following particular social practices. It describes a traditional inclination to an interconnected and systematic theory of ethnic relations (Triandis, 1989). There is a significant positive obligation of the individual in his or her everyday life in promoting solidarity in families and the well-being of members (Hofestede, 1993).

Collectivism and Ethnic-Based Alliances

African cultures are characteristically collectivist (Triandis, 1989) cultures with tendencies toward "gregariousness and group orientation" (Hofestede, 1984, p. 77). "The traditional African concept of the worth of human beings is based on the communal values of social harmony and solidarity that also emphasize individuals' obligations and duties to their community" (Hofestede, 1984, p. 78). The African communal structure means that the collectivity of people who share the same primordial characteristics such as common ancestry, language, and culture is often nowadays described as ethnicity (Haruna, 2004). Deplorably, however, the African critique against ethnicity has developed into a particular negative connotation to behaviors of individuals to mean cleavages between groups based on differentiations in ethnic identities. "This means that in many cases consensus was desired at the expense of influential opposition, tradition was promoted instead of change, and the commitment to the common good was given priority over the interests of the individual" (Hofestede, 1984, p. 81). This is what some scholars have amounted to describing as institutional backwardness because ethnicity has been compounded by the collectivist delusion of the underdeveloped world during the postcolonial era. The argument is that, collectivism, far from transcending the need for broad-based trust, served only to exacerbate its victims' backwardness (Haruna, 2004).

Traditional Economic System

African cultural structure has the hallmarks of a traditional economic system in which decisions such as the who, how, what, and for whom questions are all made on the basis of customs, beliefs, religion, and habits (Kiggundu, 1991). The system has the foundations of communalist socialist ideals based on the moral foundations of "good political order" (Hofestede, 1984, p. 62) on traditional "tribal" (Triandis, 1989, p. 112) egalitarianism and communalist solidarity, what Julius Nyerere (1968) described in his own political ideology of "Ujamaa or family hood socialism" (p. 37) as "the revival of the past collectivist communalist tradition, the sense of solidarity and the dutiful participation in social cooperation" (p. 39).

Again, deplorably, Africa's traditional economic system is believed by many to restrict individual initiative and has a lack of advanced goods, new technology, and economic growth (Jaeger and Kanungo, 1990). This is evident in an African traditional knowledge system that is constrained from supporting sustained economic growth in the region. Africa's cultural framework based on collectivism which does not appreciate individual innovation is believed to have a negative impact on its traditional economic system (Nyasani, 1997). Collectivist patterns inhibit future innovations because there is little reward or motivation for individual innovation.

> The consequence has been secrecy in the high income sectors such as medicine or indifference in the low income sectors such as medicine or indifference in the low-income sectors such as agriculture. When the innovators die, the knowledge generated is usually lost because they do not have incentive to make the innovations public. (Nyasani, 1997, p. 132)

Putting innovation as a public good, at least in the period of 10 or 15 years, without special compensation to the innovator is unambiguously bad for sustained economic growth and welfare promotion (Nyasani, 1997). No matter how efficiently cultural traditions may contribute to organizational performance, however, their influence is relatively powerless if there is no secure economic base (Jaeger and Kanungo, 1990). Socialization may proceed with the most consummate efficiency, but if the farmers cannot improve their farming techniques, if individual innovation is suppressed for lack of incentives, the community cannot long continue as a functioning and sustainable unit (Hofestede, 1984, 1993).

Deference to Authority and Politics

African cultural patterns are also grounded on unquestionable deference to authority (N'dongko, 1999). Authority in the context of Africa's cultural framework has to do with power, hierarchy, and some whose authority derives from age (Khademian, 2002). Rather than knowledge and specialized skills, deference to authority in Africa is rationalized by virtue of status, age, maturity, strength or office (Mangaliso, 2001). The concept of authority in Africa is thus a vertical political power process introduced at a very early stage and sustained by the very setting of the traditional African family itself (Nyasani, 1997). The general point is that environmental conditioning and long-standing cultural traditions demand submission, hence, "the child in Africa was muzzled right from the outset and was thereby drilled into submission to authority from above" (Nyasani, 1997, p. 129).

Early documentary evidence about Africa's social and cultural life also confirms the fundamental nature of governing by group consensus (Mbigi and Maree, 1995). For example, disputes are resolved through lengthy discussions where all involved have a chance to make their thoughts heard until some agreement is reached (Davidson, 1991). Societies in Africa are largely egalitarian and kinship bonds provide the basic framework for political models (Mangaliso, 2004).

Ecology of *Ubuntu*

Leadership in an African cultural society appears to be ecologically influenced by traditional mores and beliefs (Mangaliso, 2004). The problem of understanding this dynamic aspect of society may be approached from several points of view. Many explanations of an Afro-centric approach to leadership in Africa have been offered by many, but the scope of this study does not permit a consideration of all these hypotheses. However, the Afro-centric approach based on the value system of *ubuntu* will be developed in terms of studies by Kiggundu (1991), Mangaliso (2004), Mbigi (1997), Mbigi and Maree (1995), Nyasani (1997) and Poovan, du Topit, and Engelbrecht (2006).

One of the most dramatic attempts to explain the concept of *ubuntu* was made by Poovan, du Topit, and Engelbrecht (2006) and the subjects who have participated in their intellectual explorations. The study of these researchers and the concept of *ubuntu* which is so closely related to it, both rest upon an understanding of the forces of Africa's culture; particularly, how the cultural patterns present themselves in the management of institutions in the African milieu. It is sufficient for the purpose of this study that Poovan, du Topit, and Engelbrecht depicted with valid and reliable data analysis the dynamic nature of Africa's cultural foundations.

The intellectual device these researchers used as a basis for their dynamic exploration of *ubuntu* is a research method known as open coding. This technique ensures the precision of the research methodology used to ascertain validity and reliability from a solid ethical platform. The principle underlying *ubuntu* they revealed is, very briefly, that "traditional African values, although in congruence with many universal ethical values, place more emphasis upon collectivism, collaboration, caring, dignity and respect" (Poovan, du Topit, and Engelbrecht, 2006, p. 91). It follows that all human institutions in the African milieu, no matter how well organized they may appear to be at any particular period, are subject to influence from the fundamental African mores and traditions which they maintain within themselves. An inevitable conflict is thus bound to arise sooner or later in any society between two contradictory sets of social institutions and cultural alignments (Sansom, 2006). The *ubuntu* process investigated by Poovan, du Topit, and Engelbrecht (2006) therefore considered the impact of traditional African social values on specific characteristics of institutional effectiveness.

> The Nguni word *ubuntu*, from the aphorism; '*Umuntu Ngumuntu Ngabantu*—a person is a person because of or through others', can be described as the capacity in African culture to express compassion, reciprocity, dignity, humanity and mutuality in the interest of building and maintaining communities with justice and mutual caring. (Bekker, cited by Poovan, du Topit, and Engelbrecht, 2006, p. 73)

Since the term *ubuntu* subsumes the whole function and structure of the African society, it includes man and all the ideas, knowledge, traditions, folkways, mores and institutions which have always been part and parcel of the African culture (Ampaw, 1993; Hellsten, 2004; Mangaliso, 2001; Mbigi and Maree, 1995). As Wirth (1940) points out, "there is no society without an ethos, i.e., without shared values, objectives, preferences, and the well-founded anticipation of the members that all the others recognize the rules of the society and will abide by them" (p. 474). *Ubuntu* is therefore that ethos, the totality of human personalities, and the conscious and unconscious attitudes. The most widely accepted classification of the human personalities and values reflected in *ubuntu* is thus made by Mbigi and Maree (1995), and Yukl (2002), classified in terms of survival, solidarity spirit, compassion, respect and dignity to make up the dynamic organization of society in the ecology of *ubuntu*. The nature of these five social values is briefly considered in this study.

Survival

Survival is basic to *ubuntu* and to all social interaction and fundamental to all social organization in the African milieu (Mangaliso, 2004; Mbigi and Maree, 1995; Nussbaum, 2003; Nyasani, 1997; Poovan, du Topit, and Engelbrecht, 2006; Yukl, 2002). It can be said that society not only continues to exist by endurance, by survival, but it may fairly be said to exist in endurance, in survival. Survival of the African people involves brotherly care and common understanding and definition of problems—in the words of Mbigi, "through a collective and collaborative spirit, Africans have developed a shared will to survive" (p. 34). It is this collective and unified tradition that has kept Africa going notwithstanding the deadly odds of dire poverty and the AIDS pandemic (Yukl, 2002).

In view of the organic character of Africans' shared will to survive, it is clear that the chances of team performance are higher (Mangaliso, 2004). Africans collective and collaborative spirit built on networks of social obligations based predominantly on kinship offers the opportunity for mutual engagement and accountability which are building blocks of successful teams in modern organizations (Asante, 1991).

Solidarity Spirit

Survival among people may tend to bring about social harmony and a spirit of solidarity (Sansom, 2006). In times of difficulties people make certain mutual, if impermanent, adjustments whereby they can carry on their various activities (Elliott and Merrill, 1934). For example, it is observed in most "poor African communities in the townships and squatter camps people are obliged to share limited space, food, water and other resources" (Mbigi and Maree, 1995, p. 72). The concept of solidarity spirit may best be understood in the simple terms of its literal derivation—namely, as a process of feeling together by the majority of the members of a given society upon the important matters of their common life (Elliott and Merrill, 1934). This substantial unanimity of opinion is a product of "bonds of solidarity, which to an African consist of interpersonal, biological and non-biological bonds, are created and maintained through spiritual values" (Yukl, 2002, p. 32).

The value of solidarity spirit and the team characteristic of cohesion as it has been presented are the tendencies of members of a group to act in mutual affection and attraction (Yukl, 2002). According to Mbigi and Maree (1995), "the solidarity tendency could be the basis of building a culture of empowerment and teamwork in the workplace" (p. 5). The *ubuntu* value has the ability to create a bond between team members because it places emphasis on the achievement of tasks collectively rather than individually.

Compassion

The phenomenon of compassion is another fundamental social value of *ubuntu* (Nussbaum, 2003). Compassion is a social step toward mitigating the disorganizing effects of dilemmas of others (Elliott and Merrill, 1934). In the African milieu, there is a primary need among African people to work out ways and means for utilizing their creative energy to the end that they and others will possess a more abundant life (Poole and Van de Ven, 1989). The underlying belief amongst Africans is that all should work for each other in any human economy. Among African leaders, Julius Nyerere (1968) presents such compassionate socialism as the heritage of his own political ideology of Ujamaa or family hood socialism. In his political thought, Nyerere depicts "the sense of solidarity and the dutiful participation in social cooperation" (Nyerere, 1968, p. 112).

The effect of the social value of compassion and the characteristic of *ubuntu* will inevitably yield certain values and truths based upon the universality of human experience (Mangaliso, 2001). Helpfulness towards others creates a climate of collegiality that is based on sharing and caring (Nyerere, 1968). With a value such as compassion, the leader and team members can create a culture that promotes a vision that is shared. All members will be directed towards a shared vision because they experience belongingness in the same social network.

Respect and Dignity

The trend of respect and dignity is, in a sense, a conscious "consideration and regard for rights, values, beliefs and property" (Yukl, 2002, p. 27). Respect, from whatever point of view it is considered, is basic to understanding the African cultural society. In the midst of changing processes due to foreign influence on Africa's traditions, people cling tenaciously to certain folkways, mores, attitudes, values and ideologies (Mangaliso, 2004). These demands which the group imposes upon its members impart a certain consistency and stability to human activities and by upholding these standards members of society become dignified through respect (Pinsloo, 1995). These are the mores of society that possess an ethical sanction, also described as "the folkways with a philosophy of social welfare attached" (Yukl, 2002, p. 14) which carry the implication of the greater importance to the well-being of the group. In the African cultural milieu, therefore, the mores remain as the absolute standard to which the individual must conform if he is to remain a respectable member of the functioning group (Mbigi and Maree, 1995).

It is apparent that the process of social organization is reinforced by the "positive expectation that another will not—through words, actions or decisions—act opportunistically to one's detriment" (Robbins, 1999, p. 336). This unifying attitude is primarily the result of individual trust which the *ubuntu* values of respect and dignity reveal. These are cardinal social values in Africa's collectivist theory which states that it is "only through respecting others and according them dignity that one gains the trust of others" (Yukl, 2002, p. 17).

Post-Colonial Managerial Patterns in Africa

The breakdown of the social equilibrium in Africa may be considered from several points of view, but in this study the developed-developing world dichotomy with reference to the work of Blunt and Jones (1992), Jaeger and Kanungo

(1990), and Kamara (2006) will be discussed. The power relationships as embodied in the distinction made between "Western" management styles and work habits (teamwork, empowerment, etc.) and "African" styles and work habits (centralized, bureaucratic, authoritarian, etc.) are considered (Blunt and Jones, 1992).

A large share of Africa's social and political anarchy is laid directly at the door of the evil philosophies of slavery and colonialism. Modern Africa may therefore be considered from the standpoint of a post-colonial heritage, reflecting a theory X style of management (McGregor, 1960) "which generally mistrusts human nature with a need to impose controls on workers, allowing little worker initiative, and rewarding a narrow set of skills simply by financial means" (p. 67). The pathological manifestations of a system, namely a monolithic system of management that is discernible throughout Africa, and even throughout the "developing" world, is comparatively a recent residue of the management processes from a colonial heritage (Blunt and Jones, 1992).

The ecological aspects of organizational disabilities in Africa are manifest in lack of results and objectives orientation (Kiggundu, 1989). Typically, an inadequate utilization of capacity and lack of clear mission statement or sense of direction are general characteristics of the local organizational behavior.

The ecology of organizational disability in Africa is further illustrated in governance and decision making processes that are authoritarian and paternalistic (Kanungo and Jaeger, 1990). Communities are dominated by an institutional leadership model that is consistent with an authoritarian hierarchy style that emphasizes on control mechanisms, rules and procedures rather than performance. The importance of kinship networks is a powerful agency in introducing that authoritarian hierarchy which augments the eventual disorganization within institutions (Kiggundu, 1989).

Under the existing circumstances of organizational anarchy, of social turmoil in sub-Saharan Africa in particular, public and private sector institutions have been widely criticized as being too large, bureaucratic and change resistant (Blunt and Jones, 1992). High levels of corruption and unethical behaviors among actors are also characteristics of the organizational anarchy and social turmoil jeopardizing the status quo in sub-Saharan Africa. The lack of clear objectives, over-staffing, lack of job descriptions and job evaluation, lack of incentives, and political interference, as well as poor infrastructure and lack of systems are again some of the institutional inefficiencies identified by the Kiggundu, Jorgensen, and Hafsi's (1983) study and well documented by Dia (1993). Other observations also reveal burdens of over-staffing, underutilizations, poor pay and poor morale indicated by high turnover and absenteeism (Blunt and Jones, 1992).

Another index of institutional disorganization is given in the characterization of management principles observed to be related "to an external locus of control where events are considered not within the individual's control, where creative potential is regarded as being limited, and people are generally fixed in their ways and not malleable or changeable" (Kanungo and Jaeger, 1990).

Notwithstanding the differences in cultural environments or the different approaches taken by various management scholars in the likes of Drucker (1993), Goldratt (2004), Mangaliso (2004), Selznick, (1957), Senge (1990), Simon (1976), Nzelibe (1986), Blunt and Jones (1992), and Taylor (1919); these scholars agree that for work to produce results the right habits must be nurtured. Work habits have therefore been understood to be critical to the survival and prosperity of civilizations (Lipset, 1990). The study by Kamara (2006) thus uncovers knowledge about a correlation between good and bad independent variables of work habits. The evidence the study supports is viewed from a perspective of social change that societal development and growth are greater and achievable where standards of work habits are higher. Most of the significant cross-cultural differences in perception of work habits' effectiveness appear to be consistent with differences in cultural values and traditions. The Western participants (workers in Britain and America) in the study had similar ratings on most of the survey items for which there were significant cross-cultural differences compared to the African subjects (workers in Botswana and Sudan). In general, western workers had a higher evaluation of benefits and job climate, and basic work habits in terms of dependability, initiative and ability to meet deadlines. Notwithstanding the differences, "culture to perform, culture to learn, contribute, add value and enhance [institutional] or shareholder value is an organizational expectation for the individuals of the future" (Raelin, 2006, p. 56) and ought to be a model for all cultures, be they African or Western.

Application System of a "Governance Management" Model for Africa

"Institutions do not operate in a social vacuum. Any institution can be understood only as a part of the social matrix [or the prevailing conditions] in which it functions" (Elliot and Merrill, 1934, p. 805). The disorganized institution may therefore be considered as a manifestation of the culture patterns in that society. There is thus the need to understand the impersonal nature of the forces involved in organizational behavior if any successful reform of institutions and practices is to be undertaken. Common definitions of governance in Africa can be built up and common attitudes and values in the field of organizational behavior can only be realized by some intelligent appreciation of the real nature of the governance process.

A synthesis between local cultures and modern management techniques is an opportunity for social change (Mangaliso, 2004); a process that Beugré and Offodile (2001) described as a "culture-fit model" (p. 543), i.e. the assimilation of integrated Western management tools and techniques with Africa's cultural frameworks. The model suggests that if some of the local values or behaviors have to be changed to suit Western technical systems that have been proven to work, it has to be done. Of course, this cannot be accomplished without dissent.

It is an expected pattern in any given society for many to oppose every new development, no matter how suitable or necessary it may seem to the observer (Elliott and Merrill, 1934). The most recalcitrant citizen may eventually, however, yield to the weight of evident need or perhaps to group pressure. Public responsibility for human need comes to be accepted. The new way of doing things becomes, however, reluctantly, the accepted way and is incorporated in the mores. Each generation will tend to accept what seems valid in the old mores and work out new schemes for meeting new emergencies (Elliott and Merrill, 1934).

The creation and application of knowledge in new ways to improve organizational performance in sub-Saharan Africa is therefore at the heart of the application system of a "Governance Management" Model for Africa (see Figure 6.1. Application System of "Governance Management" Model in photospread). The application system includes not only research and synthesis of management knowledge, but also the dissemination, commercialization and application of management knowledge using technology. The application system of a "Governance Management" Model for Africa consists of four elements:

- Management knowledge and culture reservoir: Western management practices and Africa's structures of domination and influence/social values of *Ubuntu*
- Research
- Technology for good governance
- Commercialization or application

Components of the Management Knowledge and Culture Reservoir

The synthesis and application of management knowledge entails the integration of positive African cultural frameworks and proven modern organizational management practices. Much of Africa's society today is being infected by an irresponsible blame-game virus, a blame-game trap. Failing nations in Africa often blame slavery and colonialism for their lack of advancement without accepting personal responsibility for their own failures (Ayittey, 1998; Isakson, 2001). The traditional temptation to blame someone else—that the problems of Africa lie with the actions of others—must therefore be given up. Political colonialism ended over forty years ago. Africans must therefore draw strength from their collectivist culture and productively utilize it to set aside differences and look toward a common future. When standards of civic interest make this a cultural compulsive, stripped of local cultural biases and prejudices about the past, latent patterns of individual inefficiencies may be eliminated (Beugré and Offodile, 2001). Valuing good governance in sub-Saharan Africa, certainly a component of any development program (World Bank, 2001), can thus be transformed in the traditional cultural climate into a celebration of characteristics assumed to be inherent to management's principle universal nature—i.e., strong and visionary leadership, quality management, management by objectives, total quality management (TQM), just-in-time (JIT) and the critical chain management methodologies, employee empowerment, and performance-based compensation system.

Strong and Visionary Leadership

Leadership itself should aim at getting the job done (Bennis and Nanus, 1985), since governance education finds efficient ways to get jobs done. An even more concrete indication and core contextual condition of the role of visionary leadership style in generating or controlling efficiency in developing nations is shown by its relationship to recognizing problems and solving them (Bass and Aviolo, 1994).

Leaders who support and develop others, ask challenging questions, are willing to be learners themselves, see possibilities and make things happen, facilitate learning environments (Cohen and Austin, 1997). Leadership styles in sub-Saharan Africa must change to meet the development needs in developing democracies trapped in a poverty sustained by chronic corruption (Sachs, 2004). The discussion turns logically to a consideration of the direct influence of strong leadership on change and building capacity in others and to evaluate their own conduct. In this way, strong and visionary leadership is about leading by example, communicating organizational values and following them, and facilitating innovative practice (Bennis and Nanus, 1985; Deutschman, 2001). The goals of visionary leadership are realized by influencing and persuading others; guiding and setting an example (Keehley, Longmire, and MacBride, 1996). Visionary leadership's fulfilled core values of being able to show both a "hard" and a "soft" style of leadership in establishing learning and fostering sustainable social change remain the basic political values on which any contemporary progressive society must rely (French and Raven, 1958). "Hard" and "soft" leadership concern with forcefully changing structures and altering "ways-of-doing things" by being strongly guiding and directing in terms of vision and opportunities; and being encouraging and compassionate respectively (Machiavelli, 1950; van Eyk et al., 2001). By being the hard and soft leader should serve as what Machiavelli (1950) might have termed the "axis" for evaluating the various leadership strategies and ideas generated by other leadership and organizational change theorists. In this connection, the study of Machiavelli is therefore most instructive. Machiavelli's (1950) theory speaks of a prudent leader should be able "to disguise [his] character well, and to be a great feigner and dissembler" (p. 93).

A strong and visionary leadership, therefore, is one capable of identifying all necessary facets for success and works toward evaluating the alignment of these facets (Fleishman, Harris and Burtt, 1955). This point is significant in establishing expectations (French and Raven, 1958). It is also reasonable to expect that African cultural patterns which are grounded on unquestionable deference to authority would help make the difficult easier. Africans' environmental conditioning and long-standing cultural traditions which demand submission (Kiggundu, Jorgensen, and Hafsi, 1983) should be wisely exploited by a strong and visionary leader to maintain a stronger national culture of governance that is capable of enforcing laws and of adopting proven management techniques. Some of these management techniques are quality management, management by objectives, performance-based compensation, empowered performance, triple constraints management methodologies, and belief systems.

Quality Management

The general patterns of organizational trends in Africa show that most African organizations suffer from poor quality management—i.e. production inefficiencies and costly manufacturing and distribution systems, and broken service industries (Triandis, 1989). Quality management is the combination of two fields: quality management and project management. "Quality has been defined as "the totality of characteristics of an entity that bear on its ability to satisfy stated or implied needs" (Kloppenborg and Petrick, 2002, p. 47). Quality management is a field popularized by the Japanese used to optimize the performance excellence of organizations. The field involves theories and statistical methods for assessing, improving, and maintaining quality. Control charts, acceptance sampling techniques, and economic analysis tools are foundations of modern quality assurance activity (Deming, 1993; Juran, 1995). The Japanese captured significant global market shares of the automobile, machine tool, electronics and computer industries, in large part due to the application of quality management processes. "The integration of these quality approaches at all organizational levels was referred to as Total Quality Management (TQM) in the 1990s, and continues today" (Kloppenborg and Petrick, 2002, p. 49).

At the same time that quality management was developing, many events led to the need for better project management. Quality is a focus of project management (Kloppenborg and Petrick, 2002). Formal project management techniques which are systematic and standard approaches include needs to address cost, schedule, scope, and quality concerns (Deming, 1993). The use of project management teams to implement quality management process improvements, better scheduling techniques, decentralized change management and risk management decisions favor project management structures. When the performance criteria drive a project, the technically oriented project manager often feels that quality is in the driver's seat (Deming, 1993; Juran, 1995; Kloppenborg and Petrick, 2002).

Work performance in a quality environment thus includes accomplishing tasks and taking initiatives above and beyond the call of duty, along with sharing information with and helping co-workers (Deming, 1993; Kloppenborg and Petrick, 2002). This performance is typically referred to as "organizational citizenship behavior (OCB)" (Kloppenborg and Petrick, 2002, p. 53). It also includes making effective use of just-in-time practices reflected in every aspect of the organization, particularly in the production planning and control system, including inventory control, shop-floor control production, planning, purchasing, capacity planning, and distribution planning to simplify management processes (Deming, 1993; Juran, 1995; Kloppenborg and Petrick, 2002).

Management by Objectives

Management by objectives is another well-known approach to leading an organization. One of the ingredients of management by objectives is the mission statement (Dobson, 2002). The mission statement defines the organization. From the overall mission statement for the organization, each level of management develops specific mission statements for its own part of the mission. These objectives are turned into specific action lists and measurement criteria (Dobson, 2002; Kloppenborg and Petrick, 2002; See Figure 6.2. Managing Project Quality).

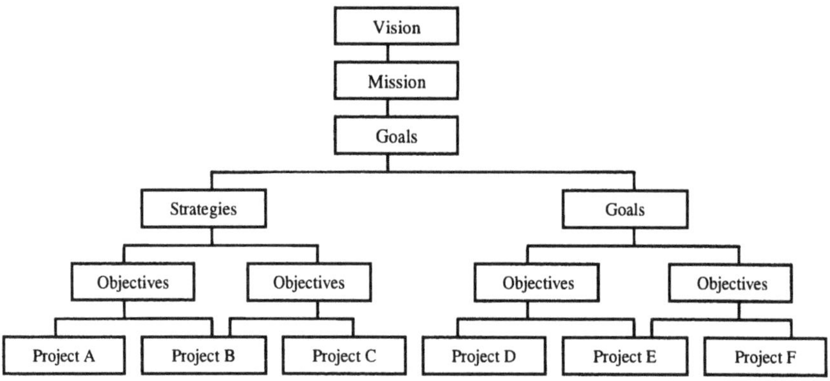

Figure 6.2. Projects link an organization's vision to strategy and results in the management by objectives approach. Source: Kloppenborg, T. J., and J. A. Petrick. *Managing Project Quality.* Virginia: Management Concepts, 2002.

Performance-based Compensation System

Developing a performance-based culture that values a direct link between work and compensation ensures a new mentality, "implying that rewards come through effort and hard work, rather than organizational politics" (Dobson, 2002, p. 54). Performance-based compensation may ultimately inspire empowered, committed, and principled performance in public employment. In addition to monetary rewards, social motivational techniques through "recognition celebrations and reward ceremonies are appropriate vehicles for reinforcing good project performance and empowering future performance" (Kloppenborg and Petrick, 2002, p. 93) of individual stakeholders (employees) in the organization. Enhancing self-respect and self-esteem, an absolute standard to which the individual must conform in the African cultural milieu, is key in motivating a workforce (Poovan, du Topit, and Engelbrecht, 2006).

Empowered Performance

Africa also needs leadership that is facilitative, aiming to mobilize all the skills, good will and know-how at the disposal of public servants. These qualities of the leader(s) are inextricably linked with the empowerment of public staff. Several scholars (Daniels and Daniels, 2004; Locke and Schweiger, 1979; Neuman, 1989; Yukl, 2002) have underscored the importance of empowerment by participation in influencing employee attitudes and behaviors. Participation provides role-expanding opportunities for individuals (Aviolo and Gardner, 2005; Neuman, 1989) from an organizational performance standpoint. The opportunity to speak up and be heard therefore indicates human resource respect for people and commitment to building community at work (Daniels and Daniels, 2004). Since most traditional African cultures encourage participation, such a management technique is not totally alien or threatening for African organizations.

Triple Constraints Management Methodologies

As leaders in Sub-Saharan Africa take up arms against a sea of organizational management troubles, they know they are pitting their brains, their hearts, and their nerves against the triple constraints of time, cost, and performance (Dobson, 2002). But why do it the hard way? African leaders and managers should just stand on the shoulders of giants, as Isaac Newton (Gleick, 2003) first observed, and they have the opportunity and the privilege of using what these giants have developed to get their jobs done. "Good managers borrow [ideas], great ones steal [them]. That is how a project management body of knowledge [evolved] in the first place: real-life project managers confronting real-life challenges sharing their tools and solutions" (Dobson, 2002, p. 71). The tools and solutions they shared have provided the opportunity to excavate hidden resources and opportunities within each project. "Unlocking, [for instance,] the mysteries of critical path, [managers are able to] find slack and the ability to reallocate resources. Through effective risk planning, [they] eliminate many problems before they have a chance to occur" (Dobson, 2002, p. 71).

Belief Systems

The extent to which traditional belief systems in Africa help to stem corruption has never been entirely researched. However, an analysis of the centrality of the *isangoma*, or traditional healer in employee's well-being maintenance in South Africa disclosed salient facts (Mangaliso, 2004). Some companies in South Africa are reported to have taken full advantage of the power of the *isangomo* as the following real-life case illustrates.

> Faced with large-scale pilfering, one company tried everything—including peer monitors, fingerprinting, and police investigations—to stop it. After all efforts to stop the pilfering had failed, the CEO finally called in an *isangoma*. The *isangoma* told the employees that the person who had stolen the goods would die from a spell cast on all employees if he/she did not confess within 24 hours. Within eight hours, an employee confessed. In this case, foreign-evolved management tactics, such as peer control, police investigations, and fingerprinting, did not work. (Mangaliso, 2004, p. 30)

Though management and the workers came from entirely different worldviews, the successful strategy engaged employees in their own worldview. In the broadest sense, if a large proportion of the workforce believes in the existence of meso-cosmic spirits, it would be strategic to retain the services of *isangomas*. By retaining the services of company *isangomas*, or commissioning *isangomas* as paid commissioners in Anti-Corruption Commissions to help address corruption in Africa would result in mutually beneficial outcomes for governments and public servants (and the *isangomas*).

Technology for Good Governance

With instantaneous communication and with enormous increases in contacts, the interests of civilized peoples can now effortlessly overlap (Magno and Serafica, 2000). Science has therefore made possible the most important of material peace-time developments. The mobilization of information technology (IT) is thus deemed crucial in fostering competitive development in the context of a rapidly changing global economy. "Increasingly, strong IT capacity is perceived to make a difference not only in the marketplace but also in the field of governance" (Magno and Serafica, 2000, p. 5). Governance could be seen in broad terms as a system for steering and coordinating collective action. New modes of policy consultation should be experimented to improve citizen engagement in the policy deliberation process. Information tools such as electronic web sites should be utilized to allow various stakeholders to present their perceptions on cultural and management issues. Democratic politics could be enhanced by increasing transparency and accountability, as well as facilitating accurate decision-making and public participation (Magno and Serafica, 2000; OECD Papers, 2006).

In this regard, an all-Africa web portal as a super forum for the discussion and exchange of governance experiences will allow an active debate on culture and development in Africa. The portal should provide entries where people are afforded the opportunity to discuss the various cultural archetypes of Africa, ask questions, provide suggestions and take positions on whether some cultural mores are worth holding to or Africa will be better of eradicating them. A portal of this nature thus has the advantage of accelerating the speed for conducting public consultations (Magno and Serafica, 2000). Concerned stakeholders would be able to express their opinions directly through the net and could also be an information network linking various research institutions, international and local organizations, other government agencies and ultimately, the local end users.

Commercialization and Application

Commercialization and application involves: 1) the development of technology-based products and services based on new knowledge technologies that will help institutions increase operating efficiencies and revenue collection; 2) facilitation of efficient operations by using new technology to support management processes like quality management, management by objectives, and the triple constraints management methodologies; and 3) government and nongovernmental organizations that apply new knowledge and technology to enhance social, cultural, and environmental quality of life.

Development of technology-based products will therefore help countries in Africa to become knowledge societies. Commercialization and application will support governance in Africa through innovative product development, also supporting goals and broad strategies for use of IT in government as well as in other aspects of the economy.

Conclusion

Out of the morass of dismal management and degenerate corruption in most sub-Saharan African countries (Ayittey, 1992, 1998) has come the acute recognition of the societal demoralization and stagnation entailed in this study. Even in societies with unlimited natural abundance, the society that is ill-managed faces a discouraging outlook that induces a liking for idleness and self-indulgence, impairs creative and technical skills, and creates a tendency to blame others for failures (Elliott and Merrill, 1934). The ultimate goal, therefore, is to inculcate competence-based management practices that emphasize delivery of service needed for development, and rewards or sanctions reflecting performance and merit. A strong and visionary leadership can be trusted to determine what cultures are conducive to better management practices and what represents a threat to basic public administration. As the study shows, any civil service reform cannot be disengaged from the issues of improved governance as they affect accountability, rule of laws, and transparency. The study, therefore, argues the case for a governance approach to civil service reform on the basis of a framework for a "governance management" model. This approach contends that management practice in sub-Saharan Africa must integrate modern management techniques and traditional cultural values in order to raise organizational performance to efficient standards and minimize the incidence of lethargy and corruption.

The "governance management" model approach can therefore be adapted to work with the alternative approaches previously considered in various World Bank (2001, 2003) studies for dealing with different aspects of the civil service riddle. These approaches include:

- The comprehensive institutional approach on effecting structural and functional changes needed to correct the patrimonial distortions affecting the performance of core government functions;

- The enclave technical approach on building or reinforcing the organizational, managerial and technical capacity that will improve the performance of existing institutions; and

- The hybrid of the comprehensive institutional and the enclave technical approaches, building on their strengths.

Implications for Research

Development in Africa has been an illusion and it has not been associated with the progression of a high degree of political accountability, and this may well continue to be the case (Bongyu, 2006; Davidson, 1992). Even the well-governed parts of tropical Africa, is stuck in a "poverty trap, too poor to achieve robust, high levels of economic growth and, in many places, simply too poor to grow at all" (Sachs, 2004, p. 123). Specifically, Sachs' (2004) findings illustrate the complementary roles of low national saving rates and negative economic growth rates; the dismal health conditions which are by far the worst on the planet, and the soaring population which are adding ecological stresses to the economic strain. The overall tone of this diagnosis of Africa may be pessimistic, albeit justified. The point is, the vicious poverty cycle could only be avoided when policy makers create self-reliant systems with checks and balances and massive commitment (Sachs, 2004).

The conceptual culture-fit model of Beugré and Offodile (2001) which proposes to amalgamate modern management techniques into indigenous cultures in sub-Saharan Africa is also a laudable direction. Blecher (2006), Kiggundu (1991), Mangaliso (2001) have made similar insights on building African leadership attempts to move beyond the (often ideologically driven) theses on the role of leadership in African societies by focusing on visionary leadership that incorporates a spirit of *ubuntu*. In doing so, Blecher (2006) develops a definition of visionary leadership as a pattern of decisions and actions made with the primary (although not exclusive) purpose of enhancing social welfare through "authentic leadership, grounded in Africa" (para. 2).

However, it is recommended that the application of any "culture-fit" model or any model of "governance management" has to be supported by strong and visionary leadership, which is a fundamental argument of this study. A "state-society synergy, that [suggests strict and authoritarian] governments and mobilized communities can enhance each other's developmental efforts" (Evans, 1995, p. 178), is strongly suggested to start reversing the dismal trends of underachievement in Africa. The use of power to good ends which characterizes today's Machiavellian duels in politics and in corporations, even in charitable not-for-profit institutions (McAlpine, 1999) is suggested. The focal point of Machiavelli's (1950) work is built on suggestions of specific action points for strong and stable governance. Machiavelli's reasoning is that good leadership makes people peaceful and obedient to rule.

Inopportunely, however, the cultural argument is raised whenever the underachievement of Africa's institutions is debated. But, whether culture can actually facilitate or inhibit development is a subject that has not been adequately covered by experts in sociology and anthropology. This is because most experts disagree as to whether culture matters. Political philosophy, nationalistic bias, educational background, psychological training, religious affiliation, and all other factors which influence opinion affect the scholars who make pronouncements on culture and the indigenous African workplace (Kroeber and Kluckhohn, 1952). Some scholars even romanticize Africa's cultural past by arguing that "Africa's ancient empires, such as Ghana, Mali, Songhai, and Oyo, are known to have had complex economic infrastructures and large-scale armies, which developed some modern management concepts" (Nzelibe, 1986, p. 43). Most common is the pervasive argument that the development of the principles of management in Africa was disrupted by contact with the Western world, contact marked by decades of economic exploitation, and social oppression (N'dongko, 1999; Nzelibe, 1986). The point is, it is difficult to turn the clock back to pre-colonial times, but it may be possible to more fully integrate the positive African cultural mores and proven principles in the management of organizations to create sustainable "learning organizations" (Senge, 1990, p. 37) in Africa. Social scientists, in collaboration with management experts, should therefore start looking into what cultural underpinnings may contribute to Africa's development and how these opportunities can be included in Africa's development processes; and what other cultural issues may be the cause of Africa's underachievement, and how these threats can be excluded from Africa's development processes. After all, "cultures change, cultures adapt, and cultures are ambiguous" (Elliott and Merrill, 1934, p. 59).

Bibliography

Ampaw, Akoto. "Empowerment and the Limits of Political Liberalism." *Empowering People: Building Community, Civil Associations and Legality in Africa,* 189–97. Toronto: University of Toronto, Centre for Urban and Community Studies, 1993.

Artadi, Elsa Vila., and Xavier Sala-i-Martin. "The Economic Tragedy of the Twentieth Century: Growth in Africa." *The Africa Competitiveness Report* (2004): 1–17.

Asante, Molefi K. *Afrocentricity.* Trenton, NJ: Africa World Press, 1991.

Avolio, Bruce, and William J. Gardner, "Authentic Leadership Development: Getting to the Root of Positive Forms of Leadership." *The Leadership Quarterly,* 16, no. 3 (2005): 315–338.

Avolio, Bruce J., William L. Gardner, Fred O. Walumbwa, Fred Luthans, and Douglas R. May. "Unlocking the Mask: A Look at the Process by Which Authentic Leaders Impact Follower Attributes and Behaviors." *The Leadership Quarterly* 15 (2004): 801–23.

Ayittey, George B. N. *Africa in Chaos: A Comparative History.* New York: St. Martin's Press, 1998.

———. *Africa Betrayed.* New York: St. Martin's Press, 1992.

Babbage, Charles. *Passages from the Life of a Philosopher* (Martin Campbell-Kelly, ed.). Farnborough, Hants., UK: Gregg International, 1969.

Bahemuka, J. M., and J. L. Brockingdon. *East Africa in Transition: Images, Institutions and Identities.* Nairobi: University of Nairobi Press, 2004.

Banks, J. A., Banks, and C. A. McGee. *Multicultural Education.* Needham Heights, MA: Allyn & Bacon, 1989.

Barczak, Gloria, Edward F. McDonough, and Nicholas Athanassiou. "So You Want to Be a Global Leader?" *Research Technology Management,* 49, no. 3 (2006): 28–35.

Bass, Bernard M., and Bruce J. Avolio. *Improving Organizational Performance through Transformational Leadership.* London: Sage, 1994.

Bennis, Warren G., and Burt Nanus. *Strategies for Taking Charge.* NY: Harper Collins, 1985.

Beugré, Constant D., and O. Felix Offodile. (2001). "Managing for Organizational Effectiveness in Sub–Saharan Africa: A Culture-Fit Model." *International Journal of Human Resource Management,* 12, no. 4 (2001): 535–50.

Blecher, Taddy. "Building African Leadership." *Finweek* 1 (2006): 98.

Blunt, Peter, and Merrick L. Jones. *Managing Organizations in Africa.* New York: Walter De Gruyter, 1992.

Bongyu, Moye G. "African Underdevelopment: From Policy Failure to Policy Failure." *PA Times,* 29, no. 7 (2006): 5–8.

Burns, James M. *Leadership.* New York: Harper, 1978.

Coase, Ronald H. *The Firm, the Market, and the Law.* Chicago: University of Chicago Press, 1990.

Cohen Burton J., and Michael J. Austin. "Transforming Human Services Organizations Through Empowerment of Staff." *Journal of Community Practice* 4, no. 2 (1997): 35–50

Courpasson, David. "Managerial Strategies of Domination: Power in Soft Bureaucracies." *Organization Studies* 21, no. 1 (2000): 141–61.

Damen, Louise. *Culture Learning: The Fifth Dimension on the Language Classroom.* Reading, MA: Addison-Wesley, 1987.

Daniels, Aubrey C., and James E. Daniels. *Performance Management: Changing Behavior that Drives Organizational Effectiveness.* n.p.: Performance Management Publications, 2004.
Davidson, Basil. *The Black Man's Burden: The Curse of the Nation State.* London: James Currey, 1992.
———. *African Civilization Revisited.* Trenton, NJ: Africa World Press, 1991.
———. *The African Genius: An Introduction to African Cultural and Social History.* Boston, Toronto: Atlantic Monthly Press, 1969.
Deming, W. Edwards. *Quality, Productivity, and Competitive Position.* n.p.: Quality Enhancement Seminars, 1993.
Deutschman, Marian. "Re-defining quality and excellence in the nursing home culture." *Journal of Gerontological Nursing* 27, no. 8 (2001): 28–36.
Dobson, Michael S. *The Triple Constraints in Project Management.* Virginia: Management Concepts, 2002.
Dia, Mamadou. "A Governance Approach to Civil Service Reform in Sub-Saharan Africa." *Africa Technical Department Series,* 225. Washington, DC: The World Bank, 1993.
———. "Development and Cultural Values in Sub–Saharan Africa." *Finance and Development* (December 1991): 10–13.
Drucker, Peter F. (1993). *The Practice of Management.* CA: Collins.
———. "Management and the World's Work." *Harvard Business Review* (1988): 65–76.
———. "Management's New Role." *Harvard Business Review* (1969): 49–54.
Elliott, Mabel A., and Francis E Merrill. *Social Disorganization.* New York: Harper & Brothers, 1934.
Esfahani, Hadui. S., and Maria. T. Ramirez. "Institutions, Infrastructure, and Economic Growth." *Journal of Development Economics,* 70 (2003): 443–77.
Fleishman, Edwin A., Edwin F. Harris, and Harold E. Burtt. *Leadership and Supervision in Industry.* Columbus, OH: Ohio State University, Bureau of Educational Research, 1955.
Folger, Robert, and Daniel P. Skarlicki. "Unfairness and Resistance to Change: Hardship as Mistreatment." *Journal of Organizational Change Management* 12 (1999): 35–50.
French John, and Bertram H. Raven. "Bases of Social Power." *Studies in Social Power* (1958): 150–67.
Geertz, Clifford. *Old Societies and New States: The Quest for Modernity in Asia and Africa.* IL: Free Press, 1963.
Gleick, James. *Isaac Newton.* New York: Pantheon, 2003.
Goduka, I. N. (1996). "Challenges to Traditionally White Universities: Affirming Diversity in the Curriculum." *South African Journal Higher of Education* 10, no. 1 (1996): 27–36.
Goldratt, Eliyahu M. *The Goal: A Process of Ongoing Improvement.* MA: North River Press, 2004.
Griffiths, Stephanie. "The Spirit of 'ubuntu'." *Communication World,* 21, no. 4 (2004): 46–46.
Graham, Harrison. "The World Bank, Governance and Theories of Political Action in Africa." *BJPIR,* 7 (2005): 240–60.
Haruna, Peter F. (2004). "Rethinking Administrative Globalization: Promises, Dilemmas, and Lessons in Ghana." *Administrative Theory & Praxis* 26, no. 2 (2004): 185–212.
Hellsten, Sirkku K. "Human Rights in Africa: From Communitarian Values to Utilitarian Practice." *Human Rights Review* 5, no. 2 (2004): 61–85.

Hofstede, Geert. Cultural Constraints in Management Theories." *Academy of Management Executive*, 7 , no. 1 (1992): 81–94.

———. "National Cultures and Corporate Cultures." *Communication Between Cultures.* Belmont, CA: Wadsworth, 1984.

Hope, Kempe R. "Toward Good Governance and Sustainable Development: The African Peer Review Mechanism." *Governance* 18, no. 2 (2005): 283–311.

Isaksson, Anders. "Financial Liberalization, Foreign Aid, and Capital Mobility: Evidence From 90 Developing Countries." *Journal of International Financial Market, Institutions and Money* 11 (2001): 309–38.

Jaeger, Alfred M., and Rabindra N. Kanungo. *Management in Developing Countries.* London: Routledge, 1990.

Jung, Carl. *The Spirit in Man, Art, & Literature (The Collected Works of C. G. Jung),* Vol. 13. ed. Adler, G.; Read, H.; and W. McGuire, 1996.

Juran, Joseph M. *Managerial Breakthrough.* NY: McGraw-Hill, 1995.

Kamara, K. S. Survey Analysis: *Work Habits and Organizational Performance in Western and African Work Environments.* Knowledge Area Module II. Walden University, 2006.

Kaufmann, Daniel, Aart Kraay, and Pablo Zoido-Lobatón. *Governance Matters.* Washington, DC: Policy Research Working Paper 2196. n.p.: 1999.

Keehley, Patricia, Laura Longmire, and Sue A. MacBride. *Benchmarking for Best Practices in the Public Sector: Achieving Performance Breakthroughs in Federal, State, and Local Agencies* (97th ed.). San Francisco: Jossey–Bass, 1996.

Khademian, Anne M. *Working with Culture: The Way the Job Gets Done in Public Programs.* Public Affairs and Policy Administration Series. NY: CQ Press, 2002.

Kiggundu, Moses N. "The Challenges of Management Development in Sub-Saharan Africa." *Journal of Management Development* 10, no. 6 (1991): 32–47.

Kiggundu, Moses N., Jan J. Jorgensen, and Taieb Hafsi. "Administrative Theory and Practice in Developing Countries: A Synthesis." *Administrative Science Quarterly,* 28 (1983): 66–84.

Kloppenborg, Timothy J., and Joseph A. Petrick. *Managing Project Quality.* Virginia: Management Concepts, 2002.

Marx, Karl. *Das Kapital,* edited by Frederick Engels. Lanham, MD: National Book Network, 1996.

Mitter, Swasti, and Sheila Rowbotham. *Women Encounter Technology: Changing Patterns of Employment in the Third World.* The United Nations University. New York: Routledge, 1995.

Lederach, John P. *Preparing for Peace: Conflict Transformation across Cultures.* Syracuse, NY: Syracuse University Press, 1995.

Lipset, Seymour M. "The Work Ethic—Then and Now." *Public Interest* (1990): 61–9.

Locke, E. A., and D. M. Schweiger. "Participation in Decision Making: One More Look." *Research in Organizational Behavior* 1 (1979): 265–339.

Lunnan, Randi, Jon E. B. Lervik, Laura E. M. Traavik, Sølvi M. Nilsen, Rolv Petter Amdam, and Bjørn W. Hennestad. "Global Transfer of Management Practices across Nations and MNC Subcultures." *Academy of Management Executive* 19 no. 2 (2005): 77–80.

Machiavelli, Niccolò. *The Prince.* New York: Random House, 1950.

Mangaliso, Mzamo P. "Building Competitive Advantage from ubuntu: Management Lessons from South Africa." *Academy of Management Executive* 15, no. 3 (2001): 23–33.

Mbigi, Lovemore, and Jenny Maree. *Ubuntu. The Spirit of African Transformation Management*. Ransburg: Knowledge Resources, 1995.
McAlpine, Alistair. *The New Machiavelli: The Art of Politics in Business*. New York: Wiley, 1999.
McGregor, Douglas. *The Human Side of Enterprise*. New York: McGraw-Hill, 1960.
Magno, Francisco, and Ramonette Serafica. "Information Technology for Good Governance." *Public Administration and Development* 8, no. 2 (2000): 125–34.
Ndaba, W. J. *Ubuntu in Comparison to Western Philosophies*. Pretoria: Ubuntu School of Philosophy, 1994.
N'dongko, T. "Management Leadership in Africa." *Management of Organizations in Africa: A Handbook of Reference* (1999): 99–123.
Neuman, J. E. "Why People Don't Participate in Organizational Change." *Research in Organizational Change and Development* 3 (1989): 181–212.
North, Douglass C. *Institutions, Institutional Change and Economic Performance*. Cambridge: Cambridge University Press, 1990.
Nzelibe, C. O. "The Evolution of African Management Thought." *International Studies of Management and Organization*, 16, no. 2 (1986): 6–16.
OECD Papers. Part II: *Governance and Capacity Building: Africa's Critical Frontier*, 5, no. 12 (2006): 14–28.
Poole, M. S., and A. H. Van de Ven. Using Paradox to Build Management and Organization Theories. *Academy of Management Review* 14, no. 4 (1989): 562–78.
Prinsloo, E. D. *Ubuntu from a Eurocentric and Afro-centric Perspective and Its Influence on Leadership*. Pretoria: Ubuntu School of Philosophy, 1995.
Pruijt, Hans D. *Job Design and Technology: Taylorism vs. Anti-Taylorism*. New York: Routledge, 1997.
Quelch, H. *Karl Marx: The Poverty of Philosophy*. CA: Prometheus, 1995.
Runciman, W. G. *The Origin of Human Social Institutions*. Oxford University Press, 2001.
Sachs, Jeffrey, John W. McArthur, Guido Schmidt-Traub, Margaret Kruk, Chandrika Bahadur, Michael Faye, and Gordon McCord. "Ending Africa's Poverty Trap." *Brookings Papers on Economic Activity*, 1 (2004): 117–240.
Saleh, Shoukry D. "Western Management Techniques and Developing Countries: The Kenya Case." *Engineering Management International* 3 (1985): 91–99.
Sansom, Richard. *An Essay on Progress in Civilization*. http://evansexperientialism.freewebspace.com/essay_on_progress.htm (accessed October 26, 2006).
Selznick, Philip. *Leadership in Administration*. New York: Harper & Row, 1957.
Senge, Peter. *The Fifth Discipline*. New York: Doubleday, 1990.
Senghor, Leopold S. *On African Socialism*. Stanford, CA: Stanford University, 1965.
Simon, Herbert A. *Administrative Behavior: A Study of Decision–making Processes in Administrative Organizations* (4th ed.). New York: Free Press, 1997.
Taylor, Frederick W. *The Principles of Scientific Management*. New York: Harper & Brothers Publishers, 1919.
Tsutsui, William M. *Manufacturing Ideology: Scientific Management in Twentieth Century Japan*. Princeton University Press, 1998.
Tylor, Sir Edward Burnett. *Researches into the Early History of Mankind and the Development of Civilization*. Adamant Media Corporation, 2005.
Weber, Max. *Economy and Society*. New York: Bedminster Press, 1968.
Wertheim, Edward G. *Historical Background of Organizational Behavior*, 2004. www.scribd.com/doc/6926402/Historical-Background-of-Organizational-Behavior (accessed July 9, 2010).

Wheatley, Margaret. *Leadership and the New Science: Discovering Order in a Chaotic World.* San Francisco, CA: Berrett–Koehler Publishers, 2001.

Wirth, Louis. "Ideological Aspects of Social Disorganization." *American Sociological Review* 5, no. 4 (1940): 472–82.

World Bank. Assessing World Bank Support for Trade, 1987–2004. An IEG evaluation. http://www.worldbank.org/ieg/trade/docs/trade_evaluation.pdf (accessed November 17, 2006).

———. *Sub-Saharan Africa: From Crisis to Sustainable Growth.* Washington, DC: World Bank, 1989.

Yukl, Gary. *Leadership in Organizations.* Englewood Cliffs, NJ: Prentice Hall, 2002.

Chapter 7
Grounded Theory and African Higher Education Transformation

Ishmael I. Munene

Introduction

Of the various Western-generated qualitative research designs, the least utilized in African studies is the grounded theory. While other qualitative designs such as case study, ethnography, phenomenology, and historical research have been widely used in the study of African societies, grounded theory has yet to make its mark. A cursory look at research programs in African universities and research training programs mounted by the Council for the Development of Social Sciences in Africa (CODESRIA), the Organization for Social Science Research in Eastern Africa (OSSREA), offers little evidence of any articulation of the significance of grounded theory research in the development of African epistemology. Yet of all the Western-oriented research designs, it is grounded theory that lends itself very well to the study of African societies, in particular the study of African universities undergoing significant transformations.

Arising from these preliminary observations, a number of questions are worth asking. What is grounded theory? Why has it been overlooked in the study of African issues? What makes it attractive as a design for the study of African societies and institutions? Grounded theory as a research strategy was first articulated by Glaser and Strauss (1967) as they studied dying patients in the 1960s. Generally it denotes the generation of theory from data systems generated through the constant comparative method (Strauss and Corbin, 1990). At the core of grounded theory is the belief that a theory should be grounded in the research data collected rather than as data used to fortify an already existing theory. Differently put, this theory-development does not come "off the shelf" but is generated from the experiences of research participants.

Returning to the issue of the dearth of grounded theory studies on African issues, it is logical to postulate that this is a function of three interrelated factors, all linked to Western research traditions. First is the bifurcation of research knowledge into two contrasting paradigms: *quantitative* approach with its positivist orientation emphasizing a single reality and the collection of numerical data versus the *qualitative* approach with its post-positivist orientation emphasizing multiple realities and the collection of non numerical data. The outcome of this divergence has been the elevation of the status of the quantitative research paradigm because it is perceived as more objective, highly rigorous, tightly controlled, and less messy. Qualitative research on the other hand is perceived to be of a lower status because it is perceived to be more subjective, less rigorous, highly flexible, and often messy.

The second factor, not unrelated to the first, is theory affirmation and verification in positivist research. A critical underpinning informing social science epistemology is the notion that there are great theories out there; all researchers need to do is to collect data to affirm them. Quantitative approaches, due to their objectivity, are the most suited for this task. Generation of new theories is outside the realm of a social scientist and those who attempt to do so are treated with suspicion. This is tied to the third factor, namely the training of African researchers. As Swayerr (2004) and Shabani (1996) revealed, the typical model of an African researcher is one who is Western-trained and espouses research values inherent in Western academic institutions—individual, discipline-oriented and university-based adhering to the tenets of the dichotomy between quantitative and qualitative approaches. Small wonder then that grounded theory—which involves active theory development—has received minimal attention in the study of African societies and institutions.

In spite of this paucity, grounded theory merits attention in African studies. With its emphasis on theory development as opposed to theory development, grounded theory offers opportunities for Afro-centric researchers to develop theories that capture the authentic situational context in the continent. Rather than trying to mesh data to fit into Western theoretical proscriptions, Afro-centric researchers can genuinely develop theories grounded in empirical data collected from the field that explains complex relationships. In addition, for institutions such as universities undergoing massive transformations and where there is a scarcity of adequate explanatory theories, grounded theory offers a rich alternative to generate theories that capture the intricacies of such changes.

Major Pioneers in Grounded Theory Research

As a research design within qualitative research approach, grounded theory has a fairly recent history. The methodology was first articulated by two sociologists Barney Glaser and Anselm Strauss (Glaser and Straus, 1967) in their study of terminally ill patients where they emphasized the ethnographic approach in sociological studies. They considered contemporary theories to be ill-suited for the study participants since *a priori* theories were not "grounded" in the actions, interactions, and processes of the patients. Their collaborative endeavor produced such classics like *Awareness of Dying* (Glaser and Strauss, 1965) and *Time for Dying* (Glaser and Strauss, 1968). In spite of their initial collaboration in the development of this family of qualitative research, the two pioneers differed substantially about what constitutes the meaning and procedures in grounded theory. Glaser criticized Strauss's approach to grounded theory as too prescriptive and structured in the mold of positivistic approach to research (Glaser, 1992).

A more recent addition to grounded theory has been the constructivist grounded theory (Charmaz 2006; Clarke, 2005). Both Charmaz and Clarke are critical of contemporary grounded theory approaches suggesting that it has given way to positivist orientations to the detriment of post-positivist leanings as was anticipated. Clarke advocates the need to incorporate postmodern perspectives including the political nature of research and interpretation, reflexivity on the part of researchers, moving away from an "all knowing analyst" to the "acknowledged participant." She further calls for "social situations" to form the unit of analysis in grounded theory and identifies three sociological modes as being pertinent in the analysis of situations, situational, social world/arenas, and positional cartographic maps for collecting and analyzing qualitative data. Unlike Charmaz, Clarke is more inclined toward a radical infusion of postmodern perspectives in grounded theory and leans on the post-structural writer, Michael Foucault, to help in the refinement of the grounded theory discourse.

While cognizant that constructivism offers an important addition to grounded theory, the analytical procedures expounded by Glaser and Strauss (1967) and by Straus and Corbin (1990) continue to inform a great deal of grounded theory research strategy. It is with this in view that the grounded theory method provided in this chapter will be based.

Major Publications Using Grounded Theory

Just like its relative short history compared to other qualitative research methods, the number of works that employ grounded theory is comparatively short though research and interest in the field is growing rapidly. In this section we focus our attention on classical methodological texts along with research studies that have employed grounded theory in a variety of study areas. This should provide panoramic overview of the development and application of this qualitative methodology in a variety of contexts.

As mentioned before, the genesis of grounded theory is traced to the sociological research undertaken by both Barney Glaser and Anselm Strauss on terminally ill patients at the medical school of the University of California, San Francisco, which resulted in three significant publications. In *Awareness of Dy-*

ing (Glaser and Strauss, 1965), the researchers delineated the theory on the influence of awareness on the interaction with dying people. Their theoretical construct distinguished between closed awareness, suspicion, mutual deception and open awareness each of which determined the type of interaction between the patient and the nurse and between the patient and relatives.

In *Time for Dying* (Glaser and Strauss, 1968), the researchers used grounded theory to identify "dying trajectory" as a relational construct that captures the various dimensions of dying such as duration, projected remission of illness or periods of improvement, and time of expected death. This trajectory has an effect on organization of work and sentiments of both staff and family. These two products of grounded theory methodology led to the publication of the first methodological textbook, *The Discovery of Grounded Theory* (Glaser and Strauss, 1967). Premised on the need to discover theory from field data, this book had three objectives: It sought to legitimize qualitative research, demonstrate the possibility of building theory from data, and to critic structural-functionalist researchers such as Talcott Parsons. Since then a number of outstanding methodological textbooks have been published including *Basics of Qualitative Research: Grounded Theory Procedures and Techniques* by Anselm Strauss and Juliet Corbin (Strauss and Corbin, 1990).

The evolution of grounded theory could hardly have been possible without the existence of academic outlets for studies that have used the methodology. In this regard, the following journals have been central in promoting grounded theory studies:

(a) *The Grounded Theory Review: An International Journal,* a publication of the Grounded Theory Institute (http://www.groundedtheory.com), is published by Barney G. Glaser, one of the founding fathers of grounded theory. It is an international peer-reviewed journal for the advancement of classic grounded theory research and scholarship.

(b) *International Journal of Qualitative Studies in Education* (popularly known as QSE) is the premier qualitative research journal in the field of education. QSE publishes peer-reviewed empirical research employing a variety of qualitative methods and approaches, such as ethnographic observation and interviewing, grounded theory, life history, case study, curriculum criticism, policy studies, narrative, ethnomethodology, social and educational critique, phenomenology, deconstruction, genealogy, autoethnography, etc.

(c) *Anthropology and Education Quarterly* (AEQ as it is popularly known) is the journal of the Council on Anthropology and Education, a professional association of anthropologists and educational researchers which is a section of the American Anthropological Association. It publishes qualitative studies in the field of education.

(d) *The Qualitative Report* (http://www.nova.edu/ssss/QR), a free online journal published by the Graduate School of Humanities and Social Sciences at Nova Southeastern University in Florida. It publishes articles on theory, methodology, and research outcomes from a variety of disciplines using the various qualitative research designs including grounded theory.

Higher educational studies using grounded theory are few and far between. A search on all major databases yielded very few studies suggesting either unwillingness to use it or unfamiliarity with the same. At any rate, we did identify some studies which have utilized it in the study of various aspects of higher education. These will be discussed briefly.

In *Grounded Theory: An Alternative Approach to Research in Higher Education*, Conrad (1982) applied grounded theory to the study of academic change in American universities. By way of constant comparative method and theoretical sampling, the cornerstones of any grounded theory, Conrad used data from four institutions to develop an explanatory theory to account for academic change. The uniqueness of Conrad's study was the use of a number of mini case studies (the four institutions) to delineate propositional constructs into a theory of academic change. In addition he used broad organizational and sociological perspectives on change to guide the initial phase of data collection.

Kezar (2004) also extended this theme of change in higher education with his investigation of the consequences of radical change in governance. The researcher combined the tenets of both case study and grounded theory approach to investigate radical change in governance because grounded theory provided detailed examination of the data while the case study provided the bounded context in which to focus the study. Kezar identified two theoretical propositions: 1) radical change process is likely to have more negative consequences than the positive features of the new system put in place, and should be implemented cautiously; 2) no governance system is ideal, each has its own weaknesses that need to be examined and altered on a continuous basis. Radical change does not solve these problems but instead can conceal them.

Another grounded theory focusing on aspects of institutional governance was that conducted by Creswell and Brown (1992) which examined how college and university departmental chairs interact with faculty members. They identified the chairs' roles which they labeled as "providing, enabling, advocating, acting as a mentor, encouraging, collaborating, and challenging." Chairs performed different roles at different times depending the level of the faculty member with whom they were interacting. Chao and Good's (2004) grounded theory study focused on nontraditional student perspectives on college education. The theoretical model generated from the study identified career development, financial investment, motivation, support system, life transition, and hopefulness as factors interacting in a dynamic way to explain nontraditional students' perception of college.

Research Questions on Grounded Theory Methodology

The use of grounded theory as a research methodology does raise some important questions. Of these questions, the following are particularly significant:

(a) Does grounded theory actually come up with a concrete theory or merely identify constructs and their interrelationships?

(b) Other than coming up with a theoretical model, how else does grounded theory differ from other qualitative research designs, especially the case study?

(c) Of what practical policy relevance does grounded theory provide which other qualitative research designs cannot?

(d) Are there issues, contexts, or situations that are more amenable to grounded theory methodology or is it applicable to all?

Major Concepts in Grounded Theory Research Strategy

Two methodological strategies are at the core of grounded theory: the constant comparative method and theoretical sampling. Without them, it would practically be impossible to distinguish grounded theory from other qualitative research designs. Additionally, both are inextricably interwoven in the theory generation phase of a study. Thus, for a clear appreciation of grounded theory research strategy it is important that the role of these two methodological strategies in grounded theory be delineated and clarified. The two strategies are:

(a) *Constant Comparative Method*: A multi-pronged inductive strategy for integrating a multiplicity of data sources, the constant comparative method is the genesis as well as the conclusion in the creative generation of a theory. It commences when a researcher collects data, codes it into categories which are abstracted on the basis of comparing data incidents against each other. As the process unfolds, the researcher begins to view the categories in theoretical terms manifested in their unique properties: their dimensions, relationships to other categories and conditions under which it is maximized or minimized (Conrad, 1982). The term constant underscores the repetitive nature of the process which comes to a close when repeated comparison yields no additional categories.

(b) *Theoretical Saturation*: Strauss and Corbin (1990) recommend that in the delineation of categories, data should be collected to the point of theoretical saturation. This point is reached when no new data is emerging that is relevant to the established categories, where the emergent categories are not clearly linked to the phenomena under investigation or where it lacks a clear relationships with the categories already established. The conclusion of the category generation phase dovetails into the theory development one. At this stage emphasis is placed on the development of a smaller number of higher level concepts and their relationships. Further refinement of the relationship leads to the development of a theory, presented in a discussion format or a set of propositions.

Theoretical sampling is a key ingredient in the development of the theory. "To say that one samples theoretically" according to Strauss and Corbin (1990, p. 177) "means sampling on the basis of concepts that have proven theoretical relevance to the evolving theory." The concepts have to show consistency in their presence or absence, and through coding they have attained the status of categories. This means that the initial data collection forms the basis of delineating concepts which forms the building blocks for a primitive theory. Initial data collection is guided by the study's research questions and, later on, by the dictates of theoretical sampling. Data is collected from a multiplicity of sources, sorted, analyzed, and coded in an attempt to generate concepts, their properties and relationships (Creswell, 2007; Strauss and Corbin, 1990). This coding process is the beginning of the transition from empirical to conceptual and theoretical view of data by identifying the underlying patterns. It is this primitive conceptual theory that guides the subsequent data collection; additional data is only relevant when it fits the stipulated theoretical criterion. This continues until all major concepts and their relationships have been theoretically saturated.

The theoretical model that emerges from grounded theory basically consists of an underlying pattern of concepts, their properties and relationships. This includes the *causal conditions* that precipitated the core *phenomena* under investigation; the *strategies* and tactics undertaken in response to the core phenomena; the *context*, the location of events or incidents pertaining to the phenomena along a dimensional range; the *intervening conditions*, broad and specific factors that influence the strategies; and the *consequences* of the strategies. We explore how this theoretical model is relevant to the transformation of African higher education in the next section.

Transformation Turbulence: An Application of Grounded Theory to African Higher Education Transformation

To illustrate the wealth of opportunities for theory development that grounded theory affords in African studies, we apply this approach to the study of African higher education. Specifically we focus on the radical transformation that most public universities are experiencing, the transition from state funded universities to state owned but privately funded institutions. The study was conducted in 2005–2006 and data collection took place in Kenya in the summer of 2005.

Research Problem and Questions

Higher education transformation has increasingly become an important policy concern presenting both opportunities and challenges. Globalization and the attendant notions of marketization and privatization have increasingly come to dominate the higher education transformation discourse (Altbach, 2001; Bok, 2003; Gibbons, 2001; Ntshoe, 2004a and 2004b; Stromquist, 2007). While substantial scholarship on stakeholder anxiety due to institutional transformation exists in the developed world, studies from the developing world, in particular Africa, are only beginning to enter into the academic discourse. To address this research gap, this grounded theory study was designed to answer the following questions:

1. Why has the process of marketization and privatization expanded in public higher educational institutions in Kenya?
2. What is the nature and process of the marketization and privatization that has taken place?
3. What aspects of marketization and privatization in Kenya's public higher education have lead to increased stakeholder anxiety?

Theoretical Sampling: Kenyatta University

In tandem with the parameters of theoretical sampling, the study began by identifying the university in Kenya that best exemplified the questions at hand. Kenyatta University (KU) was selected for a variety of reasons. As the second largest university in the country after the University of Nairobi (UoN), it had an enrollment of over 15,000 students (2005). It is located outside downtown the city of Nairobi approximately 20 kilometers, a peri-urban institution striding the fringes of both the city and rural limits. This is important because other than the urban UoN, the rest of Kenya's public universities are rural thereby providing a unique challenge in diversifying their revenue base through entrepreneurial activities. Unlike the University of Nairobi which began as a complex multi-campus institution with a multiplicity of programs, KU began as a constituent college of the University of Nairobi offering educational programs. Its sudden enrollment growth, introduction of additional programs, and the purchasing of two additional campuses are the results of efforts to align itself with the market. As such, it provided a good setting for in-depth study of university transformation.

Constant Comparative Method and Empirical Data Collection

A visit to Kenyatta University identified a large array of data sources, both primary and secondary. Primary data sources were interviews: (a) senior level university administrators including the vice-chancellor (university president), the deputy vice chancellor (finance and administration), the registrar (finance and administration), the deputy finance officer responsible for income generating activities, four deans (Business, Education, Environmental Studies and Human Sciences, and Humanities and Social Sciences) and directors of income generating activities, self-sponsored programs and institute of open learning; (b) two full professors who had served the institution for over twenty years; and (c) four union leaders, two from each of the academic staff union, UASU (University Academic Staff Union) and the middle grade staff union, UNTESU (Universities Non-teaching Staff Union).

Primary data was also collected through open-ended questionnaires from (a) six departmental chairs, one from each school, with high enrollment of privately-sponsored fee-paying students namely, Business Administration, Biological Sciences, Educational Administration and Planning, Environmental Planning and Management, History, Archaeology and Political Studies, and Hospitality and Tourism Management; and (b) five student leaders.

Data from memos, the strategic plan, newspaper articles and newsletters from various stakeholders at the institution including students, unions and the university was also collected. National level data was obtained from government documents including the Ministry of Education, Science and Technology policy documents (ministerial speeches), the 2004–2009 National Development Plan, and the 2005 National Economic Survey. These enabled us contextualize the reforms in a national context.

With such an array of data sources, analysis began with the collection of data from the first interview data. The first two interviews provided the entry points in which the researcher began the coding process for an incipient theory. Using this initial coding, it was possible to abstract some key concepts regarding university transformation, the conditions under which it occurs, and the consequences. In other words, we began to build some primitive theoretical constructs about the relationships between the concepts. This primitive theory provided the frame of reference for additional data collection; constant comparative method required that the researcher moves back and forth between empirical data and conceptual constructs. Through this process, some concepts were discarded due to insufficient confirmatory data or disconfirmed by new empirical evidence. Finally, theoretical properties began to materialize as concepts and relationships were explored, developed, refined, and tested against new data collected from the various sources.

Transformation Turbulence: A Grounded Theory of African Higher Education Transformation

In this section, the grounded theory model for university transformation to a market university is presented in Figure 7.1. In the sections that follow, the relationship between the various constructs in the model will be explained in detail.

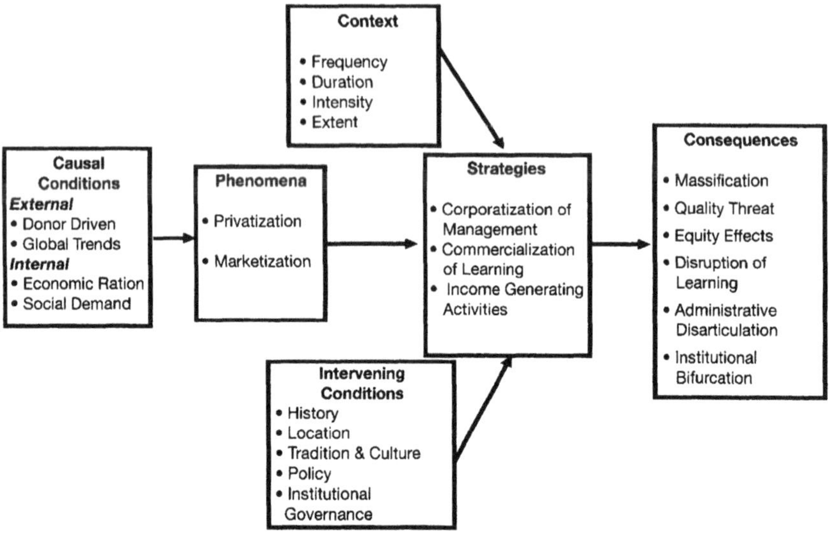

Figure 7.1. Theoretical Model for Transformation to a Market University and the Effects

Causal Conditions of Phenomena Related to a Market University

Two broad conditions were associated with the development of marketization and privatization phenomena at Kenyatta University. These are (a) external conditions related to donor demands and global trends, and (b) internal conditions unique to Kenya namely, economic factors link to government financial rationalization as well as the increased internal demand for higher education. External donor demands articulated by multilateral institutions such as the World Bank and the IMF required that the government reform its financing of higher education by giving attention to promoting private financing, introduction of tuition charges, cost-recovery for boarding and accommodation services, and a need-based loan scheme for those unable to meet the cost of education. These market and privatization movements were perceived to be global trends which Kenya had to embrace since ". . . globalization means you try to do what others are doing so that you are not left behind" as one respondent put it. Globalization was inextricably interwoven with both marketization and the commoditization of academic knowledge. As globalization had taken shape, universities had transformed their academic programs in order to tap into the emerging education market.

Internally, the Kenyan government budgetary allocation displayed significant disparities between the various sectors. Education consumed the largest share, over 38 percent and the bulk of this was devoted to teacher pay. Furthermore, of the current expenditure, teachers' salaries and university costs had the lion's share. Elementary and secondary schools, in spite of their large enrollment, were allocated far less than the universities. This constituted another rationale for cutting university funding, insisting that they generate their own revenues through market mechanism. This entrepreneurial model of development for public universities was enunciated by the country's minister for education:

> This is a turning point in the development of our public universities, where they are being called upon to adopt business-like financial management styles. It is also a point in time when universities have to plan well ahead about resources expected to be coming from sources other than the exchequer. . . . Time has come to seriously take account of the universities potential to generate income internally. . . . Income from such sources should be exploited and treated as definite sources of university revenue. (cited in Kiamba, 2004, p. 55)

Phenomena Resulting from External and Internal Pressures

Both external and internal causal conditions resulted into two closely interrelated categories of phenomena as perceived by the respondents: (a) marketization and (b) privatization of university programs and activities. Marketization was manifested in the increased adoption of market-oriented ethos in academic programs and activities. Respondents noted that marketization of university programs would accrue financial resources to meet costs: ". . . especially with the increase of the salaries for academic staff members; that was going to cause a lot of strain to the university and as a result the university tended to be focused to make sure that we are dealing with programs that are really adding business to the university. Those that are otherwise irrelevant, needed to be phased out or the departments required to rethink and reorganize themselves to become more relevant and more market oriented" (Dean). Bridging this financial gap has necessitated the need to adopt a market-based approach to university operations. Academic programs, therefore, were seen as an important revenue stream and the institution entrepreneurial.

Increasingly, the university also acquired norms of a private institution with privately-sponsored students paying market-rate tuition and studying side-by-side with their public-sponsored counterparts. Privatized too were services such as boarding and accommodation in order to assure cost-recovery of the services provided. By privatizing some of its services, the university was implementing the state's goal of providing services through private financial resources:

> [T]he central thrust of the new policies is to rely on market forces to mobilize resources for growth and development with the role of central government increasingly confined to providing an effective regulatory framework and essential public infrastructure and social services. The government will limit direct

participation in many sectors and instead promote private sector activity. (1994–1998 Development Plan, cited in Kiamba, 2004, p. 55)

Context in Which Survival and Coping Strategies Developed

Strategies for survival and coping were developed in response to the new dispensation of marketization and privatization of higher education. The development of these strategies was governed by contextual factors related to the causal condition. These are the (a) frequency, (b) duration, (c) intensity and (d) extent of both the external and internal causal condition. The enormous pressure for university transformation had dual external impetus, donor conditionality for financial assistance as well as global trends that favored the market principles in the financing of higher education. Internally, the pressure came from government budget rationalization plans and a burgeoning social demand for higher education.

The pressure was continuous in frequency—a decade long, from 1990 to 2000—due to the ever-present demand for higher education and the government's budgetary constraints in financing higher education and global surge in entrepreneurial state and private universities. This demand was of a very high annual growth granted the number of high school graduates every year and the limited higher education opportunities available in state-funded higher education opportunities in the country. The pressure for transformation was of high intensity and localized to undergraduate and graduate programs with high labor market value. High school graduate sought university education opportunities; unemployed university graduates sought programs with a high labor market orientation. Under these conditions, marketization and privatization were deemed to be appropriate transformation strategies for public universities. Marketization would realign the university programmatically into the market and privatization would infuse private resources for institutional growth and operations. In words of one dean "people want to read, people want to be in school . . . universities have to be really be very innovative on how they raise funds and this is one way of doing it."

Intervening Conditions Influencing Marketization and Privatization as Survival and Coping Strategies

Alongside the contextual variables, there were also intervening conditions; broad and general conditions that influenced the strategies adopted by the university. The conditions included (a) history, (b) location, (c) tradition and culture (d) policy environment, and (e) institutional governance. As a relatively young public university with only twenty years of existence as an independent institution, Kenyatta University had grown under the shadows of the premier and preeminent University of Nairobi for which it was a constituent college for over a decade. As Kenyatta College, it specialized in the training of high school teachers with an S1 (secondary one) certification from 1969 to 1975. In 1975, education degree programs at the University of Nairobi were transferred to college and the institution became a constituent college of the university. In 1985, it became a full-fledged university with degree programs in Arts and Humanities instituted in 1986. The brief history of full-fledged university status and limited programs limited the extent to which programmatic and organizational initiatives were available to serve as a spring board for large scale entrepreneurial activity. Nonetheless, this limitation also provided an opportunity for the university to initiate new programs as seen in the establishment of the Schools of Public Health and Law.

Kenyatta University, in contrast to the University of Nairobi, is located in the peri-urban area of around 25 miles from the city of Nairobi. It is proximate to the southern rural districts of central province of Kenya along the Thika Highway. Though this location gives it access to the Thika industrial-urban center 30 miles away, the university has still to deal with the reality that it faces tough competition from the University of Nairobi for the lucrative clientele in Nairobi city. The University of Nairobi has a strategic location in downtown Nairobi providing easy access to the institution which, coupled with the large number of academic programs, has enabled the university attain an unsurpassed success in mounting evening and weekend courses with high enrollment. Kenyatta University's acquisition of St. Anne's campus in downtown Nairobi was a strategic move to tap into the city clientele base.

Besides history and location, tradition and culture influenced privatization and marketization strategies. The non competitive working culture and tradition of the public sector turned out to be inhibitive to the needs of a competitive market- and customer-oriented work environment. Traditional public financial management principles and traditional collegial academic governance model were perceived favorably, by academics and staff, than new businesses-oriented models which imposed severe constraints on the development of an entrepreneurial culture.

Two policy factors had diametrically distinct impact on strategies. The macro-level national policies were useful in terms of system-steering of public universities into entrepreneurship and privatization. These were articulated in national documents such as the national development plans, economic surveys and policy papers from the Ministry of Education. On the other hand, policy deficit at the local institutional level resulted in a constraining environment for the development of income-generating activities and their modus operandi. Initiatives were based on the personality of the vice-chancellor; one dean stated: "[W]hen you ask why K.U [Kenyatta University] has gotten into this, I think, I would like to give credit to the former vice-chancellor."

Institutional governance was also a constraining variable. Role conflict between top university leaders, traditional governance structure, and new collective bargaining units and the decline of faculty power provided avenues of con flict which was inimical to transformation goals of the university. In absence of clear-cut governance structure that empowers all stakeholders, buying into the reforms seemed problematic.

Strategies for Marketization and Privatization

Within the framework of the context and intervening variables as presented hitherto, the phenomena of marketization and privatization lead to the development of four main strategies for survival and coping. The three strategies were (a) corporatization of management, (b) commercialization of learning and (c) development of other income-generating activities. We now turn our attention to these strategies.

Corporatization of Governance

Corporatization of the management sought to infuse private sector management ethos in the operations of the university. At the core of this strategy was to depoliticize institutional governance:

> Political changes in Kenya heralded the appointment of Chancellors who are not the head of state as was the case previously. This calls for reforms in the management structures to accommodate the new dispensation and encourage good governance principles. In Kenyan public universities, the administrative structures have been highly hierarchical and centralized. In the planned period, Kenyatta University will put in place strategies that will institutionalize the use of democratic principles in decision making and responsive administrative and management structures. (Kenyatta University Strategic Plan 2005–2015: xi).

Among the changes were the de-politicization of the university chancellorship after the head of state relinquished the position; A non-political chancellor allowed the university a larger democratic space in which to undertake decision making and increase institutional autonomy. Another de-politicization strategy was the competitive recruitment of the vice-chancellors on a performance contract rather than appointment by the head of state; this would ensure institutional accountability to the key constituents and the market.

Besides changes in chancellorship and vice-chancellorship, other transformations aimed at the corporatization of management included administrative reconfigurations involving the abolishment of executive deans, mergers, and downsizing of departments; this was aimed at achieving controlling costs, administrative efficiency, and aligning departments to the markets, as articulated in the university's newsletter:

- Establish operational efficiency in the realms of management of academic programs in order to meet changing markets.

- Formulation and implementation of a system that would facilitate optimal utilization of human, financial and physical and other resources in the university.
- Enhancement of innovative responses to shifting emphasis towards the development of a Kenyatta University brand.
- Enhancement of a system, which will lead to a learner and more efficient administrative framework. (Kenyatta University *The Weekly*, 2004, p. 3)

As part of the corporatization of governance, two trade unions were registered. The faculty union, the University Academic Staff Union (UASU), and the middle level staff union, Universities Non Teaching Staff Union (UNTESU) were given recognition and collective bargaining instituted.

The student government and leadership were re-engineered to reflect the new corporate governance model. From the previous hierarchical model of student government the Kenyatta University Students Association (KUSA) had undergone a radical transformation resulting in a decentralized guild model of student government and leadership. This re-engineering had enabled the association shed its previous image of a quasi-political activist organization with affiliation to political interests beyond the university to one that has trappings of a corporate organization addressing the needs and problems of its immediate stakeholders and clients, the students.

Commercialization of Learning

Commercialization of learning was reflected in two activities, the privatization of academic programs, the privatization of accommodation and auxiliary services. The Self-Sponsored Program, SSP, was the most conspicuous manifestation of the privatization of academic programs. Under SSP students were admitted as private students did not receive government loans and had to pay full tuition. Learning delivery for SSP students occurred in three modes: the evening format, distance learning with occasional instruction at regional centers, and through online delivery under KUeL, Kenyatta University E-Learning Center.

Commercialization had become a critical revenue stream for the university. In 2005, the university raised nearly Ksh 1 Billion (US $14 Million). Indeed, SSP income financed the 2004 faculty salary after the state failed to honor its promise to meet the cost of the award; SSP revenue contributed to continued institutional stability and labor relations harmony. This demand-driven enrollment also allowed the academic departments, to reexamine, modify, and innovate curricular: "I could call it a revolution whereby most of our institutions are looking for market-driven programs and these programs seem to target across the population" noted one dean. Academics were willing to modify their hitherto elite view of university admissions to more egalitarian and instrumental ones.

Second only to SSP programs the privatization of accommodation services was the most visible manifestation of the marketization of public universities services. With the introduction of cost-sharing and the subsequent withdrawal of government subsidies in the mid-1990s, university students met the full cost of food and beds in the residential halls. Those unable to pay are entitled to loans provided by the Higher Education Loans Board, HELB. The strategic goals of the policy were to divest accommodation issues from academic ones while ensuring the beneficiaries met the full market cost of the same.

Another strategy in the marketization of the university was the establishment of Income Generating Activities (IGA), which refers to revenue generated through other non-tuition activities or programs. Among the envisaged IGA activities included research grants and contracts, leasing property, and revenue from patents and innovations. In the 2005–2015 university strategic plan, three percent of the revenue was expected to be derived from IGA. Very little had taken place by way of developing IGA: "I can say," noted one senior academic administrator, "that the only thing I have seen is self-sponsored students bringing more funds. I have not seen anything else that has generated funding." Nonetheless, the five restaurants on campus were the most visible income-generating activities. However, owing to a variety of managerial, organizational, and socio-cultural factors, these enterprises had failed to register impact as important revenue streams for the university.

Consequences of Marketization and Privatization

These strategies were not without significant ramifications, including (a) massification, (b) quality threat, (c) equity effects, (d) disruption of learning, (e) administrative disarticulation, and (f) institutional bifurcation. Marketization and privatization had succeeded in transforming the university from an institution dependent on the state for its financial survival to one which could generate additional revenue for its operations. Nevertheless, the strategies adopted for survival came at a cost.

The most noticeable consequence was massification, the sudden surge in student population. From a student population of 9, 952 in 2001, the number had reached 16,055 in 2005 representing a 62 percent growth in four years. The number of self-sponsored students also exceeded the government sponsored ones in the same year. This massification became the sphere of contest among various stakeholders due to the threat it posed to academic quality and impact on faculty workload. Massification was not matched by increase in the number of teaching staff, library and laboratory facilities as well as staff development opportunities. At university's main campus, no new building had been constructed since the mid-1990s even though the number of students had doubled; the university library had not seen any expansion in seating as well as in resource-holding capacity since the late 1990s; and computing laboratories for faculty and students were chronically in short supply.

In addition, new academic hires could not embark on their PhD programs work due to excessive workload; they taught large classes throughout the year with no break. Bottom line considerations superseded academic quality considerations. As an academic staff union official observed:

> I have some suspicion that given the overwhelming numbers that have come in against the persisting lack of human resource base, physical facilities and the non-adoption of new teaching or delivery approach that this is not necessarily going to impact positively on academic program. People are overstretched here and they are even going to be more overstretched. I think that we are going to have many problems. As for academic staff professional welfare, there isn't much.

Equity effects were another consequence of the institutional transformation. The privatization of residential services had a deleterious effect on students from lower socio-economic background. Unable to subsist on the boarding and lodging stipend, these students employed an array of risky coping strategies. A popular coping strategy was the illegal food preparation in the residential halls which were unsuited for the activity. Thus, there were reported cases of power outages, short circuiting, and fire outbreaks in most residential halls. Electrical fire was a constant worry and a danger for those living in the university residential halls. Another coping strategy was entrepreneurship. A good number of students sold everything from CDs to electrical items, from alcohol to foodstuffs, and also did repair work on stereos, shoes, and clothes. The more enterprising had found the university residential halls restrictive and had move to the nearby village slum where they built themselves successful businesses. Other students opted to find cheaper accommodation in the neighboring unhygienic village where they were exposed to a variety of health and security risks:

> One Kilometer from the university, past a thick kei apple fence and a disused railway line, beyond a dusty footpath and into a slum village, students haggle over the price of vegetables, maize flour, meat and alcohol. The slum is appropriately called KM (short for kilometer, as it is about that distance from the campus). It also means Kiwanja Moto (hot field). Strange things happen there. . . . The entrance to KM makes you sneeze as dust billows above the make-shift structures. Used to dust particles, the students seem to have developed resistance to all this and a visitor is easily picked out from the crowd. . . . Sanitary services are awful. Raw wastes flowing slowly are common here. (Muiruri, 2005, pp. 7–9)

Therefore, the privatization of accommodation services had exacerbated socio-economic stratification within the student community.

Disruption of learning was another outcome of university transformation. The conflict between the faculty and university administration over the 35 percent devolution of income earned from the Self Sponsored Programs had led to two faculty strikes within one year. Failure by the university administration to implement the devolution policy had not only precipitated work stoppage but also heightened tension and suspicion between the two constituents: "I, brothers and sisters," noted the faculty union secretary-general, "want to refer to the agitation for the devolution of the 35 percent academic service provider. While the struggle for devolution has resulted in some hope, the agitation for implementation is yet to bear fruit." Success in generating additional revenue was accompanied with challenges of how to empower the revenue generating units financially.

Alongside disruption of learning, administrative disarticulation was another outcome of the transformation. SSP coordination was the most challenging managerial hurdles. A multiplicity of administrative structures to run the programs resulted in conflicts over role and responsibilities among the various heads of departments. Admission into SSP programs was via different programs and offices. Most, 41 percent were admitted directly through the SSP office (the central administrative unit of all self-sponsored students and admission office for all programs not handled by other offices), 28 percent through the Institute of Continuing Education (primarily teachers seeking college level degrees in order to gain promotion), 22 percent through the Institute of Open Learning (those outside the City of Nairobi and the vicinity) and 9 percent through the Post Graduate Diploma in Education Program (for teachers seeking teacher certification). These myriad of offices was also a source of conflict over timetabling, appointment of adjunct faculty, scheduling of site visits outside campus, and financial jurisdiction over income derived from the program.

Administrative disarticulation was also manifest in Program duplication. As academic departments raced to generate revenue by creating marketable courses, conflicts over similar courses being offered by two different departments were legendary. The turf war and competition for students between Geography Department and the Department of Textile and Family Consumer Sciences over which department was best suited to offer tourism and leisure management courses demonstrated how economic expediency superseded disciplinary considerations in decision about academic programming.

Administrative disarticulation also occurred when departments of differing programmatic orientation were merged during the process of administrative reconfiguration. The most-cited case was the merger of the Department of Textile and Family Consumer Sciences with the Faculty of Environmental Studies to form the School of Environmental and Human Sciences. This, in turn, contributed to insider-outsiders feelings among faculty in Human Sciences and provided a sphere of contest in resource allocation between academics in Environmental studies and those in Human Sciences.

Institutional bifurcation was no less visible as a consequence of transformation than the aforementioned. The first level of bifurcation was between faculty and departments teaching discipline with high labor market orientation such as those in the schools of business, public health, and engineering and those teaching in departments with a low labor market orientation such in the schools of humanities, pure and applied sciences and education. Faculty teaching in high-demand programs enjoyed additional income throughout the year in contrast to their counterparts teaching in low-demand programs. This was accentuated by the second level of bifurcation, between the basic knowledge (mode 1), which is discovery and long term, and applied knowledge (mode 2), which is applied and short term. The perceived importance of departments offering applied knowledge courses with a high labor market orientation and a high income faculty had raised questions about the public good of the university. Basic knowledge and faculty teaching in these disciplines were perceived as less strategic in the new dispensation.

Conclusion

As seen from the foregoing analysis, grounded theory has remarkable potential in enhancing African studies. In particular, it is suited for studies focusing on African higher education undergoing radical transformation since studies in this area are only beginning to make headway. This is reinforced by the scarcity of adequate explanatory theories in higher education. Therefore, grounded theory is first and foremost useful in theory development. The methodological approach, encompassing constant comparison and theoretical sampling, is designed to facilitate the creative development of theory.

In addition, grounded theory is useful due to its in-built flexibility in the treatment of data. As a qualitative research design, grounded theory has all the advantages of flexibility that characterizes these designs. It can be used in combination with other qualitative designs including ethnography, phenomenology, and case studies as well African-generated research approaches. This is particularly important in African studies where we need a triangulation of different research approaches in order to gain a comprehensive and exhaustive study of the society. Grounded theory can thus be a powerful tool linking Western and African research methodologies in order to develop appropriate and relevant theories in the study of African societies and institutions.

Even with its perceived advantages, grounded theory has some limitations in the study of African societies and institutions. Though the constant comparative technique ensures that data collection is cyclic, the theory generated is essentially a pattern of relationships between various constructs. This relationship, however, is linear in structure which calls into question as to whether this is in keeping with an Afro-centric world view which is cyclic and holistic in nature. This linear view of the world is a serious constraint in attempting to adjust grounded theory to the study of African societies and institutions.

Another constraining variable is the terminology used to denote the various attributes of the theory. In most cases, these terminologies will be as non-African as they are foreign. Take the case of concepts like globalization, marketization and privatization which we have used in our illustration. Questions arise as to whether these concepts have the same meaning for Africans as they do for non-Africans and if not, how a grounded theory researcher reconciles these discrepancies. This is a research challenge that is not easy to resolve.

Bibliography

Altbach, Philip G. "Higher Education and WTO: Globalization Run Amok." www.bc.edu/bc_org/avp/soe/cihe/newsletter/News23/text001.htm (accessed December 10, 2005).

Bok, Derek. *Universities in the Marketplace: The Commercialization of Higher Education*. Princeton: Princeton University Press, 2003.

Chao, Ruth, and Glenn E. Good. "Nontraditional Students' Perspective on College Education: A Qualitative Study." *Journal of College Counseling* 7 (2004): 5–12.

Charmaz, Kathy. *Constructing Grounded Theory*. London: Sage Publications, 2006.

Clarke, Adele E. *Situational Analysis: Grounded Theory after Postmodern Turn*. Thousand Oaks, CA: Sage Publications, 2005.

Conrad, Clifton F. "Grounded Theory: An Alternative Approach in Higher Education." *Review of Higher Education* 5, no. 4 (1982): 259–69.

Creswell, John W. *Qualitative Inquiry and Research Design: Choosing Among Five Approaches*. Thousand Oaks, CA: Sage Publications, 2007.

Creswell, John W., and Martha L. Brown. "How Chairpersons Enhance Faculty Research: A Grounded Theory Study." *Review of Higher Education* 16, no. 1 (1992): 41–42.

Gibbons, Michael. "Globalization in Higher Education: A View for the South." *SRHE International News* 46 (2001): 4–12.

Glaser, Barney G. *Basics of Grounded Theory Analysis*. Mill Valley, CA: Sociology Press, 1992.

Glaser, Barney G., and Anselm L. Strauss. *Time for Dying*. Chicago: Aldine, 1968.

———. *The Discovery of Grounded Theory*. Chicago: Aldine, 1967.

———. *Awareness of Dying*. Chicago: Aldine, 1965.

Kezar, Adrianna L. "Consequences of Radical Change in Governance: A Grounded Theory Approach." *Journal of Higher Education* 76, no. 6 (2004): 634–68.

Kiamba, Crispus. "The Experience of the Privately Sponsored Studentship and Other Income Generating Activities at the University of Nairobi." *Journal of Higher Education in Africa* 2, no. 2 (2004): 53–73.

Muiruri, Mugo. "Learning to Live in Slums Where Students Learn Survival Tactics." Inside Story, *Daily Nation* (2005), 7–9.

Ntshoe, Isaac M. "Higher Education and Training Policy and Practice in South Africa: Impacts of Global Privatization, Quasi–Marketization and New Managerialism." *International Journal of Educational Development* 24 (2004a): 137–54.

———. (2004b) "The Politics and Economics of Post-Apartheid Higher Education Transformation." *Comparative Education Review* 48, no. 2: 202–21.

Shabani, Juma. *Research Management in African Universities*. Unpublished Mimeo, Association of African Universities, 1996.

Strauss, Anselm C., and Juliet Corbin. *Basics of Qualitative Research: Grounded Theory Procedures and Techniques*. Newbury Park, CA: Sage Publications, 1990.

Stromquist, Nelly. "Internationalization as a Response to Globalization: Radical Shift in University Environments." *Higher Education* 53 (2007): 81–105.

Swayerr, Akilagpa. "African Universities and the Challenge of Research Capacity Development." *Journal of Higher Education in Africa* 2, no. 1 (2004): 213–42.

Chapter 8
Rural Development in the Era of Neoliberal Hegemony: Poststructuralist and Postcolonial Methodological Critique and Theoretical Analysis

Samuel Zalanga

Introduction

Katherine Snyder wrote a book, *The Iraqw of Tanzania: Negotiating Rural Development*, based on ethnographic research on rural development among the Iraqw Da'aw people of Northern Tanzania (Snyder, 2005). The goal of this chapter is to critically examine some themes raised in her book within the broader context of the debate on neoliberalism, globalization, and poststructuralist and postcolonial critique of these hegemonic ideologies and the institutions and discourses that represent them. Specifically, some of her research findings will be used to interrogate the empirical validity and long-term trajectory of living under neoliberal hegemony. In this way, her research will be employed to connect the existential struggles of grassroots people in Sub-Saharan Africa to the forces of the international political economy dominated by powerful corporations and their ideologues. The chapter is divided into four broad sections.

The first section is a brief review of neoliberalism with particular reference to the theory, its public policies and its implicit vision of history and society. The second section presents an analytical summary of some selected relevant themes from Snyder's book. In this section, insights from Paulo Freire's ideas on anti-dialogical education and development were incorporated in order to critically evaluate the impact of globalization on public education and the day-to-day life and struggles of subaltern people in Tanzania. Professor Dudley Seers' criteria for evaluating development were also highlighted in this section of the chapter. The third section of the chapter focuses on some profound ideas and insights from the work of poststructuralist scholar Foucault, and the following postcolonial scholars: Frantz Fanon, Homi Bhabha, and Gyatri Spivak. The section argues that Snyder's research is exemplary as it empirically illustrates some of the critiques of development and modernity by poststructuralist and postcolonial scholars. It demonstrates how complex social theories can be translated into empirical referents, thereby illustrating their validity or inadequacy. The fourth section builds on the third section by drawing methodological insights from poststructuralist and postcolonial social theorizing to critique conventional research on development and public policy analysis in Africa. Without stating it categorically, the argument is made that insights from the work of scholars in different scholarly traditions (i.e., not African studies) can help us forge a new trend in the area of scholarly research on Africa that focuses on subaltern people's struggle for social liberation and emancipation. The final section is the conclusion and it highlights among other things that neoliberalism is not just an economic theory but a moral philosophy with great implications for what we consider as the meaning of life, the meaning of social relationships in human community, and what constitute the good society. The answers to these questions are beyond the narrow confines of neoclassical economics. The conclusion also asserts that authentic African development cannot take place unless African identity discovers an autonomous foundation outside the orbit of Western identity and unilinear vision of development. The paper begins by providing an overview of the neoliberal theory of economics and its vision of history and society.

Neoliberalism: Theory and Vision of History

The goal of neoliberalism, or what in some circles is referred to as supply-side economics or market fundamentalism, is to bring about economic prosperity in a society through the hyper-pursuit of efficiency in the allocation of scarce resources. The debate in this context is about what is the appropriate role for the government in economic policy? The desire of neoliberals is to promote economic growth, reduce unemployment (but not necessarily eliminate it), and to keep the rate of inflation very low. The entrepreneurs in the economy need to be given utmost support by the government. If the entrepreneurs or producers produce more, this will generate increased employment and tax revenue in the economy (Friedman and Friedman, 1980). They believe that if the private sector is supported and it is functioning optimally, this sector alone would generate widespread demand that can bring about sustained economic growth and prosperity in the society. Thus, government intervention in the economy, if there should be any, should be in the area of supporting the private sector (i.e., entrepreneurs) (Harvey, 2005).

As the businesses in the private sector expand, they will create jobs and employment opportunities. The practical implication of this is that government should not provide direct support to persons in the middle and lower classes. Such persons are not trusted in terms of having a good sense of judgment to use scarce financial resources productively. Rather, such financial support is provided to the corporations and wealthy people in society who presumably will invest the money in productive activities by buying factories, machinery, and raw materials necessary for the expansion of the economy (Heilbroner and Thurow, 1994).

One major effect of this policy position is that the social cost of creating economic growth and prosperity in the whole society is shifted to the middle and lower classes. The upper social classes, the wealthy, and corporations are subsidized by receiving tax breaks and concessions to pay lower tax rates on business profits and capital gains. In effect, public policy promotes regressive taxation and redistribution of wealth from the bottom of the social structure to the top. Supply-side economics promotes a welfare program that only benefits the rich, wealthy, and corporations (Huff, 1993).

Neoliberalism assumes fundamentally that wherever two or more parties are engaged in voluntary market exchange, such exchange is assumed to take place freely and not under any compulsion. "Both parties to an economic transaction benefit from it," according to Friedman because the participants in the transaction presumably did so voluntarily and therefore naturally all benefit from it (Friedman, 1962, p. 55). It is not envisaged that one would engage in a transaction that will negatively impact his or her welfare. This means neoliberals see free exchange as the default state of affairs, and therefore denying people the opportunity to participate in such transaction lowers the potential for them to improve their welfare.

Neoliberals also assume that exchange in the marketplace will automatically lead to the division of labor, and as division of labor increases productivity, the conditions of free exchange will ensure that the fruits of the division of labor are shared for the benefit of everyone. To restrict free exchange in the marketplace therefore means restricting the division of labor and thus negatively impacting the rate of productivity in society. Overall, this will affect the rate of economic growth in a society and the welfare of everyone (Bhagwati, 2004).

Although capitalism expanded in the twentieth century and created more opportunities in spite of the Great Depression, the economies of advanced industrial societies especially in Britain and the United States in the mid-1970s were characterized by budget deficit, high inflation, and high interest rates. In the United States, this was partially precipitated by the government's involvement in the Vietnam War. This crisis of accumulation was used by neoliberals to reassert the ideology of classical liberalism with even more radical reinterpretation. The social context and mood in the late 1970s led to the legitimization of the neoliberal social order as the only viable one, because there was presumably no other alternative. It is at that moment that the neoclassical counter revolution in economics took off (Harvey, 2005).

In terms of concrete public policies, neoliberalism amounts to a profound jettisoning of some of the basic principles of Keynesian economics. Keynes' ideas constitute the philosophical justification and foundation of the postwar welfare state. He maintains that the market mechanism alone cannot guarantee a stable and prosperous economy for everyone (Keynes, 1964). Consequently, the state needs to intervene to regulate the operation of the market and support the socially disadvantaged. This established the philosophical foundation and justification for the postwar welfare state. The state needs to engage in public spending when the economy is experiencing depression and aggregate demand is low. By cutting taxes and increasing public spending, the economy will be rejuvenated. On the other hand, when the economy is going through rapid expansion, the state needs to regulate the expansion by raising interest rates so as to reduce inflation. Keynes hopes that everyone could be employed and the welfare state will discourage the possibility of economically marginalized social groups from creating social movements that will politically capture power and transform the capitalist system out of frustration, thereby creating an authoritarian system. This, in his view, is highly possible if capitalism was left alone to operate on its own without meaningful state intervention.

The proponents of neoclassical counter revolution in economics disagree in some fundamental ways with Keynes' theory, policy implications, and programs. To fully appreciate why the counter-revolution succeeded, one needs to examine several factors that changed the social context and therefore provided the necessary support for the change (Todaro and Smith, 2006, ch. 3). First, the revolution in economic thinking coincided with the emergence of governments in Britain, the United States, Canada, and West Germany that respects absoluteness of supply-side economics. Second, there was at this time a diminution in the role and influence of international organizations that defend the interest of Third World countries, the poor, and socially marginalized people of the world in general. These organizations, which are often affiliated with the United Nations, are: the International Labor Organization (ILO), the United Nations' Development Program (UNDP), and the United Nations' Conference on Trade and Development (UNCTAD).

Finally, neoliberal personalities took control of strategic decision-making positions in the World Bank and the International Monetary Fund (IMF) in the 1980s. Numerous neoliberal policies were subsequently imposed on Third World countries through the World Bank, IMF, and other multilateral and bilateral institutions that mediated the economic relationship between Third World and developed countries (Harvey, 2005; Toye, 1993). Some proponents of the neoclassical counter-revolution, however, see the roles of the World Bank and IMF as equivalent to states' intervention in the economy and society, which create more problems than solutions by distorting the operation of the market mechanism. They, therefore, recommend the dissolution of the institutions (Lal, 2000).

There are specific ways that neoliberalism has profoundly impacted Third World countries. The countries were instructed about the need to create free markets for the sake of free trade. This means dismantling all restrictions to free trade and putting in place infrastructure that will promote free market and trade. Third World governments were also told that they should desist from planning and regulating the economy. The market mechanism should replace the state's effort at regulating the economy and by implication society and its social institutions (Harvey, 2005).

Neoliberals, in their prescription to Third World countries, also assert that the slow or low level of economic development in the Third World was not in any way caused by unfair or exploitative relations between the Third World and developed countries. Rather, Third World states' intervention leads to irrational policy decisions and the misallocation of scarce resources because of the failure to allow the market mechanism to direct the allocation of scarce resources in an efficient and productive way. The way out of this quagmire for Third World countries was to institute the competitive operation of free market. Third World governments were also counseled to privatize any state enterprises that they own. Doing so will create a conducive environment for attracting foreign private investment, which will generate a big push and stimulate economic growth and entrepreneurship. They were also to deregulate all their markets (e.g., financial markets), promote production for export, and remove any government regulation in the economy that distorts the free operation of the market mechanism. For the market mechanism to function effectively in regulating the economy and society, all price distortions in the economy have to be eliminated (Todaro and Smith, 2006).

In the new economic dispensation, the overriding goal of Third World countries should be to promote efficiency and growth in the economy. The pursuit of efficiency is assumed to be the best and most realistic way to promote economic growth and prosperity in the society. In effect, the panaceas to Third World problems have nothing to do with changing the structure of the national and international political economy. The goal is to promote a *laissez faire* economic system in the Third World where the invisible hand will bring about the magic of the marketplace (Harvey, 2005). In support of their policy prescriptions to Third World countries, neoliberals point to the success stories of South Korea, Taiwan, and Singapore as examples illustrating the efficiency of the free market and *laissez faire* approach that neoliberals and neoconservatives promote. They contrast such success stories with the dismal failure of state intervention in the economies of Africa and Latin America (De Soto, 2000). It is in this respect that the analysis of the impact of globalization on Tanzania becomes pertinent as partial verification of the claims of neoliberalism to create a celestial economic social order. In the next section, the empirical findings of Snyder's ethnographic research are highlighted and used as empirical data to interrogate the claims of neoliberalism.

Katherine Snyder: The Ambivalent Nature of the Discourse and Practice of Modernity and Development: Views from the Margins of Tanzanian Society

"Development" in the view of the Iraqw people of Tanzania, when carried out properly, will lead to escape from tradition and to living in "European ways" (Snyder, 2005, p. 2). The author insists that development is an ideologically loaded concept, but this understanding does not seem to preclude experts from using it as a scientifically robust organizing principle that can transform people's lives across time and space. In brief, development in the minds of the Iraqw people can be considered as virtually everything that falls under the discourse of modernity, which contrasts itself with tradition.

The author conducted extensive field work in the region of Iraqw Da'aw in Tanzania. This region is known for its relative geographical isolation and comparatively lower level of participation in the "modern world" compared to other regions and communities in Tanzania. As Tanzania was colonized by the Germans and later the British, modernity and development meant increasingly bringing diverse pre-colonial people under the hegemony of the modern nation state. This process impacted the lives of the people of Iraqw Da'aw as it did that of many social groups in Tanzania with varying consequences. Rural communities in Tanzania such as Iraqw Da'aw have been continuously changing because of social forces operating at the regional, national, and global levels.

A major theme that Snyder attempts to elaborate through her study of the Iraqw Da'aw is the discourse of development. In her study at the grassroots level, she delineates how local people perceive development. For the local people, development implies a lack of backwardness. Yet, it is also not a fixed phenomenon because what it means to be developed changes over time. The discourse of development at the grassroots level is used to interpret the lives of people in the sense that it is used as a measuring rod to evaluate how someone performs.

Interestingly, Snyder discovers that even at the grassroots level, people have some ambivalence about this kind of discourse on development. Development means a broadening of the idea of the community the locals are involved in. It means to be part of the larger global community, which brings about some advantages, but also many disadvantages (e.g., the insecurity of farmers as they depend more on the market, which is shaped by ideological parameters situated beyond their nation). The locals see development as characterized by selfishness, individualism, and the eroding sense of community. They believe that when people act out development, modernity changes their lives, cultural practices, behavior, and their idea of involvement in the local community.

Development is also seen by the locals as justificatory ideology on the part of the state for its intervention in the lives of people and local communities with a view to reorienting and reordering them. Interestingly, there has been consistency in the exposition and articulation of development discourse from the colonial to postcolonial period. There is clearly a strong sense of ambivalence among the locals with regard to what development is all about. Many people associate development with destructive things such as the atomic bomb and rural to urban migration by the young, which even though it has the potential to make a positive contribution, in reality it has had devastating consequences on the countryside as unemployment is high in the cities. The people of Iraqw Da'aw are concerned that development is not really concerned about "fairness, justice, and egalitarianism" (Snyder, 2005, p. 10).

While at the meta-narrative level people assume that modernity means one thing, at the grassroots level, Snyder, using ethnographic research, establishes the fact that modernity is perceived as a process with diverse manifestations leading to what she calls "multiple modernities." She found a strong understanding of modernity as seeing the world temporally in unilinear progression. The idea of unilinear progression is at the core of the contrast between modernity and tradition. Although in theory these are abstract conceptual categories, Snyder finds them to be also evaluative categories that are used to rank people, individuals, and countries (2005, p. 12).

The Global and the Local: Tanzanian Society in the International Political Economy

Globalization in Tanzania, as in other societies, should be viewed in very broad terms and not restricted to the economic dimension that became hegemonic in the 1990s after the war of ideas between the Chicago School of economics and Keynesianism. Based on Snyder's research findings, globalization should be conceptualized broadly to include the diffusion of socio-cultural values and institutions that have their deep roots in Western culture, psyche, and history. Yet, these socio-cultural values and institutions have been immersed in social scientific discourses that have arrogated to themselves ontological status that transcends space and time in terms of their validity. Consequently, globalization is a refurbishment of modernization theory of economic development and cultural change that flourished in the immediate postwar era, when the goal of Western nations was to defeat the specter of communism (Inkeles and Smith, 1974). The only difference is that this time, it is modernization theory with a sense of absolutism and grandeur, given the collapse of socialism and communism. This is where historical facts about the developmental experience of Western nations are converted into historical necessities for Third World countries. Neoliberalism under this hegemonic economic regime becomes the natural and presumably "scientific" course of human history.

Farmers in Tanzania were encouraged in the postcolonial period as part of the new development strategy (especially with neoliberal economic reforms) to cultivate cash crops. In the past, the farmers had cultivated cash crops, and in spite of the fact that the state kept some of the surplus from the sale of the cash crops through its marketing boards and cooperatives, it helped stabilize prices for the farmers. Neoliberal reforms initially raised hopes that farmers would earn more from directly selling their produce in the market. This expectation, however, turned out to be naïve as the prices of the cash crops collapsed in the world market with farmers having no insurance protection such as from the marketing board to help them absorb the drop in prices. This means in the contemporary era, the farmers are on their own; neither the neoliberal state nor the global economy gives them any protection. Furthermore, the fluctuation in the price of primary commodities makes life difficult for many ordinary farmers looking for stability and sustainability (Snyder, 2005, p. 164–65).

Neoliberal policies require the government to privatize many hitherto state-owned businesses for the sake of efficiency, profitability, and productivity. The statistics for this might be impressive, but it has not brought about any meaningful transformation in the lives of ordinary rural Tanzanians. This raises the question of who sets the criteria for evaluating the success of neoliberal reforms. Should it be the International Monetary Fund and the World Bank or the ordinary people of Tanzania based on their life experiences? (Snyder, 2005). For many ordinary citizens of Tanzania and the Third World in general, privatization is equal in effect to auctioning the country to foreign investors and the few who are rich in the country (Mihevc, 1995). The evidence at hand suggests that improving the lives of the poor entails more than simple state intervention (i.e., dirigisme) or the privatization of public enterprises (Evans, 1995).

Structural Adjustment Programs (SAP) implemented in Tanzania has resulted in the dirigiste state withdrawing from its effort to be a welfare state. Increasingly, people are encouraged to live a life that is epitomized by the Horatio Alger myth (i.e., through hard work and determination alone, you can raise yourself by your bootstraps). Yet from the point of view of many ordinary Tanzanians, SAP has polarized the society into the rich and the poor; it has turned people to become more selfish and involved in personal aggrandizement. Interestingly, under Dr. Nyerere, Tanzania worked hard to forge a society based on cooperation, harmony, and community development. One might argue that even if it can be proven that globalization in theory and practice can lead to a win-win situation for all persons involved in it, in practice, people have to have the necessary skills, experience, cultural capital, and wherewithal to take advantage of the opportunities. Unfortunately, the majority of ordinary people in Tanzania and the Third World in general are ill-equipped to participate productively and meaningfully in the global market (Snyder, 2005).

The debate about development and globalization in Tanzania and internationally is essentially, then, a debate about the structure of power and inequality in the international political economy and the ability to produce a discourse that will legitimize the current neoliberal hegemony or subvert it. Unfortunately, at the grassroots level in Tanzania the subversive discourse is carried out in the form of witchcraft accusations, sorceries, and the use of divinations. In practice, all these are attempts by the powerless, the marginalized, and socio-economically disenfranchised people to subvert or get even with those who are powerful and successful in the current global neoliberal regime of development.

There is no well-organized and coherent grassroots people's movement that challenges neoliberal ideological hegemony in a strategic way. It is almost as if this is the end of history. But the question one needs to ask is what does the future hold in store if the only *constructive act of subversion* rural Tanzanians can afford is articulated in the form of witchcraft and curse? This, indeed, punishes the few that are making efforts to escape poverty since they are most likely to be attacked by witchcraft.

Given that we are now living in an overwhelmingly globalized world, if Tanzania or any developing society is to succeed, it will need not only to invest highly in its human capital in the form of education, but also to provide a kind of education that will be competitive in the global economy. Yet even this idea is problematic given the diminutive role of Tanzania in the global economy. If the country tailors her educational programs to primarily fit the needs of the global economy, this would mean creating another form of dependence (i.e., academic and intellectual). Unless the interests of global corporations are equivalent to the needs of the local population, without careful consideration, educational institutions may look more international and attend less to domestic concerns. Unfortunately, even though Tanzanian secondary schools have massively increased in number, they are not well-equipped with the necessary facilities, especially the basic minimum that is needed for competitive education in the global political economy (Snyder, 2005). Furthermore, given the background of some of the students, learning English is a Herculean task. Yet a good speaking and writing ability of English is a huge cultural capital in the contemporary global economy.

To complicate the problem for Tanzania and many developing societies, often the students that go to secondary school develop high expectations and taste (Todaro, 1992). But they soon come to terms with the fact that after their graduation, they cannot realize their high expectations and taste because of the 30 percent unemployment rate among the youth in Tanzania. Many of the youth resort to wasting time in beer-drinking places to displace their frustration. It is partially due to this fact that parents resist sending their children to school. When the children acquire "modern taste" in school, they look down upon their parents at home, who in any case are finding it difficult to pay the school fees. With unemployment of secondary school graduates very high, many parents appropriately see the secondary education of their children as a poor investment. Consequently, admission into secondary schools has dropped to less than seven percent in Tanzania (Snyder, 2005).

The educational situation in Tanzania can be better understood from Paulo Freire's analysis of education as cultural invasion. Freire discusses cultural invasion as a critical component of the theory of anti-dialogical education (1997). The aim of cultural invasion is conquest. In Freire's own words:

> The invaders penetrate the cultural context of another group, in disrespect of the latter's potentialities; they impose their own view of the world upon those they invade and inhibit the creativity of the invaded by curbing their expression. (1997, p. 133)

It is clear that cultural invasion results in oppressed people losing their originality, or at least they are under the threat of doing so. The manner in which Freire conceptualizes cultural invasion is such that any development strategy or knowledge that is imposed from the outside and not representing and building on the concerns, aspirations, and challenges of the oppressed and socially marginalized groups would amount to cultural invasion by the elites into the social context of the poor.

Related to the above is the fact that the cultural invaders could use their knowledge of the oppressed against the oppressed because the invaders have no commitment to dialogical education but rather continued domination of the oppressed. In a sense, this is similar to the argument by Habermas when he asserts that the aim of technical-rational knowledge is to facilitate prediction and social control. Such control, when in the hands of people not committed to social justice, can become an instrument of domination and oppression (Habermas, 1981).

Freire argues that if cultural invasion is successful, it creates a feeling of inferiority among the people subjugated. Under such conditions, the social institutions of the subjugated society reflect the structure of domination instituted by the dominant group at the macro level. The macro-institutional structures in turn shape micro-relations within social organizations such as the family. Thus, he sees a connection between macro- and micro-processes and suggests, for instance, that parent-child relations and socialization within the family are significantly molded by the broad structure of domination at the macro-level (Freire, 1997). In many respects, Snyder documents how micro-social relations such as gender relations, weddings, parent-child relations, and relations between the older and younger generation among the Iraqw Da'aw people are shaped by the global forces of modernization that are impacting the country and the local community. Freire's argument is therefore substantiated by Snyder's research conclusions.

In reflecting on the main elements of cultural invasion, Freire provides a theoretical framework for explaining development and underdevelopment at the national and community level. If development is the capacity for subjects working in collaboration with each other to create and recreate social reality, thereby making history, then all the elements of cultural invasion negate that.

But by far, the greatest source of frustration is the fact that the mainstay of Iraqw Da'aw economy is agriculture, which is highly dependent on the vagaries of prices in the world market. With the high cost of farm input, limited off-farm employment, and the lack of expansion of the economy, widening inequality and stagnation create a sense of hopelessness and bleak future for the youth (Snyder, 2005). We can easily conclude that frustration and hopelessness in Tanzania is not just among the youth. Indeed, it exists among parents and the elderly who see the community going through continuous decline because of social problems such as: the lower fertility of livestock; less quantity of milk from the cattle; lower agricultural productivity; poor market prices; increased rate of divorce; increased premarital childbirth; and widespread infection of the HIV/AIDS virus.

The foregoing indicates the internal contradictions in the operation of globalization in Tanzania, which is also true for other parts of the world, both developed and developing. The Tanzanian government and people evaluate their nation's performance in the global economy differently from the World Bank and IMF (Snyder, 2005). This brings to mind Dudley Seers' remarkable observation in his seminal critique of the conventional meaning of development. He asserts:

> The questions to ask about a country's development are therefore: What has been happening to poverty? What has been happening to unemployment? What has been happening to inequality? If all three of these have declined from high levels, then beyond doubt this has been a period of development for the country concerned. If one or two of these central problems have been growing worse, especially if all three have, it would be strange to call the result 'development' even if per capita income doubled. (1969, p. 3)

Ordinary rural Tanzanians rarely see the benefits of globalization or market reforms trickling down to them. Yet they are told that their country is one of the best success stories. Moreover, many are concerned that globalization is simply creating an environment where young people are aping foreign culture not only from the West but Arab culture too through watching satellite television, which has penetrated rural Tanzania (Snyder, 2005). Snyder's book leaves us with a feeling of ambivalence about the discourse and practice of development and modernity at the grassroots level. She is not anti-development but intends to impress on the reader to not think simplistically about development in the era of market fundamentalism. Ultimately, it is the quality of life of the ordinary citizens of Tanzania and the Third World that should be the measure of development, not the validity of an elegant econometric equation. Snyder's findings can be interpreted and illuminated using some poststructuralist and postcolonial ideas. The next section attempts to do just that.

Insights from Poststructuralist and Postcolonial Social Theorizing: Implications for Development and Public Policy Research and Analysis

This section of the chapter explores some ideas of Foucault (1972, 1973, 1979), a French poststructuralist scholar, and insights from the work of three postcolonial theorists: Fanon (1968, 1986); Bhabha (1986); and Spivak (cited in Landry and MacLean, 1996; Spivak, 1988). In the next section I highlight some significant social implications from the work of the theorists that have bearing for research in development and social change, and public policy analysis in Africa.

Foucault's idea that would be the main focus of discussion here is his work on discourse and power (1972). He interprets and analyzes discourse as one form of power that is exercised by experts, such as those in the International

Monetary Firm (IMF) and the World Bank that played a critical role in conceptualizing and implementing neoliberal economic reforms in Africa. Experts are supposed to make statements that are rational and systematic. The statements are not randomly made but made within the context of "rules" that govern the experts' area of specialization. At the core of discourse is what Foucault refers to as "serious speech act" which is a statement made by a professional making knowledge claim and providing procedures for the validation or verification of the statement. Foucault argues that knowledge claims are made within epistemological fields or contexts. Within every epistemological field or context, there are rules that specify who is qualified to say what and about what. Whether a statement counts as knowledge or not cannot be decided in abstraction but within the context of an epistemological field or scope (Foucault, 1973, p. 191). Unfortunately, the Iraqw people have no expert grounds to participate in the formulation and implementation of the discourse of neoliberalism.

Discourses according to Foucault could be studied from archeological and genealogical methods. The archeological study of discourse looks at their structures as systems. The main elements of the structures are examined in order to see how the different elements of the structure relate to each other and how together they constitute a systematic whole. The genealogical study of discourse examines how it came into existence and how its validity or legitimacy is rooted in social practices that themselves are not put on the table for formal discussion e.g., the institution of power (Foucault, 1980, p. 84).

Since discourses are rooted within institutions of power, as the institutions of power change, then the discourses will also change. Thus the archeological and genealogical study of power is equivalent to the study of structure and process i.e., diachronic and synchronic analysis. According to Foucault, any kind of knowledge is tied to some practical or empirical consideration. In this case the shift from classical liberalism to Keynesianism and the welfare state followed by the neoliberal counter revolution in economics spearheaded by the Chicago School of Economics is an excellent example of how social and economic conditions and shifts in political coalitions lead to changes in dominant economic discourses (Toye, 1993).

Foucault asserts that every institution of power produces a kind of discourse to justify itself. The discourse becomes knowledge, and the institution of power guarantees the legitimacy of the knowledge. Thus power, truth, and knowledge are inextricably interconnected. One tends to presuppose the other in mutually reinforcing ways. Truth for Foucault is not a substance or some piece of information that has essence that is constant and unchanging for all times. For him, truth is made what it is by a set of rules that every society through its dominant institutions establishes in order to make a distinction between what is true and what is not, thereby attributing the special status of power to what is defined as truth. Foucault defines truth as follows:

> Truth is not outside of power. . . each society has its own regime of truth, its general politics of truth. . . There is a combat for the truth, or at least around the

> truth, as long as we understand by the truth not those true things which are waiting to be discovered but rather the ensemble of rules according to which we distinguish the true from the false, and attach special effects of power to "the truth." (1980, p. 131)

In effect, rules that are used to define what is true and false are set by specific people in power depending on historical time and the specific society or social-cultural context in reference. Furthermore, since the people in power change from time to time, there will always be varying "regimes of truth." For this reason, there will always be politics around the competition for power. Every regime of politics is a struggle over truth or the redefinition of the truth (Foucault, 1980, p. 131). Some forms of knowledge and power expressed through institutions and disciplines are aimed not at liberating or emancipating people but making them productive persons while also rendering them docile in the interest of those who have established hegemonic control. The relevant point to note here is how all the most powerful institutions shaping the dominant economic discourses for the developing world are neither close to Africa's subaltern people nor influenced by them. The subalterns are not represented in sophisticated econometric models.

Foucault is suspicious of research projects that earn their validity from theories that are totalizing in their knowledge claim. Globalization discourses and epistemologies that consider themselves scientific suppress local knowledge by treating such knowledge as myth. But Foucault's approach is aimed at resurrecting or rediscovering knowledge that was hitherto de-legitimized by globalizing and totalizing discourses (e.g., neoliberalism). Instead of the subjugation of such local knowledge, he wants to resurrect, rediscover, and reconstruct them which would however be difficult because of the hegemony of globalizing discourses (Foucault, 1980). Foucault's sympathies here are similar and consistent with Freire's given that he values the input of locally generated knowledge by people in the community. In effect, both Foucault and Freire would agree that what Snyder unraveled among the Iraqw Da'aw people of Tanzania is cultural invasion.

Foucault is not opposed to science as such but opposed to sciences or scientific knowledge that are affiliated to institutions of power, where power is concentrated and hegemony is created. He calls for the "union of erudite knowledge and local memories" which he hopes will inform local struggles and the tactics used to carry out such struggles (Foucault, 1980, p. 83). The Foucauldian concept of power however is not about binary relations in society. He sees it as having multiple manifestations and operating at different levels.

Foucault's social theoretical framework of analyzing society starts not with an inherently essential conception of human beings that exists *a priori*. Rather, he turns total and universal theory upside down by saying that it is not humans with inherent essence and consciousness that constitute the subjects shaping history. Rather human beings are socially constructed by their social environment. This means that as different social environments are characterized by different institutional power structures, they will produce different regimes of truth and discourses, and all these would unevenly shape the consciousness and "essence" of people depending on their social and cultural context (Foucault, 1972, p. 142). Thus instead of seeing human beings as historical subjects rooted in certain essential, timeless, and changing qualities, Foucault sees human beings as having no one single essence. Consequently, one cannot legitimately derive a universal theory of history or totalizing vision of history, because that is only tenable when there is a single essential human nature.

Frantz Fanon was a West Indian from the island of Martinique who studied psychiatry in France and later fought on the part of Algeria in the Algerian armed struggle for independence from France. His anti-colonial critiques were contained in his two books: *The Wretched of the Earth* (1968); and *Black Skin, White Masks* (1986).

Part of Fanon's work focused on the development of human identity which in my view is central to any strategy of pursuing development as freedom to use Amartya Sen's idea (2000). He did not agree with the idea that human beings developed an identity that is coherent and settled once and for all. He was influenced by the work of Jacques Lacan (see Benvenuto and Kennedy, 1996), the French psychoanalyst. Lacan's theory asserts that the construction of social identity and ego in the conscious self was never coherent but permanently schismatic. Ego construction in Lacanian psychoanalysis involves a process of alienation and so the individual ego is never internally harmonious. It is constructed in relation to an "Other" whoever that "Other" is.

The work of Fanon and other postcolonial scholars was to appropriate the framework that Lacan used in his psychoanalytic theory to explain ego construction. They used it to explain the personality of the "colonizer" and the "colonized." In this respect, Fanon saw Western social identity which is traditionally construed as coherently rational as actually uncertain and internally discordant, inharmonious and alienated. Fanon believed that the black "Other" was necessary for the construction of the white colonizer's image. The white colonizer sees the black "Other" as the contrast rather than a mirror confirming his or her white colonizer identity. Similarly, Fanon asserts that the historical and economic context of colonialism shaped the social construction and development of a black identity that was necessarily based on the white "Other" (Fanon, 1986, p. 161).

The implication of Fanon's analysis is to undermine the coherent universalism and essence of humanity that is embedded in Western discourse of development. If the white colonizer's identity is built on the idea of contrast and opposition to the colonial "Other," any approach to development that grew out of such a worldview will never truly liberate the colonized. The colonized should therefore look for an alternative route for their liberation and emancipation, because in so far as they subsume themselves and their identity under the white colonizer's project of modernity, they will neither develop an authentic ego nor social identity, let alone liberate themselves. It is impossible to think of meaningful development taking place in Africa without an authentic social identity that is African. While Fanon's ideas are seminal in postcolonial studies and have inspired other scholars, some scholars have appreciated but also critiqued his analysis.

Homi Bhabha (1986) is a Lacanian theorist working at the University of Chicago. Building on ideas that are consistent with Foucault's, he rejects simple binary categorization as too totalizing and encompassing. Thus in critiquing Fanon, he asserts that Fanon came up with just two binary personalities (i.e., the Third World "Other" and the First World "Same"). In effect, Bhabha is asserting that Fanon's analysis is founded on a single type of personality for the whole colonized Third World people. In the case of Africa, this means from Tunis to Cape Town.

Bhabha also asserts that while Fanon presents the actions of white colonizers to Third World people as based on Western arrogance, the reality is different and more complicated. Bhabha maintains that the Orient or the "Other" is presented in Western discourse in a manner that suggests Westerners are ambivalent towards the "Otherness" of the Orient or one might say African by implication. Thus he notes that given the way Westerners represent the Orient, they betray more of anxiety than arrogance. Although there was assertiveness on the part of Western colonizers, looking at the whole gamut of representation, it was as complex, contradictory, and ambivalent as it was anxious and assertive. For instance, if Westerners' representation of the Orient was simply based on arrogance, then one would naturally expect that when the Orient imitates Westerners, the Westerners would find it affirming and fulfilling. On the contrary, they find it actually subversive. In effect, successful assimilation by the black "Other" can constitute a threat and uneasiness in the sensibilities of Westerners. For instance, at one point, the goal of the West was to make Japan open to westernization. But when Japan became very successful and excelled more than the United States in some areas (e.g., automobile manufacturing), Japan was perceived as a threat to Western hegemony and invincibility, and this created negative backlash at Japanese success and expansion in the U.S. market.

Still on the question of identity and development, the work of Gayatri Spivak (cited in Landry and MacLean, 1996; Spivak, 1988) provides an important insight with regard to whether the "colonized" has one single identity and if it does, does it ever speak with one voice or multiple voices? The main contribution and critique by Spivak grew out of her critical examination of the "subaltern studies group" in India. The aim of the research was to rediscover the suppressed voices of subaltern groups i.e., groups that are subordinated along the lines of class, caste, gender, and race. It was assumed that these groups and their social agency in resisting and subverting colonialism in India were marginalized or suppressed in colonial historiography. The goal of the subaltern studies group in India then was to recover and give this group its rightful place in history as conscious historical subjects and agents of change. In this respect, they are perceived as people that have created and led counter hegemonic movement in terms consistent with the social analysis of subversive and progressive change by Antonio Gramsci (1972).

Such an analysis surely seems to empower and recognize the role of subaltern people in history by affirming them as conscious historical subjects pursuing their interest rationally. Furthermore, they are seen as having the capacity to bring about change. The problem that Spivak identifies in this situation is that in the process of critiquing colonial historiography, the subaltern studies group in India, according to her, have built their case simplistically on the Western discourse of the enlightenment (i.e., conscious historical subjects with a voice of their own that is presumably coherent and articulate).

Spivak asserts that this is a major mistake because the idea of a single, coherent colonial subject with single consciousness and an independent voice did not exist in history. The social position that colonial subjects occupied was contradictory and their role was multiple, depending on the social-cultural context and situation. Using the case of women for instance, she said women filled the subject position of class, ethnicity, and gender. If this was really the case, she notes there was never a coherent subject position that speaks with one voice for women. Sometimes the subject's voice is of ethnic identity, sometimes class identity, and at other times gender or religious identity. This means there is no one coherent subject position that women occupied or even men occupied, for that matter. If this was the case, then there was no one single coherent voice of the colonial subject and to impute one would amount to creating a fictitious reality that never existed in history. What then are the social implications of the ideas of Foucault, Fanon, Bhabha, and Spivak for Third World development research and public policy analysis? This will be the subject matter of the next section.

Social and Methodological Implications of Poststructuralist and Postcolonial Theorizing for Research in Development and Public Policy Analysis in Africa

The first key lesson that one can deduce from the literature examined in this paper is how do we conceptualize and study development and modernity? While there are extensive definitions and official documents defining what those concepts are, Snyder uses the ethnographic approach to unravel what these concepts really mean. While no one embarks on a research project without having some thoughts or ideas in mind, Snyder decided to keep her thoughts at bay and explore what development and modernity means through observing and participating in the daily lives of the people and the community of Iraqw Da'aw. What do development / modernity mean in terms of the empirical reality surrounding the lives of the people? This kind of research is time consuming and requires patience. But when executed successfully, it helps us interrogate the official discourse of development by comparing it with the lived experience of people at the grassroots level. The national government and multilateral agencies might produce elaborate documents on development policies and programs but ultimately whether these ideas are translated into reality or not is reflected in the lives of the people.

Instead of making any *a priori* assumption, the daily interaction with people provides insights into issues of social class, social differentiation, gender inequality, climate and ecological changes, rural-urban migration, and satellite television as a kind of global cultural intrusion into the local community, and witchcraft. The challenge of the researcher is to decipher the ways in which development and modernity are translated into the lives of people in rural communities. It is obvious that for many people in the Iraqw Da'aw community, their quality of life and welfare have declined in spite of claims by neoliberal experts that neoliberal reforms would lead to greater development for all (see Havery, 2005; Friedman, 1980). Of course what this means is that irrespective of the aggregate data at the national level, ultimately, the lived experience of the people is the final arbiter as to whether development is a progress in the lives of the people or not.

Related to the above is the need to evaluate development by not just examining the relationship between input and output in a production equation, i.e., "The Harrod-Domar Growth Model" (Todaro and Smith, 2008). Rather, in order to really understand the process of development we have to carefully document the mechanisms through which development policies conceptualized by multilateral agencies like the International Monetary Fund (IMF) and the World Bank are sold to leaders of Third World countries, and then they are translated into reality by way of implementation. Often we know the input and output, but there is not much attention paid to the mechanism and process through which the public policies are implemented and how they affect the lives of the people now and by implication in the future. A method of research that has been used to document this kind of phenomenon is *"institutional ethnography"* (Smith, 1978).

Institutional ethnography was originally developed "to better understand women's everyday experiences by discovering power relations that shape those experiences. Today this methodology has been extended to the ideologies that shape the experiences of any oppressed group" (Babbie, 2001, p. 287). Its main goal is to study the day-to-day lives of subaltern groups in order to unravel how the social processes and mechanisms of operation of institutions and organizations shape the existential struggle and social realities of people's lives. Using this method, one is able to illuminate forms of oppression and social marginalization that are subtle and insidious but yet are not easily unraveled or highlighted by traditional research methods. The critical issue is starting with the ordinary lived experience of the socially marginalized social group in order to understand how institutional and organizational relations of power shape the configuration of the experience of people. Campbell elaborates what institutional ethnography is as follows:

> Institutional ethnography, like other forms of ethnography, relies on interviewing, observation and documentation as data. Institutional ethnography departs from other ethnographic approaches by treating those data not as the topic or

> object of interest, but as "entry" into the social relations of the setting. The idea is to tap into people's experiences. (1998, p. 57)

In effect, institutional ethnography connects the "micro-level" experiences of everyday life with institutions and organizations operating at the "macro-level" both nationally and internationally. Both Foucault and Freire would be comfortable and supportive of this research methodology because of its ability to unravel systems of domination and oppression, thereby helping to subvert them.

Foucault's focus on discourse as a kind of power that shapes what becomes truth is central to any research study that is attempting to explain the goals and process of development. The important question here is who sets the contours of the discourse on a particular public policy? Who sets the framework of the discourse and who gets to participate in shaping the content of the public policy, and the process and mechanism for its implementation? Furthermore, who sets the criteria for determining its success and failure? Joseph Stiglitz argues that in the many meetings he participated in on global issues of development when he was the chairperson of the United States' Council of Economic Affairs, nobody in the meetings directly represented the interests of poor people (Stiglitz, 2006). In theory, government officials are supposed to do that as part of their official responsibility, but in reality, powerful interests groups like corporations end up having a disproportionate amount of influence on the position taken by government officials. Related to this is the role that power plays in defining the truth. Foucault's conceptualization of power sees it as something that exists in a diffused manner. It is not just concentrated in one place. Consequently, it is not enough to examine power relations vertically and focus only at the top, or examine it at the international and national levels only. Instead, Foucault would suggest that at every level in the chain of command or network of human relationships, we need to isolate who has the power to say what, on what issues, and note how such persons are able to shape development discourse and programs? Shaping development discourse involves negotiation between people with different levels of power at the international, national, local, community level, and indeed even in the family. For instance, what role women, young people, and poor peasants play in shaping the development discourse? Indeed, using the concept of "bio-power," Foucault's social analysis suggests that we should examine the mechanism and process through which external systems of hegemonic control and domination get internalized and reproduced in our bodies and psyche. In effect, we end up controlling ourselves instead of being controlled.

Muhammad Yunus documents the androcentric bias of economic reasoning and the financial industry in his book, *Creating a World Without Poverty: Social Business and the Future of Capitalism* (2007). Similarly, in the documentary, *Small Change, Big Business* (Aardenburg and Films for the Humanities & Sciences, 2005), Yunus articulates how one of the major obstacles the Grameen Bank faced in implementing microcredit programs for women in Bangladesh was the resistance of some men. In particular, some religious mullahs on Islamic theological grounds were opposed to the increased role and power that women would have in the family and in the community when they receive the loan and start generating income. The mullahs used religious scriptures to assert that the women who collect the loan will go to hell because God has predestined some people to be rich while others to be poor, and this is the way of things. Often the critique of power and how it corrupts development focuses on people with formal positions in the national government bureaucracy or at the international level. But Foucault's understanding of power as diffused means we have to observe its covert and overt use and manifestation in all human relationships whether they are formal or informal. For instance, in many parts of Sub-Saharan Africa religious leaders who may not have any official political designation still have great leverage in shaping public opinion, morality and ethics of people, especially at the grassroots levels (Alidou, 2005; Corten and Marshall-Fratani, 2001; Maxwell, 2007).

Foucault's analysis of discourse and power also has the important implication that local knowledge has value and as Freire would argue, any public policy or development program that excludes the insights of or the local knowledge of the people in a community is tantamount to a kind of cultural invasion. Of course Foucault is not saying that local knowledge is the only thing that public policy or development program should be based on. Rather, he suggests that the local knowledge should constitute an integral part of any knowledge claim that will inform the public policy or development program. James Scott argues along the same line in his book: *Seeing like a State: How Certain Schemes to Improve Human Condition Have Failed* (1998). His central argument based on empirical studies was that state projects based on high modernist ideology while in and of themselves are not necessarily bad, they easily turn into an instrument of control and domination because of over-simplification of complex social-cultural reality such as was in the case in communist Russia and China, and in the case of Tanzania's Ujaama socialism. Such projects often fail because the state elites based the programs on naïve optimism and simplistic application of high level instrumental rationality, science, and technology, while ignoring the local knowledge and sensitivities of the local and ordinary people. Consequently, such state projects of modernization did not receive a wide sense of ownership beyond the coercive level or beyond those who rigged the process to their advantage. Scott makes his case as follows:

> These state simplifications, the basic givens of modern statecraft, were I began to realize, rather like abridged maps. They did not successfully represent the actual activity of the society they depicted, nor were they intended to; they represented only that slice of it that interested the official observer. They were, moreover, not just maps. Rather, they were maps that, when allied with state power, would enable much of the reality they depicted to be remade. . . . My case is that certain kinds of states, driven by utopian plans and an authoritarian disregard for the values, desires, and objections of their subjects, are indeed a mortal threat to human well-being. Short of that draconian but all too common situation, we are left to weigh judiciously the benefits of certain state interventions against their costs. (1998, p. 3, 7)

Scott is not by any means suggesting that utopian projects are only on the left of the political spectrum. Indeed, what he refers to as state intervention encompasses neoliberal economic reforms that are implemented by governments all over the world. Neoliberal reforms represent utopian projects to the extent that the neoliberal state becomes subordinated to the interest of capital and the primary role of government becomes transforming the social institutions, social structures and social attitudes of people to be conducive for the operation of free trade and the free market. Free trade, free markets, and deregulation will increase efficiency and productivity, and promote economic growth, thereby creating a Nirvana of economic prosperity.

Related to this, Habermas (1972) asserts that all projects of knowledge production have human interests that guide them. For instance, he identified the following research interests, each of which is characterized by different human interests and research methodologies: a) empirical-analytic sciences; b) practical knowledge which aims at promoting communicative action, i.e., increase hermeneutical understanding; c) emancipatory knowledge which is the realm of critical social science and the goal is promoting the social liberation of human beings. What this means is that in consonance with Freire, any knowledge claim that will inform public policy, whether its source is local or external to the community, the human interest behind the knowledge should be investigated and interrogated to see whether its goal is to simply predict and control society in an amoral manner (i.e., dominate efficiently) or promote social liberation and increase hermeneutical understanding among diverse groups of people. In doing this, the goal is to move the analysis beyond abstract formalism to the realm of practical reality.

Fanon raises an important issue that has profound implications for research on development and public policy. One can reframe Fanon's concern by asking whether Africans can become liberated with dignity if their approach to development and identity formation is subsumed under Western concept of development and identity. Fanon treats identity formation and development as central to any serious attempt at development. But if African people are told directly and indirectly that to develop means to acquire Western identity and institutions when Western identity itself is incoherent and schismatic since it developed in opposition to the "Other," then trying to be Western will create a deficient, confused, and distorted African identity. It will pigeon-hole African identity into an inferior status and it will lack the autonomous capacity and vitality to shape its destiny since it is using Western identity and achievement as its guidepost when that identity (i.e., Western) is developed in opposition to the non-Western "Other."

Unfortunately not much emphasis is paid in Africa to making a connection between identity formation and national development. Yet it is evident from Fanon's analysis that insofar as Africans subsume their identity under the Western ideal they can only develop at great social cost if at all. Fanon's preference is for Africans to look for an alternative development strategy that resituates African identity outside the orbit of Western identity but not prejudiced against it.

Doing so will require a high level of consciousness and determination and a committed crop of elites that are not only courageous but well informed about the politics and political economy of development. It is obvious that it will be easier for Western nations to control and dominate Africa if Africans subsume their identity and development under the Western model i.e., unilinear model of human progress and development.

Foucault complements Fanon on this when he asserts that Western theoretical models of development which are total and universal are based on a single universal conception of human essence and nature. The problem is if there is any such concept at all, it exists at a high level of abstract formalism. Concrete human nature and essence according to Foucault always develops within concrete socio-cultural and historical context. What this means is that Western theories of development were developed based on a perception of human beings within a specific socio-cultural and historical context but that, historically and socially, specific human identity or essence was ascribed the status of universality across time and space. African identity, while sharing much in common with other people, has to be understood within the continent's socio-cultural and historical context. This entails developing either new theories of development from scratch, or, if this is too demanding and unrealistic, then we need to interrogate all theories based on the socio-historical reality of African people and come up with an alternative. A step in this direction is Bangura's concept of Ubuntugogy. Bangura (2005, p. 20) defines *Ubuntugogy* as follows:

> [T]he essence *of ubuntugogy* is that it is imperative and urgent for African educators to be concerned about broader education as well as training and to be concerned about approaches to learning and teaching which are undergirded by humanity or fellow feeling toward others. When *ubuntugogy* is considered along with the idea of the socialization effects of educational environments and the possibilities of a reinforcement of these notions and contexts, the implications for an African educational process appear vital.

Ubuntugogy is derived from the root word "*ubuntu*" which in one African language means a worldview that sees one's human dignity and humanity as something that is inextricably interconnected with that of other human beings and therefore compelling the need for mutual recognition and respect. A point that needs to be added here is that given the dynamic forces of change within and outside Africa that are compelling the region to change as the socio-cultural and historical context changes, *ubuntu* and ubuntogogy need to be dynamic in order to take into consideration the phenomenal development that have taken place in the twentieth century across the African continent and the realities and challenges of the twenty-first century (Van der Walt, 2010 forthcoming). Furthermore, given that human societies have engaged in cultural exchanges from time immemorial, ubuntugogy, while rooted in African socio-cultural and historical realities, should not preclude Africans from adopting and adapting ideas from other societies and cultures where there is some elective affinity or fit.

Homi Bhabha's analysis can be translated into a counsel for those engaged in negotiating development programs and public policies. Whether it is at the international or national level, it is a legitimate question to ask whether elites' treatment of the masses is a manifestation of arrogance or hubris on the part of the elites or is it a behavior based on fear and ambivalence? For instance, in an article titled, "Jealousy as a Class Phenomenon: The Petite Bourgeoisies and Social Security," Abram de Swaan (1989) argues that the middle classes in Europe, in particular, the *petite bourgeoisies* opposed the extension of social security benefits to the working class because the middle class feel insecure and jealous that if the lower classes were to get what they have there would be little or no distinction in the status of the two classes. He asserts:

> Behind middle-class protests there may have been 'vigilance in maintaining and guarding something': jealous of a working class that stood to gain the security which once had been the sole privilege of the propertied classes. It is not easy to document this group feeling adequately. It was often hidden behind more elaborate ideological stances, if it was expressed at all. And it may only be uncovered by studying private sources, such as personal correspondence, diaries, and letters to the local press. (cited in Curtis and Tepperman, 1994, p. 343)

Thus in order to keep their distinctive status, the *petite bourgeoisies* opposed the progress of those below them. Such behavior is more a product of fear, envy, and a relative sense of insecurity than an outright expression of arrogance and hubris. What this means is in evaluating how Western professionals engage in the discourse of development and the process of implementing the programs that come out of that, are they conceptualizing and implementing the programs in a manner that would guarantee and perpetuate their privileges out of the fear of losing their special privileges, or is it just a sheer expression of hubris rooted in the spirit of Rudyard Kipling's (1899) "White Man's Burden"? Bhabha's analysis suggests that we must not draw quick conclusions or make generalizations about this. Instead, we should look carefully and case by case to see what motives inform the logic of the interaction between Western people and professionals with the "Other?" Are there variations among different types of Western engagements or are they all the same? The answer to these questions can have significant bearing on the substantive strategies that are adopted by subaltern people in their struggle for social liberation and emancipation. It will help them in avoiding a paranoid attitude towards all Westerners or living under a kind of siege-mentality, which can affect their ability to cultivate a healthy working relationship with Westerners or local elites that are authentically trying to help them in their struggle for social emancipation.

Finally, Spivak also provides insights from her critique of the subaltern studies. She maintains vehemently that while we should remain committed to subaltern struggles, we must be careful not to treat all subalterns as one amorphous group, but identify the nuances of variation within the group and indeed the multiple identities that anyone individual from the subaltern group can have. We should avoid reductionism in understanding people's identity across Africa. These multiple identities need to be negotiated. Without examining, documenting and analyzing the variation within the subaltern group and how the multiple identities of a person can shape his or her preferences and support for public policies, development programs or public policies will fail because they have either reduced or simplified the complex nuances and variation among the various subaltern groups into one formal category, which is given salience at the expense of the others. This is similar to the conclusion that Scott (1998) arrived at. What this implies for instance is the fact that people may be oppressed but for different reasons, and the process of oppression may also be different e.g., gender, religion, social class, ethnicity, political affiliation etc. Furthermore, this means we cannot just assume that the experience of oppression by women is the same given that some women are highly educated, some are from upper social class backgrounds, while some are illiterate and peasant farmers. Even though they are all women, their experiences vary because of several other variables that mediate or tamper with their gender experience and identity. Research in development and public policy must take this into cognizance and understand that we cannot use one policy blueprint as the panacea because of complex variation at the grassroots level across Africa. Ultimately, the concrete consequences of a development program or public policy cannot be fully determined *a priori*, because the social and historical context of the implementation is a key factor in determining the real consequences.

Similarly, political scientist Michael Sandel (1983) and philosopher Alasdair MacIntyre (1984), both of whom are communitarians in their scholarly orientation, are in agreement with Spivak even though they come from different scholarly traditions. Sandel and MacIntyre assert that the idea of the individual as someone who is fully human but existing in isolation and making rational choices outside a network of human relationships, community, and obligations is fictitious. They both critiqued the concept of the neoclassical individual that is a canon of Western liberalism and modernity, just as Spivak too is critical of that. The real individual is always rooted in one kind of social status or another that is accompanied by roles which shape his or her identity and relationship to others in a community. Often there is a conflict between or among different status positions and roles, which have to be negotiated. We cannot therefore assume that simply because people belong to the subaltern group, they therefore have one and only one identity. Neither can one universal public policy effectively address their social predicaments, or that when implemented, a particular public policy will have the same consequences on all persons in the subaltern group. What this means in practice is a paradigm shift from top-bottom conceptualization and implementation of development programs to one that is more "bottom-up" even though this may be time consuming and does not preclude progressive ruling elites from providing leadership and guidance.

Conclusion

This chapter uses Katherine Snyder's findings as empirical data to interrogate neoliberalism. In doing this, the main elements of neoliberalism were highlighted. It is obvious that neoliberalism is not just an economic theory, but it is also a moral philosophy given that the social implications and consequences of the theory affect social justice, democracy, and the struggle for equality in human societies. This much is supported by Katherine Snyder's empirical data.

The chapter highlights how the ideas of poststructuralist and postcolonial scholars can be used in combination with *"institutional ethnography"* to document the lived experiences of the oppressed and then use it to interrogate the structure and process of social institutions and the programs they implement. Instead of relying just on official discourses and statistics about the efficacy of development programs implemented, the lives and existential experiences of subaltern people become part of the data to be used to evaluate the efficacy of programs.

The chapter calls for a paradigm shift in research on development and public policy analysis in Africa that will privilege the voices of subaltern groups (who represent the great majority of people in Africa) in order to create conditions that will enable them to participate actively in shaping the discourses of development and the process of public policy implementation. Yet, it warns that there is a wide range of variation within and among subaltern groups, and so because of their multiple identities, we should guide against reducing the complexity to one single issue that is of interest to us. Such expedient reductionism would lead to program failure when the programs fail to take into cognizance the nuances and variation across the continent and within regions in different countries.

Finally, the chapter asserts in agreement with Fanon that Africa cannot be socially liberated or emancipated in so far as its development and social identity is subsumed under that of the West as represented by its dominant elites. Fanon is not against adopting and adapting ideas from other parts of the world to help improve Africa's situation in so far as they make meaningful and constructive contribution to the struggle for social liberation, but he believes that Western identity did not develop in social and historical vacuum. Rather, it developed in a particular social and historical context and in opposition to the "Other" whether that "Other" is Africa, the Orient, the East, or Latin America. Given this, building an authentic African identity on a social identity that originally opposed itself to Africa as an "Other," is a project in human misadventure. Yet it must be confessed and asserted that conceptualizing and envisioning African social identity and development outside the orbit of Western identity and development will require extraordinary courage, maturity, broadmindedness, humility and commitment to human dignity and emancipation among Africans, especially its leaders and youth. It will require an African elite vanguard that is visionary and selfless in its thinking and actions, and also confident, but yet willing to work in partnership with the oppressed people of the continent and progressive minds in all regions of the world (including the West) who are willing to commit themselves to the progressive emancipation of the oppressed (wherever they are and whoever they are) from their predicament.

Bibliography

Alidou, Ousseina. *Engaging Modernity: Muslim Women and Politics and the Politics of Agency in Postcolonial Niger* (Women in Africa and the Diaspora). Madison: University of Wisconsin Press, 2005.

Aardenburg, M., and Films for the Humanities & Sciences (Firm). *Small Change, Big Business: The Women's Bank of Bangladesh 10 years Later.* Micro Credit for Women: The Story of the Grameen Bank. Princeton, NJ: Films for the Humanities & Sciences, 2005.

Babbie, Earl R. *The Practice of Social Research* (8th Ed.). Belmont, CA: Wadsworth/Thomson Learning, 2001.

Bangura, Abdul K. "Ubuntogogy: An African Educational Paradigm that Transcends Pedagogy, Andragogy, Ergonagy, and Hetagogy." *Journal of Third World Studies* 22, no. 2 (2005): 13–53.

Benvenuto, R., and R. Kennedy. *The Works of Jacques Lacan: An Introduction.* London: Free Association, 1986.

Bhabha, Homi K. "The Other Question: Difference, Discrimination and the Discourse of Colonialism." *Literature, Politics and Theory* (1986): 148–72.

Bhagwati, Jagdish. *In Defense of Globalization.* Toronto: Oxford University Press, 2004.

Campbell, Marie L. "Institutional Ethnography and Experience Data." *Qualitative Sociology,* 21 (1998): 55–73.

Corten, Andre, and Ruth Marshall-Fratani. *Between Babel and Pentecost: Transnational Pentecostalism in Africa and Latin America.* Bloomington: Indiana University Press, 2001.

De Soto, Hernando. *The Mystery of Capital: Why Capitalism Triumphs in the West and Fails Everywhere Else.* New York: Basic Books, 2000.

de Swaan, Abram. "Jealousy as a Class Phenomenon: The Petite Bourgeoisies And Social Security." In *Haves and Have–Nots: An International Reader on Social Inequality,* edited by James Curtis and Lorne Tepperman, 339–45. Englewood Cliff: Prentice Hall, 1989.

Evans, Peter B. *Embedded Autonomy: States and Industrial Transformation.* Princeton, NJ: Princeton University Press, 1995.

Fanon, Frantz. *Black Skin, White Masks.* London: Pluto Press, 1986.

———. *The Wretched of the Earth.* New York: Grove Press, 1968.

Foucault, M. *Power / Knowledge: Selected Interviews and Other Writings.* Trans. C. Gordon. New York: Pantheon Books, 1980.

———. *Discipline and Punish: The Birth of the Prison.* New York: Vintage Books, 1979.

———. *The Order of Things.* New York: Vintage Books, 1973.

———. *Archaeology of Knowledge.* Trans. A. M. Sheridan Smith. New York: Harper & Row, 1972.

Freidman, Milton. *Capitalism and Freedom.* Chicago: University of Chicago Press, 1962.

Friedman, Milton, and Rose Friedman. *Free to Choose: A Personal Statement.* New York: A Harvest Book, 1980.
Freire, Paulo. *Pedagogy of the Oppressed.* New York: The Continuum Publishing Company, 1997.
Gramsci, Antonio. *Selection from the Prison Notebooks of Antonio Gramsci,* edited by Q. Hoare and G. N. Smith. New York: International Publishers, 1972.
Habermas, Jurgen. *The Theory of Communicative Action: Reason and the Rationalization of Society.* Boston: Beacon Press, 1981.
———. *Knowledge and Human Interest.* Trans. Jeremy J. Shapiro. Boston: Beacon Press, 1972.
Harvey, David. *A Brief History of Neoliberalism.* New York: Oxford University Press, 2005.
Heilbroner, Robert, and Lester Thurow. *Economics Explained* (Revised ed.). New York: Touchstone, 1994.
Huff, Daniel D. "Upside–Down Welfare." *Public Welfare* (1993): 36–40.
Inkeles, Alex, and David H. Smith. *Becoming Modern: Individual Change in Six Developing Countries.* Cambridge: Harvard University Press, 1974.
Keynes, John Maynard. *The General Theory of Employment, Interest and Money.* New York: Harcourt, Brace & World, 1964.
Kipling, Rudyard. "The White Man's Burden." *McClure's Magazine* 12, no. 4 (February 1899).
Lal, Deepak. *The Poverty of Development Economics* (2nd revised and expanded U.S. ed.). Cambridge: MIT Press, 2000.
Landry, Donna, and Gerald MacLean (Eds.). "Subaltern Studies: Deconstructing Historiography." In *The Spivak Reader: Selected Works of Gayatri Chakravorty Spivak,* 203–35. New York: Routledge, 1996.
MacIntyre, Alasdair. *After Virtue.* Notre Dame: University of Notre Dame Press, 1984.
Maxwell, David. *African Gifts of the Spirit and the Rise of Zimbabwean Transnational Religious Movement.* Athens: Ohio Tate University Press, 2007.
Mihevc, John. *The Market Tells Them So: The World Bank and Economic Fundamentalism in Africa.* London: ZED Books LTD, 1995.
Sandel, Michael. *Liberalism and the Limits of Justice.* Cambridge: Cambridge University Press, 1983.
Sen, Amartya K. *Development as Freedom.* New York: Anchor, 2000.
Scott, James C. *Seeing Like a State: How Certain Schemes to Improve the Human Condition Have Failed.* New Haven: Yale University Press, 1998.
Seers, Dudley. *The Meaning of Development. Eleventh World Conference of the Society for International Development,* New Delhi, 1969.
Smith, Dorothy E. *The Everyday World as Problematic.* Boston: Northeastern University Press, 1978.
Snyder, Katherine A. *The Iraqw of Tanzania: Negotiating Rural Development.* Cambridge: Westview Press, 2005.
Spivak, Gyatri C. "Can the Subaltern Speak?" In *Marxism and the Interpretation of Culture,* edited by C. Nelson and I. Grossberg (Eds.), 271–313. Urbana: University of Illinois Press, 1988.
Stiglitz, Joseph E. *Making Globalization Work.* New York: W.W. Norton & Company, 2006.
Todaro, Michael. *Economics for a Developing World: An Introduction to Principles, Problems and Policies for Development* (3rd ed.). London: Prentice Hall, 1992.

Todaro, Michael P., and Stephen C. Smith. *Economic Development* (9th ed.). Boston: Addison Wesley, 2006.
Toye, John. *Dilemmas of Development* (2nd ed.). Oxford: Oxford University Press, 1993.
Van der Walt, J. L. "Ubuntugogy for the 21st Century." *Journal of Third World Studies,* Spring (Forthcoming 2010).
Yunus, Muhammad. *Creating a World without Poverty: Social Business and the Future of Capitalism.* Philadelphia, PA: Public Affairs, 2007.

Chapter 9
Culture, Communication and Socio-economic Development in Post-Colonial Ghana

Ivor Agyeman-Duah

Introduction

Long before the UNESCO Convention on The Protection and Promotion of the Diversity of Cultural Expressions in 2005, traditional ways of communication existed in all societies in Africa as elsewhere. Depending on which cultural setting one found himself in the 64 dialects and various sub-cultures of the Republic of Ghana, there were traditional instruments and institutions of communication. Apart from the dialects, art was engaged in not for its own sake. Many artistic works had symbolic meanings or implications—clothes were specifically designed to remember historical dates, moments of victories, migrations, and funeral of heroes. Apart from wearing such clothes, they were kept as cultural or historical relics for future generations.

The Kente Cloth, perhaps the pride of Ghana as a cultural product comes in stripes bearing historical fruits—the popular one of "*Fatia fata Nkrumah*" goes beyond the matrimonial bliss of Ghana's Kwame Nkrumah's crossing over to take an Egyptian wife—it marked an epoch in decolonization in the 1960s and Pan-African agenda that embraced Africans south of the Sahara with the Mediterranean culture of Arabs. That was the way in which artists in Ghana chose to write history.

The Akan Adinkra symbols and styles for designing clothes were not only artworks but also proverbial expressions of the religious sentiments and their philosophical contemplations. Long before it became an international expression—it was associated with copyright abuse whose punishment was too punitive at least among the Asantes. A chief called Adinkra in what was formerly the Ivory Coast—who imitated by creation the Golden Stool of Asante (believed to have descended from the skies on the commands of Okomfo Anokye, the spiritual advisor of the pre-eminent first king of Asantes-Osei Tutu) in the early 1700s—was sanctioned and beheaded for not having authority or consent of the king of Asante. A popular song is to this day played at the palace of the king of Asante: "*Ye de bre bre becgee Adrinka.*" Today the symbol has become part of global culture. In an art exhibition commissioned by the Heritage Lottery Fund in the United Kingdom—*From Courage to Freedom* as part of the bicentenary of slave trade—were the works of a Ghanaian, Owusu Ankomah. He was described in the gallery brochure as drawing "on geographically diverse sources such as Adinkra signs from Ghana, graffiti from New York and capoeira from Brazil. In a trilogy of paintings created specifically for this project, Ankomah declares his vision, a manifesto of love and understanding to fill the space between past and future."[1] Recently, according to the brochure, "there had been collaboration with the designer Giorgio Armani to develop a line of clothing for the Red Campaign, generating income for the Global Funds to fight AIDS in Africa."[2]

The Asante gold weights—whose famous British collector, Peggy Appiah died in 2006, has toured many places in the world—perhaps seen as cultural exhibition only but they were originally created as currency exchange in the Asante economy of the sixteenth century. They were used as purchasing power in trade among the people and their neighbors and later with the European traders in the Asante hinterland. Only later, through conquest of the Empire did the currency system collapse to assume artistic appreciation.

Other forms of traditional communications may sound atavistic today. Over a century ago, villages in Ghana congregated in a moonlight evening to listen to folk tales, histories of their villages including little wars of independence from their immediate neighbors or villages. They did so with singing by women at the fire side as the men drank to the adoration of their wives and children. What may seem to the observer as pure socialization had important communication linkages. The youth got to learn their histories and inheritance systems especially the land economy. To this date, many family lands are undocumented and claims to land ownership depends on the power of oral history. Thus, the ability for smart men to remember family tales of ownership and property fifty years ago had stood them in good stead.

In the palace of the king of Asante to this day, Mondays and Thursday are used to adjudicate land disputes or title claims—by individuals within the same clan—Aduana, Bretuo, Oyoko and the others or sometimes inter-clan claims to vast land which is not only critical for development-farming basically but in some areas where there are mineral deposits—such as gold and diamonds, enormous wealth. Judgments at many of these hearings are given with little documentary provision but the power of memory by elders of families. Thus, people with weak remembrance of what the elders told them at the fireside decades ago, no matter if they were genuine claimants, could lose to others who made use of the same history but may not genuinely be connected.

Obi te mpanyinsem, meaning someone understands the stories of the elders or told by the elders, is therefore a common saying to victors in such disputes at the palaces of Akan chiefs.

In Northern Ghana—among the Dagombas and Gonjas—there is no documentary access on the rights of succession to titles and property. Traditions and customs are largely unwritten. Festivals have been celebrated there as in other parts of Ghana for years, some annually, but the custodians of the cultures hardly forget (Proverb Tete wo beak).

There are as well, drums—Talking Drums of the Akans, Kete, Fontomfrom, Adowa, xylophones from Northern Ghana, and flutes which before they became entertainment instruments, were functional instruments of communication.

In the colonial era, it was easy to mistake the utility of these instruments for other things. Wilks examined the Golden Axe which was Asante's diplomatic symbol but which was seen by the British as one of violence. But as the keeper of the Axe, Prince Boakye Tenten explained, "The true meaning of the Axe is this, the Axe is a fetish—we believe that some mysterious powers attaches it. Amanquatta, the bearer of the Axe, has never failed in any mission on which he has been sent, and we believe that whatever request we make, if that request be supported by the presence of that Axe, that request will be granted…" (Agyeman-Duah, 1999, p. 28–29) Two Asante proverbs support this: "However hard a case may be, we don't use an axe to cut it but we settle it with our mouths." The other says, "Whatever problem you meet on the way, does it need an axe to cut it?"

To use the Axe as a peaceful tool and to dissociate it from the British miscommunication, it was given in 1881 as a gift by the Asantehene to Queen Victoria through the British Captain Barrow and currently rests at the London museum.

Post-Colonial Changes

It was the immediate post-independent era in the 1960s that with population rise and urbanization, intellectuals, especially expatriates and locals at the Institute of African Studies, University of Ghana, recorded oral traditions and histories. It added to what earlier missionaries from the Basel Mission, anthropologists and historians like Evans Pritchard and R. S. Rattray did. Joseph Agyeman-Duah's *Asante Stool Histories*, the works of Ivor Wilks on *Wa and the Wala* as well as, the ancient empire of Akwamu came later. The shift from relying on the power of memory to provide documentation in Asante for instance had to do with the inevitable social changes or progress and the inadequacy of memory alone to preserve cultural heritage and grow the rural economy. But it also had to do with the spread of first, colonialism, and thus Westernization and some of its biproducts such as technology—electricity to the rural areas, education which served as a transition from tradition to modernity; a process which made it easier for example, to tape record or video the reminiscences of the village elders for prosperity; usage of combine harvesters and other agricultural instruments, and fertilizers instead of dependency on hoe and shifting cultivation as strategies for agricultural growth and production.

Modernity

The importance of culture in development is recognized by the 1992 Constitution of the Republic of Ghana. Article 270 (1) says, "The institution of chieftaincy, together with its traditional councils as established by customary law and usage, is hereby guaranteed."

Further, (2) "Parliament shall have no power to enact any law which a) confers on any person or authority the right to accord or withdraw recognition to or from a chief for any purpose whatsoever."[3] Apart from this, the same Constitution Article 242 (d) on Decentralization and Local Government, says of appointments of people to serve in districts/rural legislative assemblies: "Other members not being more than thirty percent of all the members of the District Assembly, appointed in consultation with the traditional authorities and other interest groups in the district."[4]

The interesting point is, it is not only constitutional guarantees that ensure that chiefs as custodians of culture have influence but the caliber of modern chiefs. The constitutional expert who helped to draw the 1992 Constitution, Prof. Dr. Nana S. K. B. Asante, worked as a UN constitutional expert before going to Ghana as an important chief and on top of that, the President of the Ghana Academy of Arts and Sciences. Another important chief who helped in the making of the same Constitution—Nana Otuo Siriboe is chairman of the Kwame Nkrumah University of Science and Technology Council. There had been a former central government statistician who is a chief—Nana Dr. Oti Boateng and earlier before him, Nana Wereko Ampem II (Chief of Amanonkrom) who became the first Government Statistician and first Chancellor of Ghana's premier, University of Ghana. The current Ga Mante was a senior public administrator in Ghana's public service.

Thus, by legislative powers as well as the strong credentials of chiefs, chieftaincy as part of culture has influence in the development paradigm.

The Theories

It is not only through this that the importance of culture in socio-economic development could be measured. Sen does not underestimate the power of culture in development and argues for others safeguarding themselves against powerful Western cultures: "This concerns the overwhelming power of Western culture and lifestyles in undermining traditional modes of living and social modes" (Sen, 1999, p. 240). Stiglitz discusses the successes of the Meiji Japan's rapid industrialization in the early twentieth century because the Japanese combined their own cultural values to "establish stable political institutions and they were quick to adopt the Western technology they had seen during the Iwakura missions to Europe and the United States in the 1870s" (Stiglitz, 2005, p. 11).

The proof in Ghana is not only because land acquisition as part of production has had huge cultural implication in the last four hundred years but a situation that has also been accepted by the country's development partners—the multilateral institutions of the World Bank and the International Monetary Fund and also governments. The Government of German has over the years invested money in the Ghanaian economy because it believed in the role of culture and traditional systems propelling economic growth. Its Ambassador to Ghana, Peter Linder, was reported in The Public Agenda of March 2007 to have said: "there is empirical evidence that at least 90 percent of Ghanaians—both rural and urban believe in and depend on the traditional authority system for organizing their lives.

"It has become even clearer that chiefs will wield a strong influence on the lives of the people."[5] The Ambassador continued: "Therefore, it is of great importance that traditional values, traditional ruling systems and traditional legislation interact with the structures of a modern democratic system in such a way that harmony, co-existence and complementary effectiveness are ensured."[6]

One area where traditional systems have however not been able to interact with structures of a modern economy is land economy and the negative consequence could be high. The World Bank agreed to a proposal in the 1990s to site an Inland port at Ejisu-Juaben district in the Ashanti Region. This was to help decongest goods at the Tema Harbour since over fifty percent of goods at this port were eventually off-loaded to the Northern Sector of the country. After the sword-cutting ceremony, a Queen mother of the area who traditionally "owned" the land was able to mobilize youth and unleashed violence in the area such that the government had to relocate the 400-acre port to Boankra, another village. Over a decade was wasted on litigation to convince a traditional Queen, clearly unmindful of the economic gains to her rural economy, of a modern inland port.

A similar incidence occupied in a village near Sekondi-Takoradi where a Chinese Company, E.C. Technology, which anticipated a West Africa Free Zone Project (in collaboration with the Ministry of Trade and Ministry which has given the license), acquired hundreds of acres of land to manufacture high-tech computers, bicycle assembling, pharmaceuticals, and food industry.

The World Bank and some Chinese banks expressed interest in this project but the chiefs of the areas—"owners" of the land—had deliberately inflated the land price to $240 million thus making investment in other areas so difficult. For years the project had been at a standstill and the chiefs were unmindful of the hundreds of jobs that could come out of it for the many unemployed youth drifting to the urban centers and of the general modernization of the locality.

Public Policy and Cultural Players

Cultural productivity is public and private sector engagements. Government makes public policy through which business enterprises operate. The first cultural policy for Ghana was largely drawn by the distinguished ethnomusicologist, J. H. Kwabena Nketia in 1957. It was thirty-six years later in 1983 that it saw a revision, a second revision in 1990 until the latest one of 2004—which was still a revision of the original. Until 2006, the National Commission on Culture was Ghana's main agency for formulation of cultural policy and its implementation. By 2007 it was an agency under a new Ministry of Chieftaincy and Culture. This Ministry had 1,800 public servants across the country and for the first time in many years had its own budget—the 2007 budget of 73 billion cedis (for emoluments, investment, and administration and infrastructure development) instead of reliance on government imprest.[7] Though this amount was a small percent of the country's GDP, the policy was supposed to create a Cultural Trust Fund to support economic development of the arts. It has to date not started.

This new cultural policy was counted as one of the achievements of the Commission even though that in and of itself did not answer to the issue of whether culture was being used enough for economic development.

Of the sixteen distinguished members who wrote the policy, five were university teachers, three were chiefs, one was a journalist, one was a revered minister, one was a musician, there was an MP, and there were others. The composition missed out on economists, statisticians, and development practitioners. Thus the outlook reflected more of moral preservation and acknowledgement of culture then the business dynamics of it.

Chapter 6 of the policy—The Culture Industry Article 10.1 of it, Economic Development, Crafts, and Rural Industry, talks of: "the State shall recognise that economic development is human centered. Hence culture should occupy the centre in every national planning." Article 10.2 of the chapter even goes beyond this: "the state shall recognise the contributions of rural communities to the entire development process, especially agricultural development, and ensure that industrialization is introduced in a manner compatible with the development needs of rural dwellers with a view to preserving their dignity and heritage."[8]

The intention is clear but the motivation of culture leading to economic growth is still a slow process. Cultural tourism has however led the way. Tourism is the fourth largest foreign exchange earner in the country.

But then, culture like the macro-economic framework itself as illustrated easier would have to be supported or stimulated from multilateral sources—through Aid or grant.

Thus, the sector could be subjected to the same debate as to whether the economy of Ghana or Africa should be Aid-dependent or should wean itself of it and look for other models of growth. Development economists including Easterly (2006) have argued about the "uselessness" of Aid to Africa and how it does not work.[9]

The policy of the Ghana government from 2001–2009 as articulated at The Chatham House by President Kufuor (March 2006)[10] was that Ghana in its current development could not do without Aid. This is empirically reflected on the general Aid inflows to the economy and the high dependence of the cultural sector on bilateral and multilateral support. Even dividends of the culture policy were externally reflected when according to a Ghana News Agency report of May 11 2007, The European Community through The European Development Fund (EDF) provided a grant of two million Euros "to assist in the development of culture and the arts." A cultural initiative support program to administer the grant would support cultural associations and foundations; individuals, artists, program managers, managers of cultural centers, arts critics, sound and light engineers, and groups of practitioners "necessary for the functioning of the sector."[11]

At the least, the grant definitely would advance cultural enterprise to another level but like other sectors of the economy, grants have previously been given to individuals and the small- and medium-scale businesses by the Ministry of Trade and Industry but growth rates in these industries were still low in questioning the basis of or attitude of beneficiaries to government grants or microcredit.

The question that the rest of this chapter would implicitly examine in terms of potential for cultural growth is whether, at its current level of development, should weak cultural institutions and industries be strengthened or re-built before grants disbursement or whether there should be a dual development (side by side).

Infrastructure and Institutions

There is the Ghana Export and Promotion Council (GEPC), an agency of the Ministry of Trade and Industry that helps with promotion of cultural goods. A unit-General Promotion Division has a sub-unit on handicraft which helps with the export of hundreds of listed cultural products with the exception of antiques and endangered species; also chemicals used in decorating handicrafts are to be stated and in the case of drums, the skin of the animal must be certified by a veterinary officer.

The twenty people who work in this outfit do so with non-governmental bodies such ATAG, GETRADE, Craft Export Consult, West Africa Trade Hub and Delata Ventures that exports to mainly USA, UK, and Germany. Under the general classification, Non-Traditional Export (NTE) Trade, data released by the GEPC in 2005 indicated positive progression in cultural goods: the handicrafts sub-sector recorded in 2005, 3001 percent increase revenue of $20.8m compared to a year earlier of $5.2m.[12] Other culturally related production saw steady progression in the rural economy according to the data: "Overall growth in the nontraditional sector has been significant within the past ten years. In 1996 for instance, total export earnings from NTE stood at $276m as against $777m in 2005." The projections are that NTE could contribute $1 billion to the economy by 2010.[13]

Non-Governmental Organizations

If the earlier reference to the Kente and Adinkra cloths were cultural symbols, they were first and foremost industrial products of important value in the rural economy. In the Kwabre and Ejisu-Juaben districts in the Ashanti region, the traditional fabric or industrial sector is the second source of occupation after farming. In the village of Bonwire in the Ejisu-Juaben District, where Kente has been produced for centuries, about a quarter of the population (2,000) work in the industry—from selling of the cotton (often imported from Asia), weaving of the strips, repairing of the machines, and sales of finished products in the locality and outside of it. The same number also works in the industry in the Asonomanso and Ntonso in the Kwabre District. But how to expand the rural economy for it to meet the demands of the urban and international patrons is the problem-lack of technology to improve the centuries-old machinery, lack of access to capital for producers from the banks—state and private—are really limiting the impact that the cultural industry could make to economic development.

Even with the EDF grant of $2 million discussed above, how much of it was accessed by cultural practitioners in the villages and districts who were engaged in cultural production and exports as against the urban players and institutions. Further, how much of this got to the local and foreign consultants before real disbursements?

The Asanteman Council Example

The most revolutionary of non-governmental intervention was the Promoting Partnership with Traditional Authorities Project (PPTAP) an initiative of the Asantehene Otumfuo, Osei Tutu II which was supported by The World Bank. The Asante King had argued strongly in the early 2000 that: "Traditional leaders must assert themselves and utilise the abundant influence they possess in partnering government to deliver social and economic benefits. Whether it is in the field of advocacy on health issues, or in the arena of ensuring that children go to school under hygienic conditions, or else in the preservation of cultural heritage, chiefs have a key role to play.'[14]

The Bank, with the consent of the Government of Ghana, gave a grant of $4.5 million to the Asanteman Council and $500,000 to the Akyem Abuakwa Council (which had, following the former, also presented a proposal to the Bank) to plan and implement development projects in their traditional areas.

The objective of the PPTAP was improvement in the general living standards of people with beneficiary communities contributing ten percent of cost with consultants from various fields tasked to help. The Asanteman Council secretariat for PPTAG was deliberately independent of Government for political reasons but was at the same geared towards working within its Poverty Reduction Programme.

The implementation of the PPTAG focused on: a) Primary Education; b) Preventive Health Care; c) Cultural Heritage Preservation; and d) Capacity Building. It effectively began on July 28, 2003 after preparatory work and ended on June 2006 as it tested the experiment of the Bank which was "a project established to ascertain whether traditional leaders are up to the task of contributing significantly to socio-economic development of their communities."[15]

Benefits in Education

By the end of implementation period, tremendous achievements had been made. Forty primary schools in eighteen districts in the Ashanti and Brong Ahafo regions that were really deprived—uncompleted buildings without roofs, those made of mud, and makeshift structures—were rescued. Each school befitted, according to the report published by the Asanteman Council and the World Bank in 2006, "from a package of a six-room classroom block, a library equipped with furniture and books, a storeroom, head teacher's office and a teacher's common room." More importantly, each package also included a borehole, two flat teachers' quarters and toilet facilities. One of the schools even had solar panel facility to pump water into an overhead tank. The importance of this was also a safeguard against numerous water-borne diseases in the communities.

Health

The results at the health sector were equally interesting. The PPTAG report said, "complemented the work of the Ghana Health Service in two categories: in Community Based Growth Promotion and in Community Based Surveillance. Under the former bicycles, weighing scales, steel trucks were distributed to communities and under the latter, demographic healthcare registers including birth, deaths and incidence of disease were sorted out."[16]

Cultural Heritage

The Cultural Heritage Preservation aspect of the PPTAG was concerned more with direct economic benefits to the communities—preservation of artifacts and sites that were of socio-cultural significance. It assessed and took stock of cultural heritage assets in twelve big paramouncies (communities). It did this through collaboration with The Consultants for Training and Development (CONTRAD) the Bureau of Integrated Rural Development (BIRD) and the Culture, Education and Technology Network (CETNET) for research in six paramouncies which included moveable and immoveable assets. Immoveable assets studied included royal palaces, shrines, birth places, ceremonial smocks, and according to the report of the PPTAG, included Osei Tutu Nyame Kesse, the first church in Ashanti built in the sixteenth century.

This collaboration led to the inventory of cultural assets, artefacts, monuments and their publication which served as a reference for tourism and the training of cultural handicrafts producers.[17]

Capacity Building

This component of PPTAG was "to build the fiscal, administrative and management capacity of traditional rulers…to develop business plans for participating paramouncies and to train their respective leaders and secretariats to facilitate, monitor the implementation of the project under their jurisdiction."[18]

By the end of the implementation period, some successes had been made. In a long tribute to this success, Mats Karlsson, World Bank Country Director for Ghana wrote: "The Asantehene's focus and what has been achieved on education, HIV/AIDS and other health issues, capacity building for traditional authorities, and community development through the help of these communities' cultural heritage with the support provided under this project can be considered very laudable."

Conclusion

There is no doubt that culture is important in the running of the modern Ghanaian economy. This is supported by the country's Constitution and other legislations that have established cultural institutions like regional cultural centers, the National House of Chiefs and its regional bodies as well as the powers invested in chiefs.

Its importance is also reflected in loans and grants made available for assessment by multilateral partners especially The World Bank and the IMF either for improvement in the core cultural institutions and capacity building for cultural productions or as accessories to other economic productions. Culture is increasingly being factored into all economic and development proposals including the biggest bilateral grant of $572 million given to the Ghana Government as part of the Millennium Challenge Account provided by the United States Government.

Yet policies evolved over the years only gave respect and recognition to cultural institutions and personalities without examining the multi-economic dimensions of culture in development.

The immediate post-independent era saw a great interest in the arts and culture which was due in part to a re-definition of the Ghanaian or African personality which itself was a project of Nkrumah's pan-African policy. That period, especially from 1957–65 saw huge infrastructural developments such as institutions of learning foremost among them, the Institute of African Studies, and the museums and monuments boards. But the policy was more to psychologically condition the Ghanaian and give him confidence in the management of their own affairs and less as culture adding to GDP.

The decline of the Ghanaian economy (partly as a result of low export earning from traditional cash crops) and coincidentally, the overthrow of the Nkrumah regime in 1966, led to some institutional collapse.

The early part of this centenary has seen the resurgence of culture in the calculation of development and the expectations from the Ghana government should be that of policy revival to resurrect collapsed cultural industries and even build new ones. With an appreciable infrastructure, policy makers could engage in medium to long-time advocacy role that would not only encourage more inflow of transnational capital and bilateral grants but that, Ghanaians in the Diaspora who contribute about $2 billion (a quarter of GDP) to the economy could invest in the cultural sector. Companies could be encouraged to enlist on the Ghana Stock Exchange.

There is sometimes doubt about the viability of cultural industries but a typical doubt turned into huge success was the establishment in 1995 of the only palace museum in Ghana, Manhyia Museum to mark the Silver Jubilee of the late Asantehene Otumfuo, Opoku Ware II. The Museum is made up of nineteenth-century cultural items and registers annually about 1.2 million tourists (strengthening the tourism industry) and is the second source of revenue earner (after Stool lands); it has souvenir shops and employs about thirty people (including board members). The long-term objective is its expansion with the help of The British Museum that would cover earlier centenaries of Asante's history.

The establishment in 2006 of the Ministry of Culture and Chieftaincy was laudable. But a year after its establishment, there was no distinction between it and supposedly the subordinate National Commission on Culture. It is not as clear which of the two bodies formulates policy and which implements it, let alone a policy that can take advantage of offers by multilateral institutions.

Once that is done, it would be a first step towards the realization of the inevitable role of culture in development.

Acknowledgments

I would like to thank Jonathan King, Keeper of the Department of Africa, Oceania and the Americas, British Museum in London, and to Claude Ardouin and Zagba Oyortey, West Africa Sectional Head and consultant respectively, for inviting me to present the first draft of this paper in March 2007 at The Centre of Anthropology. A revised version was later (in November 2007) presented at the invitation of Abdul Karim Bangura, past President of the Association of Third World Studies (ATWS) at its annual meeting held in Lima, Peru. These presentations without doubt have shaped this essay.

Notes

1. See brochure "From Courage to Freedom" (October 2007 Gallery). The exhibition was part of an educational program titled "Bitter Aftertaste: Sugar, the Slave Trade and the Arts of the Atlantic World" that ran from February 21–April 2007.

2. See "From Courage to Freedom" (2007).

3. See *Constitution of the Republic of Ghana* (1992) chapter 22, 164–68.

4. See *Constitution* (1992) chapter 20, 150–55, for greater detail.

5. *The Public Agenda* (2007) March 2, 2007, 1–2 (A biweekly development-oriented newspaper published from Accra).

6. See the same report in Public Agenda (2007), 1–2.

7. Interview with Lillian Bruce-Lyne, Chief Director of Ministry of Chieftaincy and Culture on February 15, 2007.

8. See *The Cultural Policy of Ghana* (2004) published by National Commission on Culture, especially 42–43.

9. William Easterly's book, *The White Man's Burden: Why the West's Efforts to Aid the Rest Have Done So Much and So Little Good*, is one of anti-Aid arguments that has generated controversy in the Aid as strategy for growth debate.

10. See Kufuor (2007) 50 years of Ghana Independence: Prospects and Challenges for Accelerated National Development. At The Chatham House on March 13, 2007.

11. See Ghana News Agency (2007) May 2007 report, 1.

12. See *The Akoben*, a newsletter of the Ghana Export and Promotion Council (GEPC) of 2005. In particular the article, "Export Performance," 18. Also interview with L. Akwasi Agyeman Prempeh, General Manager on February 20, 2007 in Accra.

13. See *The Akoben* (2005), 18–19.

14. The Promoting Partnership with Traditional Authorities Project (PPTAP) Report 2006, produced by Yankah and Associates for the Asanteman Council and The World Bank.

15. See PPTAP Report (2006), 9–10.

16 See Health—Ensuring the Longevity of the People, PPTAP Report (2006), 15.

17. See Cultural Heritage Preservation, PPTAP Report (2006), 18–19.

18. See Report, 18–19.

Bibliography

Agyeman-Duah, Ivor. *The Asante Monarchy in Exile*. Ghana: CIR Publishers, 1999.
Easterly, William R. *The White Man's Burden: Why the West's Efforts to Aid the Rest Have Done So Much and So Little Good.* New York: Penguin, 2006.
Sen, Amartya. *Development as Freedom*. New York: Random House, 1999.
Stiglitz, Joseph, and Charlton, Andrew. *Fair Trade for All–How Trade Can Promote Development.* Oxford: Oxford Press, 2005.

Chapter 10
The African State: An *Ubuntu*/Communal Paradigm

Abdul Karim Bangura

Employing a combination of African-centered Multiplex, *Sankofa,* and Pluridisciplinary research methodologies, this chapter draws upon theories in the fields of Political Science, Sociology, and Peace and Conflict Resolution to suggest that the *Ubuntu*/Communal paradigm is a healthy alternative for (a) Africans to create a link between culture and political parties in order to develop representative political organization, efficient states and deeper democratic governance; (b) civil society organizations to advocate overall programs for democratic reform in Africa; and (c) African political party leaders, political elite in general, and leaders of marginalized groups in society to engage in activities geared toward better representation and change. Consequently, the essay entails seven interrelated sections. The first section, the introduction, presents the nature of the problem, definitions of the major concept (i.e., the state), major research questions, and the essence of the study. The second section discusses the abovementioned research methodologies used to guide the study. The third section presents late Guinean President Sékou Touré's treatise on a dialectical approach to African culture. The fourth section reviews and synthesizes the many competing theories/paradigms that have been used to study the pre- and post-colonial African state in order to delineate their differences, similarities, and where they overlap. These Eurocentric and Africancentric theories/paradigms range from the realist to the idealist: Structuralist, Weberian, Federalist, Marxist/Instrumentalist, Neo-Marxist/Neo-instrumentalist, Anarchist, Pluralist/Polyarchist, Institutionalist/Neo-Weberian, Developmental Statist (Thandika Mkandawire), Human Rights Statist (Willy Mutunga), African Socialist (Mwalimu Julius Nyerere), Social (Adebayo Olukoshi), and *Fundi wa Afrika* (Mueni wa Muiu). The fifth section reviews and suggests the *Ubuntu*/Communal paradigm as an alternative to the discourse on the African state. The sixth section discusses South African, Liberian, Sierra Leonean, Rwandan, and Swaziland case studies as evidence for the *Ubuntu*/Communal paradigm. The final section entails the conclusion and suggestion based on the substantive findings from the preceding sections.

Introduction

The following sobering observation by Costa Hofisi, a doctoral student at the University of Fort Hare in South Africa, is a poignant point to begin the discussion in this chapter, for it captures the nature of the problem of the African state:

> Without being "pessimistic in diagnosis" and "optimistic in prescription," the African state has failed to develop despite its declared commitment and preoccupation with development. The prospects of meeting the millennium development goals (MDGs)—one of which is poverty alleviation—get dim as the year 2015 draws near, consequently making the United Nations to summon an emergency summit. The number of poor in sub-Saharan Africa is expected to rise from 314 million in 2001 to 366 million in 2015. (Hofisi, 2008)

Given this grim assessment of the African state, which is a common theme among the overwhelming majority of observers of the continent, it is only appropriate to start with the problem of defining the term *state*, even if the reader may feel frightened at the thought of another definition of a clearly over-defined phenomenon. The intention, however, is not to suggest a *new* definition, but to stress an important point, i.e., there seems to be no *final* definition of *state*, only suggestions of what it should imply.

Consequently, the concept of *state* should be an open one which will continue to be redefined as our knowledge of the phenomenon increases and as new problems emerge to be solved by the state. The intellectual preoccupation with the phenomenon of the state, to give it a new content and to come up with suggestions about how to promote it, is therefore part of the research process in the social sciences. When definitions of *state* are talked about, the effort is geared toward research orientations or foci of interests. To avoid the concept altogether would create more havoc than it solves.

To begin with, while the term *state* often encompasses all institutions of government or rule, ancient and modern, the modern state system reflects many characteristics that were first consolidated in Western Europe beginning in the fifteenth century when the concept *state* also inherited its contemporary meaning. As a result, the term is often used strictly to refer to modern political systems.

In casual parlance, the words *country*, *nation,* and *state* are often used interchangeably. But more strictly, however, the terms can be denotatively distinguished as follows: (a) *country* refers to a geographical area; (b) *nation* refers to a people who share common customs, origins, and history, albeit the adjectives *national* and *international* also refer to matters dealing strictly with *states*, as in *national elections*, *international relations*; (c) *state* refers to a set of governing institutions with sovereignty over a definite territory.

In terms of its etymology, according to historian Douglas Harper (2007), the term *state* and its cognates in other European languages—*état* in French, *staat* in German, *stato* in Italian—were derived from the Latin word *status*, which means "condition" of "status." And, as Quentin Skinner (1989) points out, the revival of the Roman law in fourteenth-century Europe saw the Latin term *status* employed to refer to the legal standing of persons such as various "estates of the realm" (noble, common, and clerical) and particularly the special status ascribed to the king. The term was also used to refer to certain Roman notions that date back to the days of Cicero (106–43 BC) that dealt with the "condition of the republic" as in *status rei publicae*. Over time, the term continued to lose its reference to particular social groups and was applied to the legal order of the entire society with its enforcement apparatus.

Another rendering of the word *state* is that it originated from the medieval *state* or regal chair upon which the monarch or the head of state would sit. Metonymically, the term *state* became used to refer to both the head of state and the power entity s/he represented. The two frequently quoted references of these different meanings commonly attributed to King Louis XIV of France are (1) *L'État, c'est moi*, meaning "I am the State," and (2) *Je m'en vais, mais l'État demeurera toujours*, meaning "I am going away, but the State will always remain." One can find a similar association of terms being used in referring to government as having authority: for example, as a September 17, 2008 *Inter Press Service* news headline written by Najum Mushtaq reads, "Kenya Parliament May Soon Consider New Abortion Rights Law."

Also, according to Robert H. Jackson and Carl G. Rosberg (1982), the term *state* has both an empirical (*de facto*) and juridical (*de jure*) connotation. In the empirical sense, an entity is a state if it is an organization that has a "monopoly of legitimate violence" over a specific territory, *à la* Max Weber (more on him and his ideas later). An often-cited example in Africa is the Somali region of Somaliland, which is an entity that imposes its own legal order over a territory even though it is not legally recognized as a state by the international community. In the juridical sense, an entity is a state in international law if it is recognized as such by the international community, even if it does not actually have a monopoly on the use of force over a territory. A current example of this type of state in Africa is the Democratic Republic of Congo.

Furthermore, the concept of the state has been distinguished by Norberto Bobbio (1989) from two related concepts with which it is oftentimes conflated. One is the notion of the state as a form of government or regime such as a democracy or dictatorship that identifies a single aspect of the state: i.e., the way the highest political offices are filled and their relationships to one another. It is absent of the other aspects of the state such as the effectiveness and efficiency of the bureaucracy that may be paramount to its everyday functioning. The other notion of the state is as a form of political system which refers to the instruments of political power.

Still, some scholars such as David Easton (1990) have argued that the concept *state* is too imprecise and loaded to be employed productively by political scientists and sociologists and, therefore, should be substituted by the more comprehensive term *political system.* And, according to Easton, a *political system* refers to a collectivity of all social structures that work together to yield biding decisions in a society. Connoting a broader concept, a *political system* would encompass the political regime, the political parties, and various other similar political bodies.

In light of the preceding discussion, this essay seeks to investigate the following major research questions: (a) How can Africans create a link between culture and political parties in order to develop representative political organization, efficient states, and deeper democratic governance? (b) What can civil society organizations do to advocate overall programs for democratic reform in Africa? (c) What can African political party leaders, political elite in general, and leaders of marginalized groups in society do to engage in activities that are geared toward better representation and change? It is my belief that the answers to these questions lie in the dialectics of African culture, the theories/paradigms that have been employed to explore the nature of the African state, and the *ubuntu*/communal paradigm, supported by a sample of case studies from different countries across Africa. But before discussing these aspects, it behooves me to first describe briefly the African-centered research methodologies that guide this essay. Thus, the essence of this paper hinges upon the fact that it is grounded on sound Africancentric theoretical and methodological approaches, albeit not ignoring relevant Eurocentric approaches where they are germane.

Research Methodologies

Undergirding this chapter is a combination of three African-centered research methodologies: (1) Multiplex, (2) *Sankofa*, and (3) Pluridisciplinary. Descriptions of these approaches follow.

First, in our book, *Peace Research for Africa: Critical Essays on Methodology* (Bangura and McCandless, 2007), I argue that since war and other forms of violent protracted conflict between groups of human beings are among the most complex phenomena in the social world, such complexity has many causes. Not only do warring groups have competing or incompatible goals, they also have profoundly contested narratives and competing discourses concerning the same supposedly factual situation on the ground. Such violent conflicts are often characterized by contested geographies, material resources, human agencies, identities, epistemologies, mythologies, outcomes, and even competing cosmologies and religious beliefs. In addition, each side to a violent and prolonged conflict is not so much trying to *convince* the other side of the righteousness of its own world view as much as to *kill* or vanquish the opponent and destroy the opposing epistemic, knowledge, or community.

Multiplex methodology is an approach that looks at violent conflict as an explosive human encounter that exists when a specific kind of relationship is established between the groups when the conflict originates. The approach focuses on the fact that this relationship is an extreme variety, if not *the* extreme type, of social relationship established between any individuals, groups, and societies. It exists because one or both sides perceive a manifest or latent conflict, which can be defined more precisely as a perceived or real incompatibility of interests, goals, or need satisfaction, such as identity, access, or ownership, due to blockage or thwarting efforts of the other group.

As such, Multiplex methodology pays particular attention to the use of case studies, in which contested geographies, human agencies, and epistemologies are central issues in peace and conflict studies. This is mainly because violent conflict always unleashes the unforeseen. The problem, then, from a methodological point of view, is how to capture and investigate the composite complexity of this phenomenon in which knowledge claims, and Truth itself, is almost always in contention. Multiplex analysis, therefore, proceeds in the following three stages:

(1) *Epistemic encounter* is the reality of contested social constructions between two or among more knowing subjects or communities. This can be the profoundly contested encounter in which a subject confronts, not an "objective reality," but another knowing subject whom s/he is trying to kill. Each party in the conflict then tries to present his/her rendition of the reason of the conflict from his/her vantage point, characterizing the perspective of the opponent as false.

(2) *Empirical encounter* refers to the contesting subjects with their material world, as they each seek the substance and resources with which to carry out the struggle, or to dominate and win complete control. For example, an actor would label the conflict by using a concept that can invoke a patriotic feeling from his/her fellow citizens in order to gain their support in a conflict.

(3) *Self-reflective or Cartesian encounter* is what the subjects in such deadly competition reflect upon, and how they incorporate their individual identities and roles into the conflict.

In essence, there is a *clash of realities* in a violent human conflict, in which each side is persuaded that it possesses the ultimate truth. Such compound realities require compound methods of investigation and inquiry, if we are to understand and ideally prevent such strife in Africa in the future.

Second, as I state in a forthcoming book (Bangura, in progress), derived from Adrinka of the Akan people of West Africa, the concept of *Sankofa* is transliterated from the Akan language as *Se wo were fi na wosan kofa a yenki*, whose literal translation in the English language is, "It is not taboo to go back to the source and fetch what you forgot." The source is the African culture, heritage, and identity. It is the power within all Africans. In essence, *Sankofa* means that as Africans move forward into the future, they need to reach back into their past and take with them all that works and is positive. *Sankofa* is employed by Pan-Africanists all over the world to promote the notion that African people everywhere must *go back to their roots in order to move forward*. The visual and symbolic representation of *Sankofa* is a mythic bird that flies forward while looking backward with an egg—symbolizing the future—in its mouth.

In terms of the development of *Sankofa* methodology, the history of this endeavor is quite young and only four scholars can be dubbed as major pioneers: Vincent Hardin, Elleni Tedla, Derrick P. Alridge, and Barbara J. Little. *Sankofa* methodology can be traced back to Vincent Hardin's 1986 concept of *the river*, albeit he did not use the term *Sankofa* itself, but extended the concept by using the analogy of a river. Hardin pointed out that he and his African ancestors are on the same river of struggle and that they share the same moment in time in a somewhat spiritual sense (Alridge, 2003, p. 29). As Hardin put it,

> I knew that what I wanted and needed to write about was something that had never been developed in one work: a narrative, analytical, and celebrative history of the freedom struggle of Black people in this country, beginning before there was a country. I was especially concerned to try to convey its long, continuous movement, flowing like a river, sometimes powerful, tumultuous, and rolling with life; at other times meandering and turgid, covered with the ice and snow of seemingly endless winters....Somehow I believed that my vow to keep faith with the creators and the children of the river would also lead me to be faithful to the truth of their experience as I saw it, read it, felt it. I knew that I must not be afraid to let that commitment speak for itself, to let my own baptized voice be heard. (quoted in Alridge, 2003, p. 29)

In 1995, Tedla developed a *Sankofa* educational approach as a measure of time by looking at African educational history on a circular plane rather than as a linear process. She began by employing a *holistic approach* that involves studying Africans by observing and recording the commonalities that exist amid their diversity. This approach is in contrast to Western approaches that present a fragmented perspective of Africans by focusing solely on the diversity of African people. She then used a *non-deficit approach* that involves critically assessing the merits of non-African ideas and institutions employed in African societies.

In 1999, Alridge wrote several articles in which he employed the concept of *Sankofa* and *the river* metaphor to connect W. E. B. Du Bois' thinking to the conditions of Blacks and their education today. Instead of examining Du Bois as a historical figure who wrote and spoke about Black education, Alridge presented Du Bois' ideas within the time frame when he lived while conceptualizing how his thinking continues to be relevant. Alridge employed the concept of *Sankofa* to help him move beyond rigidly linear conceptions of time to see the connections among the insights to be gained from Du Bois' ideas over time (Alridge, 2003, p. 29).

While Alridge used the concepts of *Sankofa* and *the river* as ways of thinking beyond the linear construct of time predominant in Western culture, he also argued that historians must be careful not to transport events, places, and people from the past to draw grand, sweeping conclusions about a problem or issue in the present. This type of scholarship, he further argued, ignores space and time and disregards the impossibility of duplicating past circumstances in the present. Consequently, he added, such an approach is likely to produce anachronistic interpretations of the past and future. He suggested, however, that researchers begin to address "presentism" by acknowledging that the present in some ways influences their research, given their position in the present, and by showing similarities between historical contexts surrounding past and present events (Aldridge, 2003, p. 29).

Finally, Barbara J. Little recently (2007) developed the *Sankofa historical archaeology* approach which involves asking questions about the past that relate to the present to help the researcher move toward a considered and intentional future. She believed that our interest in the past is drawn from our circumstances in the present and our hopes for the future; thus, the questions asked by historical archaeologists are inspired in the same way. She was fascinated by the challenges in promoting interest in and caring about "someone else's past" within an increasingly diverse population. She believed that historical archaeology offers opportunities for researchers to become aware of our common humanity and our common struggles. Given the current cynicisms and despair, she saw archaeology as a discipline that can offer glimpses into the human story as a source of hope and renewal. It is her desire, therefore, that we can all hope that respect—or at least tolerate and perhaps even celebrate—will flow from the present to the past and back again to the present.

And third, in our book mentioned earlier, *Peace Research for Africa: Critical Essays on Methodology* (Bangura and McCandless, 2007), I suggest that Pluridisciplinary methodology involves the use of open and resource-based techniques available in the actual situation. It has, therefore, to draw upon the indigenous knowledge materials available in the locality and make maximum use of them. Indigenous languages are, therefore, at the center of the effective use of this methodology.

What this suggests is that the researcher must revisit the indigenous techniques that take into consideration the epistemological, cosmological and methodological challenges. Hence, the researcher must be culture-specific and knowledge-source-specific in his/her orientation. Thus, the process of redefining the boundaries between the different disciplines in our thought process is the same as that of reclaiming, reordering and, in some cases, reconnecting those ways of knowing, which were submerged, subverted, hidden, or driven underground by colonialism and slavery. The research should, therefore, reflect the daily dealings of society and the challenges of the daily lives of the people. Towards this end, at least the following six questions should guide pluridisciplinary research:

(1) How can the research increase indigenous, endogenous, or local knowledge in the general body of global human development?

(2) How can the research create linkages between the sources of indigenous knowledge and the centers of learning on the continent and in the Diaspora?

(3) How can centers of research in the communities ensure that these communities become "research societies"? Put differently, how can research centers ensure that the societies in which they are based see them as working for the societies' interests?

(4) How can the research be linked to the production needs of the communities?

(5) How can the research help to ensure that science and technology are generated in relevant ways to address problems of the rural communities where the majority of the people live, and that this is done in indigenous languages?

(6) How can the research help to reduce the gap between the elite and the communities from which they come by ensuring that the research results are available to everyone and that such knowledge is drawn from the communities?

In sum, as in Africancentric methodology, Molefi Kete Asante's suggestion that, in the analysis of what he calls the "three fundamental Afrocentric themes of transcendent discourse: (1) human relations, (2) humans' relationship to the supernatural, and (3) humans' relationships to their own being" (1987, p. 168), that if done with an awareness of the interrelatedness of these themes, a greater understanding of the African being will be acquired, is applicable to a mixture of Multiplex, *Sankofa,* and Pluridisciplinary methodologies as well.

A Dialectical Approach to African Culture

In his essay appropriately titled "A Dialectical Approach to Culture" (1989), late Guinean President Sékou Touré argues that the path of tribulations the concept of culture has undergone has been long, as the opinions of "committees of intellectuals" cancel one another out in a sterile dialectic. These groups, he notes, bring incomprehension and a hollow humanism as they timidly deal with the historical truth of the greatest calamity known to history: i.e., imperialism. According to Touré, the intellectuals in countries where a capitalist regime isolates the general populace from scientific and technical attainments must constantly fight to retain their false "freedom" and constantly question themselves in vain about the future of a decadent economic and social structure. The helpless intellectuals somehow construct a cultural policy in order to strengthen a society whose upheavals are the undeniable symptoms of degeneration, and use the faded light of their poor autocratic reason to seek a new cultural conscience, they sink into skepticism or, rather, into the terror of a future overshadowed by capitalism (Touré, 1989, p. 3).

Touré points out that the European trends have dominated the inquiry of cultural problems in Africa. For a long time, he notes, contemporary Anglo-Saxon anthropology, obsessed with justifying the reactionary ideas of colonialism, cited Africa as the home of backward peoples who should be forced to accept colonialist humanitarian civilization. He argues that history has shown that revolutionary maturity cannot be the object of an edict which imperialism would never permit. The Anglo-Saxon school of thought, he notes, gave birth to pseudo-realism in line with David Hume's successors—Alfred Vierkandt's disciples, "culturalists" such as Anton Grabner and Bernhard Ankerman, and functionalists like Bronislaw Malinowski—assumed that they had discovered the basis of African culture. Due to their hatred of historical materialism, these scholars produced a flood of disjointed monographs in which they denied the class war and the imperialists' exploitation of Africans, reducing the phenomena instead to an anti-scientific cultural pluralism (Touré, 1989, pp. 3–4).

Archaeologists' pickaxes, Touré suggests, had evidently not reached the African culture that lay too deeply buried under the irremovable heap of dirt left behind by the colonialists, which Africans have now succeeded in uncovering. He notes that the anxiety to extricate an authenticity which was for obvious reasons unrecoverable led Lucien Lévy-Brühl, who was already blind, to present a fairly accurate "prelogism" of African culture. As Touré puts it, "In any case there is no difference of concept between the black man unaware of the logical categories of the classical world on the one hand, and the idea of the essentially sensitive black man as a sort of passive, wax creature, only fit to remain at a primary intuitive level in his perception of the outside world, on the other" (Touré, 1989, p. 4).

Thus, for Touré, it is no accident that African states had to dedicate a symposium to a topic such as that which unites them: "African culture and its realities." He recalls that as late as the 1960s, many pages were devoted to another topic that seemed quite provocative at the time: i.e., "A black man is a human being." He therefore argues that it is incumbent upon Africans to reestablish themselves in a field such as culture, because they are emerging from a long period of eclipse during which the most elementary attributes of man, notably those of his creativity, were contested and denied to Africans (Touré, 1989, p. 4).

According to Touré, a well-nurtured Eurocentric prejudice is that Africans played no role in the general task of shaping civilization. Africans were accused of being without history and without culture because it was necessary that it be so. He points out that Europeans slaughtered Native Americans while at the same time admiring their temples and palaces, and admitting that they murdered the men and took over their lands. He mentions the fact that with their quest to conquer and dominate others, Europeans destroyed millennial civilizations in Asia, but they never denied the existence of these civilizations as such and never contested the quality of their craftsmanship and their human attributes. He further states that when it came to Africa, Europeans' first notion was not to exterminate the men with the sole idea of seizing their treasures, but to treat them as beasts to be sold into slavery and as they pleased, sold on the spot or exported to America, or even killed when their capabilities and selling prices no longer assured adequate profits. To guarantee the success of such a venture, he adds, a preliminary step was taken by Europeans to ease their conscience to believe that slavery with its attendant savagery was a question of dealing with beasts and not human beings. He further states that by Europeans alleging the barbarity of Africans and denying that they have a culture and civilization made it justifiable to Europeans to estrange Africans from the human race (Touré, 1989, p. 4–5).

Despite all this dehumanization of Africans by Europeans, according to Touré, time did not stop, and progress continued to strengthen in the face of opposition and exploitation. Africans began to pay more attention to their legends, the epic poems, and the tales passed by word of mouth from generation to generation of the Griots. He adds that archaeology finally penetrated the various continents, thrusting deep into the depths of history and the soil to reveal and revive the remains of entombed cultures. He goes on to provide the following definition and attributes of culture which reveal that even without archaeological research and tales of the Griots, ordinary common sense was adequate to realize the absurdity or rather the class-consciousness of those who managed to imagine Africans as a cultureless people (1989, p. 5):

> By culture, we mean all the material and immaterial works of art and science, plus knowledge, manners, education, a mode of thought, behavior and attitudes accumulated by the people both through and by virtue of their struggle for freedom from the hold and dominion of nature; we also include the result of their efforts to destroy the deviationist politics—social systems of domination and exploitation through the productive process of social life.
>
> Thus culture stands revealed as both an exclusive creation of the people and a source of creation, as an instrument of socio-economic liberation and as one of domination.
>
> Culture implies our struggle—it is our struggle.
>
> Culture—as both the expression and the result of the relationships between man and society on the one hand and nature on the other—is found among all peoples and is inherent in the very process of life. A culture is to be found wherever conscious life exists.
>
> Culture is the sum total of the material and spiritual values created by humanity throughout its history. This creation is both continuous and necessary. It is the corollary, the yardstick and the result of man's action to adapt to his environment so that he can both survive and flourish. It is inspired by the instinct for survival at the first stage and by the awareness of the laws of existence at a higher stage. Therefore it first obeys a simple biological law regulating survival

> of the individual and the species before obeying a more complex psychological and socio-economic law. Now the instinct for self-preservation and the need for self-fulfillment are common to all societies and peoples. Every people must struggle to exist by creating the material means of its existence.

Thus, Touré asserts that Africans, like all peoples, have come along the long road of history through recurrent conflicts whose overall result has been increasing success. He notes that despite momentary slow downs, stagnation and setbacks, Africans have created material values, created spiritual values, and contributed to the creation and development of global culture. He adds that material cultural production and spiritual cultural production are dialectically linked and exercise a reciprocal influence on each other. He argues, however, that the absolute priority must rest with material production, which itself participates directly in the concrete action of humans (Touré, 1989, pp. 5–6).

The course of history and the succession of the development of African culture, Touré points out, have closely mirrored the course of the development of productive forces. The culture's initial simplicity, low intellectual level, and slow rate of progression were the results of the weakness of humankind's position and the precariousness of his/her existence. Then as time progressed, following the development of productive techniques, African culture developed, became diversified, took on shades of meaning, and incorporated science, technology, literature, music, dancing, and sculpture (Touré, 1989, p. 7).

Thus, according to Touré, the whole African cultural evolution, this progressive qualification, is subordinated to reason, to the law of gnoseology, to the transition from ignorance to an increasingly deeper and more exact degree of knowledge. Consequently, for him, any anthology of African culture that situates it outside the realm of reason, of rational thought, of the law and of gnoseology, downgrades it and deviates it from its true end, which is to qualify mankind, and sacrifices it to the myth of singularity and specificity (Touré, 1989, p. 7).

Competing Theories/Paradigms on the State

In this section, I review and synthesize the many competing theories/paradigms that have been used to study the pre- and post-colonial African state in order to delineate their differences, similarities, and overlaps. This treatise regards the state from a political standpoint only, not from the juristic—sociology, as I understand the concept, being both a philosophy of history and a theory of economics. Thus, at least a synopsis should be presented about the general nature of the political theories on the state, the relationship between the state, on the one hand, and factions and fractions, and the ruling class as a whole.

As Colin Flint and Peter Taylor (2007) point out, most political theories of the state can roughly be classified into two categories. The first category comprises the "liberal" or "conservative" theories, which treat capitalism as a given, and then focus on the function of states in capitalist society. These theories tend to see the state as a neutral entity separated from society and the economy. Robert Dahl and Francis Fukuyama are frequently identified with this school of thought. The second category is composed of Marxist theories which see politics as intimately connected with economic relations, and then emphasize the relation between economic and political power. They see the state as an instrument in the hands of the upper class to serve their own interests. Karl Marx (although he never developed a theory of the state, but he is said to have intended to do so eventually), Ralph Miliband, Nicos Poulantzas, Jürgen Habermas, Antonio Gramsci and Michael Foucault are frequently cited as belonging to this school of thought.

Two other prominent theories of the state are the state autonomy/institutionalist and the anarchist. The first theory postulates that the state is an entity that is somehow impervious to external social and economic pressures, and has its own interests. Theda Skocpol and G. William Domhoff are prominently identified with this theory (Sklair, 2004). The second theory states that the state is undesirable, unnecessary, and harmful, and calls for the promotion of a stateless society, or anarchy. Pierre-Joseph Proudhon, Max Stirner, Peter Kropotkin, Emile Armand, Lawrence Jarach, and John Zerzan are strongly identified with this theory.

The Eurocentric and Africancentric theories/paradigms that have been employed to study the African state include the Structuralist, the Weberian, the Federalist, the Marxist/Instrumentalist, the Neo-Marxist/Neo-instrumentalist, the Anarchist, the Pluralist/Polyarchist, the Institutionalist/Neo-Weberian, the Developmentalist, the Human Rights, the African Socialist, the Social, and the *Fundi wa Afrika*. Since these theories/paradigms are numerous, for each one, only a brief description and one work that used it to study the African state are presented. Given the space constraints of this chapter, no attempt is made here to rehash the charges and countercharges among these schools of thought. The interested reader can be better served by consulting the sources discussed in this section.

Proponents of the Structuralist perspective see the state as a political association with effective dominion over a territory. The entity usually includes the set of institutions that claim the authority to make rules used to govern the exercise of coercive violence for the people in that territory, and its status as a state often hinges upon being recognized by a number of other states as having internal and external sovereignty of the territory.

Earlier major scholarly works on Africa were dominated by the Structuralist perspective when examining the state. For example, Leslie Rubin and Brian Weinstein (1974) in their discussion of the organization of the contemporary African state, identify three characteristics. The first characteristic is that Europeans drew frontiers for about forty-five states enclosing thousands of precolonial political systems entirely or partially. They note that boundaries were often carelessly drawn, an action that will have important consequences on interstate relations within Africa for many years (Rubin and Weinstein, 1974, pp. 50–51).

The second characteristic is that Europeans made internal administrative divisions such as provinces, regions, and circumscriptions, which are still generally used, although with different names. These divisions, which were set up to facilitate governance, recruitment of workers, and unify the control communications, sometimes corresponded with previous divisions among African political systems, but often they did not. This situation upset traditional patterns of communication and loyalty that have led to long-term effects (Rubin and Weinstein, 1974, p. 51).

The third characteristic is that Europeans developed administrative laws, procedures, and styles based on their own models in Europe that have proven difficult to discard. The colonialists formed local armed forces for their purpose of maintaining order over the newly defined states and to carry out the judgments of courts and administration. They also established patterns of centralization and decentralization of power that still contribute to differences among English-speaking, French-speaking, and Portuguese-speaking states (Rubin and Weinstein, 1974, p. 51).

Advocates of the Weberian (1994) notion of the state identify it as a collectivity of institutions in terms of Max Weber's definition: i.e., an organization that has a "monopoly on the legitimate use of physical force within a given territory." The entity may include the armed forces, civil service or state bureaucracy, courts, and police.

Weber's notion of patrimonialism buttresses Thomas M. Callaghy's work (1984) on Zaire (now the Democratic Republic of Congo). Callaghy argues that the patrimonial character of the late President Mobutu Sese Seko Nkunku Ngbendu wa Za Banga (born Joseph-Désiré Mobutu) during his rule laid the foundation for the Zairian state's decay. He characterizes this decay in terms of its declining capacity to rule or to maintain the conditions for the operation of its eroding productive infrastructures. He identifies three areas of decline. The first area is the increasing inability of the state to relate national means to policy ends which is evident in the inefficiency of public administration, security forces, economic policies, etc. The second area is the shrinkage of credibility, as citizens became increasingly convinced that the state is incapable of carrying out accustomed functions. The third area is the decline in probity that is manifested in a culture of blatant corruption.

Purveyors of the Federalist idea of the state look at it as a conglomeration of political units, not completely sovereign by themselves, but in some cases partially or co-sovereign, that are subject to a constitution that defines the federal union. It is no exaggeration to state that very few federal political systems in the world have been studied more than that of Nigeria because of that country's enormous size, very large population, ethnic complexity, and abundance of crude oil.

As Oladimeji Aborisade and Robert Mundt retell a very familiar story to many, from the time that the British colonial authorities first considered the matter, some form of federal organization seemed necessary because of the colony's size and ethnic complexity. Early nationalist leaders such as Nnamdi Azikwe and Obafemi Awolowo also advocated a federal arrangement for independent Nigeria. As the unitary Richards Constitution proved quite unpopular in all areas, a federal system composed of three regions was established as the basis for Nigeria's move to independence in 1954. In what emerged as a uniquely Nigerian scenario, two of the regions, the Eastern and the Western, gained self-governing status in 1957; the North got its own in 1959. Thus, by independence a decentralized federal system was already in place in Nigeria. The Constitution of 1960 was explicitly federal, with responsibilities divided between the federal government and the three regions. Since then, federalism has been a constant in all of the country's constitutions: 1963, 1979, and 1989. It was also the overwhelming choice during the 1994–1995 Constitutional Conference convened by the then head of state, the late Sani Abacha. According to Aborisade and Mundt, it is difficult to imagine a stable political structure in Nigeria that does not take into consideration the devolution of power at least to the leaders of the three major ethnic groups (2001, p. 117): (1) the Igbo who are the majority in the Southeast, (2) the Yoruba who are the majority in the West, and (3) the Hausa who are the majority in the North.

Promoters of the Marxist/Instrumentalist perspective of the state see it as an entity that is determined by its position in a capitalist society. Following Karl Marx's comment in his book, *The Communist Manifesto*, these scholars maintain that the state is but an executive committee for managing the common affairs of the *bourgeoisie*. Its leading proponent, Ralph Miliband (1983), argues that the state is an "instrument" in the hands of the ruling class used to dominate society by virtue of the interpersonal ties between economic elites and state officials. Members of these groups, he points out, come from the same background and, therefore, share the same interests and linked together through an array of interpersonal and political ties.

An example of a scholarly work in which the Marxist/Instrumentalist perspective is employed to discuss the nature of the state in Africa is Osagyefo Kwame Nkrumah's classic *Class Struggle in Africa* (1970). In this book, Nkrumah identifies two groups of classes that have emerged in the African state due to colonialism and neocolonialism: (1) the *Privileged Classes,* comprised of the bureaucratic *bourgeoisie*, officers of armed forces and police, intelligentsia, professional class, compradors, etc.; and (2) the *Oppressed Classes,* comprised of workers, peasants, small farmers, and traders. He notes that the African *bourgeoisie*, the class that thrived under colonialism, is the same class that is benefiting under the post-colonial, neocolonial era. He states that the *bourgeoisie's* basic interest hinges upon preserving capitalist economic and social structures; it is therefore allied with the international monopoly capital to exploit the masses whose aspirations can only be fulfilled through "scientific socialism" (Nkrumah, 1970, pp. 11–12). He defines "scientific socialism" as a universal and abiding principle that involves "the genuine socialization of productive and distributive processes," and argues that "those who for political reasons pay lip service to socialism, while aiding and abetting imperialism and neocolonialism, serve bourgeoisie class interests." He adds that "workers and peasants may be misled for a time, but as class consciousness develops the bogus socialists are exposed, and genuine socialist revolution is made possible" (Nkrumah, 1970, p. 26).

Nkrumah observes that while the African *bourgeoisie* is small in terms of its numbers, and lacks the financial and political strength of its counterpart in the developed nations, it gives the illusion of being economically strong because of its close ties with foreign finance capital and business interests. He points out that many members of the African *bourgeoisie* work for foreign firms and have, therefore, a direct financial stake in the continued exploitation of Africans by these foreign firms. Other members of this group—notably in the civil service, trading and mining firms, the armed forces, the police, and in the professions—are committed to capitalism because of their background, their Western education, and their shared experiences of occupying privileged positions. They are mesmerized by capitalist institutions and organizations, they ape the way of life of their old colonial masters, and they are determined to preserve the status quo and power inherited from them. Nkrumah adds that Africa has in fact in its midst a hard core of *bourgeoisie* who are analogous to colonialists and settlers in that they live positions of privilege—a small, selfish, money-minded, reactionary minority among vast masses of exploited and oppressed people (Nkrumah, 1970, p. 12).

Scholars who purport the Neo-Marxist/Neo-Instrumentalist notion of the state move the Marxist/Instrumentalist perspective a bit further by arguing that the question of who controls the state is irrelevant. Leading Neo-Marxist scholar, Nicos Poulantzas (1978), influenced by Louis Pierre Althusser, postulates that the capitalist states do not always act on behalf of the ruling class and, when they do, it is not necessarily the case because state officials consciously do so, but because the "structural" position of the state is configured in such a manner to ensure that the long-term interests of capitalists always dominate. Poulantzas' contribution to the Marxist postulates of the state is the concept of "relative autonomy," although his work has been attacked for its "structural functionalism."

Operating from the Dependence paradigm, which postulates that the development of the core/center countries is a direct result from the underdevelopment of the peripheral countries, Bernard Magubane (1976) points directly to the roots of the poverty of the African state, asserting that the political economy of the continent can only be understood in terms of the relation of various African states to the international power structure and the social classes this power structure birthed within the dominated formulations. He argues that the historical incorporation of Africa and its pre-capitalist systems into the evolving capitalist mode of production led to the emergence of extremely complex systems of class relations. He notes that the system was characterized by economic and political structures in which the possessing and ruling stratum was foreign and the Africans appeared in descending order of subservience and dependence. He argues that to study the class structure of modern Africa calls for the examination of the determinate mode of production, which is the colonial capitalist mode of production. He adds that in any given African region or country, social classes appear that complement the colonial relations of production.

Furthermore, according to Magubane, the social structure of the African state, when viewed in detail, reveals a fairly complex kaleidoscope: alongside interethnic distinctions, there have emerged important interclass distinctions; and alongside of modern evils, a whole series of inherited evils oppress the African masses. All these machinations, he points out, have arisen from the passive survival of antiquated modes of productions that are frozen in time by capitalism with its inevitable train of social and political anachronisms (Magubane, 1976, p. 195).

The Anarchist school of thought on the state proposes strategies for the total elimination of the state and offers replacements. There are two strands to this perspective. The first group, the "left," argues for the conformation of society to alternative group structures. It considers the state to be an institutionalization of domination and privilege. According to this group, the state emerged to ratify and deepen the dominance of the victors of history. Thus, for this group, while reflecting social interest, the state is not a mere executive committee of the ruling class, as the Marxists suggest, but a position of power over the whole society which many fractions of the ruling classes and even the oppressed classes seek to control with different and ever-changing alliances. Therefore, this group rejects the need for a state to provide for the needs of the people because it perceives the state as an oppressive force which takes away the ability of people to make decisions about things that affect their lives. Consequently, leading left-wing anarchists such as Mikhail (Michael) Alexandrovich Bakunin (1991) and Prince Pyotr (Peter) Alexeyevich Kropotkin (1896, 1897) argue for a form of socialism without the state. The second group, the "right" or "Anarcho-capitalists," led by scholars such as Murray Newton Rothbard (1975), calls for a free market guided by the invisible hand offering critical or valuable functions traditionally provided by the state.

Economist Alex Tabarrok (2004) argues that Somalia in its stateless period provides an example for an Anarchy state in Africa, as theoretically espoused by Anarcho-capitalists such as Rothbard. Tabarrok states that the Somali experience since the collapse of the state, and especially the failure of international intervention, has offered a clear challenge to elements of conventional economic, political and social order theory and the very premises under which Western diplomacy and development agencies operate. He points out that Somalia has no government but in many respects it is booming. Somalia has what is perhaps the best phone system in Africa, for example, because entrepreneurs are unburdened by any regulation. Tabarrok quotes the following from *The Economist* to support his assertion:

> There is still no proper central government but, where once there was only a handful of warlords, there are now at least 24, and that is only the serious ones. With smaller fiefs to pillage, few can now afford the $100,000 or more that it costs to wage a six-hour battle, so such battles are less common. This is what passes for peace in Somalia, and it is enough to tempt many homesick exiles to return. They bring money as well as skills and contacts. In the past few years,

> hospitals, schools, businesses and even a university have appeared. In some ways, anarchy makes doing business easier. There are no formal taxes—given how heavily-armed the average Somali is, these would be hard to collect—and no regulation whatsoever. (*The Economist*, quoted in Tabarrok, 2004)

Tabarrok further notes that on the other hand, anarchy is turning out to be quite expensive in Somalia. He again quotes the following from *The Economist* for this claim: "But the costs of chaos outweigh the benefits. You can roar through a warlord's road block unmolested if you have ten gunmen in the back of your pickup, but you have to pay your gunmen. Nationlink, one of the country's three mobile-phone operators, employs 300 guards to protect 500 staff. Everyone yearns for a restoration of stability and a proper government" (*The Economist*, quoted in Tabarrok, 2004).

Pluralist/Polyarchist scholars such as Robert Dahl (1973) see the state as either a neutral arena for competing interests or its agencies as simply another set of interest groups. Thus, according to these scholars, state policy is the output of recurrent bargaining because the state is competitively arranged. They proffer the argument that while inequality does exist in society, nonetheless, all groups have an opportunity to pressure the state to fulfill their interests. They argue that the actions of a modern democratic state are the outcomes of pressures applied by a variety of competing organized interest groups—a kind of state that Dahl calls a "polyarchy."

A frequently, if not the most, cited work that has employed the Pluralist/Polyarchist paradigm to examine the African state is the book edited by Leo Kuper and M. G. Smith titled *Pluralism in Africa* (1969) in which the authors seek to present what they call a "new" analysis of African reality. They focus on the concepts of the "plural society" and "structural pluralism" and emphasize social exclusion as a core feature of this analytical apparatus. They clarify this idea by suggesting that individuals can be incorporated into political structures either on (a) universalist terms—directly, on identical terms, as citizens; or (b) particularistic terms—in which individuals are incorporated indirectly through their membership of particular corporate sections, basically racial or ethnic groups. In particularistic structures, different groups may be incorporated on equal or unequal terms. The latter situation is "differential incorporation": i.e., a situation of "structural pluralism." In this case, a state is comprised of ordered and structurally unequal, exclusive, corporate sections.

According to Kuper and his colleagues, the situation of structural pluralism corresponds to an order of social relations. In such a case, exclusionary practices are directed at both members of the society, according to the corporate section to which they belong, and also those from outside national frontiers. The latter category of exclusion may be less significant than in the case of the nation-state, as illustrated by some of the policies of colonial states toward migrant workers. Furthermore, the order of social relations is found in the differential incorporation of social aggregates into a common political society. This incorporation may take place formally and explicitly under the law and constitution or without them. The system of differential incorporation may disenfranchise a particular section of society by withholding citizenship from its members. But, no matter how variable the system may be in its specific conditions and properties, the collective character and scope of its substantive differentiations must be rigorous and pervasive enough to be able to establish an efficient order of corporate inequalities and subordination by the differential distribution of civil and political rights and the economic, social and other opportunities that they give or withhold (Kuper and Smith, 1969).

Proponents of the Institutionalist idea of the state such as Theda Skocpol (1985), who claim allegiance to Max Weber, begin by criticizing the "society-centered" renderings of the state that emphasize the autonomy of the state with respect to social forces. For Institutionalists, the state is not an "instrument" or an "arena" and does not "function" in the interest of a single class; instead, behavior is primarily molded by the institutions in which it is embedded. Institutionalists stress the importance of interposing civil society between the economy and the state in order to explain the differences in state forms. Thus, according to them, state actors are to a great extent autonomous. Put differently, state personnel have interests of their own that they pursue independently in society, albeit not without occasional conflicts. Consequently, according to Institutionalists, since the state controls the means of coercion, and due to the fact that many civil society groups depend on the state for achieving their goals, state personnel have the possibility of imposing their own preferences on these groups. They also make a distinction between "strong states" versus "weak, soft, failed, collapsed, declined, absent, marginal, decayed, juridical or normative states," asserting that the degree of "relative autonomy" of a state from pressures in society determines the power of that state.

Ali A. Mazrui (1995) compares the characteristics of the African state to that of a refugee. Most African states, he states, are artificial, and the states and refugees are fundamentally without roots. This lack of roots and artificiality of the African state, he argues, can be traced to its colonial origins and its artificial boundaries, while the lack of roots of the individual refugee is a result of the postcolonial political traumas of disruption and displacement.

According to Mazrui, an issue that African states and refugees face is that of alienation, as both the state and individual refugees are often alienated from the societies in which they find themselves. This alienation, he points out, can be morally unsettling and can distort the ethics and standards of behavior of the refugees and of those who control the state. Under the pressure of refugee flows, he adds, what is right and what is wrong, what is bad and what is good, can undergo disconcerting mutations (Mazrui, 1995, p. 9).

Mazrui notes that in global terms, the African state has become increasingly marginalized and has been pushed into the ghetto of the global system. He mentions the fact that like the continent's refugees, many African states were already living, at least partly, on handouts by the 1990s. But the international community is feeling donor fatigue. Furthermore, he states, the end of the Cold War diverted Western investment and aid toward the former members of the Warsaw

Pact and the newly liberalizing economies of China, India, and Vietnam. He argues that the new priorities of the post-Cold War era, to some extent, meant bad news for disabled African states and displaced African people. He notes that the Francophone economies have lost the financial asylum they used to enjoy from the French franc and must now deal with the full rigors of state formation, including the danger of producing economic and even political refugees, as Anglophone Africa has been doing. He adds that the metaphor of the African state as a political refugee continues with the reality of institutional collapse, psychic bewilderment, and human dislocation (Mazrui, 1995, pp. 9–10).

Mazrui identifies the following six state functions that seem to be particularly crucial for a state to fail: (1) sovereign control over territory; (2) sovereign oversight and supervision, although not necessarily ownership, of the state's resources; (3) effective and rational revenue extraction from people, goods, and services; (4) capacity to build and maintain adequate national infrastructure—roads, postal services, telephone systems, railways, etc.; (5) capacity to render social services such as sanitation, education, housing, fire brigades, hospitals and clinics, and immunization facilities; and (6) capacity for governance and maintenance of law and order. He insists that we should not limit ourselves to these six functions when looking at the process of state failure, as we may get earlier notice of a state in decay if we work out indicators of performance in all six areas. This is because, according to him, the African state may show signs of desperation long before it has been reduced to a political refugee (Mazrui, 1995, p. 11).

The Developmentalist notion of the state is proposed by Thandika Mkandawire. In his article, "Thinking about Developmental States in Africa" (2001), Mkandawire recalls that during much of the 1980s and1990s, literature emerged suggesting that "developmental states" were impossible in Africa. He points out that the arguments proffered ranged from cultural ones about the pervasive nature of "clientalism" to structural ones on the dependence of African economies or the atypical levels of rent-seeking in African economies. He then argues that Africa has had states that were "developmental" in terms of their aspirations and economic performance. He further argues that the experiences need to be examined critically to glean useful lessons, an exercise that has been hampered by an excessive leveling of the political and economic arenas in Africa.

Mkandawire makes the following poignant observation about the African state that captures the shift in attitudes attributable not only to the dismal performance of African states during the current economic and social crisis, but also to a number of ideological, paradigmatic, and structural shifts in both the domestic and global arenas:

> If the state was given a central role in earlier views of the process of development in Africa, the situation changed dramatically in the late 1970s and 1980s. The African state is today the most demonized social institution in Africa, vilified for its weaknesses, its over-extension, its interference with the smooth functioning of the markets, its repressive character, its dependence on foreign

> powers, its ubiquity, its absence, etc. The state—once the cornerstone of development—is now the millstone around otherwise efficient markets. It is now the "rentier state", the "overextended state", the "parasitical state", the "predatory state", the "lame leviathan", "the primordial state", the "prebendal state", the "crony state", the "kleptocratic state", the "inverted state", etc. Although this inflation of epithets has reached high proportions in more recent years, the tradition itself predates the "crisis" years. Early criticism of the state in Africa came from the neo-Marxists whose own epithets to describe the pathological condition of the African state included the "petty bourgeoisie state", the "neo-colonial state" and the "dependent state". The many epithets underscore the fall from grace of the African state. It is now argued that not only has the state become dysfunctional in terms of the management of larger societal issues, but also a real nuisance in *la vie quotidienne* of its citizens, as evidenced by the "withdrawal" from state-dominated economic and social spaces. (Mkandawire, 2001, pp. 289–290)

Mkandawire goes on to describe the "developmental state" as having two components. One component is the *ideological*: i.e., a state is primarily one whose ideological underpinning is "developmentalist" if it conceives its "mission" as that of ensuring economic development, usually characterized by high rates of accumulation and industrialization. This type of state legitimizes itself by promoting sustained development, both domestically and in its relationship to the global economy. The other component is the *structural*: i.e., a state emphasizes its *capacity* to implement economic policies efficiently and effectively. Such a capacity is determined by institutional, technical, administrative and political instruments. It is the nexus between the *ideological-structural* components that distinguishes developmental states from other forms of states (Mkandawire, 2001, p. 290).

Nonetheless, Mkandawire cautions that the formulation of the "developmental state" runs the risk of appearing tautological since evidence that the state is developmental is often drawn deductively from the performance of the economy. This can produce a conceptualization of a state as developmental if the economy is developing, equating economic success to state strength while measuring state strength by the presumed outcomes of the state's policies. Mkandawire cites the fact that in Africa, one finds many examples of states whose performance up until the mid-1970s would have qualified them as "developmental states" in the sense conveyed by the preceding definition, but which now appear anti-developmental because of the hard times that have halted the economic expansion of these countries (Mkandawire, 2001, p. 291).

The Human Rights notion of the state is advocated by Willy Munyoki Mutunga in the belief that the promotion and defense of human rights are imperative for a sustainable democratic and economically vibrant state in Africa. According to Mutunga, the resistance to the violation of human rights still remains the fundamental obligation of the human rights movement in Kenya and other African countries. He therefore argues that the role of the international human rights movement is to reinforce, if it can, the internal struggles of the human rights movements in Kenya and other African states. He points out that the recent struggle for democracy, the rule of law, the respect for human rights and the basic needs of all Kenyans and other Africans have enjoyed relative success, but that there is always the danger that these gradual and positive developments can be clawed back by states that are continually becoming infamous for their violations of human rights. He adds that blatant violation of the law and the constitution, torture, murder, rape, insecurity, a collapsing economy, a cowed and dependent judiciary, corruption, and compromised security apparatuses have all made African governments insecure, frightened, and dangerous (Mutunga, 2000).

What Mutunga brings to the attention of national and international human rights movements are the chilling facts of human rights violations in Kenya in particular and Africa in general. The violations are as follows (Mutunga, 2000):

> (a) human rights' defenders ultimately face death if they persist in their project;
>
> (b) the state does not guarantee the protection of the lives and property of human rights' defenders;
>
> (c) the state encourages informal repression as a means of intimidating and denying citizens of their rights;
>
> (d) the religious and constitutional initiatives will never be given a chance to operate, and the state will encourage the subversion of their constitutional and legal mandate;
>
> (e) the state guarantees only the rights of the supporters of the ruling party and the political parties that cooperate with the ruling party;
>
> (f) opposition political parties will not be allowed to exercise their political and civil rights;
>
> (g) the ruling party and its allies in the opposition will solely determine the content of a new constitution and the management of the political succession; and
>
> (h) the international community is totally perfidious, hypocritical, unreliable, racist and cares only about its economic, social, cultural, political and military interests. The international community just pays lip service to issues of democracy, governance and human rights. The international community cannot, therefore, be relied upon to resist, even morally, the dictatorship of certain regimes.

It is Mutunga's hope that the international human rights movement is not about to become a front for capitalist interests. He therefore challenges the international human rights movement to demonstrate that human rights violations are all over the world and that the movement will resist all states in the world that violate human rights (Mutunga, 2000).

In his book, *Constitution-Making from the Middle: Civil Society and Transition Politics in Kenya, 1992–1997* (1999), Mutunga examines the constitution-making process as a specific component of the advancement of human rights in Kenya's transition politics. He places the middle class at the core of constitution-making and identifies many civil society groups that initiated the process, showing those that dropped out, at what point they did so, and which continued the struggle. He draws significant lessons accumulated over six years as the movement engaged the state and asserts the conflictual nature of state-civil society relations, existing mainly in opposition to an illegitimate, oppressive, and corrupt state (Mutunga, 1999).

Mutunga further shows how Kenya drew its democratic inspiration from anti-colonial movements, highlighting the central role of Mau Mau land and freedom fighters. He calls for the civil society to take an Africancentric approach based on the corporate project approach in its role in constitution-making. He characterizes civil society as diverse and lacking homogeneity, grounding his understanding of civil society on the central role of the non-governmental organizations (NGOs) and the Citizens Coalition for Constitutional Change (4Cs) project in Kenya. He points out that the vibrancy of civil society should be designed to put checks and balances to the excesses of a government and argues that there should be no danger for civil society to be partisan (Mutunga, 1999).

Advocates of the African Socialist perspective of the state—one of the most noteworthy being Mwalimu Julius Nyerere (1989)—see the state as a society that ensures the sharing of economic resources in a traditional African way. Thus, the African socialist state is distinct from the classical doctrinaire socialist state, which yearns for the representation of the interests of the working class. The African socialist state is also neither the opposite of the capitalist state nor a response to it, but something completely different. It is fully African, appealing to an African identity that is even stronger than anti-capitalism. The African socialist state is, therefore, a recapturing of the spirit of what it was to be African.

In his essay, "African Socialism: Ujamaa in Practice" (1989), Mwalimu Nyerere states that traditional African society succeeded in ensuring that both the "rich" and the "poor" were completely secure. When natural catastrophe brought famine, it brought it to all: "rich" and "poor." No one starved, either for food or for human dignity, because s/he lacked personal wealth; instead, s/he could depend on the wealth possessed by the community to which s/he belongs—that was and is socialism. He argues that there can be no such thing as acquisitive socialism, for the term is self-contradictory since socialism is essentially distributive: those who sow reap a fair share of what they sow (Nyerere, 1989, p. 212).

Mwalimu Nyerere points out that in traditional African society, everyone was a worker. He does not use the term "worker" simply as an opposition to "employer" but also as opposed to "loiterer" or "idler." Even the elder, who appeared to be enjoying himself/herself without doing any work and for whom everyone else seemed to be working, had, in fact, worked hard during all of his/her younger days. The wealth s/he now appeared to possess was not personally his/hers; it was only "his"/"hers" as the elder of the group which had produced it. S/he was simply the guardian of the wealth; the wealth itself gave him/her neither power nor prestige. The respect paid to him/her by the young was his/hers because s/he was older than they and had served his community for longer; and the "poor" enjoyed as much respect as the "rich" elder (Nyerere, 1989, p. 213).

Mwalimu Nyerere also notes that those Africans who talk about the African way of life and, quite rightly so, take great pride in maintaining the tradition of hospitality which is so great a part of it must keep in mind the following Swahili saying: "Treat your guest as a guest for two days; the third day give him a hoe." In actuality, Mwalimu Nyerere, asserts, the guest was likely to ask for the hoe even before his/her host had to give him/her one, for s/he knew what was expected of him/her and would have been ashamed to remain idle any longer. He adds that there is no such thing as socialism without work. A society which fails to provide individuals the means to work or, having given them the means to work, prevents them from getting a fair share of the products of their labor, needs to be put right. Likewise, individuals who can work and are provided by society with the means to work but do not do so are equally wrong. They have no right to expect anything from society because they contribute nothing to it (Nyerere, 1989, pp. 213–214).

Thus, for Mwalimu Nyerere, the first step for Africans to develop their states must be to re-educate themselves; to regain their former attitude of mind. In their traditional African society, they were individuals within a community. They took care of the community, and the community in turn took care of them. They neither needed nor wished to exploit their fellow humans. And in rejecting the capitalist attitude of mind which colonialism brought to Africa, Africans must reject also the capitalist methods which go with it. One of this is land being owned by the individual. To Africans, land always belonged to the community. Each individual within the society had a right to the use of land because otherwise, s/he could not earn a living, and one cannot have the right to life without also having the right to some means of sustaining life. But the right of Africans to land was simply the right to *use* it; they had no other right to it, nor did it occur to them to try to claim it (Nyerere, 1989, p. 214).

Essentially then, following Mwalimu Nyerere, the foundation and the objective of the African socialist state is the extended family. True African socialists do not look on one class of men and women as their brothers and sisters and another as their natural enemies. They do not form an alliance with their brothers and sisters for the extermination of the non-brothers and non-sisters. They rather regard *all* men and women as their brothers and sisters as members of the ever-extended family, which is *Ujamaa*, or "familyhood," that describes African socialism. It is opposed to capitalism which seeks to build a happy society based on the exploitation of human by human; and it is equally opposed to doctrinaire socialism which seeks to build its happy society on the philosophy of inevitable conflict between human and human (Nyerere, 1989, p. 217).

Mwalimu Nyerere concludes by stating that it was through the struggle to break the grip of colonialism that Africans learned the need for unity. They came to recognize that the same socialist attitude of mind which, in the early days, gave to every individual the security that comes with belonging to a widely extended family must be preserved within the still wider society of the nation. But Africans should not stop there. Their recognition of the family to which they all belong extended further—beyond the ethnic group, the community, the nation, or even beyond the continent—to embrace the whole society of humankind (Nyerere, 1989, pp. 217–218).

The Social state idea is proffered by Adebayo Olukoshi (2004). In his keynote address, "Toward the Restoration of a Social State in Africa," delivered at the Globalization and Sub-Saharan Africa: International Experts' Meeting convened at the European Parliament in Brussels on April 15 and 16, 2004, Olukoshi defines the Social state as one that is socially responsible or whose foundations entail a strong social policy component that is designed to address the broad social needs of the citizenry. The Social state plays a proactive role as the vanguard in social advancement of the broad boundaries in meeting the needs of the people. Olukoshi adds that the concept is also connected to the idea of social citizenship—i.e., the broad array of social welfare rights of the citizenry that is in many ways connected to the idea of the social contract between state and society—that is used in the political literature of the 1960s and 1970s, and as appeared in the discussions that took place during the reconstructions of the post-World War II European welfare states (Olukoshi, 2004, p. 1).

Olukoshi points out that the nexus between the Social state and social citizen carried the role of state and citizenship beyond the narrow idea of security that undergirded state society relations in Europe. The idea was that the state itself was a product of a process of insecurity and instability; thus, within a given territory, the contract between the citizens of the political community and the leadership of that polity hinged upon providing security, particularly the security of life within that territory. It is the introduction of the idea of a social citizen and a social state that revolutionized that narrow conceptualization of the state, as essentially a security-providing state, to transcend that compact to include issues of economic and social rights. Therefore, according to Olukoshi, the idea of social citizenship presupposes the existence of a strong proactive socially conscious state (Olukoshi, 2004, pp. 1–2).

Briefly recounting the history of the structure of the colonial African state, Olukoshi argues that the colonial state had an inbuilt contradiction which could only resolve itself in the move towards independence—a movement that was justified on the grounds that the social policies of the colonial state were restrictive and discriminatory. As he puts it,

> Most of the nationalists and strugglers for independence fought saying that they would provide health, education, generate employment where the colonial economies failed to generate enough employment to young people, and provide better social amenities to their people, like water and electricity. What the colo-

nial states were not able to provide by the way in which [they were] constituted and the way in which [they] functioned became the flip side of the nationalists' manifesto for the push for independence. This was at the core of the post-independence social contract between state and society in Africa. Despite the different leaders' different paths—the socialists, the humanists and the market friendly and so forth; irrespective of the path they chose, when you look at the form of social expenditure of the post-independence there was a strong notion of state-led development. The state was easily the biggest and the most coherent actor in the political economy at independence. Public enterprises were set up without exception from Ivory Coast, Kenya to Nyerere's socialist republic which despite critics was doing exactly what Kenyatta was doing with his market ideology. All of them put a huge outlay in social expenditure. (Olukoshi, 2004, p. 3)

After also recounting the economic and social havoc caused by the neo-liberal push of structural adjustment programs (SAPs) on African states by the World Bank, the International Monetary Fund (IMF) and Western states, Olukoshi calls for the making of effective African states that are strong and capable of organizing development as directors and leaders of the countries and in setting the boundaries of what they want, including providing the essential structure for good investment into the economy. Thus, for him, the first immediate task for Africans is to rehabilitate the Social state, which should begin with the establishment of a functioning state. This also requires the development of a full social consciousness, right from the outset, in order to avoid the errors that were made to the state interventionist models in the 1960s and 1970s. Some of these errors have to do with the manner of the organization of power (Olukoshi, 2004, pp. 5–6).

The *Fundi wa Afrika* perspective of the state is the brainchild of Mueni wa Muiu, in her essay accordingly titled "*Fundi wa Afrika*: Toward a New Paradigm of the African State" (2002). She begins by arguing that throughout history, Western interests in Africa have consistently been to have access to cheap labor, control of the economy, markets, and raw materials. The African state was therefore shaped to meet these goals. Consequently, she asserts, African goals such as self-reliance, democracy, and continental unity cannot be achieved by the present states. She therefore calls for the restructuring of the African state to retain its positive and adequately functioning elements and by incorporating the still functional remnants of indigenous African institutions. Thus, according to Muiu, the African state should determine the framework of its economic, political, and social interactions with the sub-regional, regional, and global environment (Muiu, 2002, p. 23).

This African state envisioned by Muiu is couched within the concept she calls *Fundi wa Afrika*, a new paradigm in the study of African politics. She analogizes this paradigm to her observations of building and tailoring processes in a small village in eastern Kenya as follows:

> The owner of the house decided what the needs of the family were which he/she explained to the builder. Throughout the building process the builder and the owner consulted each other and whenever anything needed changing the builder changed it based on the needs of the client. I noticed the same process when I took my material to the tailor to make some outfits for me. She asked me what my needs were and we consulted each other throughout the process. When everything was over we were both happy. It is then that I realized that the relationship between Africans and their institutions in indigenous Africa was similar to the building and tailoring processes. (Muiu, 2002, p. 23)

These observations, according to Muiu, led her to study African institutions in order to understand when and how they changed to be externally determined rather than defined by internal factors. She argues that the analysis of the African predicament can only be understood in relation to the "new Scramble for Africa," a process that led to the depletion of the continent's human resources through the simultaneous onslaught of population control policies, AIDS, wars, and a captive and servile leadership. She therefore contends that *Fundi wa Afrika* will help to counter this debilitating process by offering Africans a way out of the predicament (Muiu, 2002, p. 23).

After presenting a brief analysis of indigenous African political systems and an examination of the colonial and post-colonial state in Africa, Muiu draws many conclusions. First, indigenous African political systems were based on African culture and tradition. Second, a vibrant civil society existed and acted as a check on leaders' power. Third, political power was decentralized, making it possible for leaders to rule and the people to participate fully. Fourth, the political systems were institutionalized in the society, since they were determined by the needs and values of their members. Fifth, the trans-Atlantic slave trade permanently transformed the relationship between the rulers and the ruled. Sixth, the pattern of slavery was accelerated through colonialism as foreign powers used Africans in their own land for the maximum profit of the West. Seventh, independence simply Africanized the colonial institutions. Seventh, Westerners rewarded African leaders that served them well, just like they did during slavery. And finally, just as the abolition of slavery was used by diverse Western agencies as an excuse to meddle into African affairs, international financial institutions are using the present African predicament to shape and control African economies. Muiu therefore argues that until Africans recapture their economies, the pattern will continue. Consequently, she calls for the development of African states that are based on their own culture and values (Muiu, 2002, p. 38).

The ultimate question here then is the following: How are the preceding theories/paradigms on the African state different and similar, and how do they overlap? To begin with, the differences among the preceding theories/paradigms are ones of emphasis. The Eurocentric schools tend to emphasize the role of African states in the creation of their problems while the Africancentric schools tend to emphasize the role of colonialists and neocolonialists in the creation of those problems. Concurrently, the Eurocentric schools call for a greater role by the international community (Western countries and their financial institutions) in solving the problems of the African state and the Africancentric call for a greater role by the African states themselves in solving their own problems.

In addition to the differences among these schools, there also are areas of similarities and overlap among them. Within a defined geographical context, all perspectives see the African state as the political organization of society. The common characteristics of the state identified include the existence of sovereignty or supreme authority, clearly defined borders with population, organized form of governance and decision-making, and security for the inhabitants. The African state system is based on territoriality, and its most important feature is the existence of political offices: i.e., persons invested with roles to exercise authority over others in a given territory. Consequently, the factors identified to have contributed to the emergence of the African state were just as significant as those that contributed to its predicament.

The *Ubuntu*/Communal Paradigm

Ubuntu is a word from the Southern African Nguni language family (Ndebele, Swati/Swazi, Xhosa, and Zulu) meaning humanity or fellow feeling: kindness (Bangura, 2008).

The reason for choosing *ubuntu* as a paradigm for problematizing the African state hinges upon the following three questions: (1) Why have the Western state system inherited by Africans after independence not yielded much benefit for them? (2) Did the Western state system infiltrate African societies because Africans lacked their own? (3) What is the nature, character, mission and overall pedigree of the African state. The following paragraphs attempt to answer these questions.

In response to these questions, drawing from the treatise by Awoonor (1990) on African political systems, it can stated that Western systems are incompatible with African systems because the former (i.e., Western) are based on a concept that fragments African life derived from a Eurocentric division of labor theory which separates politics from religion and the social institutions of family, or group, or people. This fragmentation theory emanates from Eurocentric epistemology and a fundamental approach to existence which has its genesis in Greco-Roman and subsequently Judeo-Christian thought.

Thus, one of the major tenets that underlies the choice of *ubuntu* as an African state paradigm is that before we attempt any description of the political thought process of Africans, it is necessary to locate its total personality within the boundaries of its own self-perception; this means delineating African philosophy and its view of the world, both visible and invisible, its fundamental habits of thought, and its attitude towards its physical and spiritual existence.

As Awoonor (1990) also states, the African life concept is holistic—i.e., it is based on an integrative world view. All life to the African is total; all human activities are closely interrelated. This has as its underlying principle the sanctity of the person, her/his spirituality and essentiality. This essentialist view of the person confers value to her/his personhood. All else—her/his labor and achievements—flow from this value system. Even personal shortcomings cannot invalidate it.

In addition, for Africans, politics defines duties and responsibilities alongside obligations and rights. All these relate to the various activities that have to do with survival. The survival concept is continuing, dynamic and dialectical. The fundamental principle that is at the basis of this conception is a moral one. Moreover, the African moral order never defined rigid frontiers of good and evil. Good and evil exist in the same continuum. Whatever is good, by the very nature of its goodness, harbors a grain of evil. This is a guarantee against any exaggerated sense of moral superiority which goodness alone may entail. The notion of perfection, therefore, is alien to African thought. Perfection in itself constitutes a temptation to danger, an invitation to arrogance and self-glorification. The principle of balance defines the relationship between good and evil. As life operates in a dialectics of struggle, so also does good balance evil and *vice versa*.

Thus, the essence of *ubuntuy* is that it is imperative and urgent for Africans to be concerned about the broader political entity as well as to be concerned about approaches to political practices which are undergirded by humanity or fellow feeling toward others. When *ubuntu* is considered along with the idea of the socialization effects of political environments and the possibilities of a reinforcement of these notions and contexts, the implications for an African state appear vital.

In the West, individualism often translates into rugged competition. Individual interest is *modus vivendi*, and society or others are regarded as a means to individual ends. This is in stark contrast to the African preference for co-operation, group work or *shosholoza* ("work as one": i.e., team work). For example, the *stokvels* in South Africa are approximated to be 800,000. *Stockvels* are joint undertakings or collective enterprises, such as savings clubs, burial societies and other co-operatives. The *stockvel* economy might be described as capitalism with *sazi* (humanness), or, put differently, a socialist form of capitalism. Making a profit is important, but never if it involves the exploitation of others. Profits are equally shared. Thus, *stockvels* are based on the *ubuntu* "extended family system": i.e., all involved should be considered as brothers and sisters, members of the same family.

Indeed, the *ubuntu* conception of individuality may seem contradictory, since it claims that the self or individual is constituted by its relations with others. But if this is the case, then what are the relations between? Can persons and personal relations really be equally primordial? African thought addresses this (apparent) contradiction in the idea of *seriti*: i.e., an energy, power of force which makes us ourselves and unites us in personal interaction with others. This idea allows us to see the self and others as equiprimordial or as aspects of the same universal field of force. This distinctive African inclination towards collectivism and collective sense of responsibility does not negate individualism. It merely discourages the notion that the individual should take precedence over community.

Consequently, an oppressive communalism constitutes a derailment, an abuse of *ubuntu*. True *ubuntu* incorporates dialogue: i.e., it intertwines both relation and distance. It preserves the other in his/her otherness, in his/her uniqueness, without letting him/her slip into the distance.

The emphasis on the "ongoing-ness" of the contact and interaction with others on which the African subjectivity feeds suggests a final important ingredient of the "mutual exposure" mandated by *ubuntu*: i.e., respecting the *historicality* of the other. This means respecting his/her dynamic nature or process nature. The flexibility of the other is well noted in *ubuntu*. In other words, for the African humanist, life is without absolutes. An *ubuntu* perception of the other is never fixed or rigidly closed; rather, it is adjustable or open-ended. It allows the other to be, to become. It acknowledges the irreducibility of the other: i.e., it never reduces the other to any specific characteristic, conduct or function. This underscores the concept of *ubuntu* which denotes both a state of being and one of becoming. As a process of self-realization *through* others, it simultaneously enriches the self-realization *of* others.

By drawing from many works that have dealt with the concept of *ubuntu* and similar African thoughts on communalism, I (Bangura, 2005) deduced that *ubuntu* serves as the spiritual foundation of African societies. It is a unifying vision or worldview enshrined in the maxim *umuntu ngumuntu ngabantu*: i.e., "a person is a person through other persons." This traditional African aphorism articulates a basic respect and compassion for others. It can be interpreted as both a factual description and a rule of conduct or social ethic. It both describes the human being as "being-with-others" and prescribes what that should be.

Also, from the consulted works (for these works, see Bangura, 2005), at least three major tenets of *ubuntu* can be delineated. The first major tenet of *ubuntu* rests upon its religiosity. While Western Humanism tends to underestimate or even deny the importance of religious beliefs, *ubuntu* or African Humanism is decidedly religious. For the Westerner, the maxim, "A person is a person through other persons," has no obvious religious connotations. S/he will probably think it is nothing more than a general appeal to treat others with respect and decency. In African tradition, however, this maxim has a deeply religious meaning. The person one is to become "through other persons" is, ultimately, an ancestor. By the same token, these "other persons" include ancestors, who are extended family. Dying is an ultimate homecoming. Not only must the living and the dead share with and care for one another, but the living and the dead depend on one another.

This religious tenet is congruent with the daily experience of most Africans. For example, at a *calabash*, an African ritual that involves drinking of African beer, a little bit of it is poured on the ground for consumption by ancestors. Many Africans also employ ancestors as mediators between them and God. In African societies, there is an inextricable bond between humans, ancestors, and the Supreme Being. Therefore, *ubuntu* inevitably implies a deep respect and regard for religious beliefs and practices.

The second major tenet of *ubuntu* hinges upon its consensus building. African traditional cultures have an almost infinite capacity for the pursuit of consensus and reconciliation. African style democracy operates in the form of (sometimes extremely lengthy) discussions. Although there may be a hierarchy of importance among the speakers, every person gets an equal chance to speak up until some kind of an agreement, consensus, or group cohesion is reached. This important aim is expressed by words like *simunye* ("we are one": i.e., "unity is strength") and slogans like "an injury to one is an injury to all."

The desire to agree within the context of *ubuntu* safeguards the rights and opinions of individuals and minorities to enforce group solidarity. In essence, *ubuntu* requires an authentic respect for human/individual rights and related values, and an honest appreciation of differences.

The third major tenet of *ubuntu* rests upon dialogue, with its particularity, individuality, and historicality. *Ubuntu* inspires us to expose ourselves to others, to encounter the differences of their humanness in order to inform and enrich our own. Thus understood, *umuntu ngumentu ngabantu* translates as, "To be human is to affirm one's humanity by recognizing the humanity of others in its infinite variety of content and form." This translation of *ubuntu* highlights the respect for particularity, individuality, and historicality, without which a true African communal paradigm cannot reemerge.

The *ubuntu* respect for the *particularities* of the beliefs and practices of others is especially emphasized by the following striking translation of *umuntu ngumentu ngabantu*: "A human being through (the otherness of) other human beings." *Ubuntu* dictates that, if we were to be human, we need to recognize the genuine otherness of our fellow humans. In other words, we need to acknowledge the diversity of languages, histories, values, and customs, all of which make up a society.

Ubuntu's respect for the particularity of the other is closely aligned to its respect for *individuality*. But the individuality which *ubuntu* respects is not the Cartesian type. Instead, *ubuntu* directly contradicts the Cartesian conception of individuality in terms of which the individual or self can be conceived without thereby necessarily conceiving the other. The Cartesian individual exists prior to, or separately and independently from, the rest of the community or society. The rest of society is nothing but an added extra to a pre-existent and self-sufficient being. This "modernistic" and "atomistic" conception of individuality underscores both individualism and collectivism. Individualism exaggerates the seemingly solitary aspects of human existence to the detriment of communal aspects. Collectivism makes the same mistake on a larger scale. For the collectivist, society comprises a bunch of separately existing, solitary (i.e., detached) individuals.

Contrastingly, *ubuntu defines* the individual in terms of his/her relationship with others. Accordingly, individuals only exist *in* their relationships with others; and as these relationships change, so do the characters of the individuals. In this context, the word "individual" signifies a plurality of personalities corresponding to the multiplicity of relationships in which the individual in question stands. Being an individual, by definition, means "being-with-others." "With-others" is not an additive to a pre-existent and self-sufficient being; instead, both this being (the self) and the others find themselves in a whole wherein they are already related. This is all somewhat boggling for the Cartesian mind, whose conception of individuality must now move from solitary to solidarity, from independence to interdependence, from individuality *vis-à-vis* community, to individuality *à la* community.

This spirit of communalism, as Fred Lee Hord and Jonathan Scott Lee (1995, pp. 17–20) demonstrate by republishing a collection of essays by great African minds from the continent and the Diaspora, is deeply ingrained in African philosophy. From the beginnings of recorded African thought in *The Book of Coming Forth by Day*, better known as the Egyptian *Book of the Dead*, to the stirring words of Nelson Mandela today, there is a repeated emphasis on the relationship between the individual and his/her community. This emphasis is rooted in turn in the ontological framework that stresses a fundamental relational conception of reality. This ontological conception at the same time positions the human being in a network of relationships with all aspects of the world and situates his/her community in a further network of relations, including relations to God or gods, that transcend the particularities of any culture. This web of relations is a representation of a sophisticated version of humanism—what might be called relational humanism—in which the human being is essentially a web of relationships that are both social and cosmic. Thus, Hord and Lee suggest that this distinctively African perspective on humanism offers answers to the problem of grounding ethical commitments faced by postmodern theories of the decentered human subject.

African communalism emphasizes truth, righteousness, and justice. Communal testimonies are meant to bolster an individual's case for eternal life, define a set of standards for moral conduct in the community, and assure each individual has a place in the eternal network of the universe. Central to the network of communalism is the valorization of principles of egalitarianism, peace, harmony, sharing, deliberate speech and humility. Taken together, these principles constitute the framework of a moral community in which relations—between men and women and between people and gods—make up the substance of life (Hord and Lee, 1995, pp. 17–18).

Case Studies

The Transformative Impact of the South African Truth and Reconciliation Commission

The South African battle for majority rule was resolved without the country erupting into a protracted, bloody civil war. Out of the demise of apartheid, hailed around the world, the South African Truth and Reconciliation Commission (TRC) emerged to help confront the transgressions and crimes committed from March 1, 1960 until May 10, 1994. Does the end of apartheid and the granting of amnesty to some perpetrators constitute real peace, but more importantly, just beyond the absence of war, in a land recovering from huge differences? The revered Nobel Peace Laureate, Chair of the South African TRC and former Archbishop of South Africa, the Most Reverend Desmond Tutu (2000), puts forth the *ubuntu* paradigm as undergirding the peaceful changes in the South African society that emerged as a direct result of the Truth and Reconciliation Commission hearings. Indeed, the TRC has been beneficial to the healing of the wounds of South Africa, albeit not without complications for lasting peace.

Understanding the basis for the need for amnesty requires that the atrocities be detailed and evaluated. The Commission handled 21,298 statements that covered a wide variety of human rights violations, totaling 38,000 human rights violations committed during the years 1960–1994 (Posel, 2002, p. 157). The immensity and depth of criminal acts necessitated a greater disclosure of what happened and to whom. The Commission defined a "gross human rights violation" as the commitment or conspiracy to commit the killing, abduction, torture between March 1, 1960 and May 10, 1994 that was politically motivated (Posel, 2002, p. 42). Bitterness and animosity grow out of such systems that constrain and destroy the human spirit in order to maintain leverage. Unfortunately, hatred can spring from the very same process meant to redress the crimes of the past. The Commission had an immense task and deemed many applicants not eligible for consideration. Those atrocities that were tried exposed the brutal workings of apartheid from all sides. The granting of amnesty by the Commission was not meant to further harm those who suffered the most under apartheid. The process of amnesty was meant to bring a sense of closure and justice to a land that had neither.

The atrocities that were committed during the years of White minority rule qualified for amnesty considerations. No side involved in the struggle for South African freedom was exempt from examination, nor were the men and women in charge of supporting and maintaining apartheid. The struggle in South Africa was considered to be a "low-level war" waged by the African National Congress (ANC) and the White minority government of South Africa as a war where "both sides did things that seemed unforgivable at the time, things that would be hard to put behind them if they ever sat down at a negotiation table" (Moriarty, 2003, p. 15). The idea that South Africa would ever become a multi-party, democratic state on the African continent through a quasi-peaceful transition was not a prospect given much hope by any group involved in the struggle.

The history of South Africa is filled with conflict between the emerging European settler population and the indigenous ethnic groups already thriving in South Africa (Frueh, 2003, p. 40). The struggle for South African freedom took on various forms: Whites and non-Whites did fight against the system of apartheid that emerged after the National Party's victory in 1948. The development of stricter laws regulating the races and interaction of racial groups hindered wider White and non-White co-operation in the anti-apartheid struggle. As Jamie Frueh states, "Apartheid forced South Africans to live their lives as if racism were true" (2003, p. 41). The divisiveness of the laws prevented overt assistance in most cases, but also worked at forcing those that lived in the nation to conform to the social order as envisioned by apartheid's architects: a racially segregated state with all benefits flowing from a top-down paradigm.

A brutal period of repression and heightened acts of atrocities emerged in the 1980s as a result of the State of Emergency declarations by the White-led government. The repressive powers of the state of emergency declarations mobilized the military and police units to stamp out the insurrections that were becoming more pronounced and organized against the *apartheid* regime (Frueh, 2003, pp. 106–107). The cases of political prisoners, torture, poisonings, mass graves, and detainment all became clearer to the South African populace after the hearings held by the Truth and Reconciliation Commission. The violence of South Africa's past needed to be exposed and dialogued in order to construct a new level of partnership in this newly emerging democracy.

Violence did not only occur during the years of White-minority rule. Criminal acts have increased post-apartheid and violent actions between various ethnic groups emerged after the dismantling of apartheid began in 1990. During this period, the violence that erupted claimed more than 16,000 lives, a figure that exceeds all those killed during the apartheid regime and struggle against it (Taylor and Shaw, 1998, p. 13). The sudden directional change of the National Party governance forced the South African society, Whites and non-Whites, to cope with not only the decline of the apartheid system, but also to contend with a rapidly changing society of blurred social roles and opportunities (Taylor and Shaw, 1998, p. 15). One element that explains this increase in violence is an acculturation to violence. The apartheid state forcibly and brutally kept power, utilizing immense intensity and violent means to contain any action against the state. This ignited a cycle of "meeting violence with violence." This mentality, coupled with a society that has a firearm in one out of every five homes and approximately four million illegal weapons on the streets of South Africa, provides a deeper insight into the violence that dominates South African society to date (du Toit, 2001, pp. 50–51). The institutionalization of violent measures into South African society was set into motion by the White-minority government and transcended all segments of South African racial groups. The tensions that escalated during this transitional phase were to be expected as Hernus Kriel, the South African Minister of Law and Order, stated in a 1991 address: "We are in a period of change in our country, of political change, of constitutional change. And history has taught us that whenever something like that happens in a country, it is always accompanied by some sort of instability" (Taylor and Shaw, 1998, p. 13). No longer held to the confines of emergency powers and the strict adherence to apartheid-era laws, all of South Africa's citizens needed to renegotiate their places in society.

Ethnic and social connections also proved to be connections that needed to be re-negotiated. Black-on-Black violence increased, as tensions soared between Inkatha Freedom Party members and African National Congress members who battled each other in skirmishes meant to influence votes, gain new members and intimidate the opposition into submission. This period of factional fighting weakened the transitional phase and bolstered White arguments that crime and violence would multiply under majority rule. Alliances that were formed to conduct negotiations with the National Party government furthered the division and enraged constituents.

Accusations of "complicity" from the various African groups with the White government and "betrayal" by the White, Afrikaner-dominated parties created an atmosphere of distrust and intense rivalry for power. This struggle for power killed several thousand South Africans and nearly derailed the transition of power (du Toit, 2001, p. 62). The result of apartheid's legacy has been increased Black-on-Black violence. The design of the system forced Black South Africans into the most pitiful of living conditions and situations. When combined with a breakdown in regimented procedure, such as what apartheid created, and the effects of limited education, opportunities and a growing vision of what power can bring, the reasons for the ethnic clashes can be better understood.

The transformation of a society that is racially biased and restricted according to racial lines cannot occur immediately. A government can mandate appropriate actions, but the hearts and minds of the citizens ultimately possess the true power to alter a course towards better relations. Racism began from the first moment Jan van Reibeeck laid a foundation for European settlement on South African soil in 1652 (Frueh, 2003, p. 40). In order to dismantle such perceptions, intensely ingrained on the psyche of all races within South Africa, substantial time and effort must be allocated to such a cause. Apartheid was not only law; it became a way of life for all South Africans. Simply, race defined who you were and what you were capable of doing in this particular society. Frueh notes that the Calvinist conception of predestination also influenced a moral imperative that each race had certain characteristics and strict adherence to these social responsibilities were deemed necessary to obey God's laws (2003, p. 42).

It is clearly evident that any deviation from the familiar of racial beliefs will take time to undo in this polarized nation. Surveys conducted in 1996 and 1997 showed marginal changes that relate to societal integration and the social construct of Affirmative Action. There was an overall decrease in the perception that integrating schools would result in angering individuals, thereby creating an atmosphere of animosity for a learning environment. The number of respondents who disagreed with the statement that integration would be more divisive increased by over 10 percent in the span of one year. In terms of segregated communities *by choice,* the respondents who disagreed with the statement that South Africans should have the right to devise their own community according to race rose by 6.3 percent from 1996 to 1997. The overall increase does continue to a lesser extent as affirmative action issues are addressed. The perceived need for such equalizing programs only rose by one percentage point in the course of a year. How South Africa will deal with equalizing society after apartheid has yet to be fully determined. The trend is an increase in recognition of others as components of society and those recognitions are part of the healing process initiated by the Truth and Reconciliation Commission (Institute for Justice and Reconciliation, 2004).

The Truth and Reconciliation Commission set an agenda to address the wrongs of the past. Apartheid destroyed lives, family structure and created a hostile environment for all non-Whites to function in South African society. The atrocities committed to prop up the White-led regime and by those opposing the state-sponsored actions created the need for the Commission. A national dialogue that would provide answers to so many families, non-White and White, was needed to navigate the emerging South Africa: free and in need of closure. The idea that the decisions of the courts to grant amnesty should be respected increased overall within South African society. A 7.2 percent drop in respondents that agreed with the idea of disobeying the courts and seeking retribution indicates a change in thinking. That change in thinking has a strong base in the national healing from the Commission's exposure of apartheid horrors combined with the necessary ideal of forgiveness. The respondents who agreed with the statement that they are actively working towards forgiveness towards those that hurt them under apartheid increased by 5.1 percent. Any movement forward must be interpreted as a positive step in the direction of reconciliation and healing. The 2004 survey saw an increase over the previous year by 10.2 percent. The final figure proves to be the most hopeful that South Africa is maintaining the direction of unity and reconciliation (Institute for Justice and Reconciliation, 2004).

The transition from apartheid to majority rule created needs on every level. Whites wanted to maintain a standard of living unknown to most non-White South Africans. Blacks, in addition to freedom and voting rights, wanted a more egalitarian system for education, housing, and basic human needs. Asians, Indians, and Coloureds also had a list of needs for their respective groups in the new South Africa. Political, personal, and social transformations were either mandated goals or by-products of the Truth and Reconciliation Commission. Each section of transformation has helped mold South Africa into a more representative society, struggling to reconcile the very difficult past with an uncertain, yet hopeful, future. The difficulties of granting amnesty impact each transformation.

Politically, the Whites of South Africa had the most to lose in transition. Also, the regime leaders were perceived to be the most culpable in apartheid's crimes. The political transformation came with F. W. de Klerk's decision to end the insanity of apartheid and begin to dialogue with the African National Congress and Nelson Mandela. Without de Klerk's pronouncement, the relative peace of South Africa's transition would have devolved, instead, into outright civil war. The political change in South Africa was set into motion; the Truth and Reconciliation Commission helped to deliver the promises of the political change. The judicious granting of amnesty—150 out of 7,000—and the resolute pursuit for the truth from former President P. W. Botha and others who were directly responsible for crimes against humanity aided the Commission in achieving a major goal: the transition of power due to amnesty and truth (Wiessner and Willard, 1999, p. 331). The resignation of South African Whites to majority rule may have ultimately allowed for them to play a continued role in the political scene of South Africa. Amnesty for South Africa's White political elites will continue to cause debate, but so will the granting of amnesty to an accused ANC insurrectionist/freedom fighter. As the trends of reconciliation continue and perceptions alter, the political scene of South Africa appears to be transformed beyond any architect of apartheid could have ever envisioned. For all other races, full political representation was achieved in 1994 when multiparty elections were held. No longer did South Africans have to deal with the farce of the South African Tri-Cameral Parliament, essentially separate and not equal. Political transformations translate into power for the disenfranchised in South Africa. Given time and an equalization of education and other social aspects, the populace of South Africa may indeed form an even more remarkable democracy on the African continent.

Personal transformations directly impact the social transformations. These transformations are so closely related in nature because the presence of a changed individual will have an influence on each person with whom s/he has contact. How effective that influence may be evolves over time, given the resources and opportunities for growth. In her book, *A Human Being Died That Night,* Pumla Gobodo-Madikizela details her account of interactions with Eugene de Kock, a former officer in charge of death squads during apartheid. She states: "I, like every Black South African, have lived a life shaped by the violence and the memories of apartheid" (Gobodo-Madikizela, 2003, p. 6). Violence became a constant in South African life; violence shaped the futures of many lives. Gobodo-Madikizela speaks not only of her own personal transformation as a direct result of sitting on the Truth and Reconciliation Commission, but she also notes the personal transformations of others. The healing and steps toward forgiveness are crucial to making South Africa work as a democracy and as a multi-racial state founded anew on equality. Pearl Faku, a widow of one of de Kock's victims, expressed a need "to hold him by the hand, and show him that there is a future, and that he can still change" (Gobodo-Madikizela, 2003, p. 94). Power arises in surviving such immense obstacles, but it also lies in allowing those obstacles to shape an outlook that seeks the positive. Faku's personal transformation echoes that of many around the South African nation that are willing to forgive those that did such harm in order to make a better future. De Kock also becomes a focus and example of personal transformation. Eugene de Kock was required under oath to disclose the truth of his crimes to the Truth and Reconciliation Commission. His vivid descriptions of murders and clandestine operations are later juxtaposed at his recognition of his crimes, crimes that cost many people their lives, but also terrorized an entire race of people. De Kock comes to the realization that the pain he caused affected more than just the lives he terminated. All South Africans paid for his deeds, especially the non-White citizens (Gobodo-Madikizela, 2003, p. 137).

Social transformations have also resulted from the Truth and Reconciliation hearings. Increased dialogues between previously discordant groups are creating a new environment of cooperation in South Africa. Mandela's leadership through the transitional period and beyond helped ease the tensions of a new South Africa. Mandela made it acceptable and empowering to be, in his own words, "an African" (Sparks, 2003, p. 262). The ending of economic apartheid, the social legacies created and maintained by racism and the optimism of a better South Africa comprise the most important segments of social transformation (Sparks, 2003, p. 341). The process of social transformation will not be an easy one as it evolves in South Africa. The destruction of the familiar identities that apartheid assigned to all citizens now confounds and provides new challenges to all races within South Africa (Frueh, 2003, p. 178). These challenges and confusing times can be borne out, but will provide minor difficulties as society grapples with the new definitions and role reassignments that are necessary to facilitate and sustain the healing processes.

These words must be abided: "Mercy should be granted cautiously" (Gobodo-Madikizela, 2003). Mercy should be granted with utmost caution, but it must be granted. The transformation from oppressive regime to multiparty representation for all remains a significant journey for South Africa and the global community. This journey, as it evolves, will reveal the true impact that the Truth and Reconciliation Commission has had on South African society. Those that have benefited the most remain a matter of perception. The Commission, by granting amnesty to proven cases, created an environment that derailed the cycles of violence. An entire nation reeled from the horrible revelations; in that collective grief, social transformation gained a foothold and momentum in a land that stifled the most basic of rights.

The personal and social transformation must be nurtured and may take generations to fully take hold in South Africa, but the Truth and Reconciliation Commission laid the foundation for the coming together of a people so long divided. The transformation of this society has neither been without issue, nor has it been complete. Differences do exist, and all indicators point to the continuation of such disparities. Given these challenges, South Africa has made remarkable progress in the national healing that is necessary to repair the damage of a history steeped in pain, blood, and loss. The efficacy of the Truth and Reconciliation Commission will continue to be studied, not only for the impact it has had on South Africa, but for the agency for change such a device can provide other nations in conflict.

Ameliorating the Pains and Cicatrix of the War in Liberia through *Bartee*

Since the settling of freed slaves from the United States in Liberia in 1847, the Americo Liberians, as these freed slaves are known, have dominated every aspect of the Liberian political, social, and economic life. For an uninterrupted period of 150 years, the Liberian political realm was reserved only for Americo Liberians (*Africa South of the Sahara,* 2005). The Americo Liberians imposed a colonial situation over the natives. On account of the tenuous legitimacy enjoyed by the settlers and the shallow penetrative capacity of the government, they relied on powerful institutions like the Masonic Lodge and their True Whig Party to suppress and enslave the indigenes.

The enslavement of the indigenes by former slaves caught the attention of the international community in 1929 when the League of Nations investigated allegations of slave labor in Liberia. That notwithstanding, in 1930, the settlers continued to sell natives to Spanish slave traders on the Atlantic Ocean Island of Fernando Po (Ayittey, 1999). Both the United States and the United Kingdom expressed their indignation over this matter by severing diplomatic relations with Liberia for five years.

Furthermore, although Liberian history has been characterized by repression of the indigenes, there was a gradual shift from this tendency in the period following World War II. Although President William Tubman and his successor, William Tolbert, did make reforms, they were too little and too late. But even worse, Tolbert's lack of the necessary leadership skills only aggravated the situation (Zartman, 1995). It was against the backdrop of these grim circumstances that a protest was staged against a 50 percent increase in the price of the staple food: rice. The wrong handling of the protest by the police resulted in rioting, looting, and other acts of vandalism. Hundreds of people, predominantly students, were wounded and killed, while the soldiers and police joined the looting spree that ensued (Zartman, 1995).

In light of this situation, Tolbert's decision to strengthen his grip on power by containing the opposition also came too late. Strike leaders and politicians became the target of his security forces. Many were sent to jail, and press freedom was severely curtailed. And because of the instrumental role of the students in the protests, universities were also closed. In this regard, Tolbert was at the mercy of master Sergeant Samuel Kanyon Doe and his soldiers, a mercy that was never granted him. He was killed and his mutilated body displayed at the John F. Kennedy Memorial Hospital before burial with 27 others in a mass grave (Ayittey, 1999). An estimated number of 200 people also lost their lives in the wave of killings that ensued.

Led by Doe, a group of noncommissioned officers of the Liberian army were the leaders behind this violent, but successful, *coup d'état* in 1980. Doe's record on repression and ethnic monopoly over power proved to be even worse than his predecessor. Despite the massive support enjoyed by this military government at the outset, the euphoria was quick to disappear. Instead of departing from the past, Doe institutionalized tribalism. His lack of vision, coupled with his desire to strengthen his hold on power, aggravated the political as well as the economic situation of the country. Doe's ruthless handling of the attempted *coup* by Quiwonkpa from the Mano ethnic group brought rancor into the Liberian polity. Members of the Krahn (the ethnic group of Doe) and their allies, members of the Mandingo ethnic group, were appointed to all positions of importance in government, irrespective of qualification. In effect, all Doe accomplished was to crush the Americo-Liberian dynasty and replace it with a Krahn one. The same client-patron relationship that characterized the old order was alive and active again, with the difference being that Doe and his kinship and social network occupied the patron seat. What all of this spelled for the Liberians was disillusionment. The eagerly expected revolution had not happened, due to the lack of vision on the part of Doe and his lieutenants to improve the general well-being of the nation and liberate the indigenous population. As the regime's tenuous legitimacy quickly faded away, the Krahn-dominated army became Doe's instrument of coercion. It was this instrument that he effectively sought to curb all signs of opposition, except for the National Patriotic Front of Liberia (NPFL, Charles Taylor's military organization).

Notwithstanding Doe's poor human rights and governance records, the United States maintained close ties with Liberia. In fact, according to Funmi Olonisakin of the Center for Defense Studies at King's College in London, Liberia received $500 million between 1980 and 1985 (1997, pp. 349–371). The continuation of United States-Liberian ties could be associated with the Omega navigation station and the Voice of America's largest transmitter station, which were of strategic importance due to the Cold War. The withdrawal of this vital support by the United States severely undermined the ability of the government to maintain a hold on power.

With square pegs in round holes, corruption and inefficiency became the order of the day. With every indication that a violent change was imminent, the United States forced the leadership to conduct an election. This hope was dashed away when a massively rigged election returned Doe to office. The campaign leading to this election was mired in unprecedented repression of all forms of opposition (Lawyers' Committee for Human Rights, 1986). In light of this, by 1989, trouble could be sensed looming over Liberia.

On December 24, 1989, Charles Taylor attacked Liberia from the border with the Ivory Coast. This became a full-fledged guerilla war, with large-scale massacre of civilians and a complex humanitarian catastrophe. In fact, this struggle represents one of Africa's most violent eruptions in contemporary era, with a human toll of alarming proportion: 150,000 deaths (Ayittey, 1998). While Doe's nine years of rule and the civil war dismantled the old order of things, "it left in its place a more corrupt, interethnic hatreds, rule of the gun and fear and physical destruction" (Zartman, 1996, p. 94). The conventional rules of war were violated with impunity. The savage brutality with which Charles Taylor prosecuted this war, coupled with the humanitarian crisis that ensued, left the neighbors with no alternative but to abandon the old and sacrosanct policy of non-intervention into the internal affairs of a sovereign nation.

The ethnic domination of the Americo-Liberians was not the immediate cause of the Liberian conflict; yet, it was the genesis of the ethnic politics in Liberia, and it provided the background against which Doe rose to power. The role of ethnicity was glaring during the Americo-Liberian rule. The Americo-

Liberians denied political and civil rights to natives by using the ethnic line of demarcation. In this regard, one is tempted to jump to the conclusion that ethnic differences were the motivating factor. This factor, however, reveals only half the truth; to be sure, the underlying motivation for interethnic violence is more than just cultural differences and traditional hostilities (Sandbrook, 1972). Mobilization along ethno-linguistic lines in most cases provides the most viable option when demanding recognition or share of wealth and power. This explanation tends to give credence to the primordialist claim, but only to the extent that ethnicity provided the fault line for domination and suppression. In short, it would be a gross misrepresentation to infer that Americo-Liberian treatment of the natives in the manner they did was a function of just distinctiveness in their cultures. It is reasonable to infer at this juncture, however, that the Americo-Liberian motive was limited to the desire to continue to rule. But as Clapham (1996) views it, when governments deliberately limit political participation to small cliques, while subjecting the significant remainder of their nationals to exploitative and brutal rule, they lay the basis for insurgency.

Doe's ethnic division of Liberia only goes to buttress the primordial perspective once more. In a deliberate and calculated move, Doe's government cautiously planned and executed the imposition of ethnic monopoly over state power while at the same time dealing with all other ethnic groups in a ruthless manner. It is worthy of note that ethnicity and repression were clearly stated as reasons for Doe's overthrow of the Americo-Liberian dynasty. Again, the ethnic fault line forms the basis along which Doe had divided the country. It was his desire to maintain a hold on power and the threat perceived by other ethnic groups by Doe that intensified ethnic entrenchment. The Krahn ethnic group before Doe's government was indeed at the bottom of the Liberian social strata. The Krahn were "the-one-at-a-time cigarettes sellers, prostitutes and enlisted men" (Zartman, 1996, p. 100). But with state power in their hands, they quickly became the political elite. The enjoyment of the benefits of governance to a once-deprived group was seen as an opportunity to never let go. With the awareness that other ethnic groups were also competing for the same power, Doe sought to entrench his ethnic group and also the allies—the Mandingo. In essence, the ethnic configuration of the government was a move to maintain the hold on power. The decision was not a product of ethnic differences; it was a calculated move to maintain a strong grip on power. At this juncture, maybe the competition perspective may have become the explanatory factor. With the fall of the Americo-Liberian dynasty, other deprived indigenous groups suddenly realized that they, too, could develop their own dynasties.

As George Kun (unpublished, 2006) explains, Liberia is now positioned as a fusee of hope for war-ravaged nations in sub-Saharan Africa. Only a few years ago, the ineffably violent character of the civil war that raged between 1989 and 2003 mystified the world. The inundation of indiscriminate killing, ethnic cleansing, rape, and torture failed to attract even a small measure of international attention. Over two dozen peace accords and mediations equally failed to usher in a durable solution. Out of a population of three million, the war drove over

200,000 Liberians to their early graves and approximately 150,000 languished in foreign countries as refugees.

Today, the guns are silent, the *Kalashnikovas* and machetes have been taken away. In November of 2005, Liberians went to the polls to elect a new leader—the pernicious effect of the fourteen-year civil war is now antiquity. Beneath the international accolades still lies the painful reality of the war—many Liberians only need to walk outside their doors to see the graves of their loved ones. Some of the culprits of the killings and human rights' violators are now parliamentarians paid by taxpayers, "all hail democracy," a powerful jolt to their grave sense of abandonment and denial of justice. Bridging the gap between the perpetrators and the victims is a *sine quo non* to any sustainable democracy in Liberia.

Liberia, in the hope of ameliorating the pains and cicatrix of the war, has aspired to the South African model of Truth and Reconciliation (TRC). On February 21, 2006, President Ellen Johnson Sirleaf launched the country's Truth and Reconciliation Commission, envisaged by the Comprehensive Peace Agreement signed in Accra, Ghana. This pronouncement came as a welcome relief to those who committed gross human rights abuses during the civil war. Pro-Taylor fighters agree that a war crimes court is not a good idea, said one former pro-government militia commander who still goes by his war name of "General Zig-Zag."

What does this commission seek to achieve? The commission does not have the power to dispense justice. Its role, as the president propounded in her inaugural address, is to document all abuses, validate and establish the narratives of both victims and victimizers—with special attention given to women, children, the elderly, and other vulnerable members of society. The commission will provide clear and workable recommendations at the end of its mandate on how Liberia can collectively compensate for the past and move on in unity to face the future.

But can Liberia compensate for the past by truth-telling? If the commission is not empowered to dispense justice, but rather record abuses, it is even more provoking to enunciate that justice can be served by granting general immunity to those who step forward to confess their involvement in maiming, raping, torturing, and killing of civilians during the war or their political tenure. Since the launching of the TRC, Liberians on both sides have argued fervently in favor of and against the commission's work. One side, such as the Forum for the Establishment of a War Crimes Court in Liberia (FEWCCIL), aspires to the central notion of retributive justice—those who glaringly disregard basic human decency deserve to be punished.

On May 12, 2006, the Liberian youth group petitioned the Liberian government to establish a war crimes tribunal to try those who committed the most heinous crimes against the innocent Liberians. The group argued that an integral part of the rebuilding process should encompass a war crimes court. It wants perpetrators of infamous crimes, including summary executions, massacres, amputations, and rape, brought to justice.

"Justice for the people of Liberia can no longer be delayed or denied; the time has come to establish an international criminal tribunal for Liberia," urged the FEWCCIL. The axiom of retributive justice is the notion of merit and desert—Immanuel Kant uses a debt metaphor to discuss the notion of just desert. An individual who seeks the benefits of living under the rule of law without being willing to make the necessary sacrifices of self-restraint is a free rider. Retributive justice is a matter of giving those who violate human rights law and commit crimes against humanity their "just desserts."

Certainly, if individuals who bear the greatest responsibilities of human rights abuse are given blanket pardons, it will be a denial of justice for the victims and, without doubt, cement a culture of impunity where individuals continue to commit violations without fear of punishment. "In the interests of genuine lasting peace and reconciliation, we call upon this August body to pass an act that establishes the legal framework for the creation of a Special War Crimes Tribunal for Liberia," the FEWCCIL told the Liberian Parliament.

A second group, the Confederation of Monrovia Youth (CMY), told legislatures that such a court would end Liberia's culture of impunity. "Bringing the perpetrators of gruesome atrocities to court would serve as a deterrent to others and end the culture of impunity that exists in this country," the CMY said. Impunity is the failure to bring to justice and punish those responsible for serious violations of human rights and crimes against humanity. It stems from a government's overt failure to prioritize human rights.

Yet others, such as Liberia's human rights activist Jerome Verdier, dismissed these calls as being made by people "not well informed of the trend in the peace process." Certainly, Verdier's charge is well placed, considering the 85 percent illiteracy in the country; it is only natural that many Liberians are not well informed about the successes and failures of truth commissions. Nonetheless, this statement is exiguous in substance and context. From 1974 to 2002, approximately twenty-seven truth commissions have been established in different parts of the world. Uganda being the first to establish such commission has been embroiled in a civil war for over twenty years. Even so, it will be bedeviling to a Liberian who has lost a loved one to be told that the only process that can bring closure to his/her loss is a truth commission. Prosecuting those who bear the greatest responsibility is not asking for too much.

But can retributive justice also move Liberia forward? It is easy to articulate and accept the idea that Liberians should treat individuals who committed human rights violations as they deserve. Undoubtedly, culprits or human rights violations should not be allowed to live carefree lives in Liberia, paid by taxpayers, or driving around Monrovia among their victims. Still, there is a danger to glide from putative retributive justice to an emphasis of revenge or draw a wedge between Liberians. "Bringing the perpetrators of gruesome atrocities to court would serve as a deterrent to others and end the culture of impunity that exists in this country," the CMY said. Victims of the atrocities have even expressed strong support for a war crimes court. "Liberia suffered too much at the hands of warring parties; they killed us, burned down our towns, looted our food and homes. If the court will cause them not to repeat their past deeds, then it is a good idea," said Asatu Fahnbulleh, who lost three members of her family in the war.

The history of international criminal tribunals pooh-poohs the perception that prosecution of war criminals deters future brutality against innocent civilians. Fifty years after the famous Nuremburg and Tokyo trials, Bosnian Serbs, undeterred, engaged in an orgy of ethnic cleansing of Bosnian Muslims. Even more so, these trials failed to inhibit the *Interahamwe* militias and Hutu extremists from slaughtering innocent Tutsis. Yet, the International Criminal Tribunal for Rwanda is determined to bring culprits of the genocide to justice.

What is the way forward in Liberia? The truth and reconciliation commission should be one of several mechanisms for managing transitional justice in Liberia. Liberians can invoke their traditional systems of justice that have existed in their villages for time in memorial—*Bartee*, the traditional model widely practiced and honored in Southeastern Liberia, more particularly in Sinoe and Maryland Counties, by the elders to dispense justice. It is also a customary system form of community hearings used for mediation and conflict resolution.

Bartee plays a multifaceted role within the family and society, ranging from punishment, teaching the public a lesson and reconciliation within and between villages and towns. The enchantment of *Bartee* signaled the magnitude of the case or problem—the claimant and defendant, victim and perpetrator were summoned to appear before the elders to answer to the charges. The ruling of the elders was final; there was no appeal. Often the claimant will bring an action for wrong done him/her by the defendant—even so, the defendant or perpetrator of a serious crime that involved the life of another could request the *Bartee* to confess his/her wrong. S/he had to be precise about his/her wrong to enable the elders to mediate and offer a "cola nut" to the victims. Once the cola was eaten by both parties, the issue was put to rest and never to be discussed in the community or society.

Certainly, other perpetrators in Liberia have already circumvented the commissions and gone directly to their villages to request the *Bartee*. "After the war, some of us went to our towns and villages and begged for pardon. Our people welcomed us and we are all living together in harmony, but a court would divide us and the people," said Andrew Sway, a former child soldier who has returned to school since handing in his gun.

The traditional justice theory advanced here might prove less effective. Conversely, Liberians are much more keen on honoring their traditional justice or reconciliatory mechanisms than any peace paradigm promulgated by the Liberian government that involves a mere recording of abuses without any guarantees that the main perpetrators of the ignoble crimes during the war will come forward to ask their victims for forgiveness—they are all conspicuously sitting in the House of Representatives and Senate. What happens if they ignore their conscience? Then the commission will be a measly census of past wrongs or data-collection of the most toxic crimes against the people of Liberia. It will then be hollow and a formula for a circle of revenge in Liberia. Will the victims find justice in this system?

The Road to Recovery for Former Child Soldiers via the Ritual Bath in Sierra Leone

On March 23, 1991, the Revolutionary United Front (RUF) attacked a small military outpost stationed at Bomaru. The RUF, supported by the National Patriotic Front of Liberia (NPFL), quickly routed the Sierra Leone troops manning the post and also killed the two officers in charge. With this initial success, the RUF quickly opened another front in the southern province. In the following months, the RUF advanced rapidly against very little resistance in most of the encounters. For the next eight years, this situation evolved into a full-fledged war, causing untold suffering to the people of Sierra Leone. The rebel war was a product of the cumulative effects of several years of malaise that had befallen the country. So acute were these anomalies that by the late 1980s, rice (the staple food), gas, and other essential commodities became luxury items. Long lines for these essential commodities were a common scene in Freetown. When they were available, these products carried exorbitant prices. In effect, the many years of bad governance, declining social and physical infrastructure, and wrong policy choices of the Sierra Leone People's Party (SLPP) and the military juntas, and later the one-party rule of the All People's Congress (APC) were clearly beginning to take their toll. And with no genuine indication that the government was ready to institute remedial political, economic, and social reforms, a violent outburst was inevitable. The ultimate question at this point then is the following: What social, economic and political factors precipitated the civil war in Sierra Leone?

When Sierra Leone attained independence in 1961, it had already been integrated into the global world economy by the British. This enmeshment, however, only confined it to the exportation of raw materials to the industrialized world (Sesay, 1997). Hence, Sierra Leone was heavily dependent on a narrow range of cash crops such as cocoa, coffee, and palm oil. In addition, the exploitation of the country's vast minerals, which were also sources of revenue, was dominated by transnational corporations from the West that had the technology and wherewithal to undertake such ventures. This extroverted nature of the economy had ramifications for the prices of these minerals and agricultural products. Their prices were not only determined by external forces, but also susceptible to fluctuations. Due to poor performance in this sector, Sierra Leone was in the throes of serious fiscal problems by the end of the 1970s. In the late 1980s, the fiscal deficit accounted for nearly 15 percent of GDP, while inflation had gone above 100 percent (special World Bank Report on Sierra Leone, 1998). Furthermore, international reserves were dangerously low, the "parallel market premium was substantial" (special World Bank Report on Sierra Leone, 1998), and the economy was in shambles. As it did many other African states, Structural Adjustment made Sierra Leone more dependent on social networks rather than building institutions as a means of economic survival (Clapham, 1996). With poverty on the rise, anti-government demonstrations and *coup* attempts became more frequent. The government's response was brutal, which sent most of the radical opposition in finding alternative means of effecting change. Little wonder that some members of the RUF were students and other people who suffered under the APC.

As the state continued on its downward spiral, so did the social fragmentation that divided Sierra Leone. Even before independence, the society had already been polarized along several lines. The first line of division was between the well-educated and pro-Western settlers and the then less educated communities in the interior. Friction between these two groups was common towards independence, as the Creoles, who constitute only 2 percent of the population, took over most of the professional jobs and played a preponderant role in the administrative sector (Sesay, 1997). Second, ethno-regional politics divided the country into northern (Temne, Limba, Susu, and other groups) against the southern elements (mostly Mende). This ethnic division has persisted as a common denominator for political allegiance after independence. Third, the Lebanese, who first migrated to Sierra Leone in the 1880s, became the dominant economic power, wielding enormous unofficial power in political circles. This prominent role naturally attracted the hostility of less influential indigenous groups. Fourth, the British resorted to the use of the local chiefs on account of administrative prudence. This heavy reliance on chiefs for control put into the hands of these local authorities more power as to pitch them against members of the educated elite who were craving for a more prominent role in politics. In the absence of a strong state to bridge these cleavages, social fragmentation has continued unabated since independence.

The immensity of Sierra Leone's economic problems, coupled with political malaise and social fragmentation, constitute the underlying causes of the war. The ethnic dimensions of this conflict, if any, are not clear. Indeed the Mende and Temne ethnic groups have had bitter and recurring wars before the advent of colonialism. But, in this particular instance, although the insurgency started in the eastern and southern regions of the country, its leader, the late Foday Sankoh, was a Temne from the North. And although Mende account for a greater majority of the RUF membership, there also exist a considerable number of other ethnic groups. But even if the Mende factor was anything with which to contend, it should be understood against the hollowed nature of the Sierra Leone state that lost control over the political and economic space in the eastern and southern provinces. The Liberian dollar was not only more common than the Sierra Leone currency in these areas, NPFL forays and the eventual incursion by the RUF met with little or no resistance. In fact, this alienated part of the country quickly joined the rebellion.

Six years into the war, however, ethnic tendencies began to creep into the conflict after the victory of the Sierra Leone People's Party (SLPP, an eastern- and southern-based party) in the 1996 multiparty elections. Fortunately, this did not gain currency. In that regard, ethnicity becomes the wrong lens through which the war in Sierra Leone could be viewed. The permeating propensity of ethnic affiliations in a divided society like Sierra Leone had reached the threshold like most issues, including development, education, trade unions, and even politics. But to blame the schisms in Sierra Leone on ethnicity will be a misrepresentation of reality. The instrumentalist and the warlord theories may help to explain the civil war in Sierra Leone. The RUF's decision to stop hostilities in order to share power gives credence to the instrumentalist perspective as a better explanation for understanding the Sierra Leone conflict. The organization of the RUF and the manner in which Sankoh executed the war led some observers to characterize it as warlord insurgency. According to Clapham, such wars are characterized "by personal leadership, generally weak organizational structures, and still weaker ideological motivations" (1996, p. 212). In short, the main motivation was self-aggrandizement on the part of Sankoh. Even in Liberia where the war started with clearly defined groups fighting against the government (Gio and Mano ethnic groups fighting against the Krahn-based government), things had started to change by 1992. From this point onwards, and more specifically in 1994, the ethnic fault line disappeared, giving way to factional fighting (Outram, 1997). Although Outram asserts that the reason for this shift is not known, he contends, however, that evidence is compelling and clear that the configuration of the war changed from ethnic to factional.

It is estimated that during the eleven-year war, about 5,000 juvenile combatants actively participated in the conflict. While many of these children were conscripted into combat, a significant number of them voluntarily participated in the brutalities. When the war ended in 2000, the government of Sierra Leone and the United Nations jointly established the Special Court for Sierra Leone to prosecute those "persons who bear the greatest responsibility for serious violations of international humanitarian law and Sierra Leone law." (Romero, 2004). Despite this strict statutory directive, however, child combatants between the ages of fifteen and eighteen determined to be guilty of committing heinous war crimes are not subject to imprisonment; instead, they are sentenced to a truth and reconciliation mechanism where, regardless of culpability, they are ultimately released back into their communities (Romero, 2004). Thus, the major issue here is how these ex-juvenile combatants have been received in their communities.

Indeed, Sierra Leone's traditional precepts of forgiveness have made it possible for most of the people to forgive former child soldiers. As Jeremy Ginifer reports about his observations in his monograph, *Sierra Leone—Building the Road to Recovery* (March 2003), traditional reconciliation techniques, such as cleansing rituals, have made a considerable impact in terms of community relations. He adds that there were cases of ex-combatants confessing to wrongdoing and receiving forgiveness from communities all over the country.

In her monumental work, *Restoring/Rehabilitating Former Child Soldiers in Sierra Leone: The Place of Forgiveness* (2003), involving 322 participants (187 females and 125 males) and using narratives, focus groups and semi-structured interviews, Stephanie Goins tells us that Sierra Leoneans define forgiveness as having mercy and not seeking revenge against ex-combatants. Forgiveness is given by an individual, a family, or an entire community and extended to those who ask for it. She also notes that forgiveness is characterized as "togetherness," which includes such attitudes and behaviors as acceptance, sharing, and eating together. For some Sierra Leoneans, she adds, forgiveness is also about forgetting the past. She also notes that there are comparatively fewer individuals who do not want to forgive or forget. Furthermore, according to Goins, religious convictions aid in the forgiving process. The belief that God requires forgiveness for one's enemies commits the individual to forgive ex-combatants.

Even Alan White, a former Chief Investigator of the Special Court and an American, has been quite impressed by the level of forgiveness that has been demonstrated by Sierra Leoneans. As Charles Cobb, Jr. of allAfrica.com, in his article, "Sierra Leone's Special Court: Will it Hinder or Help?" (November 21, 2002), quotes White as saying, "one of the things I have enjoyed about Sierra Leone is the people. The people are resilient, very forgiving, a very, very friendly people."

Also, as Angela Stephens states in her April 16, 2004 United Nation's Wire, "A common tactic for the RUF (Revolutionary United Front), Crane (i.e., the former Special Court Chief Prosecutor David Crane) said, was to surround a town and force all the children to kill their own parents, then take the children away, making them dependent on the rebels and eventually desensitized to killing. According to the United Nations, more than 10,000 children were abducted and forced into conscription during the war." Therefore, it was baffling why Crane could not see this as a tacit acceptance of how "children" voluntarily took up arms to fight against the RUF. Indeed, an answer to the question, from one of the judges of the Special Court, on whether these "children" had a right to voluntarily defend themselves and their parents could be deduced from Crane's statement.

Thus, it is not surprising that as Kathleen Maclay (July 26, 2002) of the University of California Berkeley Media Relations Office reports, Susan Shepler, a doctoral candidate in the university's Graduate School of Education, informs us that children are most accepting of the former "child soldiers" re-entering their ranks as they acknowledge that their fate could have been anyone's. She adds that ex-combatants seem to be most helpful with one another and that the resilience of the people is inspirational.

During her almost two-year fieldwork, Shepler talked to "child soldiers," parents, and community elders, discussing their opinions about the war and what problems they perceive that the former "child soldiers" now present. She crisscrossed Sierra Leone, journeying from city to village and back, looking for the country's answers to such questions: What is childhood? What is the value of a child? What is the role of child labor? And what is the society's responsibility for educating its children? She also inquired about how relief organization intervention helps to shape answers to these questions. For the last question, she finds that often the efforts of humanitarian agencies fail because they apply foreign values and models with no "translation" or consideration of whether they will work in other settings or cultures. For example, she notes that the concept of children's rights is largely a new one in Sierra Leone and it is due partly to philosophies and programs introduced by foreign relief agencies.

The *Gacaca* Peace Initiative in Rwanda

"After the genocide I realised that Rwandans are in total darkness and we need some light somewhere and I was among the first to convince myself that one day I will speak the truth and I would call on other Rwandans to speak the truth."

—Sylvester Mwanza

Indeed, as the preceding excerpt suggests, and a BBC World Service report concurs, many years after the genocide in Rwanda in 1994, there is still a sense of disbelief among the victims and even among some of those who committed the murders. In 1994, an estimated 800,000 people were killed in a hundred days in Rwanda. Now there are about 120,000 men and women in prison awaiting trial for their involvement in the massacres. Entire communities were killed and entire neighborhoods participated in the massacres. Rwanda's genocide became the worst in a series of massive crimes committed globally in the half century since World War II (BBC World Service, November, 2000). To understand the reason for all this, one must examine the history of Rwanda, albeit briefly.

In pre-twentieth-century Rwanda, the terms *Hutu* and *Tutsi* did not carry the same political meanings they do in today's Rwanda. The pre-colonial history of Rwandan Tutsis and Hutus is a complex series of events. The date—when the Tutsis arrived and conquered the Hutu entity—is unknown. In fact, the two groups lived in perfect co-habitation: Hutus were cultivators and Tutsis were pastoralists. Also, Hutus who accumulated sufficient wealth could become Tutsis, while Tutsis who lost their economic power became Hutus.

From the seventh century until 1916, Rwanda was a highly monarchical polity. The state was organized, centralized, and hierarchical. It is fair to say that Tutsis were the dominant group that formed the warrior-aristocracy of traditional Rwandan society. While controlling and ruling Rwanda, however, the Tutsis did not monopolize the power over Hutus. In fact, traditional Rwanda was a mutually accepted organization of power. Moreover, the social cohesion of the society is illustrated by the fact that large-scale ethnic killings do not seem to have occurred.

Another aspect of Rwandan history is the existence of a strong militia tradition in the country. First playing a role of self-defense against enemies, militias then had a more economic and social role. Second, the militias had a lively cultural life with poetry, music, and dance. Also, both Hutus and Tutsis could be members of these militias. It was even not rare for a Hutu to be in command.

Colonizers of diverse horizons, the Germans and then the Belgians, transformed Rwandan society in its deepest meaning, since they came with firmly held convictions about race and racial hierarchy. Whites were obviously considered as being superior; but among Africans, certain ethnic groups were designated more worthy than others. This is how the Tutsis became superior to Hutus in the social hierarchy. Westerners had indeed a preference for the Tutsis' facial features. The Tutsis were, in general, taller and had more "European-like features." Thus, colonial authorities were largely responsible for exacerbating ethnic schisms between the Tutsis and Hutus. Therefore, the proposition that ethnicities are politicized is tenable in the case of Rwanda.

This postulate, however, is not the only one to be applicable to the Rwandan case. Indeed, wanting to make Rwanda more rigid and more controllable, in 1926, the Belgians decided that the population should be classified as Hutu and as Tutsi, with no possibility of one changing his/her group classification. All citizens were then given national identification cards which included the names of the ethnic groups to which they belonged. Thus, the complicated hierarchy of pre-colonial Rwanda was simplified, with more power concentrated to those at the top, the Tutsis, and fewer benefits for those at the bottom of the hierarchy, the Hutus. The colonialists then eliminated the Hutus' autonomous territories, reducing the status of the group and enhancing Tutsi domination under European control. The postulate that ethnic conflicts find their cause in the feeling of loss and oppression is also validated by the Rwandan case. Indeed, Hutus had lost their land and were politically as well as economically oppressed. Moreover, they also could experience and feel that the Tutsis were advantaged because of physical differences.

The 1994 genocide that occurred in Rwanda also confirms the proposition that ethnicities can be politicized from the top. Indeed, the slaughter that occurred in the 1990s "stemmed from efforts by the dictator-president Juvenal Habyarimana to wipe out his political opposition, Hutu as well as Tutsi" (Bowen, 1996, p. 100). In 1990–1991, Habyarimana began to transform an armed gang into a militia called *Interahamwe*. This militia launched its series of massacres in a village in March of 1992, and in 1993 began systematically to kill Hutu moderates and Tutsis. Throughout 1993, the country's three major radio stations were broadcasting messages of hate against Tutsis, the opponents, and against specific politicians, setting the stage for what followed. Immediately after the still-unexplained plane crash that killed President Habyarimana in April of 1994, the presidential guard began killing Hutu opposition leaders, human rights activists, journalists, and others critical of the state, most of them Hutus. Only then, after the first wave of killings, were the militia and soldiers sent to organize mass killings in the countryside, focusing on Tutsis.

Why did people obey the order to kill? For sure, as Bowen affirms, "leaders were able to carry out a plan, conceived at the top, to wipe out an opposition group. They succeeded because they persuaded people that they could survive only by killing those who were, or could become, their killers" (1996, p. 100). Indeed, by broadcasting radio messages conveying hate and portraying the Tutsi-led Rwandan Patriotic Front as a group of bloodthirsty killers, organized Hutus turned into killing groups. Bowen sums up the situation by saying that "the killings of 1994 were not random mob violence, although they were influenced by mob psychology" (1996, p. 100). The analysts who support the idea that ethnicities can be politicized would surely agree with this interpretation of the events that occurred during the massacres, and especially with what led to these events. Indeed, negative stereotyping, fear of another group—killing lest one be killed—are what the so-called leaders led the people to do. Believing that such conflicts are natural or inherent to specific ethnicities is problematic. These negative stereotypes, this fear of another group, and killing to prevent from being killed are typical causes that are said to precipitate ethnic conflicts by those who believe that there are real ethnic triggers and mechanisms in conflicts. This suggests once again that neither politicized ethnicities, nor behaviors and reactions inherent to ethnicities, are the unique variables in the Rwandan case. These two perspectives are actually intertwined.

In essence, the ethnic conflict in Rwanda is the consequence of old and entrenched rivalries of values between ethnicities and the manipulation of these ethnicities by colonizers and contemporary political leaders. Indeed, the greed of these leaders led them to build a nation-state by oppressing minorities. This created and intensified some feeling of oppression, fear, and loss that then launched the multiple genocides that Rwanda experienced. Despite all this, one is encouraged by the path towards peace upon which Rwandans have embarked.

In March of 2005, African leaders and scholars gathered at the United States Library of Congress in Washington, DC, to talk about reconciliation in Africa. The participants discussed their experiences with religion, truth commissions, the media and other culturally-based methods of reconciliation at an all-day seminar. It was sponsored by the African Section in the African and Middle Eastern Division and the John W. Kluge Center at the Library of Congress, in collaboration with the African Presidential Archives and Research Center of Boston University, the Africa Society of the National Summit on Africa, the Nigerian People's Forum, the United States Institute of Peace and the Watson Institute for International Studies at Brown University. The Samputu-Ingeli Dance Troupe of Rwanda, demonstrating how music can be a tool of reconciliation, concluded the seminar with African dances and drumming. The three-member troupe included a Hutu, a Tutsi, and a Twa, representing the three ethnic groups in Rwanda. In addition, lead performer Jean-Paul Samputu sang and played the guitar (Urschel, 2005).

In the case of Rwanda, Athanase Hagengimana, an instructor of psychiatry at Harvard Medical School and a John W. Kluge Fellow at the Library of Congress, talked about the contributions of religion to truth and reconciliation in Rwanda. Hagengimana's observations were based on his interviews and psychological assessments of more than 300 perpetrators of genocide who are currently detained in a Rwandan prison. He found the prisoners to be open and willing to describe the atrocities they committed, because many had been "saved" and were "born again." He observed that many new churches that came to Rwanda after the genocide reached out to the prisoners. Not only did the churches preach forgiveness among the victims' survivors, they also preached to the killers in prisons about the importance of the "apology." He also observed that people who had killed others have more problems than people who are grieving, as guilt is more painful than sorrow. He further stated that he had witnessed survivors who, full of religion, have healed from trauma and can reconcile with criminals.

He added that he had seen criminals be born-again, free to confess what they did, went to the families of survivors and apologized and revealed everything, and they are now functioning in the society (Urschel, 2005).

Joseph Nzabmwita, defense attaché at the Embassy of the Republic of Rwanda in Washington, DC, talked about the *Gacaca* (pronounced *Gachacha*) model of reconciliation, a traditional African village system that works on the principle of reconciling the parties and promoting social harmony rather than penalizing the guilty party. Nzabmwita believes that under the Western criminal justice system, it will take 100 years to try the cases. Thus, he asks a profound question: "So who is that justice going to benefit?" (Urschel, 2005).

According to Nzabmwita, after July 1994, at the end of the genocide in Rwanda, there were nearly one million people dead. The government was destroyed and the society dismantled. Rwandans needed to rebuild their society, so they sat down and went back to their roots—simply sitting together and discussing among themselves the truth. The truth included learning from the perpetrators where to find the dead bodies, so that families could give them proper burials. After learning the truth, healing could begin. Nzabmwita believes that through *Gacaca*, Rwandans will benefit (Urschel, 2005). Thus, a poignant question here is the following: What is *Gacaca*, and why do Nzabmwita and many Rwandans believe that it will work given the bitterness precipitated by the genocide? The following paragraphs address this question.

Constance Morrill offers a succinct definition and an explanation of the origins of the *Inkiko-Gacaca*. According to her,

> [T]he traditional *Gacaca*, which literally means a "grassy space," is commonly associated with the activities that used to take place in any open-air, grassy areas, such as the discussion and resolution of problems within the community. In the event of a conflict within the community, the parties involved in the conflict would be heard and 'judged' by an assembly of "*inyangamugayo*," or individuals accepted by everyone in the community to be those who "detest opprobrium." These were individuals whose status of "*inyangamugoya*" was acquired by virtue of their probity, old age, erudition, wisdom in decision-making, altruism or political or economic influence within the community. (Morrill, 2004, p. 3)

Morrill also notes:

> Before colonization and the introduction of written laws, Rwanda's traditional *Gacaca* system was the only "real" justice system. "Sentences" were assigned according to the nature of the act committed by the guilty party and always involved reparations to the damaged party. (Imprisonment did not figure among the penalties, as the prison system was introduced by the colonial powers.) Even in cases where the commission of a 'wrong' was incurred by an individual, the responsibility for that wrong was shared by all members of the clan or family to which the individual belonged. As a result, family or clan members were equally responsible for "making reparations" to the damaged party. If both parties agreed to the terms of reparation, they would share a drink as a

> symbolic gesture of agreement. When the 'crime' was judged to be too serious for reparation to be an adequate sentence, the judgment could call for ostracism of the members of the particular clan or family associated with the wrongdoer or 'defendant.' As the *Gacaca* 'rules' were never written, they were passed down orally from generation to generation as part of the social education of all Rwandans. (Morrill, 2004, p. 3)

She adds:

> With the advent of colonialism, the *Gacaca* institution underwent some distortion. A law passed in August of 1924 confined *Gacaca* to the resolution of civil and commercial disputes among the indigenous population. Criminal cases became the responsibility of colonial courts, and the concept of the *Inyangamugayo* also had to submit to colonial influence: instead of acquiring this status by virtue of the individual's good standing in the community, the *Inyangamugayo* were conferred their influential status by the colonial authorities, and this method was continued by Rwandan authorities even after independence. (Morrill, 2004, p. 3)

Today, the Rwandan government believes that *Gacaca*, modified as necessary to factor in the realities of modern Rwanda, will enable the justice system to find the balance between mass release and the need for some kind of accountability on the part of the accused (Duly, 2000, p. 35). But even more encouraging are the positive and peaceful developments that are taking place in the country because of this reintroduction of Rwandan traditions. Two of the many examples I find outstanding are the Village of Hope initiative in Kigali and the leadership role being played by women in the reconstruction and reconciliation programs. The following is a discussion of these two examples.

As the UN-HABITAT office in Nairobi, Kenya, reports, Village of Hope is a civil society initiative to rebuild the lives of women, mainly genocide victims. Several crimes committed against humanity like rape, torture, and mutilation left the majority of the Rwandan women traumatized. The initiative also takes care of orphans and people living with HIV/AIDS. Most of the women had been widowed and dispossessed and had no means of survival. The initiative is an extension of the Polyclinic of Hope, a project of Rwanda Women Network (RWN), which addresses shelter needs of genocide victims. The village is made up of 20 housing units and a community center. The houses were constructed from 1999 to 2000 and the center in 2002. The center is located in Gisozi Sector, Gasabo District, Kigali (UN-HABITAT, 2006).

After the genocide, Rwanda received a great amount of humanitarian assistance. Then United States President Bill Clinton visited the country in 1999 and was moved by the Women Survivors Empowerment Program. After his visit, RWN received a grant of $100,000 from the United States Department of State. The program's members decided to build houses to meet the shelter needs of the most vulnerable women in the city, the Village of Hope. They use a holistic approach, with an end goal of healing the wounds of genocide, by supporting peace and reconciliation. They also undertake awareness-raising of the rights of women, including the right to own and inherit property. The program provides space for free interaction and dialogue. It has a participatory approach in decision-making, implementing, monitoring, and evaluating activities. Weekly meetings are facilitated by the RWN staff at the Village of Hope, where women and youths share their problems, needs, and vision, and discuss solutions to issues that affect them. Some residents also participate at the RWN General Assembly and planning meetings. Village of Hope raises most of its support through donor funding. The residents are also put into groups that make contributions through "basket funds" for emergency purposes (UN-HABITAT, 2006).

The program's major achievements include construction of 20 housing units, providing shelter to approximately 120 persons, a community center that provides support to around 1,000 women and 200 youths, a youth center for youth activities, tailoring training offered to 28 women, training on greeting cards making to 32 youths, beadwork training to 14 women, knitting and weaving training to 12 women, provision of school fees for 17 secondary schoolchildren, provision of medical services, psycho-social/trauma/HIV/AIDS counseling, and seminars on gender issues. Three out of every five employees at Village of Hope are trained in the center (UN-HABITAT, 2006).

The impacts of the initiative have been felt throughout Rwanda. The spirit of volunteering has been re-cultivated among the women, who have initiated voluntary home-based care for HIV/AIDS patients in their villages. Women have willingly provided information for documenting case studies through personal interviews and testimonies. In essence, Village of Hope is a multidisciplinary initiative that deals with trauma in a post-conflict situation while at the same time providing realistic concrete solutions: i.e., shelter and livelihood. This gives the women confidence by "getting them out" of their traumatized state psychologically, physically, and economically. The UN-HABITAT office in Nairobi has certified that the initiative fully meets the basic criteria of impact, partnership, and sustainability as well as additional considerations of leadership and community empowerment, and gender equality and social inclusion (UN-HABITAT, 2006).

Theodora Ayot interrogates the various reconstruction and reconciliation programs in Rwanda in an effort to assess the degree and the impact of their political, economic, and social empowerment of women, and how women have translated and utilized this empowerment to mobilize and sensitize the grassroots as well as national levels as a means of combating the recidivist pressures that are likely to influence the recurrence of conflict. Specifically, Ayot considers the establishment of the National Unity and Reconciliation Commission in 1999 as one of the most important programs which the new government of Rwanda instituted in its attempt to deal with the challenging issues emanating from the rejection and violation of the humanistic moral code: Thou shall not kill. She assesses the place of women in the National Unity and Reconciliation Commission to determine the impact of women's efforts towards reconciliation and reconstruction in post-conflict Rwanda (Ayot, in press).

Ayot points out that in 1995, Desmond Tutu visited the village of Ntarama, just a few kilometers from the Rwandan capital, Kigali. It is in this village where the Tutsi had been killed in a church. According to Tutu, "The new government had not removed the corpses, so that the church was like a mortuary, with bodies lying as they had fallen the year before during the massacre. The stench was overpowering. Outside the church building was a collection of skulls of some of those who had been brutally done to death—some of the skulls still had *pangas* (machetes) and daggers embedded in them. I tried to pray. Instead I broke down and wept." But despite this heart rending experience for Desmond Tutu, he was so humbled when he visited the Nelson Mandela Peace Village, a new settlement that had been built through the efforts of women themselves. The women at the village were all orphans, widows, and refugees who had come together to try to forget their ethnic origins in an effort to live together in peace and build a new Rwanda. While visiting the village, Tutu spoke to the women leaders. What impressed him the most was the strength of these women and he reports his encounter and observations:

> They (women) said, 'We must mourn and weep for the dead. But life must also go on, we can't go on weeping.' How wonderfully impressive, how indomitable. Over at Ntarama, we might say, there was Calvary, death and crucifixion. Here in the Nelson Mandela Village was Resurrection, new life, new beginning, new hope. Once more it was noteworthy to see how women have this remarkable resilience and an instinct for nurturing life. (Ayot, in press)

Addressing post-conflict Rwanda through the lenses of women, Ayot provides us with the opportunity to appreciate their incredible sense of leadership that gives hope to their families and the people of Rwanda as doctors across their country's landscape. In Rwanda, women who watched helplessly as their husbands, fathers, mothers, sisters, brothers, friends, and even children were cut down with machetes have been able to pick up the pieces of their broken lives and their broken country and begin a process of rebuilding. Women have demonstrated an amazing strength and courage in the midst of the national tragedy, and it is that inner strength that enables them to survive even the most horrific conditions in which they find themselves (Ayot, in press).

According to Ayot, in concerted efforts to restore peace in Rwanda, the government of National Unity was established and it came into existence as a result of the survivors' desire to transcend the negative images that had led to the genocide. From the time of its inception in 1999, the National Unity and Reconciliation Commission (NURC) paid particular attention to issues pertaining to Rwandans, the civil society, efforts to bring the Rwandans of all walks of life together and the challenges posed by the prevailing poverty in the country. In order to ensure national cohesion, the government of national unity embarked on a number of strategies:

(a) Ensuring democratic governance: actions to ensure democratic governance since 1994 have included the passing of the genocide law to challenge the impunity which characterized acts of violence in Rwanda for three decades before 1994; adherence to the Arusha Accords of 1993 to guide the composition of the government of national unity and national assembly.

(b) Public service reforms to enhance transparency, efficiency and effectiveness in public service delivery.

(c) Promoting peace, security and unity through reconciliation programs.

(d) Creation of a community police force to enhance security at the local levels.

(e) Promoting national dialogue on the country's needs and aspirations through fora.

(f) Initiation of a decentralized process to facilitate the devolution of administrative responsibilities and support to local government units, and consolidation of the structure of local governments.

(g) Provision of social and physical infrastructure in the local administrative units is substantially supported by direct contribution from local communities, a visible evidence of the popularity of representative local government.

(h) Cooperation with the international agencies in monitoring human rights standards and reconstruction. Above all, in a remarkably short time, Rwanda has succeeded in rebuilding a functioning civil society; in particular, strong women's associations, and a free press, and employers and workers associations. (Ayot, in press)

The NURC undertook aggressive measures to organize meetings for the various groups of people in the country. Other measures included workshops and conferences whose major themes specifically addressed concerns for National Unity and Reconciliation. These attempts by the Rwandan government to deal with the post-conflict crisis culminated into the organization of various national summits where Rwandans of all levels of society, including representatives from Rwanda's Diaspora community, were present (Ayot, in press).

The NURC also organized workshops which targeted different segments of the population. The main objective was to provide an opportunity for these individuals to undergo "civic re-education" or "solidarity camps"—the *ingandos.* Demobilized soldiers (from the national army as well as from the ex-FAR) *Interahmwe* and other groups that had been repatriated to Rwanda mostly from Eastern Congo provisionally released prisoners, and others were required to stay at an *ingando* for six to eight weeks. These individuals were offered courses covering, among other areas, "their socio-economic reintegration into the society." This became a preparatory stage through which an individual could begin to make the journey back to the real world, to the new Rwandan civil society, after the ravages of the war period. It also formed part of the most important initiatives by the Rwandan government in its attempt to rehabilitate and enhance the spirit of National Unity and Reconciliation among its citizens (Ayot, in press).

In discussing the National Unity and Reconciliation Commission from a gender perspective, Ayot points out that when the Rwandan government took a bold step towards the establishment of a government of national unity, it recognized women as a formidable force within the society. Women had been both the providers for the two sides of the conflict. They took care of the sick, the wounded, the elders, the youth, and the children. Even those who went on a killing spree returned home to be fed by women as well as those in the refugee camps. Therefore, in an effort to increase the representation of women, for example, in 1999, the government split the Ministry of Gender, Family and Social Affairs into the Ministry of Family and Social Affairs and the Ministry of Gender and Promotion of Women. The latter Ministry was charged with the responsibility of developing projects that would see to it that all laws that discriminated against women were reformed. It was also given the responsibility of promoting the education and training of women (Ayot, in press). Thus, it is not surprising that today women in Rwanda constitute 56 percent of the members of the Rwandan Parliament, a world's first, including the occupation of the Speaker's chair.

The Constitution of Rwanda had allocated 30 percent of the seats in Parliament to the women. Indeed, with the elections of the year 2003, a large number of women were elected to that August house. Women garnered six out of the twenty seats in the Senate. On the other hand, in the Lower House, which comprises a total of eighty seats, women were able to garner thirty-nine seats. The Rwandan women, in actual fact, got more votes than what was expected and it even surprised their male counterparts (Ayot, in press).

The Rwandan tragedy was a wake-up call for the women, as many of them took up new professions just to keep the country running. Women constituted an overwhelming majority in the aftermath of the conflict. At the end of the ethnic warfare of the 1990s, women greatly outnumbered men. Some of the existing estimates have put it at the ratio of seven to one, and this is because of the wanton killing of so many men and the escape of so many others involved in the carnage. During the rebuilding of the country, the women's anguished voices were difficult not to hear, and they became a powerful and credible force for reconciliation (Ayot, in press).

Some of the prominent women in Rwandan civil society include Donnah Kamashazi, the representative in Rwanda for the United Nations Development Fund for Women. Others include the Chief of Justice of the Supreme Court, the Head of National Unity and Reconciliation Commission, Deputy Police Chief, and those who hold ministerial posts in the government. Like any other world community, gender imbalance is still a major issue in much of the African continent; nevertheless, when it comes to parliamentary representation, Rwanda and South Africa as well as Mozambique have deliberately made great strides towards the political empowerment of women. This was just the foundation, the beginning, not suggesting that the problems in Rwanda are already solved just because of the presence of women in that August house (Ayot, in press).

One of the major achievements on the part of women in Rwanda has to do with the land issues where women and girls had been excluded from inheriting land. According to the July 19, 2000 report by the Secretary General to the United Nations General Assembly and Security Council, under Rwandan legal system, girls could not inherit land. But as a result of the visit to Rwanda in February of 1999, and building on the earlier work of several non-governmental organizations and United Nations agencies, the special Representative for Children and Armed Conflict engaged in a dialogue with the government of Rwanda, urging it to introduce legislation that would allow girls to inherit farms and other properties. These consultative meetings led to the enactment of legislation in November of 1999 by the government which embodied, among others, the rights of girls to inherit land and other properties. The other area of concern that has received significant attention of the international community is the issue of rape as it is perpetuated against girls and women. It was the disturbing and chilling accounts of the plight of the girls and women that led to the 1998 Rome Statute of the International Criminal Court which defined rape and sexual slavery as both war crimes and crimes against humanity (Ayot, in press).

Perhaps the following testimony about the use of *Gacaca* provided by a Rwandese man who works for a non-governmental agency may serve as a poignant conclusion to this case study on Rwanda:

> My impressions are the following. The period now (mid-April) is one of mourning. Each year, we feel the weight of contention. We are in a period of wake. It is now that you feel that the population's traumas are coming out in the open. This year is worse than 1994. As time goes on, the trauma is being released. We, the NGOs and the government, do not have adequate tools to deal with this.
>
> For twelve years, we have preached the message, "we can live together." That was the first step. Now we are in the phase of Reconciliation and Justice. Should we forget the past and build a future or punish the culprits? This is a dilemma. We should combine the two. But this has its set of challenges. Classic justice [as we know it in the West] cannot solve these conflicts. We would like to recognize the blame but also reinstate populations. We use *Gacaca* Justice. It's a participatory process allowing us to talk. We are amongst ourselves, in the community. This is how we can deal.
>
> It has been a genocide by proxy—the neighbor, the friend, the family, (and) the spectator denounce the other—so the level of participation [in the genocide] was significant. *Gacaca* is a compromise between forgetting and justice. We were not accustomed to law terms of the formal system of laws; *Gacaca* is a traditional method. You sit under the tree and deal with your problems. We had to add laws, teach formal procedures to the judges. This has not been easy. Now, we have train(ed) the judges. We have 80,000 prisoners of the Genocide. We may have 800,000 to 1.5 million prisoners [by the end of this process]. This

is a large portion of the population.

We have made progress since 1995, 1996, 1997. Now fear/distrust have decreased, even if it still exists (sic). The social climate is good. But with *Gacaca,* we are going to talk about the dead. There is a "resistance movement" that would like to prevent the Justice process. Since *Gacaca* is based on informal chats, there will be no definitives (sic). But it seems to be a good system.

The question of the survivors is very delicate: how do we repair, deal with the trauma? We do not have enough systems for that.

Good governance is a topic that worries us. There would be no genocide without the state's influence. What type of power do we want to prevent a similar genocide? Past-genocidal society is very fragile. We have put in place basic institutions but citizen participation is low, governing is not very strong.

Poverty is caused by many factors. But the fact remains that the population is poor—there are official differences. For we who work in reconciliation, poverty has never been a cause of the genocide. It was not the poor that were the people undertaking the genocide. We must be clear: poverty was not the cause of the genocide.

The church is very important in Rwandan society. A difficult past since there have been clashes with the government. The Catholic [C]hurch lost its moral clout and credibility—it is said that the church did not have a good role to play in the genocide. The church is in a phase of recovery. We can see an effort at self-examination—a "Christian *Gacaca.*" The church talks, insists on basic ecclesiastical communities as a vehicle of reconciliation and listening. The bishops support the state *Gacaca.* Justice and Peace commissions are closely involved in the *Gacaca* process. The Catholic [C]hurch has chosen a more discreet profile; it does not involve itself as much in the government. Personally, I think this separation is important so that the church can reflect. There aren't even any religious writings about the genocide. Today, the Catholic [C]hurch has accepted to become a part of the society—before that, it was superior. This is a success.

It is better to talk than to ignore. It is painful, but we must talk. (007 in Africa, 2006)

Indeed, as Christian Scherrer has argued, the importance of customary law for dealing with the overwhelming consequences of genocide is widely underestimated. Thus, Scherrer suggests that in the context of future reconciliation, the genuine revival and "autonomization" of the traditional *Gacaca* system as arbitration needs more support by civil actors, local and foreign as well. He adds that the spontaneous reactivation of this grassroots scheme for arbitration and communal justice in over twenty of Rwanda's forty-seven communes has given rise to hopes. He believes that *Gacaca*, like the *Abashigantahe* used in Burundi, may greatly contribute to the restoration of the moral order. He is also convinced that self-healing forces can be revived in every society, if needed against the will of politicians and conflict actors (Scherrer, 1999).

Monarchical Rule in Swaziland

Swaziland, which gained its independence from Britain in 1968, is one of the three remaining monarchies in Africa, and its citizens are very proud of it. Led by His Majesty King Mswati III, the citizens of Swaziland rejoice in their traditions and are staunchly committed to safeguarding their rich culture, social and natural heritage for future generations. Today, not many countries can boast of the safety, stability, and peace which Swaziland enjoys, both nationally and internationally. Visitors to the kingdom feel and appreciate the warmth and friendliness of their Swazi hosts, a characteristic engendered by the nation's stability and safety (WildLife Adventures, 2007).

Several centuries ago, a people of Nguni descent moved southwards from Central Africa and a group of them settled, during the mid-eighteenth century, in the area known today as Swaziland. The kings of Swaziland date back to the royal line of Dlamini who lived in the vicinity of Delgado Bay. Records show that the Nguni had entered the territory of Swaziland around the year 1600. Under the leadership of Dlamini III, in 1750, they settled along the Pongola River where it cuts the Lubombo Mountains (WildLife Adventures, 2007).

The land was neither vacant nor sparsely populated. It was teeming with game, rich in natural resources, and a haven for raising crops and rearing cattle. Trade had been transacted from the coast for many years, and the powerful state of Shiselweni existed which the Swazi leaders sought to absorb or overcome (WildLife Adventures, 2007).

From 1903 until it gained its independence in 1968, Swaziland was a British colonial protectorate, despite sustained pressure for its incorporation into South Africa. Throughout the colonial era, the ruling Dlamini dynasty, which was led by the energetic Sobuza II after 1921, served successfully as a rallying point for national self-assertion on the key issues of regaining control of alienated land and opposing union with South Africa. Sobuza's personal leadership in these struggles made his royalist Imbokodvo party very popular, allowing it to win overwhelming majorities in the 1964, 1967, and 1972 elections. In 1973, faced with a very weak opposition party, the Ngwane National Liberation Congress, Sobuza dissolved Parliament and repealed the Westminster-style Constitution, characterizing it as "un-Swazi." A new, non-partisan Parliament was chosen in 1979. Authority remained with the King and assisted by his advisory council, the Liqoqo (Edge, 2006, pp. 185–186).

When King Sobuza II died in 1982, many observers were left wondering if Swaziland's monarchist institutions would survive, as a prolonged power struggle increased tensions within the ruling order. Members of the Liqoqo seized effective power and appointed Ntombi as the new Queen Regent. Palace intrigue, however, continued until Ntombi's eighteen-year-old son, Prince Makhosetive, was installed as King Mswati III in 1986. The new King approved the demotion of the Liqoqo back to its advisory status and has ruled through his appointed prime minister and cabinet. In 2004, Swaziland put into effect a new constitution that provides civil liberties. While critics say that the document still leaves ultimate power in the hands of the King, supporters state that democracy creates division and the monarch is a strong unifying force for the nation (Edge, 2006, pp. 185–186).

No matter what a Swazi's position on this issue, what is clearly evident is that all Swazis take great pride in what they refer to as the "Royal Treatment." This involves their treatment of visitors with courtesy and friendliness and their genuine desire to leave in peace. There are no ethnic conflicts. Old Swazi traditions are carefully guarded through colorful ceremonies to mark specific occasions during which men, women, and children in rural and urban areas wear distinctive national costumes. The major ceremonies are the colorful *umhlanga* and the *incwala*. The latter ceremony involves sacred and secret activities that require the direct participation of the King (WildLife Adventures, 2007).

Conclusion and Recommendation

Evident from the preceding discussion is the fact that the history of Africa, from antiquity to modern times, is pregnant with indigenous approaches for meeting the continent's challenges. And since most Africans still cling to many of their traditions, meeting these challenges call for a revival of traditional African methods and a mixture of approaches. Perhaps the following Bakongo tale of "How the Wives Restored Their Husband to Life" may underscore the wisdom of such a revival and the prudent use of mixed approaches.

> A certain man named Nenpetro had three wives, Ndoza'ntu the Dreamer, Songa'nzila the Guide, [and] Fulla Fulla the Raiser of the Dead. Now Nenpetro was a great hunter; and one day he killed an antelope and gave it to his three wives. They ate it, and after time complained of hunger. Nenpetro went out shooting again, and killed a monkey. They ate this also, but still complained of hunger. "Oh," says Nenpetro, "nothing but an ox will satisfy you people." So off he went on the track of an ox. He followed the tracks for a long way, and at last caught sight of it as it was feeding with two or three others. He stalked it carefully, and shot it; but before he could reload, another angry ox charged him, and killed him.
>
> Now in town, they knew nothing of all this; but his wives grew very hungry, and cried for him to come back to them. Still he returned not. Then Ndoza'ntu dreamt that he had been killed by an ox, but that he had killed an ox before he fell.
>
> "Come along," said Songa'nzila; "I will show you the road."

> Thus they set out, and marched up hill and down dale, through woods and across rivers, until toward nightfall they came up to the place where their husband lay dead. And now Fulla Fulla went into the woods and collected herbs and plants, and set about raising him from the dead.
>
> Then the three women began to quarrel and wonder into whose shimbe Nenpetro would first enter.
>
> "I dreamt that he was dead," said Ndoza'tu.
>
> "But I showed you where he lay dead," said Songa'nzila.
>
> "And I have brought him back to life," said Fulla Fulla, as the husband gradually gave signs of life.
>
> "Well let us each cook a pot of food, and take it to him as soon as he can eat; and then let him decide out of which pot he will take his first meal."
>
> So two killed fowls, and cooked them each in her own pot, while the third cooked some pig in hers. And Nenpetro took the pot of pig that Fulla Fulla had cooked, and said: "When you dreamt that I was dead, you did not give me food, Ndoza'ntu; for I was not found. And when you, Songa'nzila, had shown the others the road, I was still unfit to eat; but when Fulla Fulla gave me back my life, then was I able to eat the pig she gave me. The gift therefore of Fulla Fulla is the most to be prized."
>
> And the majority of the people said he was right in his judgment; but the women round about said he should have put food out of the three pots into one pot, and have eaten the food thus mixed. (Feldman, 1963, pp. 217–218)

Indeed, similar to the preceding Bakongo tale, prudently employing a Western approach to meet certain challenges, Africa faces may work in a particular context, but mixing Western and African methods, or employing entirely African methods, could prove to be the most reliable.

Bibliography

007 in Africa. "*Gacaca* (pronounced *Gachacha*)." April 27, 2006. http://007inafrica.blogspot.com/2006/04/gacaca-pronounced-gachacha.html (accessed June 18, 2006).

Aborisade, Oladimeji, and Robert J. Mundt. *Politics in Nigeria*. Boston, MA: Pearson Education (initially published in 1998 by Longman, an imprint of Addison Wesley Longman), 2001.

Africa South of the Sahara (Year Book). Iain Frame and Katharine Murison, eds. London, UK: Routledge, 2005.

Alridge, Derrick P. "The Dilemmas, Challenges, and Duality of an African–American Educational Historian." *Educational Researcher* (December 2003): 25–34.

Asante, Molefi Kete. *The Afrocentric Idea*. Philadelphia, PA: Temple University Press, 1987.

Awoonor, Kofi Nyidevu. *Ghana: A Political History*. Accra, Ghana: Sedco Publishing Ltd. and Woeli Publishing Services, 1990.

Ayittey, George. *Africa in Chaos*. New York, NY: St. Martin's Press, 1999.

Ayot, Theodora. "The Nature of Reconstruction and Reconciliation Programs in Rwanda: The Place of Women." *Journal of Third World Studies* (in press).

Bakunin, Michael (Mikhail). *Bakunin: Statism and Anarchy* (edited by Marshall Shatz). Cambridge, UK: Cambridge University Press, 1991.

Bangura, Abdul Karim. *Research Methodology and African Studies* vol. 2 (in progress).

———. *African Peace Paradigms*. Dubuque, IA: Kendall Hunt Publishing Company, 2008.

———. "Ubuntugogy: An African Educational Paradigm that Transcends Pedagogy, Andragogy, Ergonagy, and Heutagogy." *Journal of Third World Studies* xxii, no. 2 (2005): 13–53.

Bangura, Abdul Karim, and Erin McCandless. *Peace Research for Africa: Critical Essays on Methodology*. Geneva, Switzerland: UN University for Peace Press, 2007.

BBC World Service. "Should There Be One Court for the World?" November 3, 2000. www.bbc.co.uk/worldservice/people/features/ihavearightto/four_b/debates4.shtml (accessed June 18, 2006).

Bobbio, Norberto. *Democracy and Dictatorship: The Nature and Limits of State Power*. Minneapolis: University of Minnesota Press, 1989.

Bowen, John R. "The Myth of Global Ethnic Conflict." *The Journal of Democracy* 7, no. 4 (October 1996): 3–14.

Callaghy, Thomas M. *The State–Society Struggle: Zaire in Comparative Perspective*. New York, NY: Columbia University Press, 1984.

Clapham, Christopher. "Recent History." In *Africa South of the Sahara* (Year Book). London, UK: Europa, 2000.

———. *South Africa and the International System: The Politics of State Survival*. Cambridge, UK: Cambridge University Press, 1996.

Cobb, Charles Jr. "Sierra Leone's Special Court: Will It Hinder or Help? *allAfrica.com*, November 21, 2002. http://www.allafrica.com/stories/200211210289.html (accessed July 13, 2004).

Dahl, Robert. *Modern Political Analysis*. Upper Saddle River, NJ: Prentice Hall, 1973.

du Toit, Pierre. *South Africa's Brittle Peace*. New York, NY: Palgrave/Macmillan, 2001.

Easton, David. *The Analysis of Political Structure*. New York, NY: Routledge, 1990.

Edge, Wayne. *Africa* (Global Studies Series). Dubuque, IA: McGraw-Hill/Dushkin, 2006.

Evans, Peter B., Dietrich Rueschemeyer, and Theda Skocpol. *Bringing the State Back In*. Cambridge, UK: Cambridge University Press, 1985.

Feldman, Susan, ed. *African Myths and Tales*. New York, NY: Dell Publishing Company, Inc., 1963.

Flint, Colin and Peter Taylor. *Political Geography: World Economy, Nation-State, and Locality* (5th ed.). Harlow, England: Pearson/Prentice-Hall, 2007.

Frueh, Jamie. *The Remaking of the South African Social Order: Political Identity and Social Change*. Albany, NY: State University of New York Press, 2003.

Ginifer, Jeremy. *Sierra Leone—Building the Road to Recovery*. Monograph No. 80. March 2003. www.iss.co.za/pubs/monographs/No80/Chap2.html (accessed July 13, 2004).

Gobodo-Madikizela, Pumla. *A Human Being Died that Night*. New York, NY: Houghton Mifflin, 2003.

Goins, Stephanie. "Restoring/Rehabilitating Former Child Soldiers in Sierra Leone: The Place for Forgiveness." Stephanie Goins' Seminar Paper 9.7.03. OCMS, 2003.

Harper, Douglas. State. *Online Etymology Dictionary*. February 26, 2007. http://dictionary.reference.com/browse/state (accessed January 18, 2008).

Hofisi, Costa. "The African State and Development in Perspective." *The African Executive*.com http://africanexecutive.com/modules/magazine/articles.php?article=2914 (accessed December 3, 2008).

Hord, Fred Lee, and Jonathan Scott Lee. *I Am Because We Are: Readings in Black Philosophy*. Amherst, MA: University of Massachusetts Press, 1995.

Institute for Justice and Reconciliation (South Africa). *Report of the Second Round of SA Reconciliation Barometer Survey*, May 2004.

Jackson, Robert H., and Carl G. Rosberg. "Why Africa's Weak States Persist: The Empirical and the Juridical in Statehood." *World Politics* 35, no. 1 (1982): 1–24.

Kropotkin, Peter. "The State: Its Historic Role (pamphlet)." 1897. http://www.panarchy.org/kropotkin/1897.state.html (accessed December 12, 2008).

———. "Anarchism: Its philosophical ideal (pamphlet)." 1896. http://www.panarchy.org/kropotkin/186.eng.htm/ (accessed December 12, 2008).

Kun, George. "Competing Approaches for Ameliorating the Pains and Cicatrix of the War in Liberia." Unpublished paper, 2006.

Kuper, Leo, and M. G. Smith, eds. *Pluralism in Africa*. Los Angeles, CA: University of California Press, 1969.

Lawyers Committee for Human Rights. *Liberia: A Promise Betrayed* (a report on human rights). New York, NY: LCHR Publications, 1986.

Little, Barbara J. *Historical Archaeology: Why the Past Matters*. Walnut Creek, CA: Left Coast Press, 2007.

Maclay, K. "Child Soldiers and Childhood in Sierra Leone Studied by UC Berkeley Graduate Student." University of California Berkeley Media Relations, July 26, 2002. www.berkeley.edu/news/media/release/2002/07/26_soldr.html (accessed July 13, 2004).

Magubane, Bernard. "The Evolution of the Class Structure in Africa." In *The Political Economy of Contemporary Africa*, edited by Peter C. W. Gutkind and Immanuel Wallerstein. Beverly Hills, CA: Sage Publications, 1976.

Mazrui, Ali A. "The African State as a Political Refugee." In *African Conflict Resolution: The U.S. Role in Peacemaking*, edited by David R. Smock and Chester A. Crocker. Washington, DC: United States Institute of Peace Press, 1995.

Miliband, Ralph. *Class Power and State Power*. London, UK: Verso, 1983.

Mkandawire, Thandika. "Thinking about Developmental States in Africa." *Cambridge Journal of Economics* 25 (2001): 289–314.

Moriarty, Thomas A. *Finding the Words: A Rhetorical History of South Africa's Transition from Apartheid to Democracy*. Westport, CT: Praeger, 2003.

Morrill, C. "Reconciliation and the *Gacaca*: The Perceptions and Peace-building Potential of Rwanda Youth Detainees." *The Online Journal of Peace and Conflict Resolution* 6, no. 1, (Fall 2004): 1–66. http://www.trinstitute.org/ojpcr/6_1morrill1.pdf (accessed June 18, 2006).

Muiu, Mueni wa. *Fundi wa Afrika*: Toward a New Paradigm of the African State. *Journal of Third World Studies* xix, 2 (2002): 23–42.

Mustaq, Najum. "Kenya Parliament May Soon Consider New Abortion Rights Law." *Inter Press Service*. September 17, 2008. www.highbeam.com/doc/1p1156350076

.html (accessed December 8, 2008).

Mutunga, Willy. Memo to the International Human Rights Movement on the Murder of Father John Kaiser on the Night of August 24, 2000. *Africa Policy E-Journal.* http://www.africaaction.org (accessed December 15, 2008).

———. *Constitution-Making from the Middle: Civil Society and Transition Politics in Kenya, 1992–1997.* Nairobi, Kenya: Sareat & Mwengo, 1999.

Nkrumah, Kwame. *Class Struggle in Africa.* New York, NY: International Publishers Co., Inc., 1970.

Nyerere, (Mwalimu) Julius K. "African Socialism; Ujamaa in Practice." In *Contemporary Black Thought*, edited by Robert Chrisman and Nathan Hare. Indianapolis, IN and New York, NY: The Bobbs-Merrill Co., Inc./MacMillan Press, 1989.

Olonisakin, F. "African 'Homemade' Peacekeeping Initiatives." *Armed Forces and Society* 23, no. 3 (1997): 349–71.

Olukoshi, Adebayo. "Towards the Restoration of a Social State in Africa." Keynote Address given at the Globalization and Sub-Saharan Africa: International Experts' Meeting, European Parliament, Brussels, April 15–16, 2004.

Outram, Quentin. "Liberia: Roots and Fruits of the Emergency." *Third World Quarterly* 20, no. 1 (1999): 163–73.

Posel, Deborah G. S. *Commissioning the Past: Understanding South Africa's Truth and Reconciliation Commission.* Johannesburg, South Africa: Witwatersrand University Press, 2002.

Poulantzas, Nicos. *State, Power, Socialism.* London, UK: New Left Review, 1978.

Romero, Joshua H. "The Special Court for Sierra Leone and the Juvenile Soldier Dilemma." 2004. Northwestern University Journal of International Human Rights. http://www.law.northwestern.edu/journals/jihr/v2/8/index.htm (accessed July 5, 2004).

Rothbard, Murray Newton. "Society without the State." *Libertarian Forum* 7, 1 (1975).

Rubin, Leslie, and Brian Weinstein. *Introduction to African Politics: A Continental Approach* 2nd ed. New York, NY: Holt, Rinehart and Winston, 1974.

Sandbrook, Richard. "Patron, Clients, and Factions: New Dimension of Conflict Analysis in Africa." *Journal of Political Science* 5, no. 1 (1972): 104–19.

Scherrer, Christian P. We need a notion of justice as the base for reconciliation policies, but foremost we need the notion of prevention. 1999. *Forums.* Lund, Sweden: The Transnational Foundation for Peace and Future Research. www.transnational.org/forum/meet/scherrer_justice–reconc.html (accessed June 18, 2006).

Sesay, Max A. "Civil War and Collective Intervention in Liberia." *Review of African Political Economy* 67 (1996): 35–52.

Skinner, Quentin. "The State." In *Political Innovation and Conceptual Change*, edited by Terence Ball, James Farr, and Russell L. Hanson. Cambridge, UK: Cambridge University Press, 1989.

Skalir, Leslie. "Globalization and Class." In Timothy Sinclair (ed.). *Global Governance: Critical Concepts in Political Science.* New York, NY: Taylor & Francis, 2004.

Sparks, Allister. *Beyond the Miracle.* Chicago, IL: University of Chicago Press, 2003.

Stephens, Angela. "Forced Marriage Pursued as Crime in Sierra Leone Tribunal Cases" (United Nations Wire). *Global Policy Forum.* April 16, 2004. www.globalpolicy.org/component/content/article/163-general/29143.html (accessed July 5, 2004).

Tabarrok, Alex. "Somalia and the Theory of Anarchy." *Marginal Revolution.* April 21, 2004. http://www.marginalrevolution.com/marginalrevolution/economics/ (accessed December 15, 2008).

Taylor, Rupert, and Mark Shaw. "The Dying Days of Apartheid." In *South Africa in*

Transition, edited by David R. Howarth and Alletta Norval. New York, NY: St. Martin's Press, Inc., 1998.

Tedla, Elleni. *Sankofa: African Thought and Education.* New York, NY: Peter Lang, 1995.

———. "Indigenous African Education as a Means for Understanding the Fullness of Life: Traditional Amara Education." *Journal of Black Studies* 23, no. 1 (September 1, 1992): 7–26.

Touré, Sékou. "A Dialectical Approach to Culture. In *Contemporary Black Thought,* edited by Robert Chrisman and Nathan Hare. Indianapolis, IN and New York, NY: The Bobbs-Merrill Co, Inc./MacMillan Press, 1989.

Tutu, Desmond. *No Future without Forgiveness.* New York, NY: Doubleday Publishing, 2000.

United Nations–HABITAT. Report of the Technical Advisory Committee (TAC) 2006 Dubai (United Arab Emirates) International Award for Best Practices, Weihai, China, 2–7 September 2006. Nairobi, Kenya: UN–HABITAT Office, 2006.

Urschel, Donna. "Examples of Reconciliation: Africa's Contributions to the Global Community." Library of Congress Information Bulletin, April 2005. http://www.loc.gov/loc/lcib/0504/africa.html (accessed June 18, 2006).

Weber, Max. "The Profession and Vocation of Politics." In *Political Writings,* edited by Peter Lassman. Cambridge, UK: Cambridge University Press, 1994.

Wiessner, Siegfried, and Andrew R. Willard. "Policy-oriented Jurisprudence and Human Rights Abuses in Internal Conflict: Toward a World Public Order of Human Dignity." *The American Journal of International Law* 93, no. 2 (April 1999): 316–34.

Wolff, Robert Paul. "Anarchism." In Joël Krieger and Margaret E. Crahan (eds). *The Oxford Companion to Politics of the World.* New York, NY: Oxford University Press, 2001.

Zartman, I. William. *Governance as Conflict Management: Politics and Violence in West Africa.* Washington, DC: Brookings Institution Press, 1996.

———. *Collapsed States: Disintegration and Restoration of Legitimate Authority.* Boulder, CO: Lynne Rienner Publishers, 1995.

Chapter 11
The Efficacies of Decision-Making Styles in the African-centric Decision Making Process

Nabie Y. Conteh

The objective of this study is to test the efficacies of various decision-making styles in the African setting. Four broad categories of decision-making styles are utilized in this study. The methodology is illustrated with a complex, semi-structured problem that is often used to train and evaluate management personnel. In order to test the efficacies of these styles, two prototype systems will be constructed. The Decision Support Systems architecture serves as a control and the Just-in-Time Intelligent Decision Support Systems as the experimental architecture. The experiment will test whether the use of either of the two systems offers a significant improvement in the process of and outcome from the four decision-making styles. The chapter closes with a conclusion on the results of the experiment and their implications on Information Systems Research in relation to the African-centric decision-making process.

Introduction

Decision making is at the cornerstone of every major project and centered on the very fabric of the traditional African social, cultural, and economic settings. The central nucleus in the African community, as in all other communities across the globe is the family. The family serves as a microcosm of the larger African community. In former times, within the family unit in the general African context, the father, being the head of the family political unit, had always played a leading and in most cases even a dominant role in the major decisions made by the family. This means the decision-making process had always been autocratic. This perspective at the family level can be rightly extrapolated when we assess the nature of the decision-making process at the community level.

The decision making process is directly linked with the need for problem solving. The right choices we make in solving problems and making decisions depends on how correctly we follow the steps through in the decision making process. Whether it is a decision to marry a lady from a certain tribe or clan, choosing a piece of land for cultivation, sending a child to a certain school, embarking upon a local trade such as carpentry, welding, or training to become a blacksmith, cultivating a piece of farmland, becoming a tailor, or even choosing to become a vendor of handicrafts or wares at the local marketplace, the choices to be made are all about weighing the criteria, generating alternative choices, and choosing the best option among them. In essence, one needs to be well-informed in order to achieve productive and effective outcomes. Whether any decisions taken or choices made are going to pay off in the near or distant future or be able to achieve the desired outcomes depends on how effective and efficient are the choices made and the accuracy of the criteria evaluation (Simon, 1960). In many cases, these choices are not taken lightly and are addressed by the parents, family heads, guardians, community leaders, and local stakeholders or those endued with the final choice at the top of the hierarchy of the political structure of the villages and communities.

From the various decision-making styles outlined below, it can be rightly stated that the autocratic style is the most prevalent style in the African setting, considering that the family heads (mostly males) make decisions that are more often autocratic than not. The same is true for the socioeconomic setting and the political leadership which have been characterized by dictatorships. Communities in small villages and towns have however been governed by collective and participatory rule; this is akin to consultative decision-making styles.

This chapter addresses the effectiveness of the process and outcomes of decision-making styles in the decision-making process, and presents a methodology for determining their effectiveness.

The Merits of Non-Subject Designs

The non-subject design approach assumes that human subjects will not be used in gathering data for the simulation study and in evaluating information system architectures. Using human subjects can present some serious scientific, technical, and economic problems. It will be time consuming and potentially costly to get human subjects because of the selection, training, and motivational issues involved in the acquisition of subjects (Hoover and Perry, 1990; O'Kane and Spenceley, 1999; Power, 2002). In addition, there may be political considerations (obtaining consent from subjects and surmounting bureaucratic hurdles from the Institutional Research Board - IRB) that are involved in selecting and utilizing human subjects in experiments. Also, humans in an experimental setting may not behave the same way as they would in practice (Conteh and Forgionne, 2004a). Moreover, it would be difficult to obtain a representative sample of human subjects. Even if the sample is representative of the defined subject group, it may not be representative of the population of potential information system African-centric users. As a result, it may be difficult to generalize the results from the subject-based experiment (Conteh and Forgionne, 2003a).

Human subjects, however, may be unnecessary to conduct simulation studies of information systems, especially when information is available about African-centric user behavior. One such instance involves studies that involve decision-making support systems (DMSS). There are various studies that define decision-making behavior for the general population (Conteh and Forgionne, 2003b).

Different decision-making styles will be generated based on a stochastic process (based on random variables). This is regulated by means of the hypothesized decision-making styles as found in the literature and specifically in: Turban and Aronson's *Decision Support Systems and Intelligent Systems* (1998, pp. 62-3). Decision Style is the way and manner in which decision makers think and respond to or address problems. Decision style is also about their cognitive response to decision situations and their individual and situational differences in beliefs and values. Decision making is not linear. That is to say the emphasis, time allotment, and priorities differ from individual to individual as well as from situation to situation. Gordon et al. (1975) identified forty processes in looking at nine types of decision and Mintzberg (1973) identified seven basic styles with a lot of variations (Turban and Aronson, 1998).

Once a simulated African-centric user or Decision Maker is assigned to a certain decision-making style category, the corresponding choice logic (parameters) will be applied to his or her decision behaviors within the simulation model. Based on these parameters, values for decision variables and uncontrollable variables will be generated and entered. The simulation results, such as values for profit after tax, investment, marketing, and research and development will be obtained for the simulated quarter or quarters. Profit status reports and sensitivity analyses will be utilized in arriving at a recommended policy (set of decision variables) for the simulated business organization (Conteh and Forgionne, 2004b).

Since each simulated African-centric user will be utilizing the alternative information system architectures, the inferences need not be precise. Moreover, sensitivity analysis can be used to test outcome and process sensitivity for inferred values.

The suggested approach can be used to generate a very large number of simulation runs for the full variety of potential African-centric users within a very short time. More importantly, the approach is timely and cost effective. Since all potential African-centric users are considered, rather than a sampling, the approach is likely to be more generalizable than human subject based experiments.

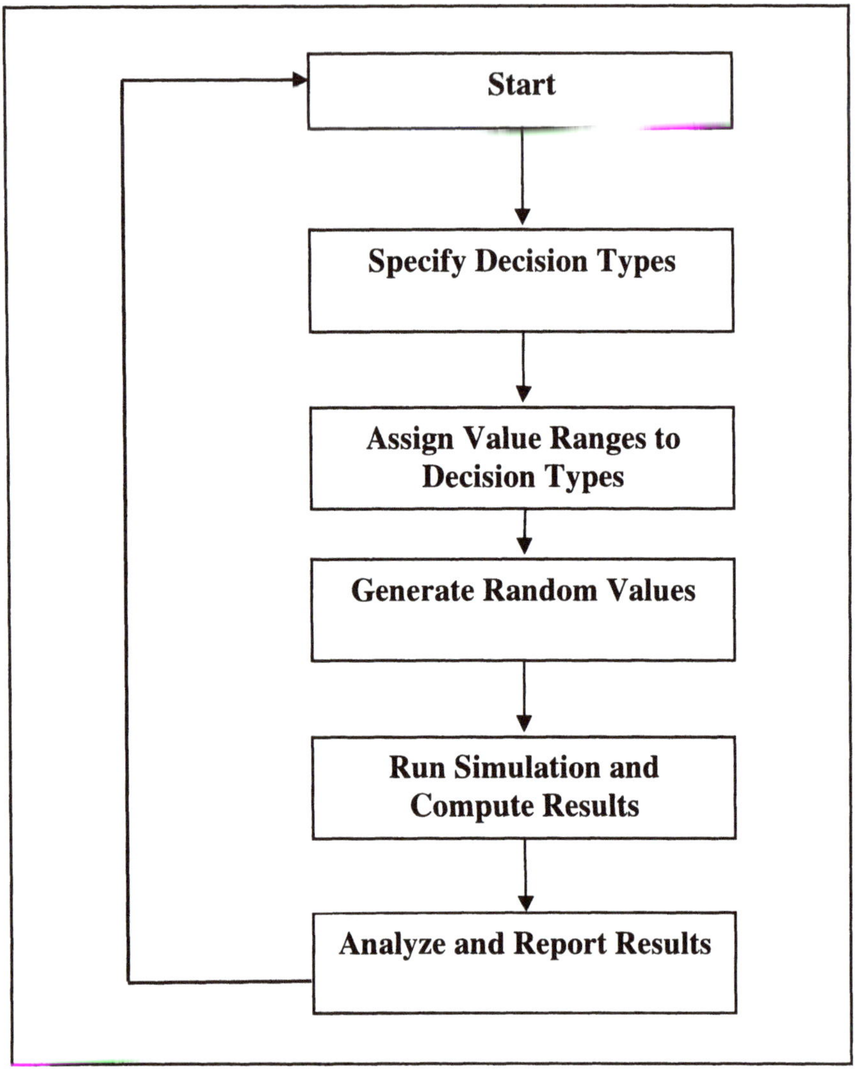

Figure 11.1. Simulation: Experimental Design

Simulation Models

The objective of this simulation study is to test the efficacies of Decision-Making Styles in the African-centric Decision-Making Process, that is, whether the autocratic African-centric decision-making style offers a significant improvement in the process of and outcome from decision-making in comparison to other existing decision-making styles. The data in Table 11.1, adapted from Aronson and Turban's *Decision Support Systems and Intelligent Systems* (1998, pp. 62–63), summarizes the variety of potential generic human behaviors. The succeeding sections will cover specific African-centric decision-making styles and how they relate to the generic styles covered in the literature.

Table 11.1. Cognitive Style Decision Approaches

Problem-Solving Dimension	Heuristic	Analytic
Approach to Learning	Learns more by acting than by analyzing the situation and places more emphasis on feedback	Uses a planned sequential to problem-solving; learns more by analyzing the situation than by acting and places less emphasis on feedback
Search	Uses trial and error and spontaneous action	Uses formal rational analysis
Approach to Analysis	Uses common sense, intuition, and feelings	Develops explicit, often quantitative, models of the situation
Scope of Analysis	Views the totality of the situation as an organic whole rather than as structure constructed from specific parts	Reduces the problem situation to a set of underlying causal functions
Basis for Inferences	Looks for highly visible situational differences that vary with time	Locates the similarities or commonalities by comparing objects

Source: Adapted from Turban, Efraim J., and Jay E. Aronson. *Decision Support Systems and Intelligent Systems*, Upper Saddle River, NJ: Prentice Hall, 1998.

In effect, Table 11.1 defines the major classes of African-centric users for DMSS and their potential behaviors.

In a simulation study, ranges of values for the controllable actions and key events can be obtained. Using the characteristics from Table 11.1, we can draw reasonable inferences about the values of actions and events within the ranges for the various classes of African-centric users.

Decision-Making Matrix

Based on the literature the following African-centric user types are proposed and utilized for the purpose of assigning values for input into the interface for the decision variables and uncontrollable variables: Analytic-Autocratic, Heuristic-Autocratic, Analytic-Consultative and Heuristic-Consultative types.

Decision making styles are described on the basis of two dimensions: 1) the amount of information used and (Analytic/Heuristic); and 2) the number of alternatives considered (Consultative/Autocratic). According to Hunsakers (1981) four classes of decision styles are proposed based on the combined influence of these two dimensions (Hunsakers, 1981): analytic-autocratic; analytic-consultative; heuristic-autocratic; and heuristic-consultative.

African-centric Decision-Making/Policy-Making Styles of Political Regimes

Based on the literature and the studies consulted on leadership/policymaking and decision-making by political regimes in African countries such as Sierra Leone, whose pattern of leadership could be portrayed as an illustrative example among other countries in West Africa and even beyond, the following decision-making/policymaking styles: (a) Administrative-hegemonial—The regimes of Sir Albert Michael Margai, Brigadier Andrew T. Juxon-Smith, and Siaka Probyn Stevens (based on the fact that the three key institutions were the executive, the administration, and the coercive apparatus—at times with a one-party dominant auxiliary organ subordinated to the ruler); (b) Pluralist—by Sir Milton Augustus Strieby Margai (based on the notion of separation of powers, with multiparty political institutions and fairly vibrant representative structures); and (c) Party-mobilizing—The regime of Joseph Saidu Momoh. It is has been classified as such, in that it bore the characteristics of some of the participatory components of a pluralist regime with the autocratic and domineering tendencies of an administrative-hegemonial regime; (d) Personal-coercive; (e) Populist; and (f) Ambiguous—The National Provisional Ruling Council (NPRC) headed by Captain Valentine E. M. Strasser was characterized as an ambiguous regime. It was hatched as a by-product of the inability of previous regimes to deal with and tackle the crisis that afflicted public institutions and restore progress and stability have been noted (Bangura, 2007).

The criteria for classifying regime types have varied widely (Chazan et al., 1988). The civilian-military typology highlights an unclear cross between means of regime change and their outcomes. The work cited by Bangura used a similar conceptual framework, and came up with classifications based on the differentiation of leadership styles: mobilizing, conciliatory, coercive, and autocratic (Bangura, 2007).

On the other hand, the categorization of regime types is based on ideology or policy orientations: Marxist, socialist, or capitalist, while others have been drawn on the basis of degrees of competition, participation, and control. The typology of Sierra Leonean regimes used in Bangura's essay is based on the dynamic interactions between rulers and the ruled and the norms governing their interactions (Bangura, 2007).

African-Centric Research Methodology

According to Bangura, there are basically three African-centered research methodologies: (1) Multiplex, (2) *Sankofa*, and (3) Pluridisciplinary:

Multiplex is centered on the use of case studies, in which contested geographies, human agencies, and epistemologies are central issues in peace and conflict studies. This is mainly because violent conflict always unleashes the unforeseen. The problem, then, from a methodological point of view, is how to capture and investigate the composite complexity of this phenomenon in which knowledge claims, and Truth itself, is almost always in contention. Multiplex analysis, therefore, proceeds in the following three stages:

(1) *Epistemic encounter* is the reality of contested social constructions between two or among more knowing subjects or communities.

(2) *Empirical encounter* refers to the contesting subjects with their material world, as they each seek the substance and resources with which to carry out the struggle, or to dominate and win complete control.

(3) *Self-reflective or Cartesian encounter* is what the subjects in such deadly competition reflect upon, and how they incorporate their individual identities and roles into the conflict.

Sankofa is transliterated from the Akan language as *Se wo were fi na wosan kofa a yenki*, whose literal translation in the English language is, "It is not taboo to go back to the source and fetch what you forgot." The source is the African culture, heritage and identity. It is the power within all Africans. In its essence, *Sankofa* means that as Africans move forward into the future, they need to reach back into their past and take with them all that works and is positive. *Sankofa* is employed by Pan-Africanists all over the world to promote the notion that African people everywhere must *go back to their roots in order to move forward.* The visual and symbolic representation of *Sankofa* is a mythic bird that flies forward while looking backward with an egg, symbolizing the future, in its mouth.

Pluridisciplinary methodology involves the use of open and resource-based techniques available in the actual situation. It has, therefore, to draw upon the indigenous knowledge materials available in the locality and make maximum use of them. Indigenous languages are, therefore, at the center of the effective use of this methodology.

In sum, as in Africancentric methodology, Molefi Kete Asante's suggestion that in the analysis of what he calls the "three fundamental Afrocentric themes of transcendent discourse: (1) human relations, (2) humans' relationship to the supernatural, and (3) humans' relationships to their own being" (1987, p. 168) that if done with an awareness of the interrelatedness of these themes, a greater understanding of the African being will be acquired, is applicable to a mixture of Multiplex, *Sankofa*, and Pluridisciplinary methodologies as well (Bangura, 2007).

The Amount of Information Used

Heuristic African-centric users, for example, generally base their decisions on minimal information. They do not normally perform lengthy searches for information. They believe: (1) that additional information will only aid in confirming what they already know; (2) that the data will be too slow in arriving; and (3) that additional information will be confounding and distracting. To the contrary, Analytic African-centric users spend more time exhaustively analyzing information before reaching conclusions about decisions to be made.

Number of Alternatives Considered

Autocratic African-centric users or African-centric users, for example, are called "satisficers." This is because they stop searching after finding one satisfactory solution to their problems and then adopt that solution. Consultative African-centric users continue to explore multiple or additional solutions and consider a range of feasible alternatives to the problem at hand before making a decision. They are called "maximizers."

Autocratic and heuristic African-centric users focus on speed, efficiency, and consistency of their decisions. They are highly action-oriented. The plans of these African-centric users tend to hinge on short-range objectives and they prefer to work in an organizational structure with clearly defined rules and specific plans.

Decision-Making Styles

In the following sections, treats how values for the various variables are allocated with justifications for the assignment of their respective values. All of them have been tied to the generic African decision-making styles obtained in the literature and other sources. In assigning these values, special considerations have been taken to accommodate the fact that no-size-fits-all for African decision-making styles. This especially so given that the choices made by different African-centric user types vary based on the nature (traditional, formal) of the decisions to be made, and the settings (village, town, city, community, or national level), as well as the seriousness of the matter (problem or decision). Generic styles of decision making have therefore been formulated to reflect and/or encompass the broad spectrum, scope, and nature of problems to be addressed and decisions to be made.

In various African countries, public participation in administrative and legislative decision-making has become an integral and important aspect of traditional, local and non-governmental governance. However, striking the right balance between democratic participation and administrative efficiency poses some challenges for many governments. Experience has shown that a one-size-fits-all approach to public participation does not exist. Rather, consultative approaches to involve the public should be adapted to the nature of the decision process and national and issue specific circumstances should be taken into consideration, while satisfying the wishes and demands of stakeholders for a transparent and fair process. Besides taking strategic considerations about the nature and scope of public participation into account, a number of practical issues may affect the success of a consultative process, such as providing clarity about the expected input and participation from stakeholders, organizing effective meetings, or providing appropriate feedback, monitoring, and evaluation on comments received.

Considerations in Assigning Value Ranges to Decision-Making Styles

The major considerations are the decision-makers' inclinations to risk-taking which is reflected by high value ranges. On the contrary, the conservative ranges represent the non-risk taking or non-gambler types. A combination of these two extremes will mean the assignment of moderate or midranges. Other assumptions are their propensity to compare with the range of prices of their competitors in the market, ranges in the previous quarters and above all, consulting with colleagues and co-workers (Conteh and Forgionne, 2004d).

Analytic-Autocratic

Analytic-Autocratic African-centric users are highly analytic in terms of information processing. They are also autocratic with regard to their choice of alternatives and their propensity to consult with others. They utilize a large amount of information before making a decision. On the other hand, they consider very few alternatives, and consult little with other staff members. In other words, they are unilateral in their decision making. This makes them rather autocratic. Based on this combination of attributes, and given their analytic inclinations, I assume that they are moderate risk takers. They would analyze information with regard to the firm's scenario data and specifically the product prices of their organizational competitors. These reasons account for the choice of value ranges for the analytic-autocratic decisions style as espoused in Table 11.2. For example, the analytic-autocratic decision maker, being a moderate risk taker, would enter values that are not high. This risk-taking tendency is furthered tempered by the fact that in combination they are analytic. Therefore, looking at the ranges in the price column, "P" for instance, this type of decision style has the next-to-lowest range ($150-$175), after the analytic-consultative style African-centric users, who are most conservative in their choice of values. It is assumed that the African-centric user will compare and analyze prices of the competitors in the market, the market conditions, and the firm's product prices in the previous and current quarters. The competitor's price in this case is $110 and the product price in the previous quarter was $100. It is assumed the autocratic gambler type would input $200 but the analytic attribute would influence this African-centric user to input mid-way values of the range $150-$175. Such considerations and analyses will temper the African-centric user's liberal price ranges and bring them down mid-way. This explains my choice of values for this decision-style African-centric user in Table 11.3. Furthermore, looking at the marketing column "M," this decision style African-centric user also has the next-to-lowest range ($650,000-$750,000) after the analytic-consultative style, whose range is $500,000-$600,000.

Heuristic-Autocratic

Heuristic-Autocratic African-centric decision style users utilize a minimum amount of data to arrive at a reasonably satisfactory decision. *Heuristic-Autocratic* African-centric users when making their decisions prioritize certain factors like speed, efficiency, and consistency. They are highly active and results-oriented. Their plans are centered on short-range objectives and they prefer to work in a well-structured organization with well-defined rules and detailed plan descriptions. They spend very little time consulting with their work colleagues and other professionals. They tend to like reports that are brief and precise and discard or ignore long and detailed reports.

Table 11.2 shows values that a Heuristic-Autocratic African-centric user would enter for variables based on his or her predefined preferences above. Looking at the values in Table 11.3, the decision style African-centric user is not only autocratic but heuristic with the highest ranges in price "P" ($180-$200); marketing "M" ($800,000-$900,000); Research and Development "R&D" ($750,000-$850,000), etc. Like in the previous decision style discussed above, the competitor's price is $110 and product price in the previous quarter was $100. I assume that this decision type African-centric user neither analyzes information adequately nor consults to obtain information about market conditions. The African-centric user would therefore be liberal in assigning input values. That is why, this African-centric user inputs a high value, in fact the highest value for the product price in the range of $180-$200. The same is true for this African-centric user's input for virtually all the remaining variables. This means, the African-centric user neither analyzes a reasonably large amount of information, nor consults and collaborates with others. In addition, the African-centric user does not consider a wide array of alternative choices and does not compare with prices of the competitor or the external environmental data. This is also because the African-centric user is rather hasty, and has to make quick decisions. This makes the African-centric user both autocratic and non-collaborative. This also means that the African-centric user is a very high risk taker.

Analytic-Consultative

Analytic-Consultative African-centric decision style users like to process extensive information as they consider several feasible options or alternatives. They are creative and seek variety. They tend to be contemplative and rather cautious in taking action. They also utilize or adopt a long-range perspective with regard to organizational planning, and their plans are adaptive because of the many alternative choices that they consider.

Analytic-Consultative African-centric users prefer to work in organizations that are well-structured with high degree of flexibility and delegation of duties. These African-centric users like to receive long, detailed, and analytic reports. Because of these qualities, they are able to effectively use consultative and participative decision making, thereby maximizing the availability of information for decision making and problem solving.

Analytic-Consultative African-centric decision style users tend to be well-informed and open to new information. They possess a broad vision of the organization and its distinctive mission, and they tend to generate creative solutions to organizational problems. Co-workers of *Analytic-Consultative* decision makers are likely to describe them as empathetic and cooperative. The values in Table 11.2 show that the analytic-consultative African-centric user considers a wide range of alternative choices, consults with colleagues, and analyzes a lot of information before inputting values. That is why this analytic-consultative decision style African-centric user has the lowest ranges in all the columns which are closely similar to those in the scenario of Table 11.3. The values that this African-centric user inputs compare closely to those of the competitor's product price which is $100 and also the product values in the previous quarter as mentioned at the value of $110. The assumption is that such an African-centric user is abreast of market information, does a lot of consultations with co-workers and colleagues and above all analyzes a lot of information regarding the product prices of competitors. These considerations will therefore lead the African-centric user to utilize informed judgment to be able to input values close to those of the competitor and the previous quarter. This African-centric user is therefore not the gambler type who is liberal with the values that she or he enters. For instance, this decision style African-centric user has the lowest price "P" ranges ($100-$125); marketing "M" ($500000-$600000); research and development ($500,000-$600,000); the economic index "EI" (1.25–1.35); and the seasonal index "SI" (1.1–1.40). These are all values in the region of the competitors' preferences in terms of parameters. This goes to show that this type of decision maker inputs values close to how the competitors price their products. And this decision maker also consults with co-workers and does exhaustive or ample research on market trends.

Heuristic-Consultative

Heuristic-Consultative African-centric *decision style* users also rely on a minimum of information. They are willing, however, to consider several alternatives and reinterpret the information to arrive at possibly different conclusions. These African-centric users are also speedy and active in discharging their duties. They exercise some degree of flexibility and adaptability in their decision making.

Heuristic-Consultative African-centric *decision style* users prefer to work in an organization with a structure that allows them the freedom to change directions depending on the conditions.

Heuristic-Consultative African-centric *decision style* users also prefer to receive from subordinates precise communications that contain a variety of specific steps or solutions to consider during decision making or problem solving. They also prefer to work within settings that permit collaborative interactions between people and other staff member or junior co-workers. They use their popularity and charm to influence and win others, and they also induce co-workers by providing them with incentives. Given the preferences of this decision style African-centric user, the assumptions are that this African-centric user is consultative but does not consider large number of alternative choices nor analyzes a lot of information. This makes this African-centric user a semi-satisficer, in that the African-centric user's tendency to accept the first satisfactory solution to the problem that comes up is tempered by the African-centric user's consultative attribute. In other words, if the price of the competitor is $110, the heuristic attribute may lead the African-centric user to enter a 100 percent increase, putting the price at $220. The consultative tendency will however bring it down to $155–$180. Table 11.3 shows values (controllable actions and key events) that African-centric users or African-centric users belonging to this African-centric user type would enter based on the preferences as defined above.

Table 11.2 shows a summary of the characteristics of the various decision styles discussed in the foregoing sections. It specifically details the major considerations that were used in defining the decision styles.

Table 11.2. Decision-making Styles

Decision Style	Risk taker (gambler type)	Consults with colleagues	Conducts market research	Analyzes historical data
1. Analytic-Autocratic	0/X	0/X	0/X	X
2. Heuristic-Autocratic	X	0	0	0
3. Analytic-Consultative	0	X	X	X
4. Heuristic-Consultative	0/X	X	0/X	0/X

Legend: 0 = Not Applicable; X = Applicable; 0/X = Moderate / Partially Applicable.

After having entered the values, for the DSS architectures (Table 11.3), the percentages of simulated subjects for each decision type of simulated subjects were determined. To do this, a random uniform percentage of 25 were allotted to each of the four decision types. It is assumed that the four decision styles are randomly distributed in the population. In this case, a random uniform distribution is a distribution, in which any number between the minimum and maximum values is equally likely to occur. This assumption is based on the principle of insufficient reason from the probability theory. That is, if there is no empirical evidence to indicate otherwise, it is reasonable to assume that the values will be uniformly distributed within the range Conteh and Forgionne 2004c).

To execute this in SAS, the following macro code was used:

```
data test;
 %macro create(howmany);
 %do i=1 %to &howmany;
x&i = RANTBL(-127968, .25, .25, .25, .25);
```

```
%end;
%mend create;

%create(10,000);
run;
```

Another code was written to obtain the probability distribution of values in their respective ranges, input by simulation subjects for each of the variables. The example below is for the price variable range only ($150 - $175).

```
data Price;
 %macro create(howmany);
 %do i=1 %to &howmany;
x&i = 150 + (25 * RANUNI(-127968));

 %end;
%mend create;

%create(10,000);
run;
```

The examples being used here contain 10,000 simulated subjects. Further, both of the two macros above were merged with the following code:

```
data Price;
set test;
 %macro create(howmany);
 %do i=1 %to &howmany;
X&i = 150 + (25 * RANUNI (-127968));

 %end;
%mend create;

%create(10,000);
run;
```

The results obtained for these simulation runs are then embedded into the conceptual architecture of the model. This model was used to run the simulations and sensitivity analysis in order to obtain the final results and the profit before and after tax. Comparisons among the four decision styles and between the two systems (DSS & IJDSS) are made through the help of descriptive and inferential statistical analysis and conclusions.

In Table 11.3, this African-centric user has the second-highest ranges, following the heuristic-analytic type, with the exception of competitor marketing "CM" starting from price "P" ($155-$185); marketing "M" ($600,000-$780,000); economic index "EI" (1.2-1.5); research and development "R&D ($700,000-$820,000) and so on. It has though the highest competitor's marketing which is $600,000-$780,000; the reason being that this African-centric user is consultative and considers a lot of alternative choices. This makes this African-centric user to try to outsell his or her competitors by increasing the competitor marketing range.

Table 11.3. Values Based on Decision-making Styles in the DSS Architecture

DM Style	DSS							
	DV UV							
	P	PI	M	R&D	EI	SI	CP	CM
AA	150-175	0	650000-750000	650-780000	1.5-1.75	1.5-1.75	150-175	650000-800000
HA	180-200	0	800000-900000	750000-850000	1.75-2.5	2.0-3.0	200-300	630000-900000
AC	100-125	0	500000-600000	500000-600000	1.25-1.35	1.1-1.40	110-140	550-600000
HC	155-185	0	600000-780000	700000-820000	1.2-1.8	1-1.7	90-180	600000-780000

Legend: DM = Decision Making; DSS = Decision Support Systems; DV = Decision Variables; UV = Uncontrollable Variables; P = Price; PI = Plant Investment; M = Marketing; R&D = Research and Development; EI = Economic Index; SI = Seasonal Index; CP = Competitor Price; CM = Competitor Marketing; AA = Analytic-Autocratic; HA = Heuristic-Autocratic; AC = Analytic-Consultative; HC = Heuristic-Consultative

The IJDSS Research Simulation

Like in the DSS research simulation, 10,000 subjects were simulated. Input values for each simulated African-centric user were entered are based on predetermined values ranges obtained from the Academic Information Systems (AIS) manual. The design of the marketing simulation used for both the DSS and IJDSS cases comes from a software package developed by AIS. Academic information systems (AIS) provides computing, library, instructional services, instructional technology support, and web management, multimedia support services for learning and research, and other information-based resources to students, instructors, and researchers. The software package used in this study for the design of the market simulation for both the DSS and IJDSS was supplied by the Academic Information Systems.

These values, which generate maximum profits, represent the advice rendered to the simulated subjects by the IJDSS (McLeod, 1986).

These input values were chosen randomly with a uniform distribution for each simulated African-centric user based on values found in the AIS manual. These values are set on ranges. The ranges start somewhere below the values in the manual and increase up to values slightly above those shown in Table 11.4. The lower bounds were arbitrarily determined.

For example, Price for African-centric user 1 (analytic consultative) is given the following range:

Quarter 1 = 45 – 55
Quarter 2 = 40 – 55
Quarter 3 = 43 – 55
Quarter 4 = 42 – 55

The major distinction between the DSS and IJDSS is the capability of the IJDSS to render timely advice in a concise form to the African-centric user.

Table 11.4. Pricing Model Simulation for Four Quarters (Based on AIS Manual)

	Quarter 1	Quarter 2	Quarter 3	Quarter 4
Price	51	51	51	51
Plant Investment	0	0	7,000,000	0
Marketing	300,000	300,000	300,000	300,000
R & D	500,000	0	0	0
Economic Index	1.00	1.00	1.00	1.00
Seasonal Index	1.00	1.00	1.00	1.00
Competitor's Price	100	100	100	100
Competitor's Marketing	600,000	600,000	600,000	600,000

Process Measures

Process tests will be carried out to determine whether the differences in profits were brought about by the process steps. Process tests will be conducted for the uncontrollable variables for the DSS and the IJDSS respectively: DSS Economic Index (E), IJDSS Economic Index (EJ), DSS Seasonal Index (SI), IJDSS Seasonal Index (SIJ), DSS Competitor Marketing (CM), IJDSS Competitor Marketing (CMJ), the DSS Competitor Price (CP), and the IJDSS Competitor Price (CPJ).

The sample t-test for the means of the eight variables in Table 11.4 will determine whether there are significant differences in the means between the DSS and the IJDSS values of the above-mentioned variables. Significant differences between any of these variables will indicate that the IJDSS profits will be due to advice obtained for the uncontrollable variables and/or the controllable variables being tested. These process measures are based on:

1) In the intelligence phase: Process revolves around guidance on the uncontrollable input selection (Forgionne, 1999).

2) In design phase, process measures involve attaching of parameters to the general model.

3) In the Choice phase, process involves guiding the uncontrollable input selection.

In this phase, the values in the DSS are selected randomly. In the IJDSS, if the African-centric user accepts advice, then random values are replaced by advised values.

Process measures are determined by the selection of the eight decision variables that must be set by the decision maker (economic index, price, plant investment, marketing, research and development, seasonal index, competitor's price and competitor's marketing). The simulation generates the values that the simulated African-centric users would have set using a DSS, and the values that have been simulated in the IJDSS will generate the advice that the JDSS provides.

Outcome Measures

Outcome is measured in terms of profit after tax to the simulated organization. There will be a profit distribution from the DSS and a profit distribution from the JDSS. By performing the sample t-test of means on the distributions, there will be a determination whether the IJDSS improved profit. The multivariate canonical correlation analyses were carried out to determine the correlation of the variables with regards to the outcomes.

Statistical Analysis

The SAS (Statistical Analysis software) was used to perform the descriptive and inferential statistical analysis. This study utilized sample t-tests for the means of the profits (DSS and IJDSS) and also multivariate canonical correlation analyses was carried out to determine the correlation of the variables with regards to the outcomes. There was a test to ascertain whether there is a correlation between the two systems and their relation to the respective profits before and after tax and a comparison between the two.

As mentioned above in the hypothesis testing, the null hypothesis will assume that all the population means are equal, while the alternative hypothesis states that the DSS and IJDSS means are different.

The other statistical analyses that were tested were the grand mean, which is carried out by dividing the total of all data values by the total sample size. Furthermore, tests for the number of samples, the sample means, the sample variances, and the sample sizes were carried out (Jones, 2003).

Conclusions

The broad conclusion from the conducted simulation study is that the IJDSS, relative to the DSS, helps improve the process of and outcome from decision making. Moreover, from the hypotheses tested, it can be inferred that the input of the right values for the controllable variables, which in essence constitute the process steps, led to the improved profit outcomes. The following statements could therefore be deduced from the results, that:

1) The controllable variables of price, marketing, research and development (R&D), plant investment contributed significantly to the mean differences in profit between the DSS and IJDSS African-centric users.

2) The means of the uncontrollable variables were insignificant and therefore the null hypothesis could not be rejected for each one of them.

In summary, the results show that the IJDSS clearly improved organizational performance and at least two decision-making steps (design and choice). From the results obtained, of all the decision styles, the consultative African-centric style yielded most significantly to the process of and outcome of decision making and in consequence, resulted in improved organizational performance

It could safely be concluded from the results of this study that the consultative approach to decision making will yield the most productive and profitable results than all other decision-making styles. In closing, the autocratic approach which used to be the norm in decision making in the African setting at all levels, has become outmoded and is now giving way to new and modern consultative approaches to decision-making styles in the decision-making process.

Bibliography

Bangura, Abdul Karim. "Sierra Leone's Regime Types from Milton Margai to Valentine Strasser." *Patriotic Vanguard*, April 11, 2007.

———. "Ubuntugogy: An African Educational Paradigm that Transcends Pedagogy, Andragogy, Ergonagy, and Heutagogy." *Journal of Third World Studies* xxii, 2 (2005): 13–53.

Bangura, Abdul Karim, and Erin McCandless. *Peace Research for Africa: Critical Essays on Methodology*. Geneva, Switzerland: UN University for Peace Press, 2007.

Chazan, Naomi, Peter Lewis, Robert A. Mortimer, Donald Rothchild, and Stephen John Stedman. *Politics and Society in Contemporary Africa*. Boulder, CO: Lynne Rienner Publishers, 1988.

Conteh, Nabie Y., and Guisseppi Forgionne. "Simulation Modeling as an Information Systems Evaluation Tool." *Proceedings of the 35th Annual Conference of the Decision Sciences Institute*, Boston, November 22–25, 2004a.

———. "The Design of Dynamic Just-in-Time Agent Technology through Simulation Modeling." *Frontiers in Artificial Intelligence and Applications: Knowledge-Based Intelligent Engineering Systems.* IOS Press B.V., Amsterdam, Netherlands, August 2004b.

———. "The Merits of Just-In-Time Knowledge (JITkm) Management Over Knowledge Bases." *Knowledge Management Encyclopedia,* Idea Group Inc., Spring 2004c.

———. "Strategy Simulation as a Hypothesis Testing Methodology." *Eighth World Multi-Conference on Systemics, Cybernetics and Informatics,* Orlando, Florida, USA, July 18–21, 2004d.

———. "Intelligent Decision Making Support, through Just-In-Time Knowledge Management." *Proceedings of the 7th International Conference on Knowledge–based Intelligent Information and Engineering Systems,* 101–106. Oxford University, United Kingdom: September 3 – 5, 2003a.

———. "Delivering Enhanced Decision Making Support through Intelligent Just-In-Time Decision Support Systems" *Proceeding of the 34th Annual Conference of the Decision Sciences Institute,* Washington D.C, 1–6. November 22–25, 2003b.

Costello, Timothy W., and Sheldon S. Zalkind. *Psychology in Administration: A Research Orientation.* Englewood Cliffs, N.J: Prentice Hall, 1963.

Dalal, Nikunj P., and Surya B. Yadav. "The Design of a Knowledge–Based Decision Support System to Support an Information Analyst in Determining Requirements," special issue on *Expert Systems and Decision Support Systems of the Decision Sciences,* Vol. 23, no. 6 (1992).

Davenport, Thomas H., with Morton Hansen. "Knowledge Management at Andersen Consulting." Harvard Business School 9 (1999): 499–032.

Dean, J. W., Sharfman, M. P. "Does Decision Process Matter? A Study of Decision-making Effectiveness." *Academy of Management Journal* 39, no. 2 (1996): 368–96.

DeLone, William H., and Ephraim R. McLean. "Information Systems Success: The Quest for the Dependent Variable." *Information Systems Research* 3, no. 1 (1992): 61–95.

Evan, James R., and David L. Olson. *Introduction to Simulation and Risk Analysis* (2nd Edition), Upper Saddle River, NJ: Prentice Hall, 2002.

Forgionne, Guisseppi A. "Decision-making Support Systems Architecture." In *Decision-making Systems: Achievements and Challenges for the New Decade,* edited by Guisseppi A. Forgionne, Jatinder N. D. Gupta, and Manuel Mora. Hershey, PA: Idea Group Publishing, 2002.

———. "Decision–Making Support System Effectiveness: The Process to Outcome Link." *Information Knowledge Systems Management* 2, no. 2 (2000): 169–88.

———. An AHP model of DSS effectiveness European Journal of Information Systems, Palgrave Macmillan Ltd Houndmills, Basingstoke, Hampshire, RG21 6XS, England, 1999.

Forgionne, Guisseppi, and Rajiv Kohli. "Management Support System Effectiveness: Further Empirical Evidence." *Journal of Association of Information Systems* Vol. 1, no. 1 (2003), Article 3.

———. "DSS Effectiveness: The Davis–Kottemann Production Planning Experiments." *Systems Analysis Modeling Simulation (SAMS)* 26 (1996): 185–95.

———. "Integrated MSS Effects: An Empirical Healthcare Investigation," Information Processing and Management 31 (1995): 879–96.

Fulmer, William E. (October 1. 1999). Buckman Laboratories. Harvard Business School, 9–800–160. Hans W. Gottinger, Peter Weimann, *Intelligent Decision Support Systems, Decision Support Systems* 8, no. 4 (August 1992): 317–32.

Goul, Michael, Barry Shane, and Fred M. Tonge. "Using a Knowledge-Based Decision

Support System in Strategic Planning Decisions: An Empirical Study." *Journal of Management Information Systems* II, no. 4 (1986): 70–97.

Gordon, Lawrence A., Danny Miller, and Henry Mintzberg. *Normative Models in Management Decision Making*. New York: National Association of Accounting, 1975.

Holsapple, Clyde W., and Andrew B. Whinston. *Decision Support Systems: A Knowledge-Based Approach*. New York: ITP, 1996.

———. *The Information Jungle: A Quasi Novel Approach to Managing Corporate Knowledge*. Homewood, IL: Dow Jones–Irwin, 1988.

Holtzman, Samuel. *Intelligent Decision Systems*. MA: Addison-Wesley Publishing Co., 1989.

Hoover, Stewart V., and Ronald F. Perry. *Simulation: A Problem-Solving Approach*. Addison-Wesley Publishing Company, Inc., 1990.

Hunsaker, Philip L., and Johanna S. Hunsaker. "Decision Styles—In Theory, in Practice." *Organizational Dynamics* 10 (Autumn 1981): 23–36.

IDSS group, faculty of Information Technology, University of Technology Sydney; http://it.uts.edu.au/research/ (accessed September, 2003).

Keen, Peter G. W. "Adaptive Design for Decision Support Systems." *Data Base* 12 (Fall 1980); 15–25.

Keen, Peter G. W., and Michael S. Scott. *Decision Support Systems: An Organizational Perspective*. Reading, MA: Addison-Wesley, Inc., 1978.

King, R. "DSS: Complementing the Small Business African-centric User." *Proceedings of the Midwest Decision Sciences Institute*, May 1990, 168–70, with John Malley and Robert Reich.

Klein, Michael R., and Leif B. Methlie. *Knowledge-based Decision Support Systems – with Applications in Business*. New York: John Wiley & Sons, 1995.

Kohli, Rajiv. "Providing Concurrent Decision Support in Healthcare Management through Decision Technology Systems." Dissertation: University of Maryland, Baltimore County, 1994.

Lang, Christopher. "Professional and Collaborative Decision–Support: Many Ways to Improve Decision-Making." DSSResources.com, 07/11/2003.

Law, Averill M., and W. David Kelton. *Simulation Modeling and Analysis* (2nd edition), McGraw-Hill, 1991.

Li, Eldon Y. "Perceived Importance of Information System Success Factors: A Meta Analysis of Group Differences." *Information and Management* 32, no. 1 (1997): 15–28.

McLeod, Robert P. Academic Information Systems (AIS) Software Package II, 1986. Available from R. P. McLeod, 1106 Glade, College Station, TX 77840 (409): 693–1241.

Mili, Fatma. "Dynamic View of Decision Domains for the Design of Active DSS." Paper presented at 22nd Hawaii International Conference on Systems Science, Hawaii, 1989.

Mintzberg, Henry. *The Nature of African-centric Managerial Work*. Englewood Cliffs, NJ: Prentice Hall, 1973.

Moore, Jeffrey H., and Michael G. Chang. *Design of Decision Support Systems*. DATA BASE 12, nos. 1 and 2 (1980): 8–14.

O'Kane, James F., Jan Spenceley, and R. Taylor. "Simulation as an Enabler for Organizational Excellence." *Measuring Business Excellence* 7 no. 4 (2003): 12–19, MCB UP Limited, ISSN 1368–3047 (CAPE '99).

Potter, Walter D., Terry A. Byrd, John A. Miller, and Krys Kochut. "Extending Decision Support Systems: The Integration of Data, Knowledge, and Model Management." *Annals of Operations Research*, Vol. 38 (1992): 501–27.

Power, Daniel J. *Decision Support Systems: Concepts and Resources for African-centric Users*. Westport, CT: Greenwood/Quorum Books, 2002.

Power, Dan J., and Shashidar Kaparthi. "The Changing Technological Context of Decision Support Systems." In *Context-Sensitive Decision Support Systems*, edited by Dina G. Berkeley, George Widmeyer, Patrick Brezillion, and Vladislov Rajkovic. London: Chapman and Hall, 1998.

Scott Morton, Michael S. *Management Decision Systems: Computer–based Support for Decision-making*. Boston, Division of Research, Graduate School of Business Administration, Harvard University, 1971.

Sensiper, Sylvia, and Dorothy Leonard. "American Management Systems: The Knowledge Centers." Harvard Business School 9 (1998): 697–68.

Sethi, Vijay, and William R. King. "Construct Measurement in Information Systems Research: An Illustration in Strategic Systems." *Decision Sciences* 22, no. 3 (1991): 455–72.

Schmidt, J. William. "Introduction to Systems Analysis, Modeling and Simulation." *Proceedings of the 1986 Winter Simulation Conference* (1986): 5–15.

Shah, V., and G. D. Buckner. "Intelligent Decision Support Systems." *The Journal of Computer Information Systems* 31, no. 2 (Winter 1991): 61–65.

Shim, J. P., Merrill Warkentin, James F. Courtney, Daniel J. Power, Ramesh Sharda, Chris Carlsson. "Past, Present, and Future of Decision Support Technology." *Decision Support Systems* (Elsevier Science B.V.) 33, no. 2 (2002): 111–26.

Silverman, Barry G. "Unifying Expert Systems and the Decision Sciences." *Operations Research* 42, no. 3 (1994): 393–413.

Simon, Herbert. *The New Science of Management Decision,* revised edition, Englewood Cliffs, NJ: Prentice Hall, 1977.

Simon, Herbert A. *The New Science of Management Decision.* New York, NY: Harper and Row, 1960.

Sowa, John F. *Conceptual Structures*. Reading, MA: Addison-Wesley, 1984.

Sprague, Ralph H., and Eric D. Carlson. *Building Effective Decision Support Systems.* Englewood Cliffs, NJ: Prentice-Hall, Inc., 1982.

Tansley, D. Stewart W., and Clive C. Hayball. *KBS Analysis and Design: A KADS Developer's Handbook.* New York: Prentice Hall, 1993.

Toffler, Alvin. *Future Shock.* New York: Bantam Books, 1970.

Turban, Efraim J., and Jay E. Aronson. *Decision Support Systems and Intelligent Systems.* Upper Saddle River, NJ: Prentice Hall, 1998.

Turban, Efraim. *Decision Support and Expert Systems: Management Support Systems.* NY: Macmillan, 1993.

Udo, Godwin J. "Rethinking the Effectiveness Measures of Decision Support Systems." *Information and Management* 22, no. 2 (1992) 123–35.

Wagner, Harvey M., *Principles of Operations Research*, Second Edition. Englewood Cliffs, NJ: Prentice-Hall, Inc., 1975.

van Weelderen, Jim A., and Henk G. Sol. "MEDESS, A Methodology for Designing Expert Support Systems." *Interfaces*, Vol. 23, no. 3 (May-June 1993): 51–61.

Index

About the Contributors

Ivor Agyeman-Duah founded the Centre for Intellectual Renewal, a public policy advocacy organization that deals with issues of culture, communication, and economic development. He was a member of the Secretariat of the World Bank Institute in Washington, DC, looking at the role of African Diaspora in economic development and in other public policy work, is an advisor to the Andrew Mellon Foundation, New York on its Africa programme, Ituka-Aluka and previously, head of Public Affairs department, Ghana Embassy in Washington, DC, and was also the advisor on culture and communication at the Ghana High Commission in London. In academia, he has been Visiting-Scholar-in-Residence at the College of Arts and Letters, California State University, Pomona, and the League of Women's Voters Visiting Writer at the University of Nebraska. Some of his seven published books include *Some African Voices of Our Time* (1996); two editions of *Between Faith and History: A Biography of J. A. Kufuor* (2003, 2006); *Bu Me Be: Akan Proverbs* (2002, 2007) with Peggy Appiah and Kwmame Anthony Appiah); and *Pan-Africanism Caribbean Connections* (2007, coauthor). Other writings, apart from book chapters, are essays and reviews published in such journals as: *African and Asian Studies Journal* (Netherlands); *African Affairs, Journal of the Royal Africa Society* (London); *International Affairs, Journal of The Royal Institute of International Affairs*, Chatham House.

Agyeman-Duah was a research scholar at the W. E. B. Du Bois Institute for Africa and African-American Research at Harvard University; a Hilary and Trinity research-scholar-in-residence at Exeter College, Oxford. He holds graduate degrees from the London School of Economics, the School of Oriental and African Studies, London, and the University of Wales.

Abdul Karim Bangura is professor of research methodology and political science at Howard University in Washington, DC. He holds a PhD in political science, a PhD in development economics, a PhD in linguistics, and a PhD in computer science. He also is the author of sixty-one other books and more than 500 scholarly articles.

Nabie Y. Conteh is an assistant professor of information systems and computer technology at the Byrd School of Business, Shenandoah University, Virginia. He holds a PhD and MS in information systems from the University of Maryland in Baltimore County, an MBA from Ferris State University in Michigan, and a BS in information systems from the Institute of Information and Communication Technology in Enschede in the Netherlands. His research interest focuses on information systems and electronic commerce knowledge management and organizational learning, decision support systems, systems modeling and simulation, artificial intelligence/expert systems, and systems analysis and design. He has authored scholarly publications and made learned presentations in these areas.

James T. Gire, an accomplished African psychologist, is professor and head of psychology at Virginia Military Institute, Lexington, Virginia. His military rank is that of Colonel. He obtained his PhD from McMaster University in Canada. He has published widely in the area of African Psychology including a book entitled *Aging and Adult Development in the Developing World: Applying Western Theories and Concepts* (with Frank E. Eyetsemitan), published by Greenwood Publishing Group, 2003.

Ibipo Johnston-Anumonwo is a tenured professor of geography at the State University of New York College at Cortland. She holds a Master's degree from the Harvard Graduate School of Education while her PhD in Geography is from Clark University, Worcester, Massachusetts. Ibipo has been a member of the SUNY Cortland faculty for twenty-one years. Her scholarly work integrates gender and ethnicity into geographic research and curriculum. A recipient of SUNY Cortland's Outstanding Research Award, her publications include several journal articles, book chapters, book reviews, two co-edited books, and two co-authored books, among which are *Issues in Africa and the African Diaspora in the 21st Century*, and *Diversity, Multiculturalism and Social Justice* published by Binghamton University Global Publications. In 2010 she received the SUNY Chancellor's Award for Excellence in Scholarship and Creative Activities.

Ngozi Caleb Kamalu is tenured full professor of political science in the Department of Government and History, and the director of the MA Program in Political Science at Fayetteville State University. Dr. Kamalu holds BA and MPA degrees from Texas Southern University and a PhD in Political Science from Howard University in Washington, DC. Prior to joining Fayetteville State University, Professor Ngozi Kamalu taught at Howard University and North Carolina Agricultural and Technical State University, respectively.

Kenday S. Kamara attended Fourah Bay College, University of Sierra Leone, 1982–1986. He is currently an educator in the Prince George's County education system in Maryland, an organizational development consultant for Medcall Staffing and Management Consultants, Inc., and a PhD scholar-practitioner in applied management and decision sciences at Walden University, specializing in leadership and organizational change.

Ishmael I. Munene is currently an associate professor in the Department of Educational Leadership at Northern Arizona University, teaching courses in comparative education, higher education, and educational research. As an experienced scholar in higher education, he has written widely on African higher education. He has authored *The Politics & Economics of Higher Education Transformation in Kenya: Impact of Globalization, Privatization, Quasi-Marketization and New Managerialism* (VDM Verlag Dr. Muller, 2009). He has edited *Transforming the Academia: Exploring African Universities in a Comparative Context* (Nova Science Publishers, 2009). He has contributed chapters in books and encyclopedias along with journal articles in *Africa Education Review*, *Basic Education Forum*, *Higher Education*, *International Journal of Educational Development*, *International Review of Education Research in Post-Compulsory Education*, *Journal of Higher Education in Africa*, *Journal of Third World Studies*, and *Research in Post-Compulsory Education*. He has served as the Executive Secretary of the African Studies and Research Forum. He has taught at the University of Nairobi, Kenya, and at the State University of New York at Albany.

Iheanyi N. Osondu is an associate professor of geography/GIS in the Department of Social Sciences at Fort Valley State University and has previously taught in higher institutions in Africa and Europe. He earned a BA (honors) in geography/education (with a minor in history from the University of Lagos, Nigeria); an MSc in urban environmental resources planning and management from the University of Jos Nigeria, and a PhD in geography and planning from the University of Edinburgh, Scotland. He was a recipient of 2006 SPACE (Spatial Analysis for Curriculum Enhancement) Instructional award and a recipient of U.S. Department of Education Congressionally Directed Grant (2009). Osondu's current research involves the use and application of GIS (Geographic Information Systems) in solving environmental problems in Africa. He has worked in the fields of economic and population geography in Africa and North America and has published in the areas of housing and housing finance, the informal sector, African Migration, socioeconomic consequences of wars and civil conflicts in Africa, and environmental issues.

Mamokgethi Setati is Executive Dean of the College of Science, Engineering and Technology and Professor of Mathematics at the University of South Africa. She is the first Black woman in South Africa to earn a PhD in Mathematics Education, among many other distinctions. She also is the author of many reviewed articles, book chapters, and books.

Samuel Zalanga is associate professor of sociology at Bethel University, St. Paul, Minnesota. He is currently the associate editor for the *Journal of Third*

World Studies (Africa section). His broad area of scholarly interest and specialization is Development Studies and Social Change. Among his recent publications are: "Religion, Economic Development, and Cultural Change: The Contradictory Role of Pentecostal Christianity in Sub-Saharan Africa" (Spring 2010), *Journal of Third World Studies* (JTWS); and "Reforming Higher Education in Africa: Access, Equity, and Equal Opportunity" in *Transforming the Academia: Exploring African Universities in a Comparative Context* (Nova Publishers, 2009).

www.ingramcontent.com/pod-product-compliance
Ingram Content Group UK Ltd.
Pitfield, Milton Keynes, MK11 3LW, UK
UKHW021035150926
475561UK00003B/111

9 780739 165980